REALIZING
SOCIAL JUSTICE

REALIZING SOCIAL JUSTICE

The Challenge of Preventive Interventions

Edited by Maureen E. Kenny, Arthur M. Horne,
Pamela Orpinas, and Le'Roy E. Reese

American Psychological Association
Washington, DC

Published by
American Psychological Association
750 First Street, NE
Washington, DC 20002
www.apa.org

To order
APA Order Department
P.O. Box 92984
Washington, DC 20090-2984
Tel: (800) 374-2721; Direct: (202) 336-5510
Fax: (202) 336-5502; TDD/TTY: (202) 336-6123
Online: www.apa.org/books/
E-mail: order@apa.org

In the U.K., Europe, Africa, and the
Middle East, copies may be
ordered from
American Psychological Association
3 Henrietta Street
Covent Garden, London
WC2E 8LU England

Typeset in Goudy by Shepherd Inc., Dubuque, IA

Printer: McNaughton & Gunn, Saline, MI
Cover Designer: Naylor Design, Washington, DC
Technical/Production Editor: Emily Welsh

The opinions and statements published are the responsibility of the authors, and such opinions and statements do not necessarily represent the policies of the American Psychological Association.

Library of Congress Cataloging-in-Publication Data
Realizing social justice : the challenge of preventive interventions / edited by Maureen E. Kenny ... [et al.]. — 1st ed.
    p. ; cm.
  Includes bibliographical references and index.
  ISBN-13: 978-1-4338-0411-3
  ISBN-10: 1-4338-0411-5
1. Mental illness—Prevention. 2. Preventive mental health services. 3. Social justice.
I. Kenny, Maureen. II. American Psychological Association.
[DNLM: 1. Preventive Psychiatry—methods. 2. Health Promotion. 3. Mental Disorders—prevention & control. 4. Social Justice. WM 31.5 R288 2009]
RA790.5.R388 2009
362.196'89—dc22

                                                                    2008029714

British Library Cataloguing-in-Publication Data
A CIP record is available from the British Library.

Printed in the United States of America
First Edition

To Mike and Katie,
I hope we may witness the just society aspired to through this text.
Strive to maintain health and positive well-being.
—*Maureen E. Kenny*

To Evelyn L. Fullagar,
the mother-in-law we all wish for.
—*Arthur M. Horne*

To my parents, Jaime and Marion,
for their gift of life and love.
—*Pamela Orpinas*

To Mariama (Gift of God) and Aman (Peace),
because all children are gifts from God and deserve the peace
that good health and safety afford.
—*Le'Roy E. Reese*

CONTENTS

CONTRIBUTORS

Victoria L. Banyard, PhD, Department of Psychology, University of New Hampshire, Durham

Daniel Blumenthal, MD, Department of Community Health and Preventive Medicine, Morehouse School of Medicine, Atlanta, GA

Kris Bosworth, PhD, College of Education, University of Arizona, Tucson

Preston A. Britner, PhD, Human Development and Family Studies, University of Connecticut, Storrs

Larisa Buhin, PhD, Clinical Psychology Department, Chicago School of Professional Psychology, Chicago, IL

Theresa L. Byrd, DrPH, School of Public Health, University of Texas, Houston

David M. DeJoy, PhD, College of Public Health, University of Georgia, Athens

Jillian DePaul, MA, MEd, Department of Counseling, Developmental, and Educational Psychology, Lynch School of Education, Boston College, Chestnut Hill, MA

Jessica Goldberg, PhD, Massachusetts Healthy Families Evaluation, Tufts University, Medford, MA

Lisa Goodman, PhD, Department of Counseling, Developmental, and Educational Psychology, Boston College, Chestnut Hill, MA

Sally M. Hage, PhD, Department of Educational and Counseling Psychology, School of Education, State University of New York at Albany

Katie Hein, PhD, Department of Health Promotion and Behavior, College of Public Health, University of Georgia, Athens

Arthur M. Horne, PhD, College of Education, University of Georgia, Athens

Anthony Isacco, MA, Program in Counseling Psychology, School of Education, Loyola University Chicago

Francine Jacobs, EdD, Eliot-Pearson Department of Child Development and Department of Urban and Environmental Policy and Planning, Tufts University, Medford, MA

Maureen E. Kenny, PhD, Lynch School of Education, Boston College, Chestnut Hill, MA

Peggy Lorah, EdD, NCC, LPC, Center for Women Students, Pennsylvania State University, State College

Connie R. Matthews, PhD, NCC, LPC, College of Education, Pennsylvania State University, State College

James M. O'Neil, PhD, School of Family Studies, University of Connecticut, Storrs

Pamela Orpinas, PhD, MPH, Department of Health Promotion and Behavior, University of Georgia, Athens

Jennie Park-Taylor, PhD, Division of Psychological and Educational Services, Fordham University, Bronx, NY

Shanti Pepper, MA, Department of Psychology, Pennsylvania State University, State College

Le'Roy E. Reese, MD, Department of Community Health and Preventive Medicine, Morehouse School of Medicine, Atlanta, GA

Belinda Reininger, PhD, School of Public Health Regional Campus, University of Texas, Brownsville

John L. Romano, MD, College of Education and Human Development, University of Minnesota, Minneapolis

Jonathan P. Schwartz, PhD, Department of Educational Psychology, University of Houston, Houston, TX

Elizabeth M. Vera, PhD, Program in Counseling Psychology, School of Education, Loyola University Chicago, Chicago, IL

Michael Waldo, PhD, Department of Counseling and Educational Psychology, College of Education, New Mexico State University, Las Cruces

Mary Walsh, PhD, Department of Counseling, Developmental, and Educational Psychology, Lynch School of Education, Boston College, Chestnut Hill, MA

Mark G. Wilson, HSD, Department of Health Promotion and Behavior, College of Public Health, University of Georgia, Athens

John Harvey Wingfield, PhD, Prevention Research Center, Morehouse School of Medicine, Atlanta, GA

LIST OF TABLES, FIGURES, AND EXHIBITS

TABLES

FIGURES

EXHIBITS

PREFACE

This book had its origins in the Prevention Section of Division 17, the Society for Counseling Psychology, of the American Psychological Association (APA). The Section sponsored a pre-convention workshop at the 111th annual convention of the APA in Toronto in 2003 that focused on the teaching of prevention. Being aware of the need for an up-to-date and comprehensive volume on prevention, Lansing Hays, then an acquisitions editor for APA, contacted the first editor of the current book about the prospect of developing a book on prevention. Maureen E. Kenny discussed possibilities for a book on prevention with the section membership. The scope and focus of the current volume grew out of those discussions. As such, we are proud to have a number of members of the Prevention Section represented among our chapter authors. To broaden the scope of this contribution, we have also invited authors from public health, health promotion, applied developmental science, and community psychology. We thank the members of the Prevention Section for their contributions to this volume and thank APA editors Susan Reynolds and Peter Pavilionis for their support of this book following Lansing Hays's departure from APA Books. We would also like to thank Boston College graduate students Emily Andersen, Meg Connolly, and Angela Borges, who assisted in the editorial process, and University of Minnesota counseling psychology doctoral students Hyun Kyung Lee and Jason Netland for their assistance in the preparation of chapter 1.

Although the APA has published a number of books in recent years that address specific areas of prevention, such as violence and substance abuse, this is the first APA volume since *14 Ounces of Prevention* (Price,

Cowen, Lorion, & Ramos-McKay, 1988) to address prevention broadly.[1] Given the proliferation of evidence-based prevention programs since the publication of that volume and the synthesis of best practices in special issues of *American Psychologist* (July 2005) and *The Counseling Psychologist* (July 2007), the current book does not endeavor to provide an in-depth presentation and examination of model prevention programs or to replicate the discussion of best practices. This book seeks to inspire further advances in the integration of prevention theory, research, and practice in the service of promoting social justice. It is our hope that the vision presented by this volume will serve to advance discussion of prevention issues and to advance social justice efforts, thereby forging a legacy for the future.

---

[1]Price, R. H., Cowen, E. L., Lorion, R. P., & Ramos-McKay, J. (Eds.). (1988). *14 ounces of prevention: A casebook for practitioners*. Washington, DC: American Psychological Association.

REALIZING
SOCIAL JUSTICE

SOCIAL JUSTICE AND THE CHALLENGE OF PREVENTIVE INTERVENTIONS: AN INTRODUCTION

MAUREEN E. KENNY, ARTHUR M. HORNE,
PAMELA ORPINAS, AND LE'ROY E. REESE

This book is about prevention and social justice—specifically about the ways in which prevention can be used to promote social justice. Part I describes the historical and conceptual roots of this vision and ethical, research, evaluation, and training issues that are central to this vision. Part II first addresses social justice concerns related to diversity and health, which extend across multiple contexts, and then focuses on promoting health and well-being across four levels of the ecological context: family, school, workplace, and community. These chapters as a group, while not exhaustive of contemporary efforts in social justice prevention, provide an opportunity to examine the current reality of prevention practice in light of the proposed social justice vision. As such, this volume builds on prior work of leaders in the fields of prevention and social justice and seeks to advance a renewed vision of preventive interventions by integrating recent developments in theory, research, and practice.

The late psychologist George Albee was an advocate for social justice and prevention for more than 50 years. In the tradition of Albee, this book promotes a vision of prevention as a mechanism for fostering social justice. As such, we draw upon Albee's writings to inform our understanding of prevention and social justice. Despite the longevity of Albee's ideas, prevention has not fulfilled its social justice promise. Social injustice remains rampant in health status, educational and occupational attainment, and income levels. These disparities are often most poignant when comparisons across racial/ethnic groups, gender, and ability status are examined (U.S. Department of Health and Human Services, 2000). This volume seeks to promote theory, research, and practice in preventive interventions that attempt to realize social justice, while considering the barriers that hinder that progress.

Our understanding of social justice is guided by existing definitions. Bell (2007) highlights the process and goals of social justice. According to Bell, the goal of social justice is to achieve "full and equal participation of all groups in a society that is mutually shaped to meet their needs. Social justice includes a vision of society in which the distribution of resources is equitable and all members are physically and *psychologically* safe and secure" (p. 1, emphasis added). This goal is consistent with what Isaac Prilleltensky (1997) has labeled *distributive social justice*, or "the fair and equitable allocation of bargaining powers, resources, and obligations in society" (p. 5) in consideration of people's differential power, needs, and abilities to express their values. The distributive aspect of social justice is also reflected in the definition offered by Fouad, Gerstein, and Toporek (2006), who describe a just society as one in which "the distribution of advantages be fair and equitable to all individuals, regardless of race, gender, ability status, sexual orientation, physical make-up, or religious creed" (p. 1). With regard to the process for attaining social justice, Bell emphasizes the importance of collaborative and participatory processes that affirm human agency and capacity. Fondacaro and Weinberg (2002) similarly emphasize the importance of including the voice of all stakeholders in decision making and refer to this as *procedural justice*, in comparison to distributive justice, which focuses on the fair allocation of resources. Swenson (1998) identifies self-awareness and attention to power relationships as integral to practice oriented to social justice. These definitions highlight the persistence of differential power relationships and oppressive social structures in creating and sustaining what economists and political scientists call "structural maldistribution" of social resources.

Social justice typically invokes the notion of social resources as economic goods and their distribution or redistribution. Bell's definition dispels that notion somewhat. Carol Swenson goes even further in her look at social justice as the "organizing value" of the social work profession. Drawing on the work of Jerome Wakefield (who in turn draws on the work of the late philosopher John Rawls, notably his A *Theory of Justice* [1971]), Swenson makes an important distinction for social resources as *noneconomic* goods, such as self-esteem, resilience, and other protective assets—attributes that complement Bell's definition of social justice as not only physical security but also psychological security. "Social resources are most often thought to be economic in nature," Swenson (1998) observes, "but Rawls's analysis can be applied to noneconomic goods as well." She quotes from Wakefield's take on Rawls's theory to buttress her point:

> In particular, Rawls's analysis implies that some psychological traits, such as self-respect, that are closely linked to the structure of social institutions and to how people react to each other are a kind of social benefit for which justice requires an attempt at fair distribution. If this is so, then psychotherapy-style interventions aimed at imparting such psychological goods would play an integral role in a justice-oriented profession. (p. 529)

Indeed, social work's enduring professional construct of the "person-in-situation" argues for the social worker helping the client muster the social resources—public goods and services *and* psychological assets—to handle difficult situations. These are *situations* that find some relief with the social worker's social and psychological intervention, but such interventions are designed to achieve an enduring change in the *social* conditions that challenge the client. This is where counseling and clinical psychologists figure significantly in community-level interventions: To be sure, the psychologist views an intervention with a professional eye toward the psychological conditions that can be changed among clients on an enduring basis—and toward whatever environmental conditions impinge on those psychological assets.

This volume employs a public health approach in its promotion of a social justice agenda in preventive interventions. The reasons for such an approach are manifold: Public health methodology has an inherent preventive focus in its application to health problems that are either epidemic or chronic in nature and pervasive in their manifestation. A public health approach goes beyond treatment of the individual to seek out the broader causes of disease and other health problems that plague a community. Thus, public health approaches acknowledge the *social determinants of health*—genetics, socioeconomic status (SES), the cultural makeup of neighborhoods and communities, and the social bonds within and external to these neighborhoods and communities. The focus on population-based treatment strategies also acknowledges the socioeconomic differentiation in health, with those at the lower SES levels suffering worse health conditions; similarly, middle-class neighborhoods suffer more health problems than affluent communities. Hence, public health approaches seek treatments to pervasive health problems that affect broad populations rather than individuals alone.

In their focus on the social determinants of health, public health approaches put a premium on *context* in their epidemiology: How are health problems influenced by—and, in turn, how do they influence—other contexts? For example, how are aggressive/delinquent youth affected by problems in the family, at school, and in the neighborhood? How are the parents of these youths similarly affected by their own contexts outside the family, particularly in the workplace (if there is one for either or both parents)? Public health approaches are also equitable not only in their trans-contextual examination of pervasive pathologies, but also in their treatment strategies. If the targets of preventive interventions are communities that suffer multiple health problems stemming from inequalities in employment levels, income, the quality of housing, and environmental pollution, the public health dimension of such interventions seeks equitable population-based remedies—that is, remedies that embrace a broader, trans-contextual solution.

The point here is that the immediate environmental conditions targeted in a community-wide intervention depend on various contexts beyond the individual. The significance of this volume is an emphasis on the trans-contextual in the design, evaluation, and conduct of a preventive intervention. Many of the psychopathologies (or simply "bad behaviors") that are targets of interventions are influenced by other contexts. Although the consulting psychologist aims at a change in the contextual source of the psychopathology, the scope of the intervention must be within the realm of the practicable. In many cases, the source of the psychological problem is easy to isolate and identify, but not so easy to eliminate or transform. Those psychopathologies can find treatment and perhaps even enduring prevention through not only a change in social environmental conditions—more and better public services, more private sector participation, antipoverty and anticrime programs—but also through psychotherapeutic interventions aimed at facilitating individual empowerment and acceptance of (perhaps even mastery over) a client's immediate environment. Social justice in these cases does not come solely from establishing new priorities for the distribution of society's public goods (in most cases), but also from a building up of protective assets and an attenuation of risk factors within the community and within the individual.

The dual focus on social and individual change as benchmarks for successful outcomes in preventive interventions also stems from public health's social determinants and their interaction within the primary level of analysis for public policy—the community. The synergy of responsive social institutions and psychologically equipped individuals sustains a social milieu of community *wellness*, which is an interactive process at the analytical and prescriptive levels. A community can promote its own state of wellness through the actions of its constituent members, who must seek an accommodation with (or even mastery over) their immediate environments to be vibrant, contributing, sustaining units of an organic whole; their daily participation and interaction in the community is the integument that holds the community together. The community, in turn, must provide its members with an adequate level of services—public goods—be it adequate social infrastructure and housing stock, responsive institutions, proactive public services, or the like. Otherwise, the environment becomes plagued with more and more risk factors, such as crime, unemployment, pollution, and violence. The more prevalent and more toxic those risk factors become, the more they impinge on the community member's immediate environment and psychological orientation to the rest of the community. Wellness at the community and individual levels cannot thrive in such a milieu, overwhelmingly made up of those already suffering vulnerabilities in resilience, self-esteem, and other protective assets at the lower SES levels. These particular community members suffer typical psychopathologies or "bad behaviors" in reaction to deteriorating social environments. Although a community-wide intervention aspires to the goals and tasks of achieving primary prevention's framework of wellness, much remediation ensues. Thus, part of the social mandate is realized in an intervention that redirects social and psychological resources to the targeted community and its members—to approach Bell's social justice definition of physical and psychological security of a community's members. The fulfillment of that mandate, it would seem, depends on whether the reprioritization and redirection of resources is enduring—that is, whether that social justice mandate transcends the remedial to achieve transformative social change for the targeted community of an intervention. Such is the challenge of preventive interventions.

Prevention has enjoyed a long history in the fields of public health, social work, and psychology, especially within the specialties of counseling and community psychology. As described in chapter 1 of this volume, however, the prominence of prevention—especially social justice–oriented prevention—in the agenda of psychology and other professions has fluctuated over the years. Definitions and models of prevention vary widely, depending on the timing and focus of the intervention (Kaplan, 2000; Silverman, 2003). *Primary* prevention, for example, focuses on taking measures to avoid the development of psychological and physical disorders and promote health and well-being among groups who have no known symptoms. *Secondary* prevention involves early identification of health problems, followed by referral and intervention aimed at stopping the progression of disease; it usually targets "at-risk" groups. *Tertiary* prevention seeks to reduce the level of disability, distress, and dependence among individuals who have already experienced a disorder. Primary prevention is unique among the three types of prevention by including a focus on health promotion and enhancement, in addition to risk reduction (Silverman, 2003). Health professionals have historically focused mostly on tertiary prevention, which includes treatment, therapy, and rehabilitation (Vera & Speight, 2007). Although secondary and tertiary prevention can and do contribute to social justice, we maintain that primary prevention, which seeks to "prevent or forestall something unpleasant or undesirable from happening in the future"

(Albee & Ryan-Finn, 1993, p. 115) is central to social justice promotion. By seeking to reduce risk factors, such as stress and oppression, and by building protective capacities (Albee, 1982), primary prevention is synergistic with social justice in its emphasis on preventing suffering, developing individual and group resources, and promoting a more just society (Prilleltensky, 1997).

Although the case studies of interventions presented in Part II of this volume all have a preventive mandate, few arrive at a community that is poised for primary prevention. That is, most of the interventions detailed here fall within the realm of secondary or tertiary prevention, seeking to treat a prevalent and pervasive psychopathology. In fact, the primary preventive interventions examined in Part II describe modest, but tangible, outcomes in terms of social justice and wellness because the scope of the intervention is contained within a particular context(s); it is a manageable agenda that emphasizes the reduction of risk factors and the promotion of protective assets in the individual's immediate environment. To the extent that these targeted venues—be they in the educational, family, or workplace contexts—span other contexts in either an analytical or prescriptive capacity, social justice and wellness embark on a community approach, albeit in a peripheral and incremental fashion.

To be sure, prevention, wellness, and social justice do not occur in a vacuum; schools, families, and workplaces are parts of a broader community, even though the proximal bonds and relationships are becoming looser and fuzzier; yet communities know best what ails them and the causes of such ailments. How they articulate such concerns and to whom and the kind of decision making within these communities—decision making that sets priorities for the dedication and direction of new social resources—is another concern of public health approaches to preventive interventions. This concern focuses on the changing nature of the mental health profession and its powerful interface with an intervention's stakeholders in the community—what Prilleltensky (2001) calls "partnerships" and emancipatory communitarian responses to social and psychological problems that plague a community. Individuals who become empowered through psychotherapeutic interventions are also active participants in self-healing and in the healing of the community, as they become yet another community asset in the wellness equation.

Although the chapters across this volume are intended to more fully explain and examine theory, research, and practice related to prevention and social justice, we wish to orient the reader of this volume by putting forth four key dimensions central to our social justice vision of prevention and describe how these dimensions coincide with ecological theory and current developments in positive youth development and multicultural psychology.

A social justice approach to prevention recognizes the contribution of toxic social conditions, including inadequate social, physical, and psychological resources—and oppressive social structures—to the etiology of emotional and physical disorders. Adopting a public health perspective, Albee noted that to reduce the incidence of a disorder, attention should be directed toward removing the pathogen (Albee & Ryan-Finn, 1993). From a social justice perspective, this entails a change in environmental conditions or systemic change, involving a redistribution of societal resources or power (Albee & Ryan-Finn, 1993). As proponents of social justice values in mental health, Prilleltensky and colleagues (Nelson & Prilleltensky, 2005; Prilleltensky, Dokecki, Frieden, & Wang, 2007) similarly maintain that unfair social policies and structures must be changed to attain social equity. Nelson and Prilleltensky (2005) describe prevention approaches that "address the causes of the causes through social change efforts" (p. 89) as transformative. In contrast, ameliorative approaches focus on strengthening the resistance and enhancing the abilities of individuals, families, or communities to cope with negative societal forces. Thus, social justice approaches to prevention need to be evaluated as to their success in addressing "the causes of the causes" and accomplishing transformative change.

A social justice approach to prevention also recognizes that toxic social conditions are more prevalent in conditions of poverty (Albee & Ryan-Finn, 1993) and in contexts of societal oppression or inequity related to race, gender, sexual orientation, immigration status, social class, religious difference, or ability status (Albee, 1996). As such, social justice prevention needs to redress these inequities and promote respect and appreciation for diversity (Prilleltensky, 2001).

A social justice approach to prevention focuses on the promotion of healthy development, the enhancement of wellness, and the acquisition of skills and competencies that enable individuals and groups to participate fully in society (Prilleltensky, 2001). Albee and Ryan-Finn (1993) identified the enhancement of personal and group competencies as key components of effective prevention. In addition to decreasing toxic social factors, the incidence of mental disorders can be reduced by increasing resilience, self-esteem, social support, coping skills, and other competencies. Nelson and Prilleltensky (2005) also recognized prevention efforts that focus on skills and competencies as essential to social justice. Although the attainment of social justice requires structural change, individuals and groups also need the requisite skills and competencies to succeed in school, work, and relationships once social barriers are reduced.

A social justice approach to prevention also attends to issues of procedural justice. Prilleltensky and Nelson (Nelson & Prilleltensky, 2005; Prilleltensky & Nelson, 1997), for example, emphasize the importance of citizen participation and of providing opportunities for individuals and groups to identify their own goals, make their own decisions, and define themselves. Prevention is not an activity for professionals to impose on at-risk individuals but should arise out of collaboration between all relevant stake-holders to facilitate the self-empowerment of all participants. To do so, the social justice–oriented preventionist needs to be self-reflective about one's own race, power, privilege, domination, and oppression (Constantine, Hage, Kindaichi, & Bryant, 2007; McWhirter, 1998; Swenson, 1998).

In sum, we contend that a social justice perspective should recognize and remedy toxic social conditions; seek to increase equal access to adequate physical, social, and educational resources; build upon cultural strengths; and facilitate empowerment rather than blame constituents (Conyne, 2004; Goodman et al., 2004; Hage et al., 2007; Prilleltensky, 1997; Romano & Hage, 2000). From a social justice perspective, prevention thus needs to combat structural barriers that limit access to resources because of race or ethnicity and equip individuals with strengths to mitigate the negative effects of discrimination and oppression. Social justice demands, additionally, that all individuals be prepared with the skills and resources needed to fully participate in society (Prilleltensky, 1997).

In our efforts to further articulate a social justice vision of prevention, this volume adopts an ecological perspective and integrates current thinking concerning the developmental context, positive development, and multicultural psychology. We conceptualize prevention as promoting healthy and positive development across the life span. Ecological (Bronfenbrenner, 1979) and developmental contextual theories (Lerner, Walsh, & Howard, 1998) emphasize the transactional relationships among individuals and the multiple interdependent contexts in which they grow and develop. Ecological and developmental contextual perspectives have been important in directing psychology away from individual explanations of emotional disorders—which tend to blame individuals for their problems—to an increased understanding of the powerful impact of positive and negative environmental conditions on human outcomes. Indeed, evidence suggests that most psychosocial outcomes are determined by an interplay of factors (Nelson & Prilleltensky, 2005). Because individuals and groups are embedded in multilayered transactional ecological systems, interventions directed at any level must transcend that setting to have a broad and sustained impact (Silverman, 2003). This complex multilevel understanding of the etiology of mental well-being and physical health highlights the role of psychological, behavioral, physical, social, economic, political, and cultural factors. As such, the knowledge that informs human development and hence prevention efforts crosses multiple disciplines, including psychology, medicine, public health, public policy, economics, and numerous others.

In developing this book, we have sought to include authors whose expertise extends beyond the confines of the discipline of psychology. Contributors are from the fields of education, medicine, and public health, in addition to counseling and community, developmental, and organizational psychology. We believe these perspectives add depth and breadth in examining a topic that has roots in community psychology. Prevention is a multidisciplinary science that now draws from many disciplines. Several, such as law, economics, social work, sociology, and criminal justice, are not represented in the authorship of this volume (Weissberg, Kumpfer, & Seligman, 2003). Although a cadre of fields is critical to understanding healthy development from a complex, multilayered ecological framework, the dialogue is more complicated and challenging than when offered from a single disciplinary perspective.

Part I of this volume supports our efforts to articulate a social justice vision of prevention by first providing the historical context and current circumstances that mandate a social justice and positive development approach to prevention. Chapters 1, 3, and 4 elaborate on the concepts presented in this introduction with respect to the interrelationships of prevention and social justice and the role of developmental-contextual theory as a foundation for prevention. Kenny and Romano (chap. 1) describe the historical and theoretical bases for this vision and current tensions that emerge from these converging perspectives. Walsh, DePaul, and Park-Taylor (chap. 3) integrate developmental-contextual theory and research in identifying best practices for prevention. Vera, Buhin, and Isacco (chap. 4) affirm the social justice mandate that impels psychologists to embrace prevention as a mechanism for reducing health disparities and fostering social justice and provide examples of ameliorative and transformative approaches to social justice preventive interventions. Although these chapters are intended primarily to elaborate the conceptual premises for a social justice vision of prevention, they also include examples of interventions that exemplify the principles discussed in that chapter.

The chapters in Part I also discuss research, program evaluation, ethical principles, and training with reference to social justice prevention. Reese, Wingfield, and Blumenthal (chap. 2) examine the challenges in linking research and practice in prevention, especially efforts focusing on social justice. Jacobs and Goldberg (chap. 5) discuss principles and frameworks for conducting program evaluation from a social justice and developmental perspective. Schwartz and Hage (chap. 6) identify the ethical issues that are unique to prevention practice, especially when social justice is held as a key value. O'Neil and Britner (chap. 7) explain a model for university-based training in prevention for social justice.

Part II of this book contains six chapters that individually and collectively describe theory, research, and practice for fostering social justice across critical contexts of development. We invited authors with known expertise in prevention and health promotion to describe examples of social justice prevention emphasizing specific dimensions of prevention relevant across multiple contexts (diversity and health promotion) and specific contexts (family, school, work, and community). While these chapters address the practice of prevention, they also describe theories specific to the focus of that chapter and discuss research that supports theory and practice in that context. The foci of these chapters are consistent with an awareness of the importance of developmental contexts in offering equitable access to societal resources and in promoting healthy development without threats to physical and psychological safety. Matthews, Pepper, and Lorah (chap. 8) present theoretical principles and research that inform the development of diversity-affirming climates and describe the application of those principles across multiple contexts, including K–12 schools, colleges, the workplace, and the community. Byrd and Reininger (chap. 9) focus on health promotion and wellness. They define health promotion, describe and critique theories of health promotion, and present a model for community health assessment that strives to promote healthy development and social justice.

The final four chapters focus on four developmental contexts. These chapters discuss theory, research, and practice for fostering healthy families (Waldo, Horne, & Kenny, chap. 10), for promoting a positive school climate (Bosworth, Orpinas, & Hein, chap. 11), for creating healthy work organizations (DeJoy & Wilson, chap. 12), and for developing healthy communities (Banyard & Goodman, chap. 13). These chapters bring together and integrate theory, research, and practice to inform the design and evaluation of programs to promote social justice. The content, however, is not exhaustive. Although each chapter provides examples, clearly numerous other exemplars of practice might have been cited. These omissions speak to the burgeoning base of theory, research, and practice in prevention.

In this volume's concluding chapter, we reflect on the status of our renewed vision of social justice prevention, examine its application across the chapters of this book, and discuss the work that we believe remains to fully realize a vision of social justice prevention. Our involvement in this project has also strengthened our awareness of the additional work that needs to be done. Disparities in health status across ethnicity, race, and social class remain great. We hope that the content of this book will serve as a framework for research and practice and will inspire further progress in reducing the gaps between theory, research, and practice in preventive interventions that are informed by social justice goals.

REFERENCES

Albee, G. W. (1982). Preventing psychopathology and promoting human potential. *American Psychologist, 37*, 1043–1050.

Albee, G. W. (1996). Revolutions and counterrevolutions in prevention. *American Psychologist, 51*, 1130–1133.

Albee, G. W., & Ryan-Finn, K. D. (1993). An overview of primary prevention. *Journal of Counseling & Development, 72*, 115–123.

Bell, L. A. (2007). Theoretical foundations for social justice education. In Adams, M., Bell, L. A., & Griffin, P. (Eds.), *Teaching for diversity and social justice* (2nd ed., pp. 3–16). New York: Routledge.

Bronfenbrenner, U. (1979). *The ecology of human development.* Cambridge, MA: Harvard University Press.

Constantine, M. G., Hage, S. M., Kindaichi, M. M., & Bryant, R. M. (2007). Social justice and multicultural issues: Implications for the practice and training of counselors and counseling psychologists. *Journal of Counseling & Development, 85*, 24–29.

Conyne, R. K. (2004). *Preventive counseling: Helping people to become empowered in systems & settings* (2nd ed.). New York: Brunner-Routledge.

Fondacaro, M. R., & Weinberg, D. (2002). Concepts of social justice in community psychology: Towards a social ecological epistemology. *American Journal of Community Psychology, 30*, 473–492.

Fouad, N. A., Gerstein, L. H., & Toporek, R. L. (2006). Social justice and counseling psychology in context. In R. L. Toporek, L. Gerstein, N. Fouad, G. Roysircar, & T. Israel (Eds.), *Handbook for social justice in counseling psychology: Leadership, vision, and action* (pp. 1–16). Thousand Oaks, CA: Sage.

Goodman, L. A., Liang, B., Helms, J. E., Latta, R. E., Sparks, E., & Weintraub, S. R. (2004). Training counseling psychologists as social justice agents: Feminist and multicultural principles in action. *The Counseling Psychologist, 25*, 413–427.

Hage, S., Romano, J., Conyne, R., Kenny, M., Matthews, C., Schwartz, J., & Waldo, M. (2007). Best practice guidelines on prevention in practice, research, training, and social advocacy for psychologists. *The Counseling Psychologist, 35*, 493–566.

Kaplan, R. M. (2000). Two pathways to prevention. *American Psychologist, 55*, 382–396.

Lerner, R. M., Walsh, M. E., & Howard, K. A. (1998). Developmental-contextual considerations: Person-context relations as the bases for risk and resiliency in child and adolescent development. In T. Ollendick (Ed.), *Comprehensive clinical psychology, Vol. 5: Children and adolescents: Clinical formulations and treatment* (pp. 1–24). New York: Elsevier.

McWhirter, E. H. (1998). Emancipatory communitarian psychology. *American Psychologist, 53*, 322–323.

Nelson, G., & Prilleltensky, I. (2005). *Community psychology: In pursuit of liberation and well-being.* New York: Palgrave Macmillan.

Prilleltensky, I. (1997). Values, assumptions, and practices: Assessing the moral implications of psychological discourse and action. *American Psychologist, 52*(5), 517–535.

Prilleltensky, I. (2001). Value-based praxis in community psychology: Moving toward social justice and social action. *American Journal of Community Psychology, 29,* 747–778.

Prilleltensky, I., Dokecki, P., Frieden, G., & Wang, V. O. (2007). Counseling for wellness and justice: Foundations and ethical dilemmas. In E. Aldarondo (Ed.), *Advancing social justice through clinical practice* (pp. 19–42). Mawhah, NJ: Erlbaum.

Prilleltensky, I., & Nelson, G. (1997). *Community psychology: Reclaiming social justice.* Thousand Oaks, CA: Sage.

Rawls, J. (1971). A theory of justice. Cambridge, MA: Harvard University Press.

Romano, J. L., & Hage, S. M. (2000). Prevention and counseling psychology: Revitalizing commitments for the 21st century. *The Counseling Psychologist, 28*(6), 733–763.

Silverman, M. M. (2003). Theories of primary prevention and health promotion. In T. Gullotta, & M. Bloom (Eds.), *Encyclopedia of primary prevention and health promotion* (pp. 27–41). New York: Kluwer.

Swenson, C. R. (1998). Clinical social work's contribution to a social justice perspective. *Social Work, 43,* 527–537.

U. S. Department of Health and Human Services. (2000). *Healthy people 2010: Understanding and improving health* (2nd ed.). Washington, DC: U.S. Government Printing Office.

Vera, E. M., & Speight, S.L. (2007). Advocacy, outreach, and prevention: Integrating social action roles in professional training. In Aldarondo, E. (Ed.), *Advancing social justice through clinical practice* (pp. 373–389). Mahwah, NJ: Erlbaum.

Weissberg, R. P., Kumpfer, K. L., & Seligman, M. E. P. (2003). Prevention that works for children and youth: An introduction. *American Psychologist, 58,* 425–432.

I

SOCIAL JUSTICE
AND PREVENTION

1

PROMOTING POSITIVE DEVELOPMENT AND SOCIAL JUSTICE THROUGH PREVENTION: A LEGACY FOR THE FUTURE

MAUREEN E. KENNY AND JOHN L. ROMANO

A number of psychological specialties (e.g., community psychology, clinical child psychology, counseling psychology) and other disciplines (e.g., public health, social work, school counseling) have for many years engaged in research, prepared professionals, and implemented programs in the name of primary prevention. However, the commitment to the scholarship and application of prevention interventions across human development disciplines and specialties has been inconsistent. For example, in applied psychology, attention to the prevention of mental health problems and the promotion of health-enhancing behaviors has waxed and waned over the years as a history of significant accomplishments has been tempered by major challenges (Romano & Hage, 2000; Tolan & Dodge, 2005; Weissberg, Kumpfer, & Seligman, 2003). This volume benefits from the remarkable and rich history of prevention science and practice, while also seeking to learn from past triumphs and challenges in charting a path for the future.

Our vision of prevention, consistent with that put forth by Hage et al. (2007), is comprehensive: It encompasses "risk reduction" (e.g., McWhirter, McWhirter, McWhirter, & McWhirter, 2007; Mrazek & Haggerty, 1994), strength enhancement (e.g., Cowen, 2000), and social justice (e.g., Albee, 1986; Prilleltensky & Nelson, 2002) and is supported by evidence-based practices (Nation et al., 2003). In a special issue of *The Counseling Psychologist*, Romano and Hage (2000) also advocated for a broad preventive focus that includes fostering strengths and assets on the individual level and promoting institutional, community, and government policies and legislation that support personal and institutional well-being on a community and societal level. Consistent with this broad conceptualization, we contend that prevention efforts that strive to promote social justice must attend to fostering individual and group strengths and to transforming those societal structures and policies that limit social justice.

In this chapter, we present a vision of prevention that seeks to foster social justice by building strengths and reducing risks across multiple levels of society. This vision draws from historical knowledge and incorporates recent developments and initiatives in the field of psychology and mental health promotion. More specifically, our vision focuses on promoting social justice by integrating current knowledge derived from positive psychology and positive youth development, multicultural psychology, developmental psychology, and prevention research. These knowledge bases share a number of common tenets, including their emphasis on the role of context in shaping human development and recognition of individual and contextual risks and assets, which can inform the science and practice of prevention in promoting positive development and social justice. Efforts to integrate these knowledge bases also reveal areas of tension. We contend that these tensions present challenges for advancements in the field of prevention even as they provide a catalyst for further growth. A vision of prevention as a tool in promoting both positive development and social justice is ambitious. As such, we anticipate that efforts to realize this vision will be arduous, requiring study of the past challenges to prevention and close examination of the tensions inherent in both our knowledge bases and in public policy. Thus we begin this chapter with a consideration of prevention history and then describe our contemporary vision within the context of this history and the current social and intellectual milieu.

CONTEMPORARY PREVENTION AS AN ENDURING AND EVOLVING GOAL

Although the origins of prevention can be traced back to Ancient Greece—specifically to Hippocrates, the father of medicine—the history of prevention can be chronicled primarily through a series of 20th century events. In the first half of the 20th century, medical and public health practices made great strides in prevention, greatly reducing or eliminating several physical ailments and diseases. Childhood inoculations eradicated smallpox, and polio is now close to extinction. Pioneers in the field of social work, such as Mary Richmond, were early proponents of prevention. Social advocacy movements, such as the establishment of settlement houses, child labor laws, and the labor movement, were enacted in the United States to prevent exploitation and to empower disenfranchised groups. In the second half of the 20th century, several legislative initiatives on the national level sought to facilitate the empowerment of disenfranchised groups, promote personal well-being, and strengthen society overall. Examples of these laws included those to reduce poverty (President Johnson's War on Poverty), to achieve equity and social justice (the civil rights and women's rights movements), and to promote educational equity and school achievement (Head Start Program).

Following the introduction of psychotropic drugs during the 1950s, many psychiatric patients left overcrowded hospitals and received care in mental health centers in their own communities (Starks & Braslow, 2005). President Kennedy's Community Mental Health Centers Act of 1963 provided funding for community-based mental health services, including primary prevention for mental health (Spaulding & Balch, 1983). During the same period, Caplan (1964) articulated the definitions of primary, secondary, and tertiary prevention, and the specialty of community psychology was formed with a focus on primary prevention. Among the strong supporters of primary prevention during the 1960s and 1970s were a number of prominent psychologists, including George Albee, Emory Cowen, and Seymour Sarason (Cowen, 1996; Spaulding & Balch, 1983). In 1979, the first of several U.S. government reports on health promotion and prevention was published. *Healthy People: The Surgeon General's Report on Health Promotion and Disease Prevention* provided national goals to reduce premature deaths and enhance the quality of life from infancy through older adulthood. To meet the nation's health objectives, the report articulated the need for preventive health services (e.g., prenatal and infant care and immunization programs), health protections (e.g., toxic and infectious agent control), and health promotion (e.g., improved nutrition and smoking cessation). The 1979 volume has been followed by three additional reports, setting national health goals for 1990, 2000, and 2010.

In the 1990s Congress mandated the National Institute of Mental Health and the Institute of Medicine (IOM) to prepare a report on the prevention of mental illness and other problem behaviors, as well as on the promotion of mental health. The interdisciplinary group of scholars from the IOM was asked to review past and current research within the mental health domain and to offer government agencies policy recommendations to advance prevention science (Mrazek & Haggerty, 1994). One of the major contributions of the IOM scholars was their definition of prevention, first articulated by Gordon (1983), which included three categories of prevention interventions: universal (desirable for everyone in the population), selective (for those at risk for becoming ill or developing a problem), and indicated (people at high risk for developing a disorder). In addition to these categories, Gordon identified treatment and maintenance to complete the spectrum of mental health care. Although maintenance is reflected in Caplan's (1964) tertiary prevention, it is not included in the IOM prevention definition.

In the latter part of the 20th century, prevention practice and research, although still a fledgling specialty area in psychology, received increased attention as problems such as alcohol and drug abuse, social violence, depression, HIV/AIDS, school failure, and occupational and family stress became major concerns throughout the world. The International Conference on Primary Health Care (World Health Organization [WHO], 1978) held in 1978 in Alma-Ata, USSR, asserted that physical and mental health and social well-being are fundamental human rights and urged all governments and the world community to promote health and the kind of economic and social development that is integral to healthy development. The WHO policy statement on mental health issued in Helsinki, Finland, in January 2005 reaffirmed the importance of psychological and social well-being as critical to quality of life (WHO, 2005). In the United States, the most recent Surgeon General's Report, *Healthy People 2010* (U.S. Department of Health and Human Services, 2000), identifies national goals to improve the health and quality of life of Americans and to eliminate health disparities across all segments of the population. Among the leading health targets for 2010 are those related to lifestyle behaviors (e.g., physical activity, tobacco use, substance abuse, healthy sexual behavior, mental health, injury, violence, nutrition) and equal access to resources that affect health quality (e.g., environmental quality, access to health care, immunizations).

Beyond Western industrialized societies, countries across the globe use combinations of traditional and contemporary practices to promote societal health and personal well-being (Lee & Armstrong, 1995; Ngubane, 1992). Examples of these global concerns and prevention activities include those to prevent HIV in Africa (Benotsch et al., 2004), in Japan (Nemoto, 2004), and in Mexico (Pick, Poortinga, & Givaudan, 2003); school violence in the Middle East (Marie-Alsana, Haj-Yahia, & Greenbaum, 2006); and child abuse in Japan (Kayama, Sagami, Watanabe, Senoo, & Ohara, 2004).

Contemporary prevention efforts also focus on political and policy changes, such as those to reduce cigarette smoking, to increase funding opportunities for prevention research, and to build a prevention infrastructure within the National Institute of Mental Health and the Centers for Disease Control and Prevention. School-based prevention interventions for children and adolescents have become increasingly sophisticated and scientifically rigorous (Greenberg et al., 2003). Finally, professional organizations such as the American Psychological Association (APA) have given increased attention to prevention. For example, prevention was the theme of the 1998 APA Convention, and APA's Society of Counseling Psychology (Division 17) has promoted a prevention agenda through its Prevention Section, established in 2000. Clearly, the importance of prevention research, intervention, and public policy has escalated throughout the world as we advance into the early 21st century.

HISTORICAL DEVELOPMENTS AND OUR CONTEMPORARY VISION

Despite the current status of prevention as an important agenda for mental and physical health, we would be remiss to ignore the social and political forces that have shaped its history and will surely influence its future. As noted by Shore (2003), political forces have had and continue to have a substantive role in shaping the agenda of prevention and health promotion. Changes in the dominant social and political ideologies have affected the extent to which prevention has attended to both strengths and risks, the extent to which support has been offered for both primary and secondary prevention, and the extent to which prevention has attended to changing environmental and community factors, as opposed to individuals.

Early definitions of prevention as put forth during the mid-20th century were derived from a traditional public health perspective that emphasized pathology and physical illness (Bloom & Gullotta, 2003). As such, early prevention efforts focused primarily on individual change and reducing personal deficits or problems that were associated with poor health and psychopathology (Conyne, 2004). In the 1970s, Cowen (1973) added the concept of wellness enhancement as a second prong of prevention to supplement the prevailing focus on disease prevention and risk reduction

(Bloom & Gullotta, 2003). Cowen's two-pronged definition was adopted by the President's Commission on Mental Health in 1978, which proposed to increase prevention efforts and to reduce poverty. Prevention efforts throughout the 1960s and 1970s recognized the role of the social environment in the development and course of mental health problems. By the 1980s, however, prevention returned to a more narrow focus on risk reduction and an emphasis on the organic, rather than the environmental bases, of psychological disorder (Albee & Ryan-Finn, 1993).

According to Albee (2003), prevention efforts that seek to change the social order tend to be unpopular with political conservatives, who have a vested interest in maintaining the status quo. As a leading figure in the prevention field, Albee (e.g., 1986, 2003) was long a critic of psychology's emphasis on remedial/treatment approaches to intervention and to a primarily biological approach to prevention. Albee and Ryan-Finn (1993) maintain that biological and remedial approaches serve to maintain the current social order, and they advocate for proactive approaches that focus on systemic change and the reduction of oppression. The discussion of prevention set forth in this volume is highly indebted to Albee's vision. Accordingly, our vision of prevention understands the powerful role of the social context in its multiple dimensions of impact on human outcomes. Prevention, in our vision as in Albee's (2003), is conceptualized, furthermore, as a means for promoting social justice.

In addition to building on the views of historical leaders in prevention, the discussion put forth in this volume benefits from and integrates influences that have emerged in recent years. These influences have served to shift attention from a narrow preventive focus on pathology to a broader focus on wellness promotion and concerns for social justice (Shore, 2003). A social justice vision of prevention mandates an examination of the consequences of mental health interventions at the individual and societal levels and their success in fostering a more just society. We will now define social justice, describe the knowledge bases that inform a social justice vision of prevention, and then discuss the tensions that emerge from efforts to integrate these perspectives.

THEORETICAL AND KNOWLEDGE BASES INFORMING A SOCIAL JUSTICE VISION

Social Justice

Although defining social justice is complex and has been the life work of numerous scholars (e.g., Freire, 1970/1990; Rawls, 1993), definitions of social justice generally emphasize fair and equitable access to societal resources that allow all groups to participate in society without threat to their physical and psychological safety (Bell, 2007; Fouad, Gerstein, & Toporek, 2006; Goodman et al., 2004; see introduction and chap. 4, this volume). A social justice vision of prevention thus seeks to combat those societal structures, policies, and hierarchies that limit access to resources based on group or individual characteristics, including age, race, ethnicity, social class, poverty, religion, gender, immigration status, sexual orientation, and language (Davidson, Waldo, & Adams, 2006; Toporek & Williams, 2006). Following the definition of social justice, prevention should also increase access to the skills and resources that enable full participation in society (Prilleltensky, 1997). This should be done, furthermore, in a way that recognizes and builds on cultural assets and seeks to empower constituents, rather than blame them (Conyne, 2004; Goodman et al., 2004; Romano & Hage, 2000).

Whereas many social justice initiatives include prevention, not all prevention programs exemplify social justice (Davidson et al., 2006). Prevention with a social justice vision embraces social advocacy as a means for challenging social policies and structures that limit access to resources by race, ethnicity, religion, or gender in efforts to effect broader social change. Although the prevention efforts of the 1960s and 1970s emphasized the need for social change, they often disempowered the populations who were the targets of the interventions by not involving them in program development (Fondacaro & Weinberg, 2002). The goals for prevention programs at that time, and often today, were set by government officials and mental health professionals with little input from community participants. In contrast, prevention programs that seek to facilitate the empowerment of clients and address systemic barriers that limit equal access to opportunities and resources are consistent with a social justice vision.

Prilleltensky and colleagues (Prilleltensky, 1997; Prilleltensky & Nelson, 2002) propose an emancipatory communitarian framework that guides their approach to social justice. Even as this framework recognizes that social change is necessary for the attainment of social justice, it also stresses the importance of building strengths among individuals, groups, and families. Although the removal of societal barriers enhances opportunities for societal participation, an individual's capacity to make use of available opportunities is influenced by the person's own skills and resources (Prilleltensky, Dokecki, Frieden, & Wang, 2007). Social justice interventions must therefore focus simultaneously on supporting individual, family, group, and societal well-being, in addition to reducing societal barriers.

The *Report of the APA Task Force on Socioeconomic Status* (2007) focuses on socioeconomic status (SES) and social class factors that enhance or detract from optimal human functioning across the life span. The report offers seven recommendations to educators, researchers, and policy makers to strengthen attention to SES and social class variables across the psychological landscape, from research to training to practice to social advocacy. The specific recommendations to the parent APA organization are: (1) to establish a continuing committee on SES and social class; (2) to expand support for psychological research, education, practice, and public policy addressing SES and social class; (3) to strengthen clinical practice through the integration of SES and social class; (4) to improve the quality and impact of psychological research on SES and social class; (5) to encourage an increase in training and education in psychology related to SES and social class; (6) to continue advocacy efforts of social policies that improve health and well-being across the socioeconomic spectrum; and (7) to foster social class diversity and social class consciousness, thereby "opening up" the field for the next generation of psychologists. Attention to SES and social class factors is fundamental to a social justice perspective in prevention science. The work of the SES Task Force provides much needed guidance to the profession and support for implementing a social justice vision of prevention.

Developmental Psychology: Theory and Research

Developmental theories, including ecological (Bronfenbrenner, 1979) and developmental contextual theory (Lerner, Walsh, & Howard, 1998) have been critical in focusing attention on the role of multiple and interacting contexts in shaping human outcomes. These frameworks are useful, furthermore, for integrating knowledge of risk and protective factors in ways that can guide the design and evaluation of preventive interventions with the simultaneous goals of reducing risk and building competency (Bogenschneider, 1996; Kenny, Waldo, Warter, & Barton, 2002; Lerner, 2001; Walsh, Galassi, Murphy, & Park-Taylor, 2002).

Over the past 20 years, research has increased knowledge of individual and contextual risk factors and awareness of the protective factors that can foster resilience or positive outcomes in the face of significant adversity (Luthar & Cicchetti, 2000; Yates & Masten, 2004). At the contextual level, for example, high-quality schools and health care systems, supportive relationships with adults at home and in the community, and safe neighborhoods represent examples of protective factors that can reduce the negative effects of risk and provide foundations for healthy development (Yates & Masten, 2004). Contextual vulnerability factors that heighten the risk for psychological distress include community violence, poverty, racial injustice, and unemployment (Hage et al., 2007; Luthar & Cicchetti, 2000). Poverty, for example, may present developmental risks by limiting access to high-quality child care or adult supervision in the after-school hours, whereas high-quality child care and after-school care programs may conversely serve to mitigate some of the risks associated with poverty (Vera & Shin, 2006).

Positive Psychology and Positive Youth Development

Attention to protective factors and resilient outcomes has also stimulated interest in positive psychology (Seligman, 2002; Snyder & Lopez, 2002) and positive youth development (Catalano, Berglund, Ryan, Lonczak, & Hawkins, 2002; Pittman, Irby, Tolman, Yohalem, & Ferber, 2001). Although somewhat distinct in emphasis, both the positive psychology and positive youth development perspectives share an appreciation for the role of individual and contextual assets in human development and seek to promote optimal human development so that individuals may thrive, rather than merely avoid risk.

Positive psychology proposes a strengths-based approach to both therapy and prevention, seeking to promote positive traits, such as courage, optimism, and hope among individuals and developing institutions that foster responsibility, altruism, and other dimensions of citizenship (Lopez et al., 2006; Seligman, 2002). Seligman maintains that the disease model that has dominated the field of psychology does not prevent serious societal problems, such as depression and school violence, and suggests that major advances in prevention emanate from the knowledge of strengths that serve to buffer against mental illness. He thus calls for a positive approach that seeks to enhance the strengths of individuals and cultivate strength-fostering climates in the family, school, corporate world, and broader society.

Positive youth development has emerged as a universal intervention approach, which recognizes that young people need a variety of social, emotional, educational, and vocational competencies and seeks to provide the individual, familial, community, and societal resources needed to foster these competencies. Being free of risk or disease is not enough to ensure full and productive participation in society (Catalano et al., 2002; Pittman et al., 2001). Positive psychology and positive youth development thus inform the development of preventive interventions that seek to build strengths and enhance competencies.

Multicultural Psychology

Multicultural theory and research have also grown in recent years, with an awareness of the changing demographic of our communities and commitment to eliminating the disparities in social and economic opportunities currently afforded by race, ethnicity, gender, and able-bodiness. Although many prevention efforts were developed in middle-class communities and reflect Western values, advances in multiculturalism provide a growing knowledge base to inform the design of culturally relevant interventions that recognize the strengths of diverse communities. We now recognize that culturally relevant interventions must go beyond a superficial accommodation to cultural difference and attend to those "deep structures" that influence community response (Castro, Barrera, & Martinez, 2004; Kumpfer, Alvarado, Smith, & Bellamy, 2002; Reese, Vera, & Caldwell, 2006). Cultural values, which may differ by subgroup, geographic region, and educational level, should be respected in program design and delivery (Kumpfer et al., 2002). APA's "Guidelines on Multicultural Education, Training, Research, Practice, and Organizational Change for Psychologists" (2003) can be applied in integrating considerations of culture and awareness of oppressive systemic structures in the design, implementation, and evaluation of preventive interventions (Sue & Constantine, 2005).

International prevention efforts addressing cultural dimensions of ethnicity and race within a given national context will also help to inform multicultural and social justice perspectives to advance prevention. Countries across the globe, such as Mexico (Pick et al., 2003), Zambia (Gausset, 2001), and Japan (Nemoto, 2004) have addressed the HIV/AIDS pandemic through prevention. Discussion of sexual health is often discouraged in many countries, including the United States, which impedes prevention of sexually transmitted diseases and unwanted pregnancies. Sex education in schools is often controversial, and cultural norms, values, and traditions challenge sex education and prevention programs (Pick et al., 2003). As another example, a qualitative study of child abuse prevention in Japan noted that the cultural norm of female passivity often prevents mothers from seeking support and assistance when they face the challenges of child rearing (Kayama et al., 2004). Even within countries, ethnic differences and educational and health disparities are important to consider when developing prevention programs, as was discussed by Marie-Alsana et al. (2006) in the context of Arab elementary school children in Israel.

Prevention Research

Consistent with the scientist–practitioner model, prevention programs need to be designed, selected, and implemented based on current research knowledge and should be evaluated for their effectiveness when implemented in a new setting. A growing knowledge base concerning what works in prevention informs our renewed vision. The APA Task Force on Prevention, Promotion, and Intervention Alternatives in Psychology in the 1980s identified model programs, and *14 Ounces of Prevention* (Price, Cowen, Lorion, & Ramos-McKay, 1988) and the 1998 APA Presidential Task Force, Prevention: Promoting Strength, Resilience, and Health in Young People, identified additional well-researched and effective programs (Greenberg et al., 2003; Nation et al., 2003; Weissberg et al., 2003). In addition, we have found that prevention research affirms a number of principles for effective practice emanating from a social justice agenda, developmental theory and research, positive psychology and positive youth development, and multiculturalism. Prevention research (Greenberg et al., 2003; Weissberg et al., 2003), for example, reveals that effective prevention programs are tailored to the cultural context in which they are being implemented. Building on strengths, sharing power, giving voice, and leaving tools that allow for self-determination among those with whom we work are four of the six principles identified by Goodman et al. (2004) to guide social justice work. Consistent with this social justice approach, prevention outcome research (Catalano et al., 2002; Nation et al., 2003; Weissberg et al., 2003; Vera & Reese, 2000) has determined that effective programs involve diverse stakeholders in all phases of program design, implementation, and evaluation and seek to build competencies and increase health, in addition to reducing risks.

AREAS OF TENSION: A FOUNDATION FOR ADVANCES IN THEORY, RESEARCH, AND PRACTICE

The vision of prevention as a tool for social justice clearly converges with developmental theory and research, positive psychology and positive youth development, multiculturalism, and prevention outcome research, including a focus on context, attention to building strengths and reducing risks, and the importance of cultural adaptation. Although these knowledge bases reveal several common principles, efforts to integrate these perspectives reveal naturally occurring tensions and the limitations of current knowledge. We have identified five areas of tension that keep us from attaining complacency and alert us to some of the contemporary challenges for prevention theory and research.

Attention to Cultural Variation

Although developmental psychology, positive psychology, and multiculturalism bring many common emphases to social justice-oriented prevention, closer examination reveals some areas of uncertainty. Positive psychology and positive youth development, for example, seek to affirm strengths and avoid the focus on deficits that characterize some prevention and treatment modalities. Multiculturalism emphasizes the importance of considering cultural variations in the ways in which strengths are understood. Although many diverse cultural practices have been wrongly identified as maladaptive based on difference, all cultural practices cannot be assumed ipso facto to be healthy. Some cultural traditions, such as reliance on high-fat foods as a dietary staple, restrictive roles for women, or use of harsh physical punishment in child rearing, may have negative consequences that need to be considered. Frazier, Lee, and Steger (2006) note that further research is needed to advance understanding of the complex ways in which conceptions of optimal human functioning and the factors that contribute to optimal functioning vary across and within race, ethnicity, culture, religion, and social class.

Building Strengths and Transforming Oppressive Social Structures

An exclusive focus on promoting strengths could also neglect societal problems that must be addressed in the service of social justice and multiculturalism. Vera and Shin (2006) contend that to promote strengths in a "socially toxic world," it is imperative to use strategies that correct unjust social structures. Exclusive attention to positive emotions may also overlook the value of psychological states that motivate change. Although anger, for example, might be considered as a maladaptive or negative emotion to be managed, it can also serve as an impetus for collective social action among persons of color who seek to resist societal injustices (Watts, 2004). The construct of resilience, which highlights individual and community strengths in overcoming adversity, has been criticized for placing responsibility or blame on individuals rather than social structures (Luthar & Cicchetti, 2000). Watts critiques the construct of resilience further, suggesting that it applauds individual adjustment to conditions of social injustice, rather than promoting activities to change oppressive social structures.

Social Justice and Research

A simultaneous commitment to multiculturalism, social justice, and evidence-based practice may also be a source of tension. Scientific research typically emphasizes standards related to objectivity, generalizability, standardization, and neutrality in values. Social justice entails a commitment to social change, concern for community well-being, inclusion of the perspective of all stakeholders, and respect for diversity, among others. Traditional models of science have neglected social justice (Fondacaro & Weinberg, 2002), perhaps related to challenges in assessing social justice outcomes and in integrating procedural justice processes, such as including participants in program design and evaluations, with scientific methods. Yet, scientific evidence is increasingly demanded as a component of public accountability and as a requirement for continued public and private funding (Greenberg et al., 2003). Programs that are not effective, furthermore, do not serve the best interests of the disenfranchised and thus do not foster social justice. However, because findings from efficacy trials completed in experimental contexts may not be easily transferred to varied community contexts, prevention researchers need to conduct effectiveness trials under diverse, natural conditions (e.g., Prochaska, Evers, Prochaska, Van Marter, & Johnson, 2007).

Although it is clear that evaluation is essential for determining whether a specific intervention is effective, experimental scientific method may conflict with efforts to be flexible and responsive with diverse populations. For example, although scientific procedures would suggest that interventions should be delivered in a standardized manner to be replicable, efforts to be responsive to local needs suggest that program planners and evaluators should incorporate the views of local stakeholders and adapt content, procedures, and evaluation methods to fit the local context (Castro et al., 2004; Reese et al., 2006). Scientific concerns for fidelity in implementation need to be balanced with concerns for cultural and ecological validity and social change (Fondacaro & Weinberg, 2002; Yates & Masten, 2004). Mid-course changes made to be responsive to local concerns might wreak havoc on rigorous research design but may be critical to program continuation. Although clinical trials may be viewed as rigorous and valued in the scientific community, methods such as participatory action research may provide results that are more valuable for the community being served. The challenges of designing and evaluating an effective prevention program in varied community and school settings are great, but social justice demands that access to effective interventions be fair and equitable.

Multiculturalism and Structural Change

With regard to multiculturalism and social justice, the APA "Guidelines on Multicultural Education, Training, Research, Practice, and Organizational Change for Psychologists" (APA, 2003) provide guidance in the design and delivery of services to multicultural populations. Yet their application for prevention, advocacy, and outreach services intended to promote social justice remains somewhat limited (Vera, Daly, Gonzales, Morgan, & Thakral, 2006; Vera & Speight, 2003). Although macrolevel interventions are considered integral to social justice work (Goodman et al., 2004), psychologists to date have more fully articulated the applications of multicultural guidelines for practice in therapy and organizational development than in systemic interventions (Vera & Speight, 2003). Similarly, feminist and multicultural counseling theorists provide an understanding of the role of social oppression in mental health, but the theories have been applied by psychologists most often in microlevel social justice practice, rather than macrolevel intervention (Goodman et al., 2004).

Professional Barriers

An examination of the tensions revealed across these knowledge bases alerts us, moreover, to pragmatic challenges in accomplishing the proposed vision of prevention. Prevention work with a social justice agenda challenges many of the social and economic structures that support our livelihood as professionals. Within the field of psychology, for example, insurance companies typically reimburse therapy services, rather than prevention programs or social advocacy efforts (Vera & Speight, 2003). As noted by Helms (2003), social justice interventions are often delivered pro bono. Although we may seek to imbue our students with social justice values, unless they can be paid for this work, they may be forced to revise their commitments when they enter the professional world. Although recent work has begun to document approaches to social justice and prevention training among professionals (Goodman et al., 2004; Hage et al., 2007), our current experience and knowledge base in doing this remain limited. Preparing students to competently deliver prevention and advocacy interventions within a multicultural and social justice framework will require changes in our training programs, as well as our licensing requirements (Ivey & Collins, 2003). In our view, many training programs in psychology do not equip students with the skills and strategies to accomplish social change on a macro level.

CONCLUSION

We believe this is an exciting time for prevention theory, research, and practice. We are encouraged by the renewed vision and interest in prevention, but see numerous challenges as we move forward. We hope that the inevitable tides of political and social attitudes will not decrease the energies that are currently propelling a vision of prevention that focuses on context, strengths, and social justice values and is supported by research evidence.

REFERENCES

Albee, G. W. (1986). Toward a just society: Lessons from observations on the primary prevention of psychopathology. *American Psychologist, 41*, 891–898.

Albee, G. W. (2003). The contributions of society, culture, and social class to emotional disorder. In T. P. Gullotta & M. Bloom (Eds.), *Encyclopedia of primary prevention and health promotion* (pp. 97–104). New York: Kluwer.

Albee, G. W., & Ryan-Finn, K. D. (1993). An overview of primary prevention. *Journal of Counseling and Development, 72*, 115–123.

American Psychological Association. (2003). Guidelines on multicultural education, training, research, practice, and organizational change for psychologists. *American Psychologist, 58*, 377–402.

American Psychological Association, Task Force Report on Socioeconomic Status. (2007). *Report of the APA Task Force on socioeconomic status.* Washington, DC: American Psychological Association. Retrieved September 12, 2007, from http://www2.apa.org/pi/SES_task_force_report.pdf

Bell, L. A. (2007). Theoretical foundations for social justice education. In M. Adams, L. A. Bell, & P. Griffin (Eds.), *Teaching for diversity and social justice* (2nd ed., pp. 3–16). New York: Routledge.

Benotsch, E. G., Stevenson, Y., Sitzler, C. A., Kelly, J. A., Makhaye, G., Mathey, E. D., et al. (2004). HIV prevention in Africa: Programs and populations served by non-governmental organizations. *Journal of Community Health, 29*, 319–336.

Bloom, M., & Gullotta, T. P. (2003). Evolving definitions of primary prevention. In T. P. Gullotta & M. Bloom (Eds.), *Encyclopedia of primary prevention and health promotion* (pp. 9–14). New York: Kluwer.

Bogenschneider, K. (1996). Family related prevention programs: An ecological risk/protective theory for building prevention programs, policies, and community capacity to support youth. *Family Relations, 45*, 127–138.

Bronfenbrenner, U. (1979). *The ecology of human development.* Cambridge, MA: Harvard University Press.

Caplan, G. (1964). *Principles of preventive psychiatry.* New York: Basic Books.

Castro, F. G., Barrera, M., Jr., & Martinez, C. R., Jr. (2004). The cultural adaptation of prevention interventions: Resolving tensions between fidelity and fit. *Prevention Science, 5*, 41–45.

Catalano, R. F., Berglund, M. L., Ryan, J. A. M., Lonczak, H. S., & Hawkins, J. D. (2002). Positive youth development in the United States: Research findings on evaluations of positive youth development programs. *Prevention & Treatment, 5*, Article 15. Retrieved August, 1, 2002, from http://journals.apa.org .osiyou.cc.columbia.edu:2048/prevention/volume5/pre0050015a.html

Conyne, R. K. (2004). *Preventive counseling: Helping people to become empowered in systems and settings.* New York: Brunner-Routledge.

Cowen, E. L. (1973). Social and community interventions. *Annual Review of Psychology, 24*, 423–472.

Cowen, E. L. (1996). The ontogenesis of primary prevention: Lengthy strides and stubbed toes. *American Journal of Community Psychology, 24*, 235–249.

Cowen, E. L. (2000). Community psychology and routes to psychological wellness. In J. Rappaport & E. Seidman (Eds.), *Handbook of community psychology* (pp. 79–99). New York: Kluwer.

Davidson, M., Waldo, M., & Adams, E. M. (2006). Promoting social justice through prevention interventions. In R. L. Toporek, L. Gerstein, N. Fouad, G. Roysircar, & T. Israel (Eds.), *Handbook for social justice in counseling psychology: Leadership, vision, and action* (pp. 117–129). Thousand Oaks, CA: Sage.

Fondacaro, M. R., & Weinberg, D. (2002). Concepts of social justice in community psychology: Towards a social ecological epistemology. *American Journal of Community Psychology, 30*, 473–492.

Fouad, N. A., Gerstein, L. H., & Toporek, R. L. (2006). Social justice and counseling psychology in context. In R. L. Toporek, L. Gerstein, N. Fouad, G. Roysircar, & T. Israel (Eds.), *Handbook for social justice in counseling psychology: Leadership, vision, and action* (pp. 1–16). Thousand Oaks, CA: Sage.

Frazier, P. A., Lee, R. M., & Steger, M. F. (2006). What can counseling psychology contribute to the study of optimal human functioning? *The Counseling Psychologist, 34,* 293–303.

Freire, P. (1970/1990). *Pedagogy of the oppressed.* New York: Continuum.

Gausset, Q. (2001). AIDS and cultural practices in Africa: The case of the Tonga (Zambia). *Social Science and Medicine, 52,* 509–518.

Goodman, L. A., Liang, B., Helms, J. E., Latta, R. E., Sparks, E., & Weintraub, S. R. (2004). Training counseling psychologists as social justice agents: Feminist and multicultural principles in action. *The Counseling Psychologist, 25,* 413–427.

Gordon, R. S. (1983). An operational classification of disease prevention. *Public Health Reports, 98,* 107–109.

Greenberg, M. T., Weissberg, R. P., O'Brien, M. U., Zins, J. E., Fredericks, L., Resnik, H., & Elias, M. J. (2003). Enhancing school-based prevention and youth development through coordinated social, emotional, and academic learning. *American Psychologist, 58,* 466–474.

Hage, S., Romano, J., Conyne, R., Kenny, M. E., Matthews, C. R., Schwartz, J. P., & Waldo, M. (2007). Best practice guidelines on prevention practice, research, training, and social advocacy for psychologists. *The Counseling Psychologist, 35,* 493–566.

Helms, J. E. (2003). A pragmatic view of social justice. *The Counseling Psychologist, 31,* 305–313.

Ivey, A. E., & Collins, N. M. (2003). Social justice: A long term challenge for counseling psychology. *The Counseling Psychologist, 31,* 290–298.

Kayama, M., Sagami, A., Watanabe, Y., Senoo, E., & Ohara, M. (2004). Child abuse prevention in Japan: An approach to screening and intervention with mothers. *Public Health Nursing, 21,* 513–518.

Kenny, M., Waldo, M., Warter, E., & Barton, C. (2002). School-linked prevention: Theory, science, and practice for enhancing the lives of children and youth. *The Counseling Psychologist, 30,* 726–748.

Kumpfer, K. L., Alvarado, R., Smith, P., & Bellamy, N. (2002). Cultural sensitivity and adaptation in family-based prevention interventions. *Prevention Science, 3,* 241–246.

Lee, C. C., & Armstrong, K. L. (1995). Indigenous models of mental health intervention: Lessons from traditional healers. In J. G. Ponterotto, J. M. Casas, L. A. Suzuki, & C. M. Alexander (Eds.), *Handbook of multicultural counseling* (pp. 441–456). London: Sage.

Lerner, R. M. (2001). Promoting promotion in the development of prevention science. *Applied Developmental Science, 5,* 254–257.

Lerner, R. M., Walsh, M. E., & Howard, K. A. (1998). Developmental-contextual considerations: Person-context relations as the bases for risk and resiliency in child and adolescent development. In T. Ollendick (Ed.), *Comprehensive clinical psychology: Vol. 5. Children and adolescents: Clinical formulations and treatment* (pp. 1–24). New York: Elsevier.

Lopez, S. J., Magyar-Moe, J. L., Petersen, S. E., Ryder, J. A., Krieshok, T. S., O'Byrne, K. K., et al. (2006). Counseling psychology's focus on positive aspects of human functioning. *The Counseling Psychologist, 34,* 205–227.

Luthar, S. S., & Cicchetti, D. (2000). The construct of resilience: Implications for interventions and social policies. *Development and Psychopathology, 12,* 857–885.

Marie-Alsana, W., Haj-Yahia, M. M., & Greenbaum, C. W. (2006). Violence among Arab elementary school pupils in Israel. *Journal of Interpersonal Violence, 21,* 58–88.

McWhirter, J. J., McWhirter, B. T., McWhirter, E. H., & McWhirter, R. J. (2007). *At-risk youth: A comprehensive response* (4th ed.). Belmont, CA: Thompson/Wadsworth.

Mrazek, P. J., & Haggerty, R. J. (1994). *Reduced risk for mental disorders: Frontiers for preventive interventions research.* Washington, DC: National Academy Press.

Nation, M., Crusto, C., Wandersman, A., Kumpfer, K., Seybolt, D., Morrissey-Kane, E., et al. (2003). What works in prevention: Principles and effective prevention programs. *American Psychologist, 58,* 449–456.

Nemoto, T. (2004). HIV/AIDS surveillance and prevention studies in Japan: Summary and recommendations. *AIDS Education and Prevention, 16* (Supplement A), 27–42.

Ngubane, H. (1992). Clinical practice and organization of indigenous healers in South Africa. In S. Feierman & J. M. Janzen (Eds.), *The social basis of health and healing in Africa* (pp. 366–375). Los Angeles: University of California.

Pick, S., Poortinga, Y. H., & Givaudan, M. (2003). Integrating intervention theory and strategy in culture-sensitive health promotion programs. *Professional Psychology: Research and Practice, 34,* 422–429.

Pittman, K. J., Irby, M., Tolman, J., Yohalem, N., & Ferber, T. (2001). *Preventing problems, promoting development, encouraging engagement: Competing priorities or inseparable goals.* Retrieved March 1, 2003, from http://forumforyouthinvestment.org/preventproblems.pdf

Price, R. H., Cowen, E. L., Lorion, R. P., & Ramos-McKay, J. (1988). *Fourteen ounces of prevention: A casebook for practitioners.* Washington, DC: American Psychological Association.

Prilleltensky, I. (1997). Values, assumptions, and practices: Assessing the moral implications of psychological discourse and action. *American Psychologist, 52,* 517–535.

Prilleltensky, I., Dokecki, P., Frieden, G., & Wang, V. O. (2007). Counseling for wellness and justice: Foundations and ethical dilemmas. In E. Aldarondo (Ed.), *Advancing social justice through clinical practice* (pp. 19–42). Mahwah, NJ: Erlbaum.

Prilleltensky, I., & Nelson, G. (2002). *Doing psychology critically: Making a difference in diverse settings*. Basingstoke, England: Palgrave.

Prochaska, J. O., Evers, K. E., Prochaska, J. M., Van Marter, D., & Johnson, J. L. (2007). Efficacy and effectiveness trials: Examples from smoking cessation and bullying prevention. *Journal of Health Psychology, 12*, 170–178.

Rawls, J. (1993). *Political liberalism*. Cambridge, MA: Harvard University Press.

Reese, L., Vera, E., & Caldwell, L. (2006). The role and function of culture in violence prevention practice and science. In J. R. Lutzker (Ed.), *Preventing violence: Research and evidence-based intervention strategies* (pp. 259–278). Washington, DC: American Psychological Association.

Romano, J. L., & Hage, S. M. (2000). Prevention and counseling psychology: Revitalizing commitments for the 21st century. *The Counseling Psychologist, 28*, 733–763.

Seligman, M. (2002). Positive psychology, positive prevention, and positive therapy. In C. R. Snyder & S. J. Lopez (Eds.), *Handbook of positive psychology* (pp. 3–9). New York: Oxford University Press.

Shore, M. F. (2003). The political context of primary prevention and health promotion. In T. P. Gullotta & M. Bloom (Eds.), *Encyclopedia of primary prevention and health promotion* (pp. 104–107). New York: Kluwer.

Snyder, C. R., & Lopez, S. J. (Eds.). (2002). *Handbook of positive psychology*. New York: Oxford University Press.

Spaulding, J., & Balch, P. (1983). A brief history of primary prevention in the twentieth century: 1908 to 1980. *American Journal of Community Psychology, 11*, 59–80.

Starks, S. L., & Braslow, J. T. (2005). The making of contemporary American psychiatry, part 1: Patients, treatments, and therapeutic rationales before and after World War II. *History of Psychology, 8*, 176–193.

Sue, D. W., & Constantine, M. G. (2005). Effective multicultural consultation and organizational development. In M. G. Constantine and D. W. Sue (Eds.), *Strategies for building multicultural competence in mental health and educational settings* (pp. 212–226). Hoboken, NJ: Wiley.

Tolan, P. H., & Dodge, K. A. (2005). Children's mental health as a primary care and concern: A system of comprehensive support and service. *American Psychologist, 60*, 601–614.

Toporek, R. L., & Williams, R. A. (2006). Ethics and professional issues related to the practice of social justice in counseling psychology. In R. L. Toporek, L. Gerstein, N. Fouad, G. Roysircar & T. Israel (Eds.), *Handbook for social justice in counseling psychology: Leadership, vision, and action* (pp. 17–34). Thousand Oaks, CA: Sage.

U.S. Department of Health and Human Services. (2000). *Healthy people 2010: Understanding and improving health* (2nd ed.). Washington, DC: U.S. Government Printing Office.

Vera, E. M., Daly, B., Gonzales, R., Morgan, M., & Thakral, C. (2006). Prevention and outreach with underserved populations. In R. L. Toporek, L. Gerstein, N. Fouad, G. Roysircar, & T. Israel (Eds.), *Handbook for social justice in counseling psychology: Leadership, vision, and action* (pp. 86–99). Thousand Oaks, CA: Sage.

Vera, E. M., & Reese, L. E. (2000). Preventive interventions with school-age youth. In S. D. Brown & R. W. Lent (Eds.), *Handbook of counseling psychology* (pp. 411–434). New York: Wiley.

Vera, E. M., & Shin, R. Q. (2006). Promoting strengths in a socially toxic world: Supporting resiliency with systemic interventions. *Counseling Psychologist, 34,* 80–89.

Vera, E. M., & Speight, S. (2003). Multicultural competence, social justice, and counseling psychology: Expanding our roles. *Counseling Psychologist, 31,* 253–272.

Walsh, M., Galassi, J. P., Murphy, J. A., & Park-Taylor, J. (2002). A conceptual framework for counseling psychologists in schools. *The Counseling Psychologist, 30,* 682–704.

Watts, R. J. (2004). Integrating social justice and psychology. *The Counseling Psychologist, 32,* 855–865.

Weissberg, R. P., Kumpfer, K. L., & Seligman, M. E. P. (2003). Prevention that works for children and youth: An introduction. *American Psychologist, 58,* 425–432.

World Health Organization. (1978, September 6–12). *Declaration of Alma-Ata, International Conference on Primary Health Care, Alma-Ata (Kazakstan) USSR.* Retrieved on March 4, 2007, from http://www.euro.who.int/AboutWHO/Policy/20010827_1

World Health Organization. (2005, January 12–15). *Mental Health Action Plan for Europe. WHO European Ministerial Conference on Mental Health, Helsinki.* Retrieved on March 4, 2007, from http://www.euro.who.int/Document/MNH/edoc07.pdf

Yates, T. M., & Masten, A. S. (2004). Fostering the future: Resilience theory and the practice of positive psychology. In P. A. Linley & S. Joseph (Eds.), *Positive psychology in practice* (pp. 521–539). New York: Wiley.

2

ADVANCING PREVENTION, HEALTH PROMOTION, AND SOCIAL JUSTICE THROUGH PRACTICAL INTEGRATION OF PREVENTION SCIENCE AND PRACTICE

LE'ROY E. REESE, JOHN HARVEY WINGFIELD, AND DANIEL BLUMENTHAL

Advances in the field of prevention science and practice during the past 50 years have improved the human condition in significant ways. Scientists have now identified many of the risk factors responsible for a host of adverse developmental, psychological, and physical health outcomes (Albee, 1996; Biglan, Mrazek, Carnine, & Flay, 2003). Additionally, scientists understand that a number of diseases have shared risk factors and risk behaviors, an instructive finding that helps to explain the sometimes comorbid conditions experienced at an individual and community level (Flay, 2002; Hawkins, Catalano, & Arthur, 2002). Beyond being able to identify risk factors, scientists understand how many of these risk factors operate. The development of sophisticated statistical models now allows researchers and practitioners to make reasonably accurate predictions regarding the contribution of these factors in explaining certain diseases and risk behaviors (Bloom, 2006). Finally, and perhaps most germane to the focus of this volume, preventionists understand in many instances how to prevent the occurrence of causal agents, thereby arresting their detrimental effects on the health status of individuals and the larger domain of public health. One practical benefit of these advances is that incremental increases have been made in the last 30-plus years in terms of expanding the average life expectancy of U.S. citizens (Nussbaum, 2006).

Another by-product of the advances made in prevention science is that increasingly scientists and practitioners see remedial intervention (i.e., treatment) as insufficient and reactionary, particularly when such approaches are the primary methods by which risk behavior and disease are addressed (Albee, 1996). As Albee (2000a) and other early prevention pioneers who extolled the benefits of proactive (i.e., primary) preventive health strategies asserted, society is healthier when the occurrence of various risk behaviors (e.g., violence, drug abuse) and disease (e.g., cancer, cardiovascular disease) are prevented prior to their onset.

However, troubling questions continue to haunt prevention researchers, practitioners, and policy makers committed to improving the nation's health generally and in particular that of those citizens and communities disproportionately burdened by disease and premature mortality (U.S. Department of Health and Human Services [USDHHS], 2000). Specifically, in view of the advances in prevention science and practice, why do the disparate health statuses continue to exist among the poor and certain ethnic minority groups in the United States? Conversely, given the advances of the last 50 years, why is progress in ameliorating the public health burden of certain diseases or risk behaviors (e.g., cardiovascular disease, cancer, violence) seemingly stalled? Former Surgeon General David Satcher provides a salient response to the latter question in his assertion that the United States spends more on treating diseases than on preventing them (Satcher, 2006). In fact, only about 3% of the health-care dollar is spent on prevention.

Biglan (2004), among others, recently asserted that one of the most significant challenges facing the field of prevention science is the translation (i.e., dissemination and implementation) of the last 20 years of prevention research into tangible reductions in the incidence of problem behaviors and diseases (see also Elliot & Mihalic, 2004; Pentz, 2004). In an effort to assist with this challenge, the Society for Prevention Research developed a strategic plan that promotes federal- and state-level initiatives on the integration of prevention research and practice via dissemination efforts (in Botvin, 2004).

In this chapter, we identify and discuss several challenges that require resolution to realize the full benefits of preventive and health promotion efforts in improving the health status of citizens of the United States and beyond. As Kenny and Romano (chap. 1, this volume) and others (e.g., Reese, 2007) have proffered, the imperatives of prevention are clear, but the full impact of prevention and health promotion efforts will be limited until the challenges discussed in this volume are resolved.

This chapter is organized in three sections. The first section examines advances in theory and practice that inform a comprehensive model for understanding the multiple factors influencing health, followed by a consideration of some of the tenets of effective preventive and health promotion practice. The second section discusses critical questions and controversies regarding the role of social justice in prevention and health promotion. We attend to the disconnect between prevention science and prevention practice and discuss the implications of this observation for prevention work and public health in the 21st century. In the third section we respond to some of the questions we've raised by offering recommendations that highlight four strategies: economic evaluation, dissemination research, cultural relevance, and professional identity. The perspectives that inform the views offered in this chapter are guided by our experience and training in psychology, public health, and preventive medicine. It may be important for the reader to understand this point as the recommendations and challenges presented here are not specific to a particular discipline but rather reflect the multidisciplinary nature of prevention science and practice.

ADVANCES IN THEORY AND PRACTICE

As briefly mentioned earlier in this chapter, researchers in the field of prevention science have developed a broad and complex understanding of many causal agents for a variety of risk behaviors and diseases. Indeed, as Flay (2002) and others have discussed, many risk factors have an impact on the presentation of risk behavior and diseases. Likewise, for at least the last 20 years, the field has been postulating and examining various theoretical models in terms of their ability to explain risk behavior and disease. The evolution of these models has gone from individually focused models, in which etiology was only considered from the perspective of individual-level factors (e.g., health belief model, attribution theories), to models informed by understanding the broad impact of the social ecology at multiple levels as both causative and prophylactic (e.g., Bronfenbrenner, 2001; Lerner, 2005). The implications of ecological and developmental contextual theory for the design and evaluation of prevention and health programs are discussed elsewhere in this volume (see chaps. 1, 3, 9, & 13). The theoretical advances as reflected in this and other work have led to the creation of a different lexicon for how health concerns are considered.

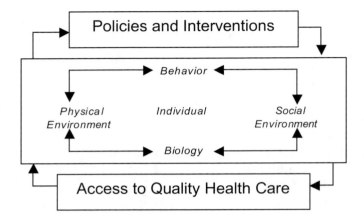

Figure 2.1. Determinants of health. From *Healthy People 2010,* U.S. Department of Health and Human Services, 2000.

Over the course of the last decade, the Healthy People initiative of the Department of Health and Human Services has adopted a framework that summarily integrates the multiple factors influencing health and disease (see http://www.healthypeople.gov for further explanation of the model). This framework highlights the interaction of the individual's behavior and biology, which is influenced by the person's physical and social environment. At the macro level, policies that support health, availability of effective interventions, and access to quality health care further determine the individual's health (see USDHHS, 2000). Figure 2.1 provides a pictorial representation of the model as depicted in the *Healthy People 2010* report and of the interrelation among the various factors.

Presently, this model has a significant influence on the federal government's public health approach to health promotion and the elimination of health disparities. It has stimulated research that includes ecological factors such as income inequality and social cohesion (see Kawachi & Berkman, 2000; Marmot, 2005; Satcher & Rust, 2006). The Centers for Disease Control and Prevention (CDC), for example, have adopted health models including ecological influences on individual health to inform their prevention and health promotion efforts.

Beyond the theoretical advances described previously, scientists also now know considerably more about the components of effective program implementation and prevention practice. In a summary of this literature, Reese and Vera (2007) maintain that investigators and practitioners must (a) have an accurate understanding of the communities in which they wish to work, (b) spend time developing positive relationships with community members and partners, and (c) conduct research or implement programs that are valued by community members. They also emphasize the importance of creating opportunities for members of the target community to actively participate in the processes that result in the development, implementation, and evaluation of interventions these communities are to receive (Lerner, 1995; Vera & Reese, 2000). Scholars in the area of community-based participatory research have spent considerable effort explicating the processes involved in the successful implementation of preventive and health promotion interventions at the community level where success is largely informed by collaborative partnerships, the generation of social capital, the promotion of community buy-in, and the development of community resources and infrastructure (Blumenthal & DiClemente, 2004).

As this brief overview highlights, the theoretical paradigms have evolved over time to reflect the complexity of the factors that influence risk behavior and disease. As a result, there is now a considerable theoretical and practical base on which preventionists can draw in their research and programmatic efforts. The challenge now is for the field to translate these theoretical tenets into practice to effectively reduce the incidence of risk behavior and disease (Biglan, 2004).

SOCIAL JUSTICE AND PREVENTION: CRITICAL CONTROVERSIES

Over the course of the past decade, a number of scholars have promulgated the critical role of social justice considerations if the health status of the general citizenry and of specific communities is to be improved in meaningful ways (see Prilleltensky & Prilleltensky, 2003; chap. 4, this volume). Consistent with effective prevention practices, these and other scholars have emphasized that social justice–oriented prevention and health promotion must promote research that is important to society (i.e., the common good), as well as research that is valued by and beneficial to program participants (see Albee, 2000b; Lerner, 1995; Reiss & Price, 1996; Vera & Speight, 2003). In the face of such assertions and convincing arguments advanced by social justice advocates, at least three central questions remain:

1. What exactly is this beast called "social justice," or more precisely how is it conceptualized within the scientific traditions of behavioral science, clinical medicine, and public health?
2. Can social justice be operationalized in a scientifically meaningful manner? Does the construct lend itself to empiricism? Is the term *social justice* polarizing in light of the sociopolitical history of health care and prevention in this country?

3. In what ways should the foci of prevention and health promotion research and practice be changed or expanded to support goals consistent with the objectives of social justice?

Addressing these and other questions will help ensure that social justice is not marginalized in the dialogue about significant constructs in effective prevention, as other constructs, such as cultural competence, initially endured (see *The Counseling Psychologist*, July 2001; American Psychological Association, 2003). Answers to these questions will also greatly assist scientists, practitioners, and policy makers genuinely committed to the principles of social justice, where all members of society are treated in an equitable manner and can rightfully expect to experience positive health. Bell (1997) defines social justice as "full and equal participation of all groups in a society that is mutually shaped to meet their needs. A current view of social justice includes a vision of society in which the distribution of resources is equitable and all members are physically and psychologically safe and secure" (p. 3). Definitions such as these are instructive from an aspirational perspective in that the scientist or practitioner has an idea of what social justice might look like optimally. In a similar manner, some of the ethical principles that govern the professional conduct of psychologists can be considered aspirational rather than practical in every instance of professional practice. Although helpful, broad definitions such as these leave considerable work for prevention scientists and practitioners as they try to translate what "physically and psychologically safe and secure" or "the common good" mean in practice and to determine how such outcomes can be achieved and measured.

Although the unequal health status experienced by many women, the poor, and some ethnic minority communities is clear, the assumption that most prevention scientists and practitioners agree with the ideas implied by the term "social justice" or the need to change these inequalities by redistributing the available health promotion resources is just that—an assumption. Additionally, there is little theoretical guidance in the prevention literature or existing measurement models for social justice as an empirically examined and understood construct. In view of the many advances in the field of prevention, perhaps the next generation of research, practice, and policy literature will make its contribution by providing testable theoretical models with empirical support for the assumptions that underlie some of the commonly agreed-on tenets of social justice. Already some important initiatives are underway in this regard, with leadership from colleagues in community psychology and community health (e.g., Blumenthal & Yancey, 2004; Wandersman, 2001; Wandersman, Goodman, & Butterfoss, 1997). The results of these and other efforts represent an important nexus for the integration of prevention theory, practice, and policy. For example, the Morehouse School of Medicine Prevention Research Center (PRC), where each of the authors collaborates, is guided by a model of community health. The model, entitled Community Organization and Development for Health Promotion (Braithwaite, Murphy, Lythcott, & Blumenthal, 1989), is informed by the following principles: (1) understand the community ecology before entering the community; (2) establish relationships with community gatekeepers; (3) build credibility and trust; (4) develop a community coalition or governance board; (5) work with the board to understand the needs of the community as identified by the community; and (6) work with the board to develop, implement, evaluate, and disseminate prevention and health promotion interventions.

The implementation of such principles is not without challenges. Certainly there is more to achieving these goals than the one-sentence descriptions offered here convey. For example, establishing partnerships with community gatekeepers also requires understanding whether those gatekeepers accurately represent the perspective of their constituents. It is instructive, however, that the Morehouse PRC has now been funded for more than 10 years by the CDC and other state and federal agencies; that the investigators and practitioners who call the PRC home have published in a number of peer-refereed journals; and, most importantly, that the partnership between Morehouse and the communities in which it works have produced a number of tangible outcomes that have improved the health of the community, increased its resources and capacity, and served as an example of what social justice in an academic-community partnership might look like.

The second central question posed previously may be a more challenging one: What does the methodology of social justice research look like, and is it consonant with the current standards for scientific rigor? In an era of randomized controlled trials as the gold standard in research and with the use of a control group often considered a minimum criterion for fundable and publishable research, how is concern for equitable distribution of resources as discussed by social justice advocates promoted? Often times, randomization and control groups, even if they are delayed-treatment control groups, are objectionable to participants of prevention programs, especially in communities with few resources and significant health problems (Reese & Vera, 2007). Schwartz and Hage (chap. 6, this volume) raise important and challenging questions regarding the ethical dilemmas that can be posed by certain research methodologies in the context of social justice. Thus, questions of the compatibility of "research" with a social justice orientation and current perspectives about what constitutes "rigor" in research remain unanswered. We believe, however, that our experience at Morehouse responds affirmatively to the first question, if you accept that the communities in which we work are not classrooms, laboratories, or charity cases, but instead partners in our work.

Our view is that social justice prevention research done well is highly rigorous. It is critical, however, that scientists pay attention to the development and use of alternative designs and research methodologies (e.g., mixed methods, participatory action research) in their efforts to implement social justice principles. It is equally important that the primary function of prevention and health promotion research—to improve health and well-being—not get lost. An example from the 2005 American Evaluation Association conference helps to illustrate the challenge and the exciting and progressive work being done to develop a shared understanding of the form and function of prevention research. During a featured conference plenary, a number of highly regarded prevention scientists questioned the real benefits and costs of various research methodologies (i.e., randomized controlled trials) preferred by some federal government funding agencies and prominently highlighted in a number of academic journals. This debate, which had become heated leading up to the conference, was followed by several position papers, representing an important effort by all who participated in, listened to, or learned from this exchange. An interesting artifact of this debate is that the term *social justice* was never used prominently in the discussions. The discourse was consistent, however, with social justice concerns for conducting meaningful and practical prevention research, where the results of effective interventions are more readily available for dissemination to affected communities. The point we wish to emphasize here is that prevention and health promotion research should not be considered an academic exercise, a point that often gets lost in scholarly exchanges regarding research and, in this case, prevention research. We assert, as have others, that the priority in our work should be to understand and prevent health problems and to promote healthy lifestyles. We contend, furthermore, that in those efforts, our intellectual interests and curiosity can simultaneously be satisfied.

In this section, we have raised a number of questions, especially in the areas of theory development, research methodologies, and prevention practice that we believe are important in giving social justice solid footing in prevention and health promotion initiatives. Efforts to move social justice prevention research to the center of the dialogue about prevention and health promotion will require sustained efforts in promoting and clarifying the benefit of such efforts for optimally promoting community health among our colleagues and government entities, such as the U.S. Department of Health and Human Services. For example, many of the important concepts (e.g., cultural relevance, social ecology, social epidemiology) and methodologies (e.g., hierarchical linear modeling) currently guiding federal initiatives have their origins in academic research. As prevention work may have a political tenor in different contexts (i.e., health policy), it is important that scientists and practitioners committed to improving health learn how to manage these processes so that their work informs effective health policy and not be viewed as an academic exercise. Many advocates of an equitable and healthy nation will never use the term *social justice*; thus it is important that our work be expressed in a manner that is understandable to our many constituencies, inclusive of those in the political arena. Advocates must be strategic and engaging in their efforts to support and help the communities to which they are committed.

BRIDGING THE GAP BETWEEN SCIENCE AND PRACTICE IN THE CONTEXT OF SOCIAL JUSTICE

Two concerns relevant to social justice and the integration of prevention science and practice are health economics and dissemination research. To be a good steward of limited fiscal resources, questions related to cost benefits and economic efficiency are important. Researchers also need to be intentionally cognizant about how an effective intervention can be translated for dissemination. In addition to economic evaluation and dissemination research, this section examines cultural relevance and the development of professional identity as two additional factors important in bridging the science-practice gap.

Economic Evaluation

Economic evaluation of preventive interventions is relatively new to the consciousness of prevention researchers and practitioners, yet its value is increasingly acknowledged. Practitioners and policy makers must now consider the practicality of prevention interventions in terms of the cost of implementation (Poston, Pizzi, & Lofland, 2006). Briefly, an economically efficient prevention program offers maximal benefits, while simultaneously minimizing the economic costs for obtaining those benefits. This is a practical necessity in the United States as many communities have limited fiscal resources, and it is consistent with the goals of prevention and health promotion interventions with a social justice orientation (Lutzker, Wyatt, & Corso, 2006). To determine the economic efficiency of an intervention, implementation costs must be considered. For example, the developer of an intervention would have to intentionally create opportunities to collect cost data on the front end to understand the real cost of implementation. If the intervention is effective, these data can assist in determining the feasibility of replicating it in different settings, depending on the availability of appropriate resources.

In particular, program developers need to consider how cost effectiveness and cost benefit inform the interpretation of an intervention's value, as this data will define what resources are necessary to replicate the positive results (Haddix, Teutsch, & Corso, 2003). Cost benefit is often viewed through the metric of dollars saved or some other common measure related to the impact of an intervention. For example, the cost benefit in terms of health-care savings for women who get mammography when recommended is that treatment is less expensive and more effective when cancer is identified at an early stage. Cost effectiveness is a form of economic evaluation that assesses different types of interventions with a shared outcome and then determines which intervention can produce the same effect at the lowest cost (e.g., comparison of a small-media campaign and a group-administered smoking cessation intervention).

Intervention effectiveness can thus no longer be considered from the sole perspective of an obtained effect size for main outcomes. Program development, implementation, evaluation, and ultimately the interpretation of effectiveness must also be considered in both economic and social terms. For example, an effective prevention and health promotion intervention that produces statistically significant changes or growth may not be able to be responsibly disseminated for replication as interventions can be cost prohibitive for many communities. The inclusion of economic evaluation can assist in divorcing purely intellectual exercises from practical prevention work by determining which interventions will work for which individuals, families, and communities and under what circumstances.

One example where these types of considerations have been intentionally considered is the Blueprints for Violence Prevention program, a clearinghouse for the dissemination of empirically supported violence prevention programs at the Center for the Study and Prevention of Violence (see Elliot & Mihalic, 2004). In a previous partnership with the Office of Juvenile Justice and Delinquency Prevention focusing on the dissemination of effective violence prevention interventions, one of the criteria for replication was whether a replication site had the budget to implement the intervention as intended. In this way, the goals of social justice are advanced by matching an intervention with both the need and the capacity to implement the intervention by a given institution or community.

Economic evaluation also allows for more meaningful integration of science and practice, as the availability of appropriate resources often determines which empirically supported strategies can by implemented. A final point is that attention to economic evaluation may lend greater credibility to terms like "evidence-based" and "best practice." Specifically, economic data will assist in framing for whom the intervention should be considered a best practice and perhaps, in this way, challenge prevention scientists to be more sensitive to issues related to resource availability and context, thereby reducing some of the acrimony between scientists and practitioners.

Dissemination

Another area that has received short shrift among prevention professionals relates to the field's dissemination, or the process of literally taking the lessons (e.g., strategies, programs) developed and determined to be effective from the research context to the context of prevention practice. Presently a number of well-developed and effective interventions are described in great detail in grant applications, conference proceedings, and journal articles, but have never been shared, let alone applied in a context outside of the funding that supported the original research. For example, cancer preventionists acknowledge that the public health burden of cancer could be significantly reduced by having effective prevention strategies disseminated and adopted by public health and clinical facilities (National Cancer Institute, 2007). Likewise, we know it is imminently possible to influence the current obesity epidemic through diet and physical activity, yet there has been limited effort and success in disseminating and implementing these strategies in schools and other community-based organizations that serve young people. Because these strategies have not been disseminated, many of the prevention practices implemented by community-based organizations and clinics are not informed by the most current, empirically-supported knowledge and strategies. Thus, the public health burden has not been reduced as significantly as it might otherwise be. Similar observation can also be made in the areas of violence prevention, HIV/AIDS, and diabetes.

These observations beg the question as to why the dissemination of effective intervention and prevention strategies is not occurring. A practical reality for most researchers, and the field of prevention more generally, is that dissemination is limited to conference presentations, book chapters, and journal articles, as described earlier. Although dissemination represents an important opportunity to integrate practice and science, many prevention professionals do not have the skills to achieve this goal outside of academic arenas.

Several federal agencies (e.g., USDHHS, U.S. Department of Education) have expanded their focus to support the dissemination of research, an acknowledgement that the benefit of new discoveries is muted if these findings are not shared and implemented by stakeholders such as public health clinics and school districts. As an example, many community-based organizations, schools, and other entities provide prevention and health promotion programs for their consumers, but if these organizations do not implement empirically supported interventions, they are unlikely to realize the desired positive effects (see Hawkins et al., 2002). The net result is that human suffering is not decreased, health is not improved, and sometimes those who are implementing interventions become demoralized. Over the last 5 years, the CDC has dedicated resources to assist researchers, practitioners, and policy makers in developing a meaningful understanding of the dissemination and translation process. Some of the lessons learned about dissemination by the CDC, a health promotion and prevention agency, have been extrapolated from the business community, specifically marketing. One result of the agency's efforts was reflected in its recent reorganization, resulting in the creation of the National Center for Health Marketing. Health marketing is "creating, communicating, and delivering health information and interventions using customer-centered and science-based strategies to protect and promote the health of diverse populations" (CDC, 2007).

We hope that one message from this discussion is that as the field considers greater integration of prevention science and practice, it will also need to become familiar with previously foreign concepts like marketing. Although dissemination, like economic evaluation, represents an important conduit for the integration of science and practice, the lack of familiarity with the basic tenets of these practices is a significant obstacle. Thus, we recommend that continuing professional development provide training in economic evaluation and dissemination processes.

Cultural Relevance

Almost without exception, issues of cultural relevance and competence have been central to discussions about how to advance the effectiveness and impact of prevention and health promotion efforts. Unfortunately, from our perspective, these issues are all too often discussed as an afterthought, a gesture at political if not cultural sensitivity. They are not given the careful and critical consideration they deserve. In a book such as this, where social justice, ethics, and meaningful prevention science and practice are the guiding values, the importance of cultural considerations should be obvious. Several contributors to this book have addressed the centrality and complexity of culture. As we have discussed economic evaluation as a "nexus" and dissemination as a "conduit" to bridging the integration of prevention science and practice, cultural relevance and cultural competence may be the linchpin to that bridge.

By cultural relevance, we mean the extent to which interventions are consistent with the values, beliefs, and desired outcomes of a particular community (Kumpfer, Alvarado, Smith, & Bellamy, 2002; Nation et al., 2003). Cultural competence, although related to cultural relevance, is distinctly different and addresses a standard whereby an individual, group, or institution demonstrates the requisite training, skills, and experience to be considered competent in working with specific or diverse populations

(Reese & Vera, 2007). The "why" for the importance and inclusion of these constructs is simple: The theories and methods guiding prevention work are value laden, and often the developers and authors of prevention programs have a markedly different cultural frame of reference from the communities receiving their preventive interventions.

In light of these realities, the prevention field faces a dilemma. On the one hand, given assumptions about risk status, most preventive efforts, especially secondary and tertiary interventions, are currently directed toward historically underserved and under-resourced communities. Alternatively, most health promotion programs might be directed to communities and individuals considered to have more resources with fewer obvious risk factors. It is important to consider how we frame our work. Lessons from the fields of social psychology and health communication are instructive on this point. Interventions that are framed from the position of health gains are often received differently by the target community than those framed in terms of health loss. For example, a community that identifies a problem of violence might respond differently to an intervention that discusses healthy and safe lifestyles versus one that focuses exclusively on violent victimization and perpetration. Approaches such as Botvin's Lifeskills program (2004) and the emphasis on positive youth development are consistent with a health gain framework. Furthermore, these efforts are consistent with a social justice perspective as they focus on promoting life skills that will enhance opportunities for success for all youth.

There are also empirical grounds for considering how interventions are presented. In a carefully controlled meta-analysis of the effects of delinquency programs across different demographic groups, the authors found programs meeting their inclusion criteria to be effective overall (e.g., reducing youth delinquency). Significant group differences for factors such as participation, acceptance of the program, and overall satisfaction were also found; these differences existed between white youth and ethnic minority youth (Wilson, Lipsey, & Soydan, 2003). Such findings exemplify the importance of integrating science and practice. The interventions studied by Wilson and colleagues were effective (i.e., science), yet factors related to prevention practice (i.e., participant satisfaction) were not equivalent in their effectiveness. A process whereby science and practice operate reciprocally may serve to enhance the effectiveness of future interventions by giving attention to factors that influence effectiveness for specific groups. In the final analysis, the careful consideration and incorporation of cultural relevance and competence have practical import for interventions not only guided by the principles of social justice and elimination of disparities but for any serious effort to bridge prevention science and practice (Reese, Vera, & Caldwell, 2006).

Professional Identity

In 1949, a training conference was held in Boulder, Colorado, to address problems specific to the field of clinical psychology. The stimulus for this meeting was the apparent disconnect between the science of clinical psychology and the application of that science in the work of practicing clinical psychologists. An important outcome of this conference was the establishment and advancement of the scientist-practitioner model as a professional identity to be promoted in doctoral training programs and in the professional conduct of clinical psychologists. The "Boulder model," as it came to be known, put forward the premise that clinical work or applied psychology should be informed by empirical science that is theory driven (Benjamin & Baker, 2000). One outcome of this conference was that clinical psychology programs began to modify their training so that students were increasingly expected to demonstrate basic competence in conducting research and clinical practice with the goal of understanding the necessary relation between science and practice. More than a half-century since that conference, the model or some variation of it has been adopted in other areas of applied psychology (i.e., counseling psychology), public health, and preventive medicine.

As the centrality of prevention and health promotion has become more important to the work of helping professionals and health care providers, the Boulder model has become especially relevant (see Vera, 2000). Belar (2000) maintains that "education and training in professional psychology requires training in the conduct of scientific research, clinical practice and their integration" (p. 249). Accordingly, training in prevention should encompass the conduct of prevention science and practice and their integration. Although the Boulder model is frequently cited and praised, the true integration of science and practice is often neither taught nor practiced. Furthermore, as Botvin (2004) suggests, new research models need to promote the active collaboration of prevention researchers and practitioners. We further assert that multidisciplinary approaches will be needed to effectively understand and resolve the challenges to obtaining and maintaining positive health at an individual, community, and society level (see Reese, 2007). Health determinants (e.g., economic status, access to health care), as shown in Figure 2.1, are not in the exclusive purview of any single academic discipline or vocational domain. In an effort to illustrate how multidisciplinary approaches are used in preventive medicine, Exhibit 2.1 features a description from one of our authors of his 30-plus years of experience in preventive medicine as a physician, prevention scientist, and chair of the Department of Community Health and Preventive Medicine.

EXHIBIT 2.1
The Multidisciplinary Nature of Prevention and Health Promotion

Prevention and public health are truly multidisciplinary fields. The range of professions involved in our Department of Community Health and Preventive Medicine at More-house School of Medicine includes behavioral science, epidemiology, medicine, social work, nutrition, nursing, and many others. From the discussion earlier in this chapter, it is clear that philosophy has a role (What, precisely, is "social justice"?), as do economists (How can one measure the cost effectiveness and cost benefit of interventions?).

Multidisciplinary work is the strength of prevention science. At the same time, it is its weakness. Focusing the knowledge, skills, and perspectives of many disciplines on the prevention of disease and promotion of health is surely more effective than a monolithic approach. However, this also means that few professionals self-identify as "prevention scientists," "preventionists," or "public health workers." Most categorize themselves by their primary discipline, such as physician, nurse, or psychologist. This is true even of those with a public health degree (MPH, MSPH, DrPH); indeed, a public health degree says little about one's area of expertise, which may be health promotion, environmental health, epidemiology, biostatistics, health policy and management, or nutrition, for example. In our own department where the primary focus is on preventive and health promotion research and practice, few of my colleagues would identify themselves as prevention scientists. What we collectively do, however, is pursue our research, practice, and training endeavors in a manner that builds upon our relative expertise. For example, it is not uncommon on a research project to see a medical epidemiologist, behavioral scientist, community activist, and health educator jointly developing everything from the research questions to the methodology to be employed in implementing and evaluating an intervention. In addition, one of our core values is that we see the communities we work in as our partners and ourselves as members of these communities.

It is ironic that many of the top positions in public health—most state or local health officers, the Director of CDC, and deans of many schools of public health—are occupied by physicians, even though physicians typically receive little education about public health or prevention in medical school. Although residency training and board certification are available in Public Health and Preventive Medicine, most physician directors of state and local health departments lack such training and certification. Rather, they are often appointed—and later fired—for political reasons. Similarly, the vast majority of health department workers lack formal training in public health or prevention; they simply learn on the job. I imagine that many of these workers probably perform more than adequately; however, in a society where financial advisors, real estate agents, barbers, beauticians, and many other service workers must have formal training, certification, and licensure, this speaks to the relatively low regard in which those who protect the public's health are held.

It is here that the benefits of multidisciplinary collaboration in the intentional integration of science and practice are clearest. As a physician board-certified in pediatrics and preventive medicine, I do not have to be an expert in psychology or social work because I have colleagues who work closely with me to whom I can refer/defer as appropriate about issues related to human behavior or mental health. At the individual level, physicians play an essential role in prevention. They give immunizations; they administer or order screening tests (e.g., Pap smears, mammograms, blood pressure measurements, a variety of blood and urine tests); they counsel patients on multiple parameters, from smoking cessation, nutrition, and exercise to safety. The preventive measures that physicians (and other clinicians, such as nurse practitioners) should offer are catalogued in the widely recognized *Guide to Clinical Preventive Services,* developed by the U.S. Preventive Services Task Force (http://www.ahrq.gov/clinic/uspstfix.htm). To be sure, many of these functions, especially counseling, could be performed as well if not better by non-physicians. However, physicians are thought of by most persons primarily as healers of the sick, and most physicians think of themselves that way. Hence, physicians often miss opportunities to offer preventive interventions and have much to learn from our prevention colleagues in the behavioral and social sciences.

Note. Prepared by Daniel Blumenthal.

CONCLUSION

Our goal in this chapter was to identify and discuss issues we view as important to the integration of social justice and prevention science and practice and ultimately to the contribution prevention will make to the improvement of public health and the reduction of health disparities. In the final analysis, we view this integration as representing two sides of the same coin where meaningful science and practice should be understood as inseparable. To repeat Botvin (2004), the challenge to the field of prevention is to translate the past 20 years of research findings to prevention practice. This statement also recognizes the extent to which the field's contributions have been minimized. In the face of continuing disparities in health status for many in this country and the global community, we must recognize the urgency of our work and how positive effects could be enhanced by increasing the reciprocity between good prevention science and practice.

Indeed, the prevention field is well positioned in terms of understanding risk and protective factors; having theoretical models that reflect the complexities of life at an individual, community, and societal level; and encompassing research and analytic methods that allow us to understand the effects of our interventions on individuals embedded in multiple contexts. Yet, as noted by former Surgeon General David Satcher (2006), although the United States is the richest nation in the world, our investment in prevention and health promotion is not commensurate with that status. As preventionists committed to social justice, we cannot allow ourselves to naively think that politics and discrimination at multiple levels do not influence support for the work we do. The crisis that continues to dominate the political and health care landscape tells us this. It is a crisis that predominantly falls on the poor, among whom ethnic minorities are disproportionately represented in the United States. When we talk about health disparities, we are not talking about middle-class America.

Finally, there is a charge to hold ourselves accountable in the stewardship of our work. The integration of prevention science and practice and the careful and intentional inclusion of the ideas discussed here require that we divorce ourselves from activities that are only "intellectual exercises." This is a luxury we cannot afford if we are serious about social justice. And if we are serious, we must stretch ourselves and the institutions where we work beyond that which is comfortable for us professionally, to that which is necessary.

REFERENCES

Albee, G. W. (1996). Revolutions and counterrevolutions in prevention. *American Psychologist, 51*, 1130–1133.

Albee, G. W. (2000a). The Boulder model's fatal flaw. *American Psychologist, 55*, 247–248.

Albee, G. W. (2000b). Commentary on prevention and counseling psychology. *The Counseling Psychologist, 28*, 845–853.

American Psychological Association. (2003). Guidelines on multicultural education, training, research, practice, and organizational change for psychologists. *American Psychologist, 58*, 377–402.

Belar, C. D. (2000). Scientist-practitioner ≠ science + practice: Boulder is bolder. *American Psychologist, 55*, 249–250.

Bell, L. A. (1997). Theoretical foundations for social justice education. In M. Adams, L. A. Bell, & P. Griffin (Eds). *Teaching for diversity and social justice: A sourcebook* (2nd ed., pp. 3–16). New York: Routledge.

Benjamin, L. T., Jr., & Baker, D. B. (2000). Boulder at 50. Introduction to the section. *The American Psychologist, 55*, 233–236.

Biglan, A. (2004). Contextualism and the development of effective prevention practices. *Prevention Science, 5*(1), 15–21.

Biglan, A., Mrazek, P. J., Carnine, D., & Flay, B. R. (2003). The integration of research and practice in the prevention of youth problem behaviors. *American Psychologist, 58*, 433–440.

Bloom, M. (Ed.). (1996). *Primary prevention practices.* Thousand Oaks, CA: Sage.

Blumenthal, D. S., & DiClemente, R. J. (Eds.). (2004). *Community-based health research: Issues and methods.* New York: Springer Publishing Company.

Blumenthal, D. S., & Yancey, E. (2004). Community based research: An introduction. In D. S. Blumenthal & R. J. DiClemente (Eds.), *Community-based health research: Issues and methods* (pp. 3–24). New York: Springer Publishing Company.

Botvin, G. J. (2004). Advancing prevention science and practice: Challenges, critical issues, and future directions. *Prevention Science, 5*, 69–72.

Braithwaite, R. L., Murphy, F., Lythcott, N., & Blumenthal, D. S. (1989). Community organization and development for health promotion within an urban black community: A conceptual model. *Health Educator, 20*(5), 56–60.

Bronfenbrenner, U. (2001). The bioecological theory of human development. In N. J. Smelser & P. B. Baltes (Eds.), *International encyclopedia of the social and behavioral science* (pp. 6963–6970). Oxford, England: Elsevier.

Centers for Disease Control and Prevention. (2007). *What is health marketing?* Retrieved October 3, 2007, from http://www.cdc.gov/healthmarketing/whatishm.htm

Elliott, D. S., & Mihalic, S. (2004). Issues in disseminating and replicating effective prevention programs. *Prevention Science, 5,* 47–53.

Flay, B. R. (2002). Positive youth development requires comprehensive health promotion programs. *American Journal of Health Behavior, 26,* 407–424.

Haddix, A. C., Teutsch, S. M., & Corso, P. S. (2003). *Prevention effectiveness: A guide to decision analysis and economic evaluation.* New York: Oxford University Press.

Hawkins, J. D., Catalano, R. F, & Arthur, M. W. (2002). Promoting science-based prevention in communities. *Addictive Behaviors, 27,* 951–976.

Kawachi, I., & Berkman, L. F. (2000). Social cohesion, social capital, and health. In L. F. Berkman & I. Kawachi (Eds.), *Social epidemiology* (pp. 174–190). New York: Oxford University Press.

Kumpfer, K. L., Alvarado, R., Smith, P., & Bellamy, N. (2002). Cultural sensitivity and adaptation in family based interventions. *Prevention Science, 3,* 241–246.

Lerner, R. M. (1995). *America's youth in crisis: Challenges and options for programs and policies.* Thousand Oaks, CA: Sage.

Lerner, R. M. (2005). Foreword: Promoting positive youth development through community and after school programs. In J. L. Mahoney, R. W. Larson, & J. Eccles (Eds.), *Organized activities as contexts of development: Extracurricular activities, after-school and community programs* (pp. ix–xii). Mahwah, NJ: Erlbaum.

Lutzker, J. R., Wyatt, J. M., & Corso, P. (2006). Violence prevention in the 21st century: Merging agendas and creating impact. In J. R. Lutzker (Ed.), *Preventing violence: Research and evidence-based intervention strategies* (pp. 279–297). Washington, DC: American Psychological Association.

Marmot, M. (2005). Social determinants of health inequalities. *Lancet, 365,* 1099–1104.

Nation, M., Crusto, C., Wandersman, A., Kumpfer, K. L., Seybolt, D., Morrissey-Kane, E., & Davino, K. (2003). What works in prevention: Principles of effective prevention programs. *American Psychologist, 58,* 449–456.

National Cancer Institute. (2007). *Division of cancer control and population sciences, 2006 overview and highlights: Dissemination and diffusion.* Retrieved October 3, 2007, from http://cancercontrol.cancer.gov/bb/2006_bb.pdf#page=111

Nussbaum, S. (2006). Prevention: The cornerstone of quality health care. *American Journal of Preventive Medicine, 31,* 107–108.

Pentz, M. A. (2004). Form follows functions: Designs for prevention effectiveness and diffusion. *Prevention Science, 5,* 23–29.

Poston, S., Pizzi, L. T., & Lofland, J. H. (2006). An overview of the economic evalution of healthcare interventions. In L. T. Pizzi & J. H. Lofland (Eds.), *Economic evaluation in U.S.: Principles and applications* (pp. 1–12). Boston: Jones & Bartlett.

Prilleltensky, I., & Prilleltensky, O. (2003). Synergies for wellness and liberation in counseling psychology. *The Counseling Psychologist, 31*, 273–281.

Reese, L. E. (2007). Beyond rhetoric: The ABCs of effective prevention science, practice and policy. *The Counseling Psychologist, 35*, 576–585.

Reese, L. E., & Vera, E. M. (2007). Culturally relevant prevention: Scientific and practical considerations of community-based programs. *The Counseling Psychologist, 35*, 563–580.

Reese, L. E., Vera, E. M., & Caldwell, L. (2006). The role of culture in violence prevention practice and science: Issues for consideration. In J. R. Lutzker (Ed.), *Preventing violence: Research and evidence-based intervention strategies* (pp. 259–278). Washington, DC: American Psychological Association.

Reiss, D., & Price, R. H. (1996). National research agenda for prevention research: The National Institute of Mental Health report. *American Psychologist, 51*, 1109–1115.

Satcher, D. (2006). The prevention challenge and opportunity: A former surgeon general renews his prescription for the American people. *Health Affairs, 25*, 1009–1011.

Satcher, D., & Rust, G. (2006). Achieving health equality in America. *Ethnicity & Disease, 16*, 8–13.

U.S. Department of Health and Human Services. (2000). *Healthy people 2010*. Washington, DC: U.S. Government Printing Office.

Vera, E. M. (2000). A recommitment to prevention in counseling psychology. *The Counseling Psychologist, 28*, 829–837.

Vera, E. M., & Reese, L. E. (2000). Preventive interventions with school-aged youth. In S. D. Brown & R. W. Lent (Eds.), *Handbook of counseling psychology* (pp. 411–434). New York: Wiley.

Vera, E. M., & Speight, S. L. (2003). Multicultural competence, social justice, and counseling psychology: Expanding our roles. *The Counseling Psychologist, 31*, 253–272.

Wandersman, A. (2001). *Program accountability system workbook PIE*. Columbia, SC: SC Office of First Steps.

Wandersman, A., Goodman, R., & Butterfoss, F. (1997). Understanding coalitions and how they operate. In M. Minkler (Ed.), *Community organizing and community building for health* (pp. 261–277). New Brunswick, NJ: Rutgers University Press.

Wilson, S. J., Lipsey, M. W., & Soydan, H. (2003). Are mainstream programs for juvenile delinquency less effective with minority youth than majority youth? A meta-analysis of outcomes research. *Research on Social Work Practice, 13*(1), 3–26.

3

PREVENTION AS A MECHANISM FOR PROMOTING POSITIVE DEVELOPMENT IN THE CONTEXT OF RISK: PRINCIPLES OF BEST PRACTICE

MARY WALSH, JILLIAN DEPAUL, AND JENNIE PARK-TAYLOR

A comprehensive vision of prevention focuses on the reduction of risk (e.g., Conyne, 2004; McWhirter, McWhirter, McWhirter, & McWhirter, 2006), the enhancement of strengths (e.g., Cowen, 2000), and advocacy for social justice (e.g., Albee, 2000). Each of these essential components of prevention requires a consideration of the integral role of culture and context in development. Risk cannot effectively be reduced without taking the contributors to the risk into account. Though contexts often create risks, they also have the capacity to generate assets and promote strengths in developing citizens, thereby establishing pathways to healthy development. Finally, adopting a social justice perspective expands the focus of prevention beyond attention to individual needs and strengths toward incorporating efforts to rebuild elements of the social and contextual structures that perpetuate risks for specific populations. For example, given the increasing evidence of the devastating impact of contextual factors, such as institutional racism, on individuals' capacity to thrive (Davis & Stevenson, 2006; Harris, Tobias, Jeffreys, Waldegrave, & Nazroo, 2006), prevention efforts must include initiating change at the systemic level.

The purpose of this chapter is to explore theoretical and practice-related issues in prevention with a focus on promoting positive development and fostering strengths and protective factors. Our exploration of prevention will include a consideration of the intersection between culture and prevention—an intersection that often leads to the emergence of both risk and protective factors. We will begin by describing developmental contextualism, a theoretical framework that has shaped the philosophy and informed the implementation of the current prevention agenda. In our discussion of this theory, we will summarize and critique the resilience literature, extrapolating from it a model of prevention that includes an orientation toward social justice and a commitment to systemic change. Finally, we will provide examples of prevention initiatives that seek to promote social justice and exemplify best practice principles related to the developmental contextual framework.

THE DEVELOPMENTAL CONTEXTUAL FRAMEWORK

The rise of prevention as a strategy for decreasing negative developmental outcomes reflects psychology's increasing knowledge of human development. Traditional theories (e.g., Erikson, 1950; Freud, 1949) explained development in terms of universal stages, focusing on the problems that could arise from the disruption of each of the stages. Though these theories were important in shaping the field of psychology, the stage theory approach failed to account for what is now recognized as the significant impact of context on development. Newer understandings of development have pointed toward the significance of context and are equally concerned with both the strengths and deficits that arise from an individual's mutually determining interactions with the environment (Lerner, 1984, 1995, 2001). The recognition that context can contribute to positive and negative outcomes gives way to the realization that some negative outcomes can be prevented or limited through efforts to create positive environments and opportunities for healthy development.

Developmental contextualism (Lerner, 1984, 1995, 2001) is a prominent example of a contemporary developmental theory. Grounded in Bronfenbrenner's (1979) developmental systems approach, developmental contextualism has been described by Walsh, Galassi, Murphy, and Park (2002) in terms of four central tenets that view development as: (1) occurring simultaneously on biological, psychological, and social levels; (2) ongoing across the life span; (3) impacted by context and vice versa; and (4) shaped by risk and protective factors.

Simultaneous Occurrence

Developmental contextualism strives to understand the whole person, attending to various personal domains, including the biological, psychological, and social aspects. These developmental levels continually and reciprocally interact with one another to profoundly shape an individual's health and growth. For example, an elementary school student who suffers from poor nutrition will not likely be able to engage fully in schoolwork or in positive social interactions with classmates. As a result, the child's academic self-efficacy and/or sense of social competence may be negatively affected. Prevention initiatives for children, though they may be targeted at a specific physical, psychological, or social need, should be mindful of the impact that change at one developmental level could have on the other levels and, in turn, the whole child. As another example, a middle-aged man going through a separation may experience a somatization of his psychological stress that interferes with his work, or he may lose access to critical social support with the loss of his partner and his or her social connections. Though prevention is often thought of as a service for children, the man in this example might benefit at biological, social, and psychological levels from a prevention program that focuses on teaching men how to identify psychological distress and seek appropriate help.

Across the Life Span

In contrast to traditional theories that have focused primarily on the first 18 years of life, the second tenet of developmental contextualism proposes that development continues across the life span. This perspective therefore endorses plasticity, proposing that the potential for redirecting the course of development is lifelong. Some new evidence suggests that primary care providers can help alter the course of mental health problems in their adult patients by educating them about psychological disorders such as depression (Muñoz et al., 1995).

In addition, prevention initiatives with children should remain aware of the impact of continuing development of relevant adults. Targeting prevention initiatives at adults (e.g., English language classes, parenting classes) could significantly increase the life chances of not only the adults themselves but the children in their care.

Though these first two assumptions about development are critical to the practice of prevention, the latter two (i.e., the impact of context on development, risk and protective factors) have particular relevance to the intersection of prevention and culture.

Context

Foremost within contemporary perspectives such as developmental contextualism (Lerner, 1995) and ecological theory (Bronfenbrenner, 1979, 1986) is the understanding that human development occurs within a range of contexts and involves a transactional relationship between an individual and these contexts (Rutter & Sroufe, 2000). Bronfenbrenner's (1979) ecological model places the individual at the center, with ever-more-distal developmental influences arrayed around the individual in a series of nested contexts called *microsystems*, *exosystems*, and *macrosystems*. For schoolchildren, microsystems would include a child's peer group, parents, and teachers. Exosystems might include school district-level decisions about curricula and federal educational policies that influence the school environment. Macrosystems might include the belief systems, resources, risks, opportunity structures, and life course options that are embedded in such overarching systems (Bronfenbrenner, 1986). As these systems interact, they mutually influence one another, giving way to a constantly evolving physical, social, and emotional environment that shapes and is shaped by the schoolchildren.

The recent view of development, which strives to understand the individual within a complex, ever-changing web of environments, provides ample opportunity for prevention initiatives to take hold in effective and meaningful ways. Instead of focusing on the once-prominent nature-nurture debate, this theoretical framework asserts that development is inextricably embedded in family, neighborhood, school, community, society, and culture, and cannot be considered in isolation from these contexts (Walsh et al., 2002). The role of each of these contexts in development suggests that psychologists cannot limit prevention initiatives to the individual level but must also intervene at the systems and sociocultural levels. Further, prevention efforts are effective insofar as they reflect the unique contexts that have already shaped and continue to shape the individual. For example, a prevention initiative that aims to encourage increased physical activity among inner-city youth should take into account an urban context, in which children encounter obstacles to physical activity such as fewer parks and unsafe neighborhoods.

Though the delivery of prevention initiatives may seem to reflect abstract and universal practices, it is now widely recognized that the effectiveness of these initiatives is grounded in the specific cultural and social context in which they are delivered (Lubeck, Jessup, deVries, & Post, 2001). Most universal prevention programs are fairly generic, having been developed for the dominant culture in the United States, which is heavily influenced by white, middle class values (Kumpfer, Alvarado, Smith, & Bellamy, 2002). Though this dominant culture is an important overarching layer in development as it informs the subcultures within it, more proximal contexts, such as family and community, profoundly shape development. In recent years, some prevention specialists have implemented programs specifically founded on the values and practices of these more local systems or subcultures within which the intended recipients are developing. These prevention programs have generally shown promising results (e.g., Resnicow, Soler, Braithwaite, Ahluwalia, & Butler, 2000). Though the success of some culturally relevant programs was limited to specific outcomes, such as participant retention (e.g., Kumpfer et al., 2002), other programs have demonstrated that cultural relevance is significantly related to greater program satisfaction and changes in the targeted behavior (e.g., Williams et al., 2006).

Risk and Protective Factors

For decades, mental health professionals focused their attention nearly exclusively on understanding "the trajectory from risk to psychopathology" (Cicchetti & Garmezy, 1993, p. 497). The environment as an intervening factor was considered only marginally for the purpose of elucidating the development of negative psychological outcomes. In recent years, attention has turned toward those elements of individuals' experience and environments that curtail or prevent negative outcomes in those who develop in contexts of risk. Examining developmental pathways that lead to resilience has become a critical task for psychologists. Knowledge of significant protective factors is crucial to promoting healthy development in the presence of risk.

Resilience is defined as "the capacity to spring back, rebound, successfully adapt in the face of adversity" (Henderson & Milstein, 1996, p. 7). It implies the presence of individual, family, or societal factors that "stem the trajectory" from risk to psychopathology, resulting in adaptive outcomes in the presence of harsh conditions (Cicchetti & Garmezy, 1993, p. 497). This construct is grounded in a belief that all individuals have the capacity for healthy development—that no environment, no matter how toxic, is a one-way ticket to exclusively negative outcomes. Resilience is based on the idea that protective factors can be promoted and strengths can be nourished to guide individuals even in the most perilous contexts. Theoretical foundations of resilience suggest that it is not a static condition, but rather that it continuously evolves through dynamic interactions between an individual and his or her environment and among his or her intra-organismic (i.e., biological, psychological, social) levels of development (Cicchetti & Schneider-Rosen, 1986). Therefore, though individuals remain susceptible to risk factors throughout their lives, they maintain the capacity to develop strengths (e.g., academic aptitude, career self-efficacy, athletic ability) or use potential protective factors (e.g., mentor support, community involvement; Masten & Coatsworth, 1998). This capacity assumes contextual conditions that do not prevent the use of protective factors.

Over the last decade, the literature has presented varied and sometimes arbitrary definitions of prevention concepts such as risk and protective factors (Masten, 2001). The struggle to define these concepts reveals complexities that challenge efforts to examine them. Masten argues that risk and protective factors are rarely pure entities and that they almost never appear in isolation. Rather, developmental risks often co-occur, with their effects cumulating toward a greater likelihood of negative outcomes. Further, risk factors are often conceptualized along a continuum, with the low-risk ends related to positive outcomes and the high-risk ends related to negative outcomes. However, low-risk factors do not indicate the presence of protective factors or adaptive outcomes, so it is important not to conclude that low risk is causally related to positive adaptation (e.g., the absence of negative discipline strategies does not indicate the existence of positive strategies). Rather, positive outcomes are more likely a product of not only low risks but also an interplay of risk factors, protective factors, and strengths. As Masten states, "competent parents (causal factor), for example, may produce fewer stressful family life events (risks), choose to live in neighborhoods with low crime rates (risks) and good community resources (assets), and be more likely to hire tutors for their children (assets)" (p. 228).

As understandings of the complex interactions between risk and protective factors have emerged, it is becoming increasingly clear that initial youth programming efforts, which focused almost exclusively on reducing risk factors, were not ideal. In the late 1990s, the pendulum swung widely as the traditional focus on risk was replaced with a near-absolute focus on building assets. It is now generally agreed that, given the complex interaction between risk and protective factors, best practices of prevention should operate on several levels. Prevention initiatives should combine a focus on reducing risk factors with efforts to establish protective factors and build strengths that buffer children from negative outcomes *and* make positive ones more likely.

Although a perspective that accounts for both risks and strengths is critical, recent understandings of prevention suggest that programs should also be designed with an awareness of the social milieu within the subculture of the school or community that is the target for the intervention (Resnicow et al., 2000). According to Cicchetti and Garmezy (1993), resilience can exist or develop along interacting levels of individual, family, and community. The culture of the family and community is relevant in the development of resilience and the effectiveness of prevention. Ultimately, prevention requires a simultaneous focus on individuals, families, and communities, promoting resilience through partnerships among schools, families, and community agencies that foster altruistic behaviors and secure relationships.

Though the construct of resilience is attractive in its contention that all individuals are capable of healthy outcomes in the face of significant contextual landmines, such a fundamental assumption can be controversial. The resilience literature has been criticized for placing the locus of control for either succumbing to or overcoming adversity too squarely on the shoulders of the individuals facing the risks (Luthar & Cicchetti, 2000). Further, resilience develops in the context of risks and contextual barriers, which occur at times as a result of arguably avoidable social inequities and systemic oppression. Some worry that an overemphasis on the promotion of resilience may allow for these inequalities and oppressions to continue. Watts (2004) suggests that resilience applauds individual adjustment to socially unjust conditions rather than seeking change in oppressive social structures. The promotion of resilience should therefore be one aspect of a multifaceted approach to prevention. Ideally, this approach would also include efforts to make lasting changes to social systems and structures as a means of preventing risk and negative outcomes for populations chronically at risk.

Culture

Whereas each of these four principles reflects a critical aspect of development, the core of developmental contextualism is the relationship between context and development. Contexts shape and are shaped by the interaction of biological, social, and psychological levels, the mutually dynamic relationship between risk and protective factors, and the continued development across the life span. A critical aspect of context is culture. Given the multicultural character of our country, and indeed our world, a discussion of developmental contextualism and prevention requires a description and explication of the role of culture in development.

Clinicians and researchers have been challenged by the question of how to properly integrate culture and prevention into practice. Despite a recent shift toward a focus on culture-specific phenomena and theories, this growing body of literature is mired by narrow, inconsistent, and ambiguous operational definitions (Johnson, 1990; Lonner & Malpass, 1994). Not only is culture defined in a variety of ways by scholars, the term *culture* is oftentimes used as a proxy to describe racial and ethnic differences (Helms & Talleyrand, 1997; Park, 2005).

Before considering culture in relation to prevention, it is important to look at various meanings of culture. A systems-oriented perspective in cross-cultural psychology conceptualizes culture as a relatively stable system of shared meanings. Alternatively, the practice-oriented view considers culture to be a continuous process of meaning making in particular persons and in particular temporal and spatial contexts. Neither theory taken alone is capable of completely explaining cultural dynamics—that is, how individuals' meaning-making activities can collectively create an enduring cultural pattern (Kashima, 2000). For example, though the systems view is common, this conceptualization of culture may result in an undue focus on the individual, particularly how he or she internalizes the culture's stable norms and values. As a result, this framework may attribute cross-cultural differences in behavior solely to within-person psychological characteristics (e.g., values) in contrast to systemic conditions (e.g., poverty, discrimination; Poortinga & Van Hermet, 2001). On the other hand, a strict practice view limits the work of researchers and practitioners because conceptualizing culture as a continuous system of meaning making stymies attempts to create a distilled understanding of the specific cultural components that have an impact on individuals within a given system.

Both the systems view and the practice view of culture, as well as the inadequacy of each of them as singular perspectives, should inform the design and implementation of prevention programs. A systems-oriented prevention specialist would incorporate the long-lasting, prevalent norms, values, and shared meanings that define the culture of the group being targeted in a program. A practice-oriented prevention specialist might consider the more immediate place (e.g., school community) and specific time within which the targeted individuals are developing. A well-designed intervention program would be constantly adapting to the changing dynamic. Both perspectives make important contributions to prevention programs, which should ideally be anchored in the stable cultural meaning of a particular group while maintaining flexibility to evolve with the interaction of individuals with closer systems, such as school, family, and community.

The shift from a deficit-oriented view of culture to a view of culture as an important source of thriving leads to an appreciation of resiliency among ethnic minority youth as well as an investigation of their specific individual and ecological assets. When this framework is applied to understanding the developmental trajectories of urban poor youth of color, the preventive focus that emerges is grounded in their particular individual and ecological strengths, rather than exclusively preoccupied with cultural deficits (Dryfoos, 1990).

PREVENTION AND SOCIAL JUSTICE

The goal of attending to the multiple cultural forces that shape individuals mirrors psychology's burgeoning awareness of and commitment to addressing psychopathology on a systemic level as well as on an individual level (Prilleltensky, 1997; Vera & Speight, 2003). A number of prevention initiatives reflect a movement to rectify deeply embedded inequities in the social landscape. The ordering principle and distributive properties of most liberal-capitalist systems tend to perpetuate cycles of oppression on the basis of social class and race. For example, growing up in poverty exponentially increases risk for negative mental health outcomes, which thereby impede efforts to overcome barriers by accessing opportunities for education and advancement (Costello, Compton, Keeler, & Angold, 2003). Interrupting this status quo requires more than intervention, which merely reacts to the predictable manifestation of problems. Prilleltensky argues that implementing exclusively reactive intervention practices to address individual issues is not only ineffective psychological practice, but also morally questionable in its failure to address the systemic causes of deleterious social conditions.

Clinical psychologists, counseling psychologists, and social workers are in a position to engage in prevention that not only reflects effective practice but also works toward social justice by creating opportunities for disempowered citizens to have more equitable access to society's benefits and burdens (Meara, Schmidt, & Day, 1996). Although the work of preventionists from various disciplines can bring about more socially just conditions, it is worth noting that the orientation toward social justice differs across professions. For social workers, social justice is the "organizing value" of their profession (Swenson, 1998, p. 527)—the direct goal and defining principle that motivates and shapes their work in achieving social justice through tangible, redistributive outcomes regarding public goods for their clients and the community. Alternatively, the work of clinical, counseling, and community psychologists has the dual focus on community and individual wellness in restoring or bolstering the equally significant noneconomic goods of self-esteem, resilience, and other individual protective assets. Although the amelioration of social inequities is a potential byproduct of prevention efforts and therapeutic interventions aimed at psychological health and wellness, bringing about a more just reorganization of social structures has traditionally not been a defining principle of psychology. Recently though, some leaders in psychology are calling for the field to more explicitly integrate social justice into its mission (Prilleltensky, 1997).

It could be argued that bolstering resilience in individuals through building skills and reducing risks perpetuates systemic inequities in the social context. From this perspective, the psychologist's traditional helping role supports clients' accommodation to an inequitable situation. In contrast to the accommodative or ameliorative modality, an activist modality engages the psychologist in advocating for the redistribution of social resources toward the ultimate preventive goal of community wellness. Psychologists diverge in their understandings of whether psychology as a field can simultaneously support both of these modalities. Exclusively espousing an activist perspective to change the system necessarily excludes the ameliorative role. One cannot support the status quo while changing it. On the other hand, it may be argued that there is room for both practices within the field. Psychologists can both work toward the intermediate goals of easing individual suffering and preventing problems in at-risk groups while simultaneously seeking the ultimate goals of system change and social justice. It may also be argued that an exclusive focus on a single goal, either the ameliorative or the activist, is insufficient as a comprehensive approach to fostering social justice and healthy development. These two roles can be viewed as coexisting along a continuum of supports that includes redistributive strategies as well as primary, secondary, and tertiary prevention.

An example of a continuum of services that includes redistributive strategies as well as primary, secondary, and tertiary prevention is the contemporary best practice approach for providing nonacademic supports for student learning (Adelman & Taylor, 2002). Primary prevention includes school-based interventions for all students, such as health and social competence programs, that seek to promote healthy development and prevent nonacademic barriers to learning that are associated with poor physical health and emotional distress (Marx, Wolley, & Northrop, 1998; McKenzie & Richmond, 1998). Primary prevention might also include systemic and redistributive change in student support systems to make available a broad range of community resources to support academic achievement for historically disempowered groups (Weissberg & O'Brien, 2004). Secondary prevention includes early intervention to identify and address student issues soon after they arise. School professionals might work with a student support team to assess at-risk students and refer them to appropriate services. Counselors can coordinate programs that address specific issues (e.g., bullying prevention, friendship groups) or specific problems (e.g., failing core subjects). Finally, tertiary prevention seeks to remedy severe and chronic problems that students face through a web of in-school and community-based services (e.g., mental health counseling, special education, medical care). Through this multilevel approach to prevention, initiatives that address existing problems, prevent problems in those who are at risk, and promote strengths for all children and community members are integrated into a comprehensive system.

PRINCIPLES OF BEST PRACTICE IN PREVENTION PROGRAMS

Several recent reviews (e.g. Hage et al., 2007; Nation et al., 2003; Weissberg, Walberg, O'Brien, & Kuster, 2003) have attempted to identify practices that contribute to effective prevention programs. We have chosen to highlight a number of these best practice principles that are particularly relevant to the effective implementation of programs that seek to promote social justice and support positive development in the context of risk. Prevention programs are more likely to be successful if they are theory-driven, promote structural change, are developmentally appropriate, are based on collaboration among multiple partners, are culturally relevant, are evaluated, and are sustained over time. Examples of prevention measures are used to illustrate the principles of prevention.

Theory-Driven

Though these examples embody best practices in diverse ways and are unique in their target problems and their modes of intervention, they share the overarching quality of being grounded in theory. Research suggests that effective prevention programs, no matter how specific or far-reaching their goal, must embrace a theory of change—that is, a supposition for how they will bring about their stated goal (Nation et al., 2003). Although a number of theories (e.g., social learning theory; Bandura, 1977) are the foundation of prevention programs that embody best practices and lead to changed outcomes (Hawkins, Clarke, & Seeley, 1993), our examples highlight the relevance of developmental principles to effective implementation practices. In particular, prevention programs that are grounded in developmental contextualism aim to both reduce negative effects of risk factors and promote protective factors and strengths at multiple levels of context (e.g., individual, family, community).

Structural Change

Consistent with a social justice orientation, effective prevention programs aim for an impact not only on individuals but also on the political structures that often create or perpetuate risks such as poverty (Hage et al., 2007). A systemic perspective and a mission to address social inequality are the natural consequences of a developmental contextual theory of change that recognizes the significant role of context in development. Theoretical recognition of the way that contextual systems perpetuate risk factors, such as persistent poverty, leads to an approach to prevention that intervenes on multiple levels (e.g., individual, school, community) to both promote protective factors and reduce risks. In short, this recognition requires intervention to make real and lasting change, not only to individuals' functioning, but also to social systems like families, schools, and communities. Exhibit 3.1 describes the Boston Connects Program as an example of a systemic intervention in school practice that works on multiple levels to address the impact of poverty on the academic achievement of urban schoolchildren (Walsh & Brabeck, 2006).

Further, Boston Connects focuses on both promoting protective factors and reducing risk factors at each of these contextual levels (see Figure 3.1).

Developmentally Appropriate

Though development occurs throughout the life span, certain formative events and critical transitions generally occur at common times during childhood and adulthood. As understood in the context of a dynamic interaction

EXHIBIT 3.1
The Boston Connects Program: A Systemic Intervention in School Practice

The Boston Connects Program is an example of multilevel strategies and collaboration among diverse partners (urban school district, community agencies, and a large university) to address the impact of poverty on the academic achievement of urban school children. In particular, Boston Connects strives to strengthen protective factors and address risk factors in elementary school children (see Figure 3.1). To ameliorate barriers to learning and strengthen positive development, Boston Connects has developed a coordinated, comprehensive, and systemic approach to the provision of non-academic supports for learning (e.g., health care, after-school programs, mentoring, social competence, and obesity prevention curricula, etc.). The prevention-intervention program works at multiple levels. At the individual and family level, Boston Connects provides an infrastructure that matches each child and his or her family with appropriate school and community-based resources and services. At the neighborhood level, Boston Connects identifies and addresses the wider range of contextual issues that impact academic achievement (e.g., lack of affordable day-care, increased prevalence of obesity, etc.). The program enables teachers, principals, and community-agency practitioners to develop collaborative, inter-professional and coordinated strategies that promote learning and healthy development in children and families. Encouraging these schools to develop new practices naturally results in a conversation regarding funding allocation and educational policy at the district and state levels. For example, representatives of Boston Connects presented evaluation data to state legislators who were debating whether to slash funding for school nurses when the state had cut back on its budget. Beyond working with the local power structures, the university partner in this intervention is well positioned to engage in the national conversation regarding social and educational policy and practice. An innovative school-community-university intervention can impact the national conversation by raising awareness of current social problems and promoting practices that address social injustices (Walsh & Brabeck, 2006).

---

between individual and context, these developmental challenges, though often brought about by external circumstances (e.g., high school graduation), resonate on several levels to influence not only the individual's life situation but also his or her sense of self and readiness to take on the next developmental challenge. Incorporating knowledge of the timing and sequence of development into program design can render delivery more meaningful for the targeted population and more effective in supporting successful life transitions (Nation et al., 2003). Exhibit 3.2 describes Tools for Tomorrow, a prevention program that exemplifies developmentally appropriate best practice in its philosophy and execution (Kenny, Sparks, & Jackson, 2007; Solberg, Howard, Blustein, & Close, 2002).

Collaboration

Effectiveness in prevention requires collaboration among various players and partners throughout the stages of design and implementation of programs (Shapiro & Renaldi, 2001). Collaboration in prevention initiatives can and should take several different forms. First, interdisciplinary collaboration between prevention programmers from various fields is crucial. Risk

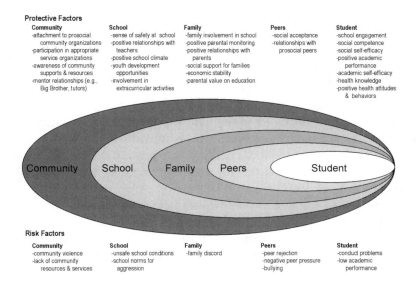

Protective Factors

Community	School	Family	Peers	Student
-attachment to prosocial community organizations	-sense of safety at school	-family involvement in school	-social acceptance	-school engagement
-participation in appropriate service organizations	-positive relationships with teachers	-positive parental monitoring	-relationships with prosocial peers	-social competence
-awareness of community supports & resources	-positive school climate	-positive relationships with parents		-social self-efficacy
-mentor relationships (e.g., Big Brother, tutors)	-youth development opportunities	-social support for families		-positive academic performance
	-involvement in extracurricular activities	-economic stability		-academic self-efficacy
		-parental value on education		-health knowledge
				-positive health attitudes & behaviors

Community · School · Family · Peers · Student

Risk Factors

Community	School	Family	Peers	Student
-community violence	-unsafe school conditions	-family discord	-peer rejection	-conduct problems
-lack of community resources & services	-school norms for aggression		-negative peer pressure	-low academic performance
			-bullying	

Figure 3.1. Risk and protective factors. Adapted from *Bullying Prevention: Creating a Positive School Climate and Developing Social Competence,* by P. Orpinas and A. M. Horne, 2006, Washington, DC: American Psychological Association; and *Healthy Teens: Understanding Social Development From Middle to High School,* by P. Orpinas, A. M. Horne, P. Reeves, and D. Bandalos, 2006, grant proposal funded by the Centers for Disease Control and Prevention (unpublished document). Copyright 2006 by the American Psychological Association. Adapted with permission of the authors.

EXHIBIT 3.2
Tools for Tomorrow: A Developmentally Appropriate Best Practice

A psychoeducational intervention, "Tools for Tomorrow" seeks to help inner-city high school students internalize the connection between school, work, and life, thereby providing them with a deeper understanding of the school-to-work transition and an increased wealth of resources to employ in navigating this life stage. Informed by developmental contextualism and seminal career development theories, this program fosters vocational exploration as a means for students to understand themselves, as well as the opportunities and barriers in their environments. This intervention occurs developmentally at a time when students are engaged in self-exploration and self-definition. As they transition into high school, they are experiencing more autonomy at home and at school and are therefore faced with determining the level at which they will engage their schoolwork. The transition to high school is also a time when risk factors, such as school disengagement, can lead to negative outcomes like academic failure and dropout. At this critical juncture, the program focuses on promoting protective factors such as a future orientation, valuing education, and career self-efficacy as well as enhancing existing strengths that may be present (e.g., high academic performance). Given that poor children are more likely to be poor as adults due to lack of resources and environmental stressors (Evans, 2004), this program promotes social justice and prevents lifelong poverty by making careers, and thereby upward mobility, more accessible (Kenny, Sparks, & Jackson, 2007; Solberg, Howard, Blustein, & Close, 2002).

factors are so complex, pervasive, and intertwined and the problems to which they give rise are so diverse that adequate prevention measures cannot be provided from the perspective of a single discipline. Given the interaction of the biological, psychological, and social aspects of the person, prevention specialists from multiple fields such as psychology, public health, social work, medicine, law, and education must integrate their varied expertise to respond effectively to the multiple levels of development as well as the varied manifestations of needs across individuals. Though interdisciplinary collaboration introduces challenges to prevention implementation, it vastly increases the potential for effective supports (Brabeck, Walsh, Kenny, & Comilang, 1997).

In addition to collaboration between professionals from different fields, effective prevention demands collaboration between the professionals and the targeted community population. Traditionally, there has frequently been a disconnect between prevention clinicians and their organizations and the targeted community. Prevention clinicians often represent universities or community agencies that tend to rely on theoretical and intellectual expertise, whereas the target community members live in the everyday reality of social inequities, such as impoverished schools and neighborhoods. As a result, prevention measures are often characterized by a striking power imbalance, in which the prevention "experts" design and deliver an intervention to a so-called "community in need." This arrangement may fail to recognize the reality that community members bring a different perspective as experts on the specific needs and strengths of their community. Over time, it has been recognized that the "answers" provided by research are more relevant if the questions and process are shaped in partnership with those in the "earthen trenches" (Jensen, Hoagwood, & Trickett, 1999, p. 206) of the community. Similarly, although university partners may be knowledgeable in the general principles of development, community members are experts in the unique strengths, needs, values, and phenomena of their particular community. To create meaningful change, these respective experts must work together to create a partnership in which knowledge acquired through study and research is applied in ways that align with a community's norms and values. Exhibit 3.3 describes Pathways/Senderos, a prevention program that exemplifies collaboration among partners in its commitment to egalitarian power sharing (Pearlman & Bilodeau, 1999).

Cultural Relevance

Best practices in prevention call for programs to be relevant to the specific life of the population of interest. In other words, effective programs are "culture-centered." According to the American Psychological Association's (2003) "Guidelines on Multicultural Education, Training, Research, Practice,

EXHIBIT 3.3
Pathways/Senderos: A Collaborative Program

Pathways/Senderos is a prevention program designed to prevent teenage pregnancy in Connecticut. The program engages in effective and egalitarian collaboration between university professionals and community members and relies on a shared vision of change, as well as a mutual respect for the expertise of the "other." Collaboration for Pathways includes five stages: joining, agreement, education, consultation and information, and evaluation (Pearlman & Bilodeau, 1999). The process of open dialogue and respectful negotiation reflects an emancipatory communitarian philosophy in its recognition that differences of worldview and expertise are outweighed by a shared hope for lasting social change and a sense of responsibility for creating that change (Prilleltensky, 1997). This partnership is thus grounded in a central philosophy of change and a shared vision of success that propel the partners through the inevitable challenges of collaboration. Supportive collaboration helps the program work towards reducing teenage pregnancy, which has been associated with subsequent vocational failure, child maltreatment, and homelessness. The program promotes strengths and protective factors through academic support, career preparation, family life education, and sex education.

and Organizational Change for Psychologists," psychologists are encouraged to use a "culture-centered" approach in their work, which acknowledges that behavior may be influenced by culture, by the reference groups to which one belongs, and by prevailing stereotypes about reference groups.

In attending to cultural difference, it is critical that prevention programs conceptualize culture not simply as a static identifier, but rather as a dynamic level of identity influenced by multiple factors such as family traditions and level of acculturation as well as local community norms (Santisteban, Mena, & Suarez-Morales, 2006). Similarly, best practices for culturally tailoring prevention programs go beyond *surface structure* language translation and cosmetic alterations to *deep structure* adaptations that are sensitive to the unique expressions of culture in particular neighborhoods, schools, and populations (Resnicow et al., 2000). Deep structural sensitivity to culture includes understanding how members of the target population perceive the cause, course, and treatment of the target problem, as well as which risk and protective factors may be particularly relevant to certain groups. Exhibit 3.4 describes Messengers for Health, a prevention initiative that exemplifies how prevention programs can be culturally relevant (Christopher, 2005).

Evaluation

Prevention practitioners have a responsibility to demonstrate effectiveness, not only because of their claim to alter the course of development but also because evaluation is the only way to ensure that prevention programs will be sustained financially. Further, documented effectiveness is crucial to continuing the shift of focus in mental health from reactive intervention to

EXHIBIT 3.4
Messengers for Health: A Culturally Relevant Program

Compared with their white neighbors, Northern Plains Indians have a statistically higher mortality rate from cervical cancer (Schmidt, 2005). This is a disease that can be treated effectively if identified early. In addition to external barriers, such as lack of female health care providers, cultural characteristics of the Apáalooke tribe can hinder women's access to early screenings and treatment for cervical cancer. For example, the collectivist culture and commitment to family on the reservation may prevent many Apáalookes, particularly women, from examining their physical health, and also from going outside the tribe for counsel and care. Messengers of Health, a partnership between Montana State University and the Apáalooke people, trains women leaders within the tribe to be health educators and advocates for their families and neighbors. In this way, the partnership capitalizes on the cultural values and practices of the tribe. Cultural practices that might pose barriers to help-seeking behaviors are fashioned into protective factors that promote good health. In addition, this program strengthens community cohesion by empowering leaders within the tribe. Tribe members trust the health education imparted to them by their fellow tribeswomen and heed their counsel. This culturally relevant program respects collective values as women are encouraged to take care of themselves so that they can be there for their families (Christopher, Christopher, & Dunnagan, 2000; Schmidt, 2005; Watts, Christopher, Streitz, & McCormick, 2005).

EXHIBIT 3.5
Evaluation of the Boston Connects Program

Researchers at Boston College and other universities are assessing the partnership's progress toward its stated goals of improving academic achievement, as well as increasing community agency involvement in schools and creating a more diverse array of supports for students (e.g., mentoring, after-school programs). Boston Connects evaluation data have shown advancement toward several of these ends. For example, students who receive services are making academic gains at the same rate and sometimes at a faster rate than students not in need of support services. In addition, the continuous evaluative feedback from a cross-section of involved parties (e.g., school-site coordinators, teachers, principals, parents), has been used to make modifications to many aspects of the program, from service delivery at the individual schools to the overarching program infrastructure.

proactive prevention. This shift is a critical element of the social justice agenda that seeks to transform patterns of social inequity. Prevention programs can impact individuals and communities in a positive and measurable manner. Evaluation of outcomes can also ensure that individual prevention interventions are continually informed by the evolving needs and strengths of the community and the national conversation regarding best practice and theory. Evaluation efforts should be comprehensive in scope, as they seek to evaluate the outcomes and the process of the prevention intervention. Finally, evaluation of prevention programs cannot be limited to quantitative outcomes but must also assess the process of implementation. Exhibit 3.5 describes the Boston Connects Program's approach to evaluation.

Sustainability

To have maximum impact, prevention programs must be imple-mented and sustained over a period of time. Short-lived prevention pro-grams have little lasting effect. The developmental research has made clear that change occurs over time, not overnight. Over time, the partners can develop true reciprocity and can learn to complement each other's strengths and limitations. Further, lasting relationships with the commu-nity allow the programs to accurately assess and respond to their evolving needs and strengths.

Sustainability is critical to prevention largely because it allows for many best practices to be realized. For example, structural change would not be possible unless prevention programs impacting those structures were sus-tained over considerable time. If a program is not sustainable, then its poten-tial for replication and for affecting change on a far-reaching scale is seriously compromised. Sustained periods of time are essential to developing the requi-site structures and processes or adapting the existing structures enough to accomplish and document the change. Further, conducting a sound, empiri-cal program evaluation takes time and cannot produce meaningful evidence of effectiveness unless the program exists over a number of years.

Currently, funding is a major obstacle to sustaining prevention pro-grams. Typically, these programs are funded by time-limited grants that often deplete before the program reaches its potential or is able to document its

---

EXHIBIT 3.6
Communities That Care: A Network Built to Last

Based in Pennsylvania, Communities That Care (CTC) are community-based preven-tion coalitions that target adolescent behavior problems (e.g., substance abuse, school dropout, violence, teen pregnancy) through a process of risk assessment and implementation of prevention initiatives (Feinberg, Riggs, & Greenberg, 2005). CTC's prevention strategy begins with the formation of a coalition of community leaders, termed a "prevention board," who undertake an assessment of the community's risk and protective factors. After prioritizing the risk factors, the board selects and supports the implementation of empirically-validated prevention programs to address the risks. CTC has been growing since the mid-1990s, when Pennsylvania initiated a compre-hensive plan to replicate CTC projects throughout the state. Funded by the Pennsyl-vania Commission on Crime and Delinquency, CTC now serves over 100 communi-ties. Though its sustainability depends on consistent funding from the state, important structural and design aspects of the program contribute to its ability to continue and grow. CTC does not rush into an unfamiliar community to remedy one problem. The community's needs and strengths are first assessed. This allows for a smooth transi-tion into the community. Further, by engaging various stakeholders to sit on the "prevention-board," the program ingrains itself into the community and secures diverse and indigenous perspectives that fortify its strategies. In addition to the individual risk and protective factors addressed in the interventions, Communities that Care engen-ders a sense of ownership and empowerment at the community level.

---

successes. It is an unfortunate reality that limited resources and personnel often must be diverted from direct service goals toward chasing down funding for program continuation. Exhibit 3.6 exemplifies a prevention intervention that has been "built to last," the Communities That Care network (Feinberg, Riggs, & Greenberg, 2005).

CONCLUSION

In this chapter, we have described prevention as a multifaceted approach to creating positive opportunities and outcomes for any person or population in danger of losing footing on the diverse pathways of healthy development. We have advocated a comprehensive approach to prevention that focuses on the reduction of risks, the enhancement of strengths, and advocacy for social justice. In addition, we have argued that effective prevention takes an inclusive view of culture, strives to understand its complex impact on individuals, and works to integrate these comprehensive understandings into prevention practice. This approach to prevention has the potential to break social patterns of inequity that seem to unfold relentlessly and tragically.

Just as these dimensions of prevention fall along a continuum, so do the goals of psychology, as they range from bettering lives and life chances on an individual level, to creating a more just and equitable society at a systemic level. Prevention represents the middle ground, a linchpin for the profession's various strategies of intensive intervention with individuals and efforts to create lasting change in social structures by working with and within them. Thus, prevention must embody the ideals and implement the best practices of psychology by recognizing the vital role of context in development, reversing trends of risk to foster resilience, maintaining a systemic perspective, and embracing the complexities of culture that unfold in dynamic levels within and around individuals.

REFERENCES

Adelman, H. S., & Taylor, L. (2002). Building comprehensive, multifaceted, and integrated approaches to address barriers to student learning. *Childhood Education, 78,* 261–268.

Albee, G. W. (2000). Commentary of prevention and counseling psychology. *The Counseling Psychologist, 28,* 845–853.

American Psychological Association. (2003). Guidelines on multicultural education, training, research, practice, and organizational change for psychologists. *American Psychologist, 58,* 377–402.

Bandura, A. (1977). *Social learning theory*. Upper Saddle River, NJ: Prentice Hall.

Brabeck, M. M., Walsh, M. E., Kenny, M., & Comilang, K. (1997). Interprofessional collaboration for children and families: Opportunities for counseling psychology in the 21st century. *The Counseling Psychologist, 25*, 614–636.

Bronfenbrenner, U. (1979). *The ecology of human development: Experiments by nature and design*. Cambridge, MA: Harvard University Press.

Bronfenbrenner, U. (1986). Ecology of the family as a context for human development: Research perspectives. *Developmental Psychologist, 22*, 723–742.

Christopher, S. (2005). Recommendations for conducting successful research with Native Americans. *Journal of Cancer Education, 20*, 47–51.

Christopher, S., Christopher, J. C., & Dunnagan, T. (2000). Culture's impact on health risk appraisal psychological well-being questions. *American Journal of Health Behavior, 24*, 338–348.

Cicchetti, D., & Garmezy, N. (1993). Prospects and promises in the study of resilience. *Development and Psychopathology, 5*, 497–502.

Cicchetti, D., & Schneider-Rosen, K. (1986). An organizational approach to childhood depression. In M. Rutter, C. Izard, & P. Read (Eds.), *Depression in young people: Clinical and developmental perspectives* (pp. 71–134). New York: Guilford.

Conyne, R. K. (2004). *Preventive counseling: Helping people become empowered in systems and settings* (2nd ed.). New York: Brunner-Routledge.

Costello, E. J., Compton, S. N., Keeler, G., & Angold, A. (2003). Relationships between poverty and psychopathology: A natural experiment. *Journal of the American Medical Association, 290*, 2023–2029.

Cowen, E. L. (2000). Psychological wellness: Some hopes for the future. In D. Cicchetti, J. Rappaport, I. Sandler, & R. P. Weissberg (Eds.), *The promotion of wellness in children and adolescents* (pp. 477–503). Washington, DC: Child Welfare League of American Press.

Davis, G. Y., & Stevenson, H. D. (2006). Racial socialization experiences and symptoms of depression among black youth. *Journal of Child and Family Studies, 15*, 303–317.

Dryfoos, J. G. (1990). *Adolescents at risk: Prevalence and prevention*. New York: Oxford University Press.

Erikson, E. H. (1950). *Childhood and society*. New York: Norton.

Evans, G. W. (2004). The environment of childhood poverty. *American Psychologist, 59*, 77–92.

Feinberg, M. E., Riggs, N. R., & Greenberg, M. T. (2005). Social networks and community prevention coalitions. *The Journal of Primary Prevention, 26*, 279–298.

Freud, S. (1949). *An outline of psychoanalysis*.New York: Norton.

Hage, S., Romano, J., Conyne, R., Kenny, M., Matthews, C. R., Schwartz, J., & Waldo, M. (2007). Best practice guidelines on prevention practice, research, training, and social advocacy for psychologists. *The Counseling Psychologist, 35*, 493–566.

Harris, R., Tobias, M., Jeffreys, M., Waldegrave, K., & Nazroo, J. (2006). Racism and health: The relationship between experience of racial discrimination and health in New Zealand. *Social Science & Medicine, 63,* 1428–1441.

Hawkins, W. E., Clarke, G. N., & Seeley, J. R. (1993). Application of social learning theory to the primary prevention of depression in adolescents. *Health Values: The Journal of Health Behavior, Education & Promotion, 17,* 31–39.

Helms, J. E., & Talleyrand, R. M. (1997). Race is not ethnicity. *American Psychologist, 52,* 1246–1247.

Henderson, M., & Milstein, M. M. (1996). *Resiliency in schools: Making it happen for students and educators.* Thousand Oaks, CA: Corwin.

Jensen, P. S., Hoagwood, K., & Trickett, E. J. (1999). Ivory towers or earthen trenches? Community collaborations to foster real-world research. *Applied Developmental Science, 3,* 206–212.

Johnson, S. D., Jr. (1990). Toward clarifying culture, race, and ethnicity in the context of multicultural counseling. *Journal of Multicultural Counseling and Development, 18,* 41–50.

Kashima, Y. (2000). Conceptions of culture and person for psychology. *Journal of Cross-Cultural Psychology, 31,* 14–32.

Kenny, M. E., Sparks, E., & Jackson, J. (2007). Striving for social justice through interprofessional university school collaboration. In E. Aldarondo (Ed.), *Advancing social justice through clinical practice* (pp. 313–335). Mahwah, NJ: Erlbaum.

Kumpfer, K. L., Alvarado, R., Smith, P., & Bellamy, N. (2002). Cultural sensitivity and adaptation in family-based prevention programs. *Prevention Science, 3,* 241–246.

Lerner, R. M. (1984). *On the nature of human plasticity.* New York: Cambridge University Press.

Lerner, R. M. (1995). Developing individuals within changing contexts: Implications of developmental contextualism for human development research, policy, and programs. In T. A. Kindermann & J. Valsiner (Eds.), *Development of person-context relations* (pp. 13–38). Hillsdale, NJ: Erlbaum.

Lerner, R. M. (2001). Promoting promotion in the development of prevention science. *Applied Developmental Science, 5,* 254–257.

Lonner, W. J., & Malpass, R. (Eds.). (1994). *Psychology and culture.* Needham Heights, MA: Allyn & Bacon.

Lubeck, S., Jessup, P., deVries, M., & Post, J. (2001). The role of culture in program improvement. *Early Childhood Research Quarterly, 16,* 499–523.

Luthar, S. S., & Cicchetti, D. (2000). The construct of resilience: Implications for interventions and social policies. *Development and Psychopathology, 12,* 857–885.

Marx, E., Wolley, S. F., & Northrop, D. (Eds.). (1998). *Health is academic: A guide to coordinated school health programs.* New York: Teachers College Press.

Masten, A. S. (2001). Ordinary magic: Resilience processes in development. *American Psychologist, 56,* 227–238.

Masten, A. S., & Coatsworth, J. D. (1998). The development of competence in favorable and unfavorable environments: Lessons from successful children. *American Psychologist, 53,* 205–220.

McKenzie, F. D., & Richmond, J. B. (1998). Linking health and learning: An overview of coordinated school health programs. In E. Marx, S. F. Wolley, & D. Northrop (Eds.), *Health is academic: A guide to coordinated school health programs* (pp. 1–14). New York: Teachers College Press.

McWhirter, J. J., McWhirter, B. T., McWhirter, E. H., & McWhirter, R. J. (2006). *At-risk youth: A comprehensive response* (4th ed). Pacific Grove, CA: Brooks/Cole.

Meara, N. M, Schmidt, L. D., & Day, J. D. (1996). Principles and virtues: A foundation for ethical decisions, policies, and character. *The Counseling Psychologist, 24,* 4–77.

Muñoz, R. F., Ying, Y., Guillermo, B., Perez-Stable, E. J., Sorenson, J. L., & Hargreaves, W. A. (1995). Prevention of depression with primary care patients: A randomized controlled trial. *American Journal of Community Psychology, 23,* 199–222.

Nation, M., Crusto, C., Wandersman, A., Kumpfer, K. L., Seybolt, S., Morrisey-Kane, E., & Davino, K. (2003). What works in prevention: Principles for effective prevention programs. *American Psychologist, 58,* 449–456.

Orpinas, P., & Horne, A. M. (2006). *Bullying prevention: Creating a positive school climate and developing social competence.* Washington, DC: American Psychological Association.

Orpinas, P., Horne, A. M., Reeves, P., & Bandalos, D. (2006). *Healthy teens: Understanding social development from middle to high school.* Grant proposal funded by the Centers for Disease Control and Prevention. Unpublished document.

Park, Y. (2005). Culture as deficit: A critical discourse analysis of the concept of culture in contemporary social work discourse. *Journal of Sociology & Social Welfare, 32,* 11–33.

Pearlman, S. F., & Bilodeau, R. (1999). Academic-community collaboration in teen pregnancy prevention: New roles for professional psychologists. *Professional Psychology, 30,* 92–98.

Poortinga, Y. H., & Van Hermet, D. A. (2001). Personality and culture: Demarcating between the common and the unique. *Journal of Personality, 69,* 1033–1060.

Prilleltensky, I. (1997). Values, assumptions, and practices: Assessing the moral implications of psychological discourse and action. *American Psychologist, 52,* 517–535.

Resnicow, K., Soler, R., Braithwaite, R. L., Ahluwalia, J. S., & Butler, J. (2000). Cultural sensitivity in substance use prevention. *Journal of Community Psychology, 28,* 271–290.

Rutter, M., & Sroufe, L. A. (2000). Developmental psychopathology: Concepts and challenges. *Development and Psychopathology, 12,* 265–296.

Santisteban, D. A., Mena, M. P., & Suarez-Morales, L. (2006). Using treatment development methods to enhance the family-based treatment of Hispanic adolescents. In H. Liddle & C. Rowe (Eds.), *Adolescent substance abuse: Research and clinical advances* (pp. 449–470). Cambridge, England: Cambridge University Press.

Schmidt, C. (2005). *Messengers of Health use traditional Crow relationships to teach about contemporary health.* Retrieved April 30, 2007, from http://www.montana.edu/cpa/news/nwview.php?article=2287

Shapiro, D. L., & Renaldi, A. (2001). Achieving successful collaboration in the evaluation of sexual assault prevention programs: A case study. *Violence Against Women, 7,* 1186–1201.

Solberg, V. S., Howard, K. A., Blustein, D. L., & Close, W. (2002). Career development in the schools: Connecting school-to-work-to-life. *The Counseling Psychologist, 35,* 705–725.

Swenson, C. R. (1998). Clinical social work's contribution to a social justice perspective. *Social Work, 43,* 527–537.

Vera, E. M., & Speight, S. L. (2003). Multicultural competence, social justice and counseling psychology: Expanding our roles. *The Counseling Psychologist, 31,* 253–272.

Walsh, M. E., & Brabeck, M. M. (2006). Resilience and risk in learning: Complex interactions and comprehensive interventions. In R. J. Sternberg & R. F. Subotnik (Eds.), *Optimizing student success in school with the other three R's: Reasoning, resilience and responsibility* (pp.113–142). Greenwich, CT: Information Age Publishing.

Walsh, M. E., Galassi, J. P., Murphy, J. A., & Park, J. (2002). A conceptual framework for counseling psychologists in schools. *The Counseling Psychologist, 30,* 682–704.

Watts, R. J. (2004). Integrating social justice and psychology. *The Counseling Psychologist, 32,* 855–865.

Watts, V. M., Christopher, S., Streitz, J. L., & McCormick, A. (2005). Evaluation of a lay health adviser training for a community-based participatory research project in a Native American community. *American Indian Culture and Research Journal, 29,* 59–79.

Weissberg, R. P., & O'Brien, M. U. (2004). What works in school-based social and emotional learning programs for positive youth development. *Annals of the American Academy of Political and Social Science, 591,* 86–97.

Weissberg, R. P., Walberg, H. J., O'Brien, M. U., & Kuster, C. B. (2003). *Long-term trends in the well-being of children and youth: Issues in children's and families' lives.* Washington, DC: Child Welfare League of America.

Williams, J. H., Auslander, W. F., de Groot, M., Robinson, A. D., Houston, C., & Hairie-Joshu, D. (2006). Cultural relevancy of a diabetes prevention nutrition programs for African American women. *Health Promotion Practice, 7,* 56–67.

4

THE ROLE OF PREVENTION IN PSYCHOLOGY'S SOCIAL JUSTICE AGENDA

ELIZABETH M. VERA, LARISA BUHIN, AND ANTHONY ISACCO

Identifying and addressing the mental health needs of underserved populations (e.g., ethnic and racial minorities, the poor, gay men, lesbians, and bisexual people) have become increasingly important in the field of psychology over the past quarter century. Despite the endorsement of the "Guidelines on Multicultural Education, Training, Research, Practice, and Organizational Change for Psychologists" (American Psychological Association [APA], 2003) and multicultural counseling competencies (Roysircar, Arredondo, Fuertes, Ponterotto, & Toporek, 2003) by professional psychology and counseling organizations, the discussion continues about how psychologists and counselors can best meet the needs of underserved communities (Constantine & Ladany, 2000; Vera & Speight, 2003). This discussion in large part centers on the ever-present remedial emphasis embedded in traditional mental health services. Specifically, most of the current multicultural guidelines and competencies have been developed around the assumption that practitioners will function primarily as psychotherapists and diagnosticians for individuals and families, roles that have been characterized as limiting and potentially inadequate, as opposed to working with larger systems such as schools (Santiago-Rivera, Talka, & Tully, 2006; Speight & Vera, 2004).

Indeed, the majority of applied psychologists devote three quarters of their professional activity time to providing traditional mental health assessment and psychotherapy services in independent practice settings (Reed, Levant, Stout, Murphy, & Phelps, 2001). More recent trends show the transition of applied psychologists from independent practice to group practice HMO network settings because of the rise of managed care (Sanchez & Turner, 2003). Unfortunately, applied psychologists who work under managed care rely on third-party reimbursement within a medical model that focuses on remediation of disorders, which may do little to address larger systemic social justice issues with an impact on mental health.

This chapter argues that prevention is a key component of psychology's social justice agenda and that, through a variety of preventive approaches, psychologists can truly begin to make an impact on the causes and consequences of injustices. The chapter comprises four sections. The first section defines social justice. The next section discusses the factors that influence the lower utilization levels of mental health services by traditionally underserved communities. The third argues that prevention is an integral part of a social justice agenda for psychologists and other mental health professionals; in many ways, it represents the best hope we have of improving the quality of life of diverse communities. The final section provides concrete examples of how prevention can address social injustices, both through direct services with individuals and public policy interventions.

SOCIAL JUSTICE DEFINED

Several scholars have criticized traditional mental health services as ineffective tools of social justice. For example, Bemak (1998) argued that the contemporary field of mental health has been markedly deficient in advocating for the social, political, cultural, and economic problems hundreds of millions of people face. The field's predominant emphasis on working with individuals has, in effect, "neutralized social and political concerns, and as a consequence, preserved traditions of neutrality and dominant paradigms" (p. 280). Furthermore, the underutilization of traditional psychotherapy by many members of racial and ethnic minority communities, especially those who are poor, has raised the question of whether such services, even when culturally sensitive, can ever adequately address the needs of diverse populations. Albee (2000a) challenged the profession to fight social injustice by expanding our scope of services to include advocacy, community outreach, and prevention.

Discussions of social justice are found in a wide variety of literatures, including psychology, education, theology, and political science. Vera and Speight (2003) present the definition of social justice as conceptualized by Bell in 1997:

the goal of social justice is 'full and equal participation of all groups in a society that is mutually shaped to meet their needs. Social justice includes a vision of society in which the distribution of resources is equitable and all members are physically and psychologically safe and secure.' (p. 259)

Although this is but one of a variety of definitions of social justice, the majority of published definitions emphasize the equitable distribution of resources and allocation of power.

One particular paradigm of social justice embraced by several contemporary scholars is referred to as a *communitarian* or *deliberative* model of justice (Heller, 1987; Young, 1990). In this model of social justice, the process of decision making and interaction that occurs at both the individual and systemic level is evaluated to identify practices of domination, privilege, and oppression. The main assumption of the model is that unjust processes inevitably lead to unjust outcomes. Thus, in this model, an outcome such as the equal distribution of resources cannot be mandated by laws, because laws do not typically address the causes of inequities. Rather, any processes that result in unequal outcomes must be scrutinized and transformed (Vera & Speight, 2003).

Typically, the process of marginalization is the main vehicle by which social injustice is maintained. Young (1990) argues that in the United States, a large proportion of the population is shunted from full participation in social life, including people of color, the poor, the elderly, persons with disabilities, women, gay men, lesbians, bisexual people, and the unemployed. For example, racism marginalizes people of color, and such marginalization negatively affects mental health and educational opportunities. Yet, because all people simultaneously possess multiple group memberships, multiple forms of marginalization are possible. For example, a person of color who is also poor may experience marginalization stemming from racism and classism (Speight, Myers, Cox, & Highlen, 1991). Furthermore, it is important to note that many individuals who experience marginalization based on one group membership (e.g., being gay or Latino) have societal privileges that are associated with other group memberships (e.g., being male and middle class). Thus, groups of individuals cannot be defined as unilaterally "oppressed" or "oppressors." Even within cultural groups where there is a history of oppression, individuals vary in the extent to which such marginalization results in negative outcomes. This is the underlying assumption behind the research on resiliency, which has found that some individuals succeed and thrive on a number of developmental outcomes even when exposed to multiple risk factors (Masten, 2001). Having acknowledged this important caveat, this chapter will discuss the potential psychological consequences of marginalization stemming from sexism, racism, classism, and homophobia; but first it will address the ways in which racism and classism have affected the use of mental health services.

UNDERUTILIZATION OF REMEDIAL SERVICES BY ETHNIC AND RACIAL MINORITY COMMUNITIES

Although individual empowerment has been a major objective of the mental health profession (Lee, 1998), the origins of many mental health problems lie in deleterious social-ecological conditions such as racism, poverty, and unemployment that pervade individuals' experiences. This is particularly true for traditionally underserved populations, such as people of color, the poor, and residents of rural communities. Although members of the aforementioned groups are often overrepresented statistically in the occurrence of particular types of mental health and social problems (which will be discussed later in this chapter), the use of services aimed at ameliorating these problems is often disappointingly low. Ironically, individuals who may be in most dire need of psychological services because of their experiences with marginalization are oftentimes the least likely to use such services (Sue & Sue, 1999).

Understanding the underutilization of traditional psychological and counseling services by these communities is a multifaceted social justice issue. One frequently cited explanation is that clients' cultural values and beliefs can be inconsistent with assumptions of mainstream psychology. For example, in some racial and ethnic communities, the cultural stigma of seeking therapy is perceived as an admission of "weakness" or a violation of cultural norms that discourage seeking help from "outsiders." Help seeking may occur more informally in such communities or be targeted toward culturally sanctioned individuals (e.g., talking with a minister, elder, or folk-healer) (Broman, 1987; Taylor, Hardison, & Chatters, 1996). A preference to seek help from a minister or folk-healer may be a perfectly effective way of dealing with problems for many people, so it is important to note that there is no assumption that the services of mental health professionals would be more beneficial. Rather, this factor is one possible reason that particular individuals may not choose to see a psychologist or social worker.

Even if an individual's cultural norms permit the use of formal counseling services, such services are oftentimes difficult to access or are unaffordable, which is particularly relevant for clients in low-income communities. For example, access to services is frequently impeded by institutional barriers, such as inadequate health insurance or a lack of evening and weekend appointments. For clients who have limited English-speaking skills in communities that lack bilingual professionals, counseling services may also be limited. Furthermore, community members may distrust the local community mental health center, hospital, or university-based services even when such services are available (Sue & Sue, 1999); this lack of trust is usually justified by historical violations of trust perpetrated by health providers (e.g., the Tuskegee Experiment). The legacy of such aberrations may perpetuate a "healthy paranoia" of health care providers. Thus, offering only traditional counseling services, even when provided by multiculturally competent service providers, may present barriers to engaging particular groups of clients who may in fact be interested in seeing psychologists.

If economic, institutional, and cultural barriers prevent underserved community members from seeking traditional mental health services, it is important to begin to offer more "nontraditional" types of services, rather than to focus solely on making our traditional services more culturally sensitive (Atkinson, Thompson, & Grant, 1993; Lewis, Lewis, Daniels, & D'Andrea, 1998; Thompson & Neville, 1999; Toporek & Reza, 2001; Vera & Speight, 2003). In several existing models of broad-based mental health service provision (Atkinson et al., 1993; Lewis et al., 1998), prevention has been identified as an important professional approach that might be particularly useful with underserved communities. Primary prevention in particular is guided by the goal of providing participants with skills and knowledge that will keep mental health problems from emerging (Romano & Hage, 2000; Vera & Reese, 2000). Thus, prevention approaches are promising alternatives for psychologists who are committed to a social justice agenda (Albee, 2000b).

PREVENTION AND THE PROMOTION OF SOCIAL JUSTICE

An important argument for prevention as a key part of a social justice agenda is not only the inadequacy of remedial services, but also the existence of ethnic and racial disparities, in particular behavioral and mental health problems that can reflect social injustices. Several sets of alarming statistics illustrate this point. Homicide has been the leading cause of death for African Americans between the ages of 15 and 34 for the last decade and the second leading cause of death for Latinos (Centers for Disease Control and Prevention, 2007). Latino adolescents have the lowest rates of high school completion (Harvard Civil Rights Project, 2004); although college enrollment increased between 1980 and 2000, the percentage of Latinos graduating from colleges is significantly lower than other ethnic groups (National Center for Education Statistics, 2005). Finally, ethnic minority youth, especially African American and Latino, have been disproportionately confined in correctional settings. Although they represent only 30% of American youth, they constitute 70% of all juvenile inmates (Sickmund, 2004).

It is worthwhile to revisit the issue of multiple types of marginalization within this discussion. Poverty and racism are relevant factors to consider in that middle class youth of color are less likely to be incarcerated than poor youth, regardless of race (Duster, 2003). These data suggest that large-scale initiatives aimed at reducing the risk factors facing particular cultural groups (e.g., poor Latino youth) in the United States are well justified. To be clear, the fact that such disparities exist is best explained by a multitude of sociopolitical factors that have put particular groups at risk for negative outcomes. A person's race or ethnicity is not a risk factor in and of itself. Rather, the type of marginalization that a poor Mexican immigrant child, for example, may experience within the school system contributes to a less than optimal learning environment, which may increase the temptation to leave school prematurely.

Given the aforementioned statistics, prevention programs in communities of color may be, quite simply, some of the best ways we have of reducing the future incidence of psychological disorders (Albee, 2000a). For example, it is much more sensible and economical, and less time consuming, to provide programs that attempt to prevent drug use and possible addiction than it is to provide rehabilitation services once addiction has occurred (Lewis et al., 1998). From a cost–benefit perspective, a large advantage that prevention holds over individual therapy is that mental health professionals can reach wider audiences using fewer resources. Prevention interventions may not only decrease an identified problem within the community but may also eliminate the development of related difficulties that occur as a result of these problems. Two recent meta-analyses (Tobler, 2000; Wilson, Gottfredson, & Najaka, 2001) provide strong evidence to support the effectiveness of using preventive approaches in reducing or preventing crime, substance use, dropout/nonattendance, and other conduct problems among adolescent youths of color.

As has been discussed previously in this volume (Kenny & Romano, chap. 1, this volume), prevention approaches generally fall into one of two categories: person-centered and environment-centered. Person-centered approaches involve directly working with clients in individual or group settings in an attempt to enhance protective factors or decrease risk factors via psychoeducational approaches or skills training. Environment-centered approaches are aimed at enhancing the quality of life or preventing specific problems of clients indirectly through strategies that enhance protective factors or decrease risk factors in their immediate context. Primarily, environment-centered approaches target public policy changes or client advocacy within important contexts (e.g., local governments). Both approaches to prevention can be powerful tools in fighting social injustice, although it could be argued that person-centered prevention focuses mainly on assisting clients to better adapt to a potentially unjust world. The next sections present concrete examples of person- and environment-centered prevention that affect social justice. To represent the importance of engaging in prevention across the life span, examples of person-centered approaches will include programs aimed at children and adults.

EXAMPLES OF PREVENTION AND SOCIAL JUSTICE

Person-Centered Prevention With Children: Preventing Racism

Vera and Speight (2003) argue that a just society can be created only if socially unjust practices are examined and altered into those that promote the psychological, emotional, physical, and economic well-being of society. One example of a problematic behavior and attitude that can be the focus of preventive interventions is the development of racist beliefs. This section discusses practical implications of recent findings in prevention research and theoretical advances in contact theory as they relate to person-centered programs for the prevention of racism in children.

The chronic stress of racism comes in a variety of forms, originally discussed by Jones (1981) and later by Thompson and Neville (1999), including individual forms such as "everyday racism" (e.g., being followed in stores, being the target of racial slurs), institutional barriers to financial or educational opportunities, cultural racism (or white supremacy; Takaki, 1993), and environmental racism (e.g., the overrepresentation of people of color who reside in environmentally polluted communities; Santiago-Rivera et al., 2006). Whether racist incidents are microaggressions or major threats to well-being (e.g., hate crimes), the cumulative toll has direct physiological and psychological consequences that put people of color at risk for a host of mental health problems such as anxiety and depression (Bryant-Davis & Ocampo, 2005; Clark, Anderson, Clark, & Williams, 1999).

Contact theory, research on the development of racial cognitions, and research on effective prevention programming cumulatively offer directions for the development of effective programs to reduce and eliminate racism in children (Buhin, 2006). Based on the aforementioned literature, several "best practices" of prevention programs are aimed at reducing and eliminating racism:

1. Provide opportunities for personally meaningful, intensive, cooperative, and repetitive interactions among members of different racial groups (Emerson, Kimbro, & Yancey, 2002; Pettigrew, 1998). Research shows that the number of interracial friendships is inversely related to an individual's age (Emerson et al., 2002). Therefore, prevention of racism should ideally start in early childhood before children learn racial stereotypes (Katz, 1983; Quintana, 1998) and when cross-racial friendships could be easily encouraged through everyday play activities. Based on the principles of social–cognitive learning theory, intervention facilitators, teachers, school administrators, and parents should model positive interracial relationships for children (Bandura, 1999).

2. Include psychoeducational programs on specific racial and ethnic groups (e.g., history and customs) as well as skill building, such as the development of general reasoning skills to apply to new situations and new racial groups to build connections with culturally different others (Pettigrew, 1998). These skills could include questioning racial stereotypes and understanding oppression and how it is perpetuated in today's society (London, Tierney, Buhin, Greco, & Cooper, 2002). Children who have already experienced racism and discrimination could be assisted in dealing with the negative effects of racism by helping them accurately attribute negative events to stigma (Crocker & Major, 1989) and by promoting a strong sense of racial and ethnic identities (Pizarro & Vera, 2001), collective self-esteem (Luhtanen & Crocker, 1992), and increasing critical consciousness (Watts & Abdul-Adil, 1997).

3. Value human commonalities as well as cultural differences in effective counseling of culturally diverse clients (London et al., 2002). Racism prevention programs should therefore include components that would teach children to find and appreciate commonalities of all human beings, as well as honoring differences among cultural groups. Quintana (1998) found that children and adolescents evidence increasingly intricate thoughts about interracial contact and oppression. Facilitating age-appropriate discussions about common human experiences, cultural differences, and cultural racism that promotes intergroup dislike may assist children in developing the sophisticated cognitive skills necessary to develop a strong sense of racial and ethnic pride and a low level of racist attitudes.

Racism prevention programs that incorporate the aforementioned components may be useful as tools of social justice for two primary reasons. First, such programs contribute to reducing the development of racist attitudes, beliefs, and practices by intervening with children whose race-related cognitions and behaviors are still in formation. Second, such programs may reduce the impact of being raised in a racist society by enhancing positive racial and ethnic identities and preventing misattributions that can lead to low self-esteem and self-confidence. Such programs could be incorporated into schools or other community venues and could be supplemented with family components. The evaluation of such programs could involve measuring the extent to which stereotypical beliefs and attitudes change, examining peer affiliations for cross-racial friendships, and even assessing the extent to which antiracist attitudes are adopted in conjunction with the programs. Regardless of the ultimate structure or location of the program, prevention programs that target the reduction of racism are excellent examples of social justice–oriented prevention work that could be introduced to schools that aim to educate children holistically.

Person-Centered Prevention With College Students: Preventing Homophobia

Lesbian, gay, bisexual, and transgendered (LGBT) individuals are often the targets of homophobia that ranges from heterosexism to violent hate crimes. College campuses have been domains in which psychologists, often through their work in college counseling centers, have made efforts to reduce such homophobia to increase the quality of life for LGBT students (Schreier, 1995). There have also been active efforts in the field to help classroom instructors and professors to promote increased understanding of sexual diversity through a variety of classroom activities (Battle, 2004; Plous, 2000). Chapter 8 in this volume discusses programs to reduce homophobia in high schools, in the workplace, and at the community level.

Schreier (1995) has argued that a hallmark of effective homophobia reduction programs should be more than just "tolerance" of sexual diversity. Rather, effective programs should aim to create a nurturing climate on college campuses where "gay, lesbian, bisexual people are seen as invaluable and indispensable parts of the culture" (p. 20). In this paradigm, successful interventions would require students to be transformed beyond mere tolerance, and to be inspired to act as LGBT allies and advocates for the rights of individuals of all sexual orientations.

Similar to the processes that underlie the amelioration of racist attitudes, research has found that students who engage in positive contact and interaction with LGBT individuals generally display more positive attitude change than those who have not had such contacts (Nelson & Krieger, 1997). Nelson and Krieger designed a preventive intervention program, delivered to undergraduate college students, consisting of a panel presentation and discussion that featured the personal narratives of four individuals who were members of the university's organization for gay and lesbian students. Each panelist delivered a brief biographical sketch; discussed the coming-out process; talked about the reactions of their family, peers, and associates to their sexual orientation; and shared experiences of discrimination. The presentation was followed by a question-and-answer period and small group discussion sessions in which students were able to have more intimate conversations with the panelists. Participants responded to a survey that included the Attitudes Toward Homosexuality Scale (MacDonald & Games, 1974) prior to and following the panel presentation. The researchers found that attitudes toward LGBT individuals became more positive after the intervention. Interestingly, they also found that gender was an important moderator in that the attitudinal change was more pronounced in women than men.

In the evaluation of this program, as is true for all such programs, it is important to note that attitudes do not necessarily predict subsequent and long-term behavior change of the participants. For example, it is unclear whether, as a function of having more positive attitudes toward LGBT individuals, participants would be more likely to confront overt displays of homophobia with family or friends. Plous (2000) designed a series of experiential activities as part of a prevention program that are aimed at helping college students learn how to respond in antihomophobic ways to such overt displays. This line of research suggests that preventing homophobia can target a variety of attitudes and behaviors, depending on the goals of the program and the baseline attitudes of the participants. The aforementioned examples illustrate another way that prevention can be used to fight social injustice in the form of homophobia.

Environment-Centered Prevention: Preventing Environmental Racism

Romano and Hage (2000), among others, have argued for psychologists to engage in prevention not just through person-centered, direct services, but through involvement in community advocacy and policy-making organizations. Albee (2000b) noted that this type of prevention constitutes a deeper level of intervention, which can be effective at mediating social change. Often referred to as *environment-centered prevention*, these interventions are systemic in nature and allow professionals to intervene within community contexts that may increase risk factors or perpetuate social conditions detrimental to underserved populations (Conyne, 2004; Vera, Buhin, Montgomery, & Shin, 2004). Environment-centered prevention is the focus of other disciplines such as community psychology, public health, and health psychology, all of which view etiologies of disorders as arising from a mixture of individual, community, and societal influences. A social-ecological perspective (Bronfenbrenner, 1986) is central to environment-centered prevention, in particular, and informs intervention strategies that complement person-centered approaches (Conyne, 2004).

To enable change, environment-centered prevention often requires the use of public policy work, outreach, and advocacy practices that enable psychologists to partner and collaborate with at-risk communities to seek solutions to their problems. Implementing environment-centered preventive interventions that facilitate social change must involve wide-ranging partnerships between psychologists, community members, grassroots organizations, public health professionals, and legislators, for example (Prilleltensky & Nelson, 2002). These efforts involve three essential steps to establishing a partnership in which community participants share in driving the intervention process: relationship building, collaborative efforts, and needs assessment (Lerner, 1995). Mental health professionals faithful to these steps increase their credibility in the community and increase the potential impact of their interventions. A prevention research agenda that is consistent with community collaboration is participatory action research, a model whose goal is to inform actions that serve the needs of disadvantaged groups with an explicit focus on social change and justice (Prilleltensky & Nelson, 2002).

Combating environmental racism provides a powerful example of environment-centered prevention aimed at social justice. Environmental racism refers to racial inequities in environmental protection and health that exist in rural, urban, and suburban settings (Santiago-Rivera et al., 2006). The term was derived from a preponderance of research that has documented a significant relationship between race and the quality of one's physical environment on a number of indices, such as air quality and exposure to hazardous waste (Mohai & Bryant, 1992). For example, as stated in Santiago-Rivera et al. (2006), African Americans and Latinos live near abandoned toxic waste sites disproportionately to their white counterparts (Bullard, 1994) and are twice as likely to be exposed to lead as any other racial group (Wernette & Nieves, 1992). Given that exposure to lead and toxic waste increase the risk of developing a variety of serious physical and mental health problems such as cancer and developmental disabilities (Bullard, 1994), it can be argued that environmental racism is an urgent social justice issue.

Santiago-Rivera et al. (2006) offer multiple suggestions for how psychologists and social workers can join the ongoing efforts of other professionals (e.g., National Resources Defense Council, Sierra Club) to prevent environmental racism via environment-centered prevention. The majority of the suggestions are examples of advocacy. Advocacy, defined as speaking up for people whose rights may be in jeopardy, can take many forms, from lobbying political leaders to joining grassroots efforts (Vera & Shin, 2006; Vera et al., 2004). One advocacy strategy could be to raise public consciousness about environmental racism by inviting speakers from relevant grassroots organizations to visit groups of people who live in affected communities, if that is not already occurring. Heightening public awareness of the existence of environmental racism and the health consequences of exposure to toxins can be done with media campaigns, participation in health fairs, and presentations within the community (e.g., church and school groups). Assisting community members to organize or affiliate with existing grassroots organizations that are addressing the problem may be another advocacy strategy that draws on existing strengths of the community. Another important environment-centered intervention would be advocating for community-based, affordable health screenings for all residents so that any existing health effects of environmental toxin exposure can be detected and treated.

Most important, joining with community members, concerned citizens, and local leaders in public policy efforts (e.g., participatory action research) to eliminate exposure to toxins may be paramount to preventing future environmental racism. In this strategy, psychologists may find themselves arranging meetings with politicians, leaders of business and industry, and other individuals who are in positions of power to legislate changes. The professional credentials and knowledge of political organizations that psychologists have can often facilitate access to policy makers above and beyond the kind of access local residents feel they might have. The social cache that comes with being a professional is a powerful tool in advocating for communities in need. Advocacy is currently being given significant attention by professional mental health organizations, such as the American Counseling Association, for its potential as an important component of social justice–driven counseling practice (Lewis, Smith-Arnold, House, & Toporek, 2004).

Evaluating the impact of one's efforts in environment-centered prevention can be challenging. Since the benefit to the community is gained indirectly, there may not be immediate effects of an intervention, but rather long-term benefits that are most apparent in future generations. For example, if a piece of legislation were passed that prohibited companies from endangering the health of community residents, or required them to be fiscally responsible for any unintended health problems, there may still be a significant number of people who will suffer the effects of pre-policy conditions. However, the future residents of a community may show significantly lower levels of health problems, which could be attributed to the new policies. Thus, the outcomes of environment-centered interventions are often more elusive to document.

The interrelated disciplines of prevention research, strength-based counseling models, and positive psychology add to the understanding and appreciation of the complex human experience and often take form through community interventions intended to serve underserved populations. According to Wandersman and Florin (2003, p. 441), "these disciplines emphasize engaging in grassroots participation, increasing interorganizational linkages, and strengthening community problem solving" serving as "catalysts for public agency and foundation initiatives" that support environment-centered prevention and other community interventions.

CONCLUSION

The delivery of psychological services to underserved populations such as racial and ethnic groups, urban youth, and people living in poverty represents a growing concern among scholars who contend that effective interventions need to address a change in the status quo of traditional counseling and psychotherapy (Prilleltensky & Fox, 1997; Vera et al., 2004). Addressing a change in the status quo requires several conceptual shifts, which in turn inform the preferred choice of interventions. The first requirement of such a conceptual shift is recognition that marginalization contributes to psychological distress and mental health disparities and plays a prominent role in specific populations remaining underserved (Prilleltensky & Gonick, 1996). Second is an understanding of ethics that extends beyond a set of codes and rules to involve a sense of personal and social responsibility to others (Giroux, 1994). Third is a focus on a strength-based counseling model that affirms the role of human strengths in buffering against mental illness (Seligman, Steen, Park, & Peterson, 2005). Fourth is an emphasis on systemic interventions that address institutions, barriers, and policies that contribute to individual stress and emotional turbulence (Speight & Vera, 2004).

Admittedly, this conceptual shift has been made by some psychologists already, such as members of the Association of Black Psychologists who have advocated for the needs of African-American communities for many years. For those psychologists not exposed to social justice training or professional experiences such as outreach, advocacy, and prevention, the shift may be more challenging (Goodman et al., 2004). Although a shift away from a counseling model that solely emphasizes individualism and remediation to a model that also emphasizes societal influences and preventive interventions might be difficult, the content of training programs can be enhanced in ways that benefit the next generation of psychologists. For those who come into the field with a commitment to social justice, there must be opportunities to acquire the knowledge and skill set necessary to become agents of change who can work with individuals, groups, communities, and policy makers. It is debatable whether the best way to provide such opportunities is to add required coursework to doctoral programs or to integrate prevention into existing coursework.

Regardless of where this debate eventually takes the field, it is clear that prevention is a critical component of a social justice agenda in psychology. Whereas social justice will result in the elimination of institutionalized domination and oppression to allow all members of society to lead "the good life," prevention aims to offer early, culturally appropriate interventions that

stop the occurrence of, delay the onset of, and reduce the impact of problems for at-risk and underserved populations (APA, 2000; Conyne, 2004;
Young, 1990).

Risk factors detrimental to psychological well-being, such as drug and
alcohol abuse, violence, school dropout, unemployment, and poor nutrition appear more frequently in the lives of people living in poverty and in
communities of color. Prevention programs, promotion of resiliency, and
community-level advocacy represent the best ways to reduce future incidence of psychological disorders (APA, 2000; Vera et al., 2004). Indeed,
effective interventions in the community, rather than in an office, "are
multicomponent interventions that generally combine individual and environmental change strategies across multiple settings to prevent dysfunction
and promote well-being" (Wandersman & Florin, 2003, p. 441).

Prevention has been shown to be at least as effective as therapy in treating a number of different presenting problems (Weisz, Sandler, Durlak, &
Anton, 2005). From a cost–benefit perspective, a large advantage that prevention holds over individual therapy is that mental health professionals can
reach wider audiences using fewer resources. This chapter proposes that prevention science is uniquely suited to design, deliver, and evaluate larger-scale,
culturally appropriate, psychological interventions with three overarching
goals: (1) preventing and/or minimizing potential damage of social injustice,
(2) boosting the resilience of at-risk populations, and (3) acting to transform
social injustices by empowering marginalized individuals. Hence, prevention
can reduce barriers that prevent marginalized individuals from pursuing traditional counseling services, and also reduce the conditions that result in mental health problems for marginalized populations by altering methods of service delivery so that they might be more accessible to underserved
communities (Vera, Shin, & Buhin, 2006).

REFERENCES

Albee, G. W. (2000a). The Boulder model's fatal flaw. *American Psychologist, 55,*
247–248.

Albee, G. W. (2000b). Commentary on prevention and counseling psychology.
The Counseling Psychologist, 28, 845–853.

American Psychological Association. (2000). *Resolution on poverty and socioeconomic
status.* Retrieved May 18, 2005, from http://apa.org/pi/urban/povres.html

American Psychological Association. (2003). Guidelines on multicultural education, training, research, practice, and organizational change for psychologists.
American Psychologist, 58, 377–402.

Atkinson, D. R., Thompson, C. E., & Grant, S. K. (1993). A three-dimensional model
for counseling racial-ethnic minorities. *The Counseling Psychologist, 21,* 257–277.

Bandura, A. (1999). Social cognitive theory of personality. In L. A. Pervin & O. P. John (Eds.), *Handbook of personality: Theory and research* (2nd ed., pp. 154–196). New York: Guilford.

Battle, C. (2004). Promoting increased understanding of sexual diversity through experiential learning. *Teaching of Psychology, 31*, 118–120.

Bell, L. A. (1997). Theoretical foundations for social justice education. In M. Adams, L. A. Bell, & P. Griffin (Eds.), *Teaching for diversity and social justice: A sourcebook.* New York: Routledge.

Bemak, F. (1998). Interdisciplinary collaboration for social change: Redefining the counseling profession. In C. C. Lee & G. R. Walz (Eds.), *Social action: A mandate for counselors* (pp. 278–292). Washington, DC: U.S. Department of Education, Office of Education Research and Improvement, Educational Resources Information Center.

Bronfenbrenner, U. (1986). Ecology of the family as a context for human development. *Developmental Psychology, 22*, 723–742.

Broman, C. L. (1987). Race differences in professional help seeking. *American Journal of Community Psychology, 15*, 473–489.

Bryant-Davis, T., & Ocampo, C. (2005). Racist incident-based trauma. *The Counseling Psychologist, 33*, 479–500.

Buhin, L. (2006). Strategies for prevention of racism in children. *Prevention in Counseling Psychology: Theory, Research, Practice and Training, 2*, 21–23.

Bullard, R. D. (1994). *Unequal protection: Environmental justice and communities of color.* San Francisco: Sierra Club Books.

Clark, R., Anderson, N. B., Clark, V. R., & Williams, D. R. (1999). Racism as a stressor for African Americans: A biopsychosocial model. *American Psychologist, 54*, 805–816.

Centers for Disease Control and Prevention. (2007). *Web-based injury statistics query and reporting system.* Retrieved December 10, 2006, from http://www.cdc.gov/nicp/wisqars/

Constantine, M. G., & Ladany, N. (2000). Self-report multicultural counseling competence scales: Their relation to social desirability attitudes and multicultural case conceptualization ability. *Journal of Counseling Psychology, 47*, 155–164.

Conyne, R. K. (2004). *Preventive counseling: Helping people to become empowered in systems & settings.* New York: Brunner-Routledge.

Crocker, J., & Major, B. (1989). Social stigma and self-esteem: The self-protective properties of stigma. *Psychological Review, 96*, 608–630.

Duster, T. (2003). *Backdoor to eugenics.* New York: Routledge.

Emerson, M. O., Kimbro, R. T., & Yancey, G. (2002). Contact theory extended: The effects of prior racial contact on current social ties. *Social Science Quarterly, 83*, 745–761.

Giroux, H. E. (1994). Insurgent multiculturalism and the promise of pedagogy. In D. T. Goldberg (Ed.), *Multiculturalism: A critical reader* (pp. 325–343). Cambridge, MA: Blackwell.

Goodman, L. A., Liang, B., Helms, J., Latta, R. E., Sparks, E., & Weintraub, S. (2004). Training counseling psychologists as social justice agents: Feminist and multicultural principles in action. *The Counseling Psychologist, 32*, 793–837.

Harvard Civil Rights Project. (2004). *Losing our future: How minority youth are being left behind by the graduation rate crisis.* Cambridge, MA: The Civil Rights Project at Harvard University.

Heller, A. (1987). *Beyond justice.* New York: Basic Books.

Jones, J. M. (1981). The concept of racism and its changing reality. In B. J. Bowser & R. G. Hunt (Eds.), *Impact of racism on white America* (pp. 27–49). Beverly Hills, CA: Sage.

Katz, P. A. (1983). Developmental foundations of gender and racial attitudes. In R. L. Leahy (Ed.), *The child's construction of social inequality* (pp. 41–78). New York: Academic Press.

Lee, C. C. (1998). Counselors as agents of social change. In C. C. Lee & G. R. Walz (Eds.), *Social action: A mandate for counselors* (pp. 3–16). Alexandria, VA: American Counseling Association.

Lerner, R. M. (1995). *America's youth in crisis: Challenges and options for programs and policies.* Thousand Oaks, CA: Sage.

Lewis, J. A., Lewis, M. D., Daniels, J. A., & D'Andrea, M. J. (1998). *Community counseling: Empowerment strategies for a diverse society* (2nd ed.). Pacific Grove, CA: Brooks/Cole.

Lewis, J., Smith-Arnold, M., House, R., & Toporek, R. (2004). *American Counseling Association advocacy competencies.* Alexandria, VA: American Counseling Association.

London, L. H., Tierney, G., Buhin, L., Greco, D. M., & Cooper, C. J. (2002). Kids' college: Enhancing children's appreciation and acceptance of cultural diversity. *Journal of Prevention & Intervention in the Community, 24*, 63–78.

Luhtanen, R., & Crocker, J. (1992). A collective self-esteem scale: Self-evaluation of one's social identity. *Personality and Social Psychology Bulletin, 18*, 302–318.

MacDonald, A., & Games, S. (1974). Some characteristics of those who hold positive and negative attitudes toward homosexuals. *Journal of Homosexuality, 1*, 9–27.

Masten, A. S. (2001). Ordinary magic. *American Psychologist, 56*, 227–238.

Mohai, P., & Bryant, B. (1992). Environmental racism: Reviewing the evidence. In B. Bryant & P. Mohai (Eds.), *Race and the incidence of environmental hazards: A time for discourse* (pp. 163–176). Boulder, CO: Westview.

National Center for Education Statistics. (2005). *The condition of education.* Washington, DC: U.S. Department of Education, Office of Educational Research and Improvement.

Nelson, E. S., & Krieger, S. (1997). Changes in attitudes toward homosexuality in college students: Implementation of a gay men and lesbian peer panel. *Journal of Homosexuality, 33*, 63–81.

Pettigrew, T. F. (1998). Intergroup contact theory. *Annual Review of Psychology, 49*, 65–85.

Pizarro, M., & Vera, E. M. (2001). Chicana/o ethnic identity research: Lessons for researchers and counselors. *The Counseling Psychologist, 29*, 91–117.

Plous, S. (2000). Responding to overt displays of prejudice: A role-playing exercise. *Teaching of Psychology, 27*, 198–200.

Prilleltensky, I., & Fox, D. (1997). Introducing critical psychology: Values, assumptions, and the status quo. In D. Fox & I. Prilleltensky (Eds.), *Critical psychology: An introduction* (pp. 3–20). London: Sage.

Prilleltensky, I., & Gonick, L. (1996). Policies change, oppression remains: On the psychology and politics of oppression. *Journal of Political Psychology, 17*, 127–148.

Prilleltensky, I., & Nelson, G. (2002). *Doing psychology critically: Making a difference in diverse settings.* New York: Palgrave MacMillan.

Quintana, S. M. (1998). Children's developmental understanding of ethnicity and race. *Applied and Preventive Psychology, 7*, 27–45.

Reed, G. M., Levant, R. F., Stout, C. E., Murphy, M. J., & Phelps, R. (2001). Psychology in the current mental health marketplace. *Professional Psychology: Research and Practice 32*(1), 65–70.

Romano, J. L., & Hage, S. M. (2000). Prevention: A call to action. *The Counseling Psychologist, 28*, 854–856.

Roysircar, G., Arredondo, P., Fuertes, J. N., Ponterotto, J. G., & Toporek, R. L. (2003). *Multicultural counseling competencies 2003: Association for Multicultural Counseling and Development.* Alexandria, VA: Association for Multicultural Counseling and Development.

Sanchez, L. M., & Turner, S. M. (2003). Practicing psychology in the era of managed care: Implications for practice and training. *American Psychologist, 58*, 116–129.

Santiago-Rivera, A. L., Talka, K., & Tully, A. W. (2006). Environmental racism: A call to the profession for community interventions and social action. In R. L. Toporek, L. H. Gerstein, N. A. Fouad, G. Roysircar, & T. Israel (Eds.), *Handbook for social justice in counseling psychology: Leadership, vision, and action* (pp. 185–199). Thousand Oaks, CA: Sage.

Schreier, B. (1995). Moving beyond tolerance: A new paradigm for programming about homophobia/biphobia and heterosexism. *Journal of College Student Development, 36*, 19–26.

Seligman, M. E. P., Steen, T. A., Park, N., & Peterson, C. (2005). Positive psychology progress: Empirical validation of interventions. *American Psychologist, 60*, 410–421.

Sickmund, M. (2004, June). *Juveniles in corrections.* Washington, DC: U.S. Department of Justice, Office of Juvenile Justice and Delinquency Prevention.

Speight, S. L., & Vera, E. M. (2004). A social justice agenda: Ready, or not? *The Counseling Psychologist, 32*, 109–118.

Speight, S. L., Myers, L. J., Cox, C. I., & Highlen, P. S. (1991). A redefinition of multicultural counseling. *Journal of Counseling and Development, 70*, 29–37.

Sue, D. W., & Sue, D. (1999). *Counseling the culturally different: Theory and practice.* New York: Wiley.

Takaki, R. (1993). *A different mirror: A history of multicultural America.* Boston: Little, Brown.

Taylor, R. J., Hardison, C. B., & Chatters, L. M. (1996). Kin and nonkin as sources of informal assistance. In H. W. Neighbors & J. S. Jackson (Eds.), *Mental health in black America* (pp. 130–145). Thousand Oaks, CA: Sage.

Thompson, C. E., & Neville, H. A. (1999). Racism, mental health, and mental health practice. *The Counseling Psychologist, 27,* 155–223.

Tobler, N. S. (2000). Lessons learned. *Journal of Primary Prevention, 20,* 261–274.

Toporek, R. L., & Reza, J. V. (2001). Context as a critical dimension of multicultural counseling: Articulating personal, professional, and institutional competence. *Journal of Multicultural Counseling and Development, 29,* 13–30.

Vera, E. M., Buhin, L., Montgomery, G., & Shin, R. Q. (2004). Enhancing therapeutic interventions with people of color: Integrating outreach, advocacy, and prevention. In R. T. Carter (Ed.), *Handbook of racial-cultural psychology and counseling* (pp. 477–490). Hoboken, NJ: Wiley.

Vera, E. M., & Reese, L. E. (2000). Prevention interventions with school-age youth. In S. D. Brown & R. W. Lent (Eds.), *Handbook of counseling psychology* (pp. 411–434). New York: Wiley.

Vera, E. M., & Shin, R. Q. (2006). Promoting strengths in a socially toxic world: Supporting resiliency with systemic interventions. *The Counseling Psychologist, 34,* 80–89.

Vera, E. M., Shin, R. Q., & Buhin, L. (2006). The pursuit of social justice and the elimination of racism. In M. Constantine & D. W. Sue (Eds.), *Addressing racism: Facilitating cultural competence in mental health and educational settings* (pp. 271–287). Hoboken, NJ: Wiley.

Vera, E. M., & Speight, S. L. (2003). Multicultural competence, social justice, and counseling psychology: Expanding our roles. *The Counseling Psychologist, 31,* 253–272.

Wandersman, A., & Florin, P. (2003). Community interventions and effective prevention. *American Psychologist, 58,* 441–448.

Watts, R. J., & Abdul-Adil, J. K. (1997). Promoting critical consciousness in young, African-American men. *Journal of Prevention & Intervention in the Community, 16,* 63–86.

Weisz, J. R., Sandler, I., Durlak, J. A., & Anton, B. (2005). Promoting and protecting youth mental health through evidence-based prevention and treatment. *American Psychologist, 60,* 628–648.

Wernette, D. R., & Nieves, L. A. (1992). Breathing polluted air: Minorities are disproportionately exposed. *Environmental Protection Agency Journal, 18,* 16–17.

Wilson, D. B., Gottfredson, D. C., & Najaka, S. S. (2001). School-based prevention of problem behaviors: A meta-analysis. *Journal of Quantitative Criminology, 17,* 247–272.

Young, I. M. (1990). *Justice and the politics of difference.* Princeton, NJ: Princeton University Press.

5

EVALUATING CONTEMPORARY SOCIAL PROGRAMS: CHALLENGES AND OPPORTUNITIES

FRANCINE JACOBS AND JESSICA GOLDBERG

Program evaluation is arguably the most directly applied of the social science research traditions and, in that sense, sits squarely at the interface between research and practice. A broad range of accepted research methods is employed to answer questions about the operations and effectiveness of programs and policies. These programs and policies are real, as are their potential and actual consequences for participants. Conscientious evaluators are aware of this fact and attempt to optimize the usefulness of their investigations. This use of evaluation results takes many forms, among them, for example, the modification of program activities or components, the decision to expand or replicate the intervention, and the development of new ideas about how to achieve cherished goals.

Mention program evaluation in a room of practitioners, however, and many head for the hills; in these circles, it is often viewed as an intrusive, objectifying, unnecessary, alienating, and alienated enterprise. Yet the impulse to weigh, measure, understand the workings of, and assess the value of objects and phenomena of interest is deeply human and is practiced by each of us, repeatedly, in the innumerable exchanges that constitute our daily lives. Why, then, is the formalized practice of program evaluation so fraught, and how can it be made less threatening and more responsive? How might evaluation of contemporary social justice programs be undertaken so as to maximize utility, preserve scientific rigor, nurture stakeholder interest, and facilitate collaborative researcher–practitioner partnerships, even as it remains faithful to the renegade spirit of the programs themselves? This is a tall order indeed.

This chapter explores the ways in which evaluators have responded to the needs of programs engaged in this often difficult process of self-analysis and critique. It begins with a brief historical overview of program evaluation in the past half-century, explicating some of the particularly thorny challenges that prevention programs have presented to evaluators over the years. Next it offers an evaluation model (the Five-Tiered Approach; see Jacobs, 1988, 2003; Jacobs & Kapuscik, 2000) that promises to address a number of these challenges and is well suited for social justice program evaluation. Using the case of a home-visiting program for young parents of newborns, this chapter illustrates how this evaluation model can be operationalized and highlights several critical lessons learned along the way about these community-based programs and about the conduct of evaluation itself.

PROGRAM EVALUATION: A BRIEF OVERVIEW

Many evaluation texts begin by commenting on how broad the definition and practice of program evaluation has become (e.g., Fitzpatrick, Sanders, & Worthen, 2004; Rossi, Lipsey, & Freeman, 2004), with evaluators plying their trade according to their own orientations. That said, the early definition of evaluation as a scientific process, meant to judge the value of a program, to determine whether or not a program achieves its promised result, remains the "default" job description.

Understanding *how* the program operates is a subsequent, but increasingly central, aspect of evaluation practice. Applying accepted social science research methods to collect and analyze the information is another key element. Rossi and Freeman (1993) underscore their view of evaluation as "disciplined, systematic inquiry"; Jacobs and Kapuscik (2000) see it as "a set of systematically planned and executed activities" (p. 3); and Mark, Henry, and Julnes (2000) speak of evaluation as "assisted sense-making," highlighting the role of the evaluator as one who communicates and disseminates what has been learned. A comprehensive definition, offered by Rossi, Lipsey, and Freeman (2004) considers evaluation (or used here interchangeably, evaluation research), as "a social science activity directed at collecting, analyzing, interpreting, and communicating information about the workings and effectiveness of social programs" (p. 2).

The basic categories of evaluation are contained in these definitions. The study of the effects of programs, interventions, or policies is called *impact, outcome, summative, result-based,* or *output-focused* evaluation; efficiency studies that consider the value of a program relative to its costs, or to the costs of programs with similar intentions, are a subset of outcome evaluation. The study of program or policy operations is called *process, implementation, formative,* or *input-focused* evaluation. The terms used within these two broad categories are not wholly synonymous, and can be used quite differently, depending on the disciplines of the evaluator, the type of program being studied, the funding source, and so forth. But the field concedes the general premise—that determining effects is a different activity, with different purposes, than is documenting program processes.

Evaluation differs from both basic and applied research in several ways. Simply stated, *basic research* intends to discover and elucidate phenomena in the universe, at least initially, for its own sake, to build the knowledge base, without any immediate application. *Applied research* generally studies phenomena in context, and its utility is obvious; that is, there are usually many functions in the real world that are or may be affected by the knowledge that is gained. For example, the recent finding that first children, on average, have higher IQ scores (Kristensen & Bjerkedal, 2007) results from an applied research study; it provokes discussions of the contributions that family dynamics make to the development of intelligence and how these mechanisms might be channeled for the other siblings' benefits. Were some enterprising soul to develop a curriculum to stimulate the intellectual development of subsequent children, it might well be the object of *program evaluation research*—investigation that is based on an actual intervention and is ultimately meant to improve the circumstances for program participants. In this way, program evaluation is the most directly applied social science research tradition.

PROGRAM EVALUATION SINCE THE 1960s

The history of the evaluation field is a footnote to the story of America's love affair with science—that is, with objectivity, testable principles, universal truths, predictable patterns, and other critical features of 20th century modernity. This history has been detailed, alternatively with affection and pique, in many evaluation texts produced over the past 30 years, so this chapter offers only the briefest introduction to it here.

Although evaluation is millennia old, modern practice in the United States began building steam in the post–World War II era and hit its stride in the late 1960s (Rossi et al., 2004). Adherents of the more quantitative social sciences (e.g., economics and psychology) were called on to evaluate the scores of new social programs that emerged during the War on Poverty.

These primarily theoretically oriented researchers brought with them the positivist orientation of their disciplines and used research tools and techniques that reflected that disposition. Their evaluations were almost exclusively impact-focused, designed to answer the "does it work?" question; the apparent assumption was that the programs were being implemented as planned, in many cases, as uniform treatments across cities, states, and populations. These input and output evaluations were later characterized as "black box studies" and roundly criticized for not attempting to understand the essence of the programs, the people under study, or the contexts in which both programs and people existed (Wight & Obasi, 1993). Not surprisingly then, over the next decades many of these early studies, however well meaning, were judged to be evaluation failures, in the sense that they did not appear to capture the spirit of the programs under investigation, nor did they provide much guidance to program directors and policy makers on how to improve operations and outcomes.

Consider now the wave of community-based, grassroots-initiated, progressive social programs that emerged in the 1970s, and the shortcomings of this early approach are particularly glaring. The core features of these types of programs, for example, "localized" components within a broad social agenda, flexible staffing, multiple stakeholders and potential beneficiaries, and desired effects in areas for which few standardized measures existed, bedeviled evaluators committed to scientifically rigorous study. Partly in response to these evaluation challenges and demands and partly as a by-product of a more general movement in social science research away from a rigid adherence to positivism, evaluators began to adopt more diversified methodologies (Johnson & Onwuegbuzie, 2004). Practitioners of the interpretive social sciences—anthropology, sociology, and clinical psychology—have been invited into the evaluation conversation, and the virtues of qualitative data slowly have become more apparent (Lincoln & Guba, 1985, 2000; Smith, 1983). In the process, participants have begun to be viewed as more than a collection of demographic variables, and in place of the implicit assumption that all programs with the same title operate more or less similarly, programs have been acknowledged as having particular characters, reflecting their local contexts (see, for example, Conner, 2004). The "black box" has been cracked open.

THE CONTEMPORARY ORIENTATION TO EVALUATION: MORE FLEXIBLE AND RESPONSIVE

The current atmosphere for evaluation, then, is more pluralistic than in years past, with varying approaches being taught and implemented by evaluators trained in a range of disciplines. Several well-practiced approaches come to mind. Patton (1978, 2000) popularized the term *utilization-focused evaluation* to represent studies that are explicitly meant for practical use, such as program improvement, staff development, intervention modification, and even funding decisions. Utilization-focused evaluators are also committed to matching their investigatory methods to the questions at hand, even if that means that less "scientific" or validated techniques and measures are chosen (Casswell, 2000). Within this orientation, there is a greater acceptance of mixed-method designs, those that make use of both qualitative and quantitative data. Critics assert that this approach sacrifices rigor for use; others argue simply that the notion of "rigor" needs to be redefined (Lawrenz & Huffman, 2002). In addition to utilization-focused evaluation, examples of other contemporary approaches include *participatory evaluation*, which suggests that program stakeholders not only be included in the framing of the study but also in its implementation (Upshur & Barreto-Cortez, 1995); *empowerment evaluation*, which emphasizes the value of capacity building for self-evaluation within programs (Fetterman, Kaftarian, & Wandersman, 1996; Scriven, 1997); and *democratic evaluation*, which acknowledges and attempts to address conceptually and procedurally the power relations inherent in the conduct of the evaluation, both on the ground between evaluator and program and within the broader culture (Ryan, 2004).

Central to all of these orientations is a deep appreciation of *program processes* —the ways in which the programs themselves are implemented by administrators and staff, adapted and used by participants, and reshaped to respond to budgetary, financial, political, and societal changes (Wight & Obasi, 2002). Attending to process, it is argued here, results in a greater understanding of how change occurs (see Weiss, 1998, for explication of application of "theory of change" considerations to program evaluation), which in turn yields improved program design, operations, and ultimately, outcomes (Rosecrans et al., 2008).

These inroads may not have come soon enough, nor gone far enough, to satisfy the demands for a new applied research paradigm from some social justice advocates and scholars. Fine (2006), for example, argues for critical research methods in social psychology—integrating social action with methods and theory—that question notions of objectivity and expert knowledge. Prevention researchers Kellam and Langevin (2003) have deconstructed the concept of *evidence*, suggesting a multiplicity of meanings and uses broader than is currently accepted among mainstream researchers and evaluators. Because there are relatively few examples of evaluations of social justice programs in the published literature, it may be that many of these progressive programs resist, or at least do not embrace, the practice. On the other hand, given the stubborn preference in the scholarly world, and also among funders and policy makers, for outcome evaluation of the traditional genre (Parker, 2004), program studies based in a critical approach to positivist research may simply not be granted the light of day in the usual outlets. Paradoxically, this situation is likely to precipitate further advances in both evaluation practice and program receptivity.

THE FIVE-TIERED APPROACH TO EVALUATION

The Five-Tiered Approach (FTA) to evaluation (Jacobs, 1988, 2003; Jacobs & Kapuscik, 2000) is a case in point. Conceived in the 1980s in response to the new generation of social programs—in particular, family support programs—the FTA is a specific application of utilization-focused evaluation. The FTA is a *developmental* model as well, viewing programs as living organisms or systems, with distinct personalities or characters. A new program or one that has just begun to serve a different clientele or work with a different funder, a program that has recently experienced a change in leadership, a grassroots program on a shoestring budget, or a stable, high-profile program being bombarded with requests for replication are good candidates for certain types of evaluation and not for others. The FTA requires that evaluators factor these program traits into their evaluation planning.

Programs also have developmental trajectories, some of which can be anticipated, whereas others cannot. New programs usually need time to sort themselves out before they establish a regular profile of services; established programs that lose their founding directors may retrench or "regress" for a time or set off on a different mission. At one stage in a program's life, new funding opportunities are sought, whereas at other times they are perceived as too overwhelming to consider. In addition, a program's interest in and capacity to support evaluation also change over time, hopefully in the direction of greater engagement and sophistication. The FTA argues that evaluators need to take all of these aspects of programs into account.

The FTA also views the whole evaluation enterprise as necessarily developmental and recommends that programs begin by working to understand their "insides" and then move to establishing possible effects. A young program might need an evaluation that helps it monitor its services by detailing the profile of clients and of individual service utilization. A more mature program might well have those data in hand and could investigate other aspects of program operations, such as client satisfaction or implementation fidelity (the extent to which the programming currently being offered conforms to the program's design). Programs that are confident they are in good working order should be encouraged to move on to outcome evaluation activities. But the information generated in these initial process-oriented stages (or "tiers," in this model) is critical, and all programs need to have cycled through them to be prepared for the later, outcome-focused investigations that should follow.

According to the FTA, the first major task for an evaluator is to match the program under consideration to an important, interesting (to the program), and answerable set of questions given what is known about it and about the resources available for the study. Those questions will lead to a particular tier of evaluation. This step often requires significant education of the potential client or program funder, since outcome evaluation remains the more popular, though often the less appropriate, genre. Once the earlier tiers have been engaged, however, the model does recommend that most programs proceed to outcome evaluation. Although the FTA is developmental, it is not linear; a program that has conducted outcome evaluation should not be considered "finished" with evaluation for all time. Rather, evaluation is a recursive or iterative process. A good evaluation raises as many questions as it answers, and often those questions send a program back to an earlier tier, to begin once again.

The Five-Tiered Approach Structure, in Brief

The five-tiered model proposes five stages, or tiers, of evaluation activities (see Jacobs & Kapuscik, 2000, for a detailed explication of the framework). Evaluation activities at Tier One produce needs and demand assessments and are usually conducted prior to the program's initiation. Evaluation activities at Tiers Two and Three are directed at program processes: they describe program staff, services, clients, and costs; examine program implementation compared to model standards; determine participant satisfaction; and provide feedback to programs for improvement. Tiers Four and Five focus on outcome evaluation activities, assessing the extent to which a program is meeting its short-term and long-term goals. The primary difference between Tier Four and Tier Five is the use of an experimental design at Tier Five; when conditions allow for such rigor, the FTA strongly endorses its use (see Table 5.1 for FTA model summary and Exhibit 5.1 for FTA in practice).

TABLE 5.1
Description of Evaluation Activities for the Five-Tiered Approach

Tier	Purposes of evaluation	Types of evaluation activities
TIER ONE: NEEDS ASSESSMENT	• Document the size and nature of a public problem • Determine unmet need for services in a community • Propose program and policy options to meet needs • Set a data baseline from which later progress can be measured • Broaden the base of support for a proposed program	• Review existing community, county, and state data • Determine additional data needed to describe problem and potential service users • Conduct "environmental scan" of available resources • Identify resource gaps and unmet need • Set goals and objectives for intervention • Recommend program model
TIER TWO: MONITORING AND ACCOUNTABILITY	• Monitor program performance • Meet demands for accountability • Build a constituency • Aid in program planning and decision making • Provide a groundwork for later evaluation activities	• Determine needs and capacities for data collection and management • Develop clear and consistent procedures for collecting essential data elements • Gather and analyze data to describe program along dimensions of clients, services, staff, and costs
TIER THREE: QUALITY REVIEW AND PROGRAM CLARIFICATION	• Develop a more detailed picture of the program as it is being implemented • Assess the quality and consistency of the intervention • Provide information to staff for program improvement	• Review monitoring data • Expand on program description using information about participants' views • Compare program with standards and expectations • Examine participants' perceptions about effects of program • Clarify program goals and design

TABLE 5.1
(Continued)

Tier	Purposes of evaluation	Types of evaluation activities
TIER FOUR: ACHIEVING OUTCOMES	• Determine what changes, if any, have occurred among beneficiaries • Attribute changes to the program • Provide information to staff for program improvement	• Choose short-term objectives to be examined • Choose appropriate research design, given constraints and capacities • Determine measurable indicators of success for outcome objectives • Collect and analyze information about effects on beneficiaries
TIER FIVE: ESTABLISHING IMPACT	• Contribute to knowledge development in the field • Produce evidence of differential effectiveness of treatments • Identify models worthy of replication	• Decide on impact objectives based on results of Tier Four evaluation efforts • Choose appropriately rigorous research design and comparison groups • Identify techniques and tools to measure effects in treatment and comparison groups • Analyze information to identify program impacts

Note. From "The Five-Tiered Approach to Evaluation: Context and Implementation," by F. H. Jacobs, 1988; in H. Weiss and F. H. Jacobs (Eds.), *Evaluating Family Programs* (pp. 37–68), Hawthorne, NY: Aldine de Bruyter. Copyright 1988 by F. H. Jacobs. Adapted with permission of the author.

EXHIBIT 5.1
The Massachusetts Healthy Families Evaluation:
A Case Study of the Five-Tiered Approach in Practice

Used by evaluators in a variety of settings, the Five-Tiered Approach (FTA) has demonstrated its utility with a broad range of programs, including financial education initiatives (e.g., Fox, Bartholomae, & Lee, 2005), teacher training and professional development programs (e.g., Deshmukh-Towery & Oliveri, 2005/2006; Easterbrooks & Jacobs, 2007), community development coalitions (e.g., Ganey & Bloomberg, 2007), family life education programs (e.g., Small, 1990), international agricultural education projects (e.g., Radha-krishna, 2001), community mental health systems (e.g., Kutash, Duchnowski, Johnson, & Rugs, 1993), mental health services (Barnes, Stein, & Rosenberg 1999), and family support programs (e.g., Duggan, Rodriguez, Burell, Shea, & Rohde, 2005).

Although our team at Tufts University also has used the FTA to evaluate a wide variety of programs, we focus here on our most extensive evaluation to date: the longitudinal evaluation of Healthy Families Massachusetts (HFM), a statewide home visiting program for first-time young parents. (See Jacobs, 2003, for a more extended description of the project in its early stages.) For more information on the Healthy Families Massachusetts program, see its website (http://www.mctf.org). HFM is administered by the Massachusetts Children's Trust Fund (MCTF), a state agency focused on preventing child maltreatment and promoting healthy family development. Primarily within young parents' homes, HFM offers individualized parenting support, information, and services to its participants, beginning prenatally and continuing until the child's third birthday. HFM aims to reduce rates of child maltreatment, prevent repeat teen pregnancy, encourage educational and economic attainment, and promote both child and parental health and well-being.

HFM services currently are provided by 26 local agencies across the state and include home visits, goal-setting activities, group-based activities, and linkages and referrals to other services. The majority of HFM home visitors are paraprofessionals, with a wide range of educational and life experiences. HFM home visitors receive extensive preservice and in-service training from MCTF, as well as regular, intensive supervision from their local program directors.

Soon after HFM's inception in 1997, the Tufts University team, composed of faculty from the Eliot-Pearson Department of Child Development and the Department of Urban and Environmental Policy and Planning, received the contract for its evaluation (the Co-Principal Investigators of MHFE are M. Ann Easterbrooks, PhD, Francine Jacobs, EdD, and Jayanthi Mistry, PhD). The first cohort study (Massachusetts Healthy Families Evaluation-1 [MHFE-1]) was initiated in 1998 and produced a final evaluation report for this phase in 2005 (for final evaluation report, see Jacobs, Easterbrooks, Brady, & Mistry, 2005). The Tufts team is presently recruiting participants for a second cohort study (MHFE-2).

The Tufts team was particularly enthusiastic about the opportunity to evaluate HFM, a promising and complex program with many goals, many potential beneficiaries, and many stakeholders. Its administrative structure was also part of the appeal; the state agency (MCTF) behaved from the outset as a learning organization (see Senge, 1990), with a demonstrated commitment to evaluation. It undertook the construction of a program management information system that was critical to the evaluation, cooperated with all data collection activities, and made a concerted effort to preserve evaluation funding, even in the face of significant state budget cuts. This posture promised to improve the state program's operations and effectiveness, as well as to contribute knowledge about home visiting to the broader practice and research fields.

Evaluations of the home visiting program already were plentiful when MHFE-1 began (see, for example, Gomby, Larson, Lewit, & Behrman, 1993; Halpern, 1984; Olds, 1993). Nonetheless, there were still important "unexplored frontiers" in the home visiting literature. For example, although these evaluations routinely presented outcome findings, little attention was given to the ways in which programs were implemented and used and what factors might account for variations; the characteristics and quality of the community-based agencies providing these services; the nature of the home visit itself; and the interpretation of participant outcomes in light of family, cultural, communal, individual program, and state policy factors.

MHFE-1, then, represented our attempt to use the FTA to frame an investigation of these and other "neglected" issues, while simultaneously addressing MCTF's need for data on participant outcomes. In the sections that follow, we briefly describe our experiences with MHFE-1 and our current plans for the second evaluation phase (MHFE-2).

Structure of the Massachusetts Healthy Families Evaluation, Phase One (MHFE-1)

MHFE-1 comprised three overlapping components: the process study, the outcome study, and the ethnography; each of these sub-studies was responsible for answering a discrete set of the project's core research questions. The goal of the process study was to understand particular elements of the program's operations and to document how participants perceived themselves to have benefited from it. The outcome study sought to determine the extent to which the desired changes accrued to HFM families. And the ethnography explored participants' beliefs about parenting, child rearing, and help seeking and the extent to which HFM services were consonant with these beliefs. Generally speaking, the process study team undertook evaluation activities at Tiers Two and Three, the outcome study team engaged in Tier Four activities, and the ethnography primarily addressed Tier Three questions, though its results informed the outcome study as well. (See Table 5.2 for an illustration of how sample MHFE-1 research questions mapped onto the FTA.)

Each team was also responsible for preparing its data to support both the data collection and analyses undertaken by the others; for instance, findings from the process study informed the outcome study, the outcome study produced data to test hunches arising from the ethnography, the results of following through on those hunches suggested additional process or outcome investigations, and so forth. This iterative quality is central to the FTA model.

Evaluation Design

In large part because HFM was intended to be a *universal* home visiting program—that is, provided to every young parent, age 20 and under, in Massachusetts—MHFE-1 did not use a comparison or control group in its evaluation design. Rather, a quasi-experimental design with comparison standards was used, relying on other sources of comparison data, such as state and nationwide historical data on key indicators and extant data from large-scale studies of adolescents and young parents. These comparison data allowed for assessments of changes across time and comparisons between groups on specific outcomes. MHFE-1 drew a sample of approximately 360 young mothers from 22 of the 31 HFM sites in operation at the start of data collection (1999). On average, these mothers entered the study at 17.7 years old and were demographically representative of teen mothers across the Commonwealth.

Data collection proceeded from January 1999 through June 2002. Participants were administered standardized questionnaires, along with a semi-structured research interview covering topics such as demographics, parenting, maternal functioning, and program participation; these data collection visits occurred at 6-month intervals over an 18-month period. Ethnographic and process data collection from HFM clients and staff occurred throughout.

TABLE 5.2
The Five-Tiered Approach in Practice: Sample Research Questions From
Massachusetts Healthy Families Evaluation-1

Tier	Sample research questions	Substudy
TIER TWO: MONITORING AND ACCOUNTABILITY	• Who is enrolled in Healthy Families Massachusetts (HFM), and how do participants use the services?	Process
	• Who are the home visitors in HFM (e.g., education level, years of experience)?	Process
	• What are staff turnover rates across sites?	Process
TIER THREE: QUALITY REVIEW AND PROGRAM CLARIFICATION	• What is the nature of the home visit?	
	• What is the range of topics covered during home visits?	Process
	• Who participates in home visits?	Process
	• To what extent is home visiting practice consonant with ethnotheories (culturally embedded sets of beliefs) of parenting and child rearing?	Process Ethnography
	• To what extent is the intervention being delivered consistently, with consistent quality, across program sites?	Process Ethnography
	• To what extent do participants utilize "non-visit" activities (e.g., phone calls, referrals, etc.), and do these collateral activities influence participant outcomes?	Process
	• To what extent do the programs, as implemented, conform to HFM model and individual program standards?	Process
	• What are the reasons for service "noncompliance"?	
	• How satisfied are participants with the program and how successful do they perceive the program to be?	Process

TABLE 5.2
(Continued)

Tier	Sample research questions	Substudy
TIER FOUR: ACHIEVING OUTCOMES	• To what extent is the program meeting its stated "distal," or long-term, goals?	Outcome
	• To what extent are the "intermediate," or short-term, objectives being achieved? These intermediate objectives include:	Outcome
	• increasing the amount, types, and quality of social support used by young parents;	
	• increasing parental knowledge of child development and enhancing parenting competence/ parenting skills;	
	• enhancing the quality of the parent-child relationship and promoting parental well-being.	
	• In what ways do characteristics of participants, programs, and communities moderate both utilization of program services and the attainment of the short- and long-term outcomes?	Process Outcome Ethnography

Note. From *Healthy Families Massachusetts Final Evaluation Report,* by F. H. Jacobs, M. A. Easterbrooks, A. Brady, and J. Mistry, 2005, Medford: Massachusetts Healthy Families Evaluation. Adapted with permission of the authors.

LESSONS FROM THE FIELD

This first cohort evaluation of the Healthy Families program (Massachusetts Healthy Families Evaluation-1 [MHFE-1]) was meant to exemplify the FTA in practice. Our team used a mixed-methods approach—developing, adopting, and adapting both qualitative and quantitative instruments and techniques that fit the precise needs of our populations and stakeholders. We made an effort to integrate Healthy Families Massachusetts (HFM) participants into the design and execution of the evaluation; through interviews and focus groups, stakeholders—from the teen mothers themselves to Massachusetts Children's Trust Fund (MCTF) administrators—were included in decisions about instrumentation, interpretation of data, and dissemination of results.

Along similar lines, MCTF and the Tufts evaluation team established and maintained a collaborative relationship throughout the course of the evaluation. MCTF has been unusually receptive to, and facilitative of, the evaluation process, even when it caused some political difficulties for the agency. We, in turn, have striven to operate in as transparent a manner as possible, providing regular feedback on the progress of the evaluation, and sharing program-related data as quickly and thoroughly as we could. For example, when results from an early sub-study analysis of service slippage suggested that a mismatch between some participants' availability for home visits and home visitors' work schedules might account for a good percentage of missed visits, MCTF revised agency contracts to require that home visitors be able to visit families outside the 9-5 workday. In a more recent example of this collaboration, for the past year, members of the Tufts evaluation team have participated in a "think tank" of key HFM stakeholders and state agency leaders, convened by MCTF to systematically review key findings from the first evaluation phase. Over the course of these meetings, committee members used the MHFE-1 findings to generate new implementation strategies for Healthy Families Massachusetts and to suggest new hypotheses and research questions for MHFE-2.

On balance we have concluded that MHFE-1 was a successful evaluation—both in the sense that it represented a sustained attempt to conduct evaluation according to FTA principles and, more important, that it produced results MCTF could use to make necessary adjustments in the HFM offerings and approach. Nonetheless, no matter how well-planned an evaluation is, as this first cohort evaluation was, the programs, their contexts, and the theoretical knowledge that informs and is informed by program behavior are constantly changing. This essential truth lends a touch of the impossible, even the absurd, to the enterprise of evaluating such a program; "attempting to hit a moving target" is a well-worn, but fitting, metaphor. Good evaluation acknowledges this as its basic operating condition, assuming, for example, that new, even more pressing questions will emerge during the course of the study, as will new and better ways to measure what is occurring. Like housecleaning or teeth flossing, one is never "done"; evaluation is an eternal discipline. However onerous that seems, a major virtue of this situation is that there is always something to learn that can be profitably applied to the next evaluation.

In that spirit, we provide brief examples of the types of education that evaluators receive, which are primarily answers to questions we didn't have the forethought to ask but wish we had and lessons on the conduct of evaluation that we might have anticipated but did not. Included here are thoughts about how we will address each of these issues in the second cohort evaluation (MHFE-2). These lessons from MHFE-1 are organized on a kind of continuum, as follows:

- Some issues fall on the "no-brainer" end, as pleasant surprises or challenges that we actually could have predicted and that had relatively straightforward solutions.
- Others were challenges that were more complicated but still "solvable," or at least the next steps to addressing them were clear.
- A final set of lessons pertained to continuing conundrums for us, and perhaps also for the field, that simply have not yet yielded to a satisfying solution.

"No-Brainers"

Of the numerous challenges, pleasant surprises, and mixtures of both we encountered during MHFE-1, we have selected two in this category. The first reflects a challenge that we should have expected and that had some modest, though noteworthy consequences for the evaluation; it pertains to our reliance on the newly developed management information system. The second represents a great pleasure for us—conducting this evaluation democratically, across disciplines—that nonetheless required considerable retraining on the parts of the principal investigators and their students.

Beware of Promising New Databases

One of the earliest indications that MCTF was serious about this evaluation was its willingness to spend considerable resources on the construction and administration of a comprehensive computerized management information system (the Participant Data System, or PDS). Data on the full complement of mothers and children enrolled in the HFM program were to be available through this system, including information about participants' program use and progress on family goals. Because the PDS would be collecting these critical data, the Tufts evaluation team did not have to develop its own mechanism to do so.

Initially, our evaluation team was thrilled at this prospect, and indeed, MHFE-1 was designed with the PDS as a cornerstone. Soon, though, technical problems with the system emerged, and these—in one form or another—persisted over the course of the first cohort evaluation. MCTF contracted with various software consulting groups, which revised and upgraded the PDS, but new glitches with its electronic transmission functionality continued to surface. We should have known better than to rely so heavily on these data, however attractive the offer.

In addition to alerting us to the possibility of technical failings, this experience reminded us of the more general limitations of too much dependence on agency administrative data—any agency's administrative data. Because this information is quantified, available, and "official," researchers and program monitors alike often assume it to be both reliable (accurately and consistently recorded) and valid (representing the constructs of interest). More often than is admitted, however, it is at least somewhat lacking on both counts.

For administrative data to be reliable, those entering the data must be both competent to do so and sufficiently committed to the documentation process. In this case, we suspect that some of the data enterers—the home visitors—had relatively poor computer skills that improved only slowly over the course of the evaluation; others were simply disinclined to put a priority on accurate record keeping over, say, visiting their clients. Regarding data validity, although home visitors received some instruction in documentation as part of their preservice training, it tended to be cursory, leaving room for interpretation. For example, home visitors across program sites had different standards about what constituted a "home visit": Some programs restricted this term to visits in the home, while others counted any kind of face-to-face contact with clients, including office visits and car rides. Furthermore, as home visitors likely did not always have the full story about what was happening with their clients, the data may sometimes have represented only their "best guesses" about a number of the required PDS indicators.

MCTF has already taken many steps toward ensuring the Participant Data System's future accuracy. The agency has switched to a more user-friendly Web-based version, stepped up documentation training, standardized data entry parameters across sites, begun to consider computer proficiency when hiring new home visitors, and created a PDS data oversight system in which the supervisor needs to sign off on each entry before it can be considered completed.

What is the proper role for a research team to play in a data system enhancement process being undertaken by the entity whose program it is evaluating? We have a large stake in this activity, since the data need to be sufficiently reliable and valid for us to feel comfortable using them for MHFE-2. Since we have developed considerable expertise in working with the PDS, we have advice to offer, and MCTF has been open to hearing it. This genre of engagement seems to us well within the bounds of an acceptable collaboration between evaluator and program. Other reasonable evaluators, however, might disagree, arguing that this conversation places us more in the role of consultants, not evaluators, and indeed, in other circumstances, with other agencies, we might feel the same. There is no simple answer here.

The Benefits of Differing Perspectives

For decades, an interdisciplinary orientation to professional work has been embraced by practitioners and researchers, at least in theory. MHFE-1 made a conscious effort to implement this approach by enlisting co-principal investigators (co-pi's) with scholarly interests and expertise that overlapped, but also extended, the project's reach. Two of the co-pi's were trained as developmental psychologists, one with a particular interest in infants and toddlers and their families and the other with interests in young children in educational settings. Over the years, these scholars have focused on parent-child relationships, including those with fathers (in the first case) and on cultural settings or contexts and development, for example, schools (in the second). The third co-pi was trained in an educational policy program and is most interested in factors that account for the variations in the delivery of programs and policies meant to be uniformly implemented.

Each was most animated by a particular set of questions and used a particular set of methods, sometimes applied to distinct subsamples, to answer them. For example, establishing the relationship between maternal characteristics (e.g., maternal depression or a childhood history of maltreatment) and substantiated maltreatment of a child enrolled in HFM required a large, representative sample and depended on longitudinal data collected in waves, using standardized measures, agency administrative data, and a project-developed interview. Understanding the nature of the relationship between home visitor and young mother, and how that relationship was related to community norms and values, required a small sample within selected communities, and ethnographically oriented observational and interview data collection protocols. Determining how HFM participants actually used the program and what accounted for the differences that emerged relied both on PDS output and on data collected from HFM staff.

Overall, the evaluation was conducted with a great respect for, and curiosity about, the perspectives that each co-pi brought to it; the co-pi's jointly administered the project, staying in close contact with one another throughout. Indeed, the starker differences in orientation among them faded somewhat, at least at the margins, as evidenced by the evolution in structure as the study progressed from three distinct substudies, to a far more integrated investigation. Nonetheless, tensions that reflected distinct disciplines surfaced repeatedly; these ranged from questioning the value of using certain measures, to the wisdom of spending additional resources on intensive data collection activities within a small group of participants, to the merits of presenting papers at certain professional conferences and not others.

In the end, however, the evaluation profited far more than it suffered from this arrangement. With all its limitations, the final report is perhaps a more broadly theoretical document, on the one hand, and a more practically useful one, on the other, than many of its contemporaries. It is also clear to us, as scholars and teachers, that such an environment provides constant intellectual provocation and encourages a breadth of thinking that does not emerge as easily in laboratories organized around a single scholar or a unified orientation to research.

Complex Challenges

If pressed to collect the most important lessons from MHFE-1 and place them under one heading, it likely would be: "It's all about relationships." The relationships referred to here are those that develop between HFM program staff and the Tufts evaluation team *and* those at play in the HFM programs themselves (e.g., between home visitors and families, between HFM program directors and home visitors, and between the state program's central staff and the individual program directors). Each of these types of relationships brings its own set of challenges to the evaluation process. The relationships between the Tufts team and MCTF staff, for example, require considerable political skill, goodwill, and delicacy by all parties to maintain the proper balance between collaboration and autonomy. And the complex webs of relationships among people *within* the HFM programs (consider the relationship between a "professional" program director and "paraprofessional" frontline workers, for example) are extremely challenging, from a research standpoint, to measure, quantify, and use in analyses. The following brief description of the home visitor–client relationship hints at the complexity that confronts evaluators of programs of this nature.

The Home Visitor–Client Relationship

We entered the evaluation knowing that the quality of the relationship between the teen parent and the home visitor would be a core component of the program. MCTF certainly saw it as such and adopted a paraprofessional home visiting model in part because the agency believed that these "lay" workers—many from the same communities as the participants—would be better able to establish and maintain critical personal connections that would keep teens involved in the program. MCTF also detailed standards for this relationship that defined how the home visitors should behave, including the proper metaphorical *distance* between participants and home visitors that should be maintained.

However potentially powerful this relationship, it is, nonetheless, only one aspect of the HFM program. Each program also selects a variety of curricula for use during home visits, constitutes local peer support groups for HFM participants, hosts social activities, makes referrals to other services, and provides wide-ranging instrumental support (e.g., transportation to medical appointments, provision of diapers, assistance with filling out college applications). In addition, although some of these young mothers appear isolated, geographically and/or by their parenting status, others live within dense social networks that offer much of the social support they seem to need or want. As a result of these variables, we remained agnostic about whether the relationship itself, independent of these other offerings, would be the main draw for many teen mothers.

MHFE-1's questions about the home visitor–client relationship related to both the substance of that relationship and its measurement. What was it about that connection that kept teen mothers involved or that drove them away? Which home visitor characteristics were particularly salient (e.g., age, parenting status, racial/cultural identification) for which mothers, and why? To what extent did home visitor behavior (such as turnover) affect participants? Which elements of the relationship were related to longer tenure in the program, greater satisfaction, or better outcomes?

We gathered data from both the mothers and the home visitors, using a wide variety of methods. The ethnographers interviewed program personnel, observed home visits, and discussed the home visitor–client relationship with the teen mothers and their families. In the research interview, teens were asked how they perceived their home visitors' role (e.g., friend, social worker, mother figure), how satisfied they were with their home visitors, and what kinds of advice they were likely to accept from program personnel. Home visits also were videotaped to gain a better understanding of the nature of the home visits themselves and to observe the ways in which the home visitor–client dynamic actually played out during the visits.

Despite these concentrated efforts, answers to the questions listed previously remained largely inconclusive (see Jacobs, Easterbrooks, Brady, & Mistry, 2005). Most teen mothers appeared well satisfied with their home visitors and with the relationship that was established. The nature of that relationship appeared to differ across individual home visitor–client pairs and also, according to our ethnographic data, by cultural community. It seems as though the relationship with one particular home visitor mattered to some, whereas the relationship as an entré into a set of services that the local HFM program offers (not with one person per se) drew in others. Not surprisingly, then, home visitor turnover appeared to affect some participants more than others, with some teens staying in the program despite gaps in service and multiple home visitors and others leaving as soon as a home visitor replacement was necessary.

Fully 75% of the respondents viewed their home visitor as a "friend," which is a more familiar role with less professional distance than the state program standards seem to intend. And whereas mothers might enjoy their relationships with their home visitors, it is unclear how much influence these home visitors are allowed to have. It does appear, for example, that mothers accepted, and made good use of, their home visitors' help in continuing their education—a major HFM goal. Yet a large percentage of mothers noted that they essentially disregarded their home visitors' efforts to influence decisions regarding family planning, another central HFM goal. Finally, no statistically significant relationships between specific home visitor–client relationship characteristics and program outcomes could be established.

The conclusion here, then, is that understanding this rich, varied relationship is a worthwhile pursuit—one far more difficult than we expected—and with the experiences of MHFE-1 in hand, we will be able to do it better this time around. We have embarked, for instance, on a series of focus groups designed to investigate how participants at all levels of the HFM program (MCTF administrative staff, program directors, home visitors, and participants) understand and enact the proper professional distance between the home visitors and their clients. Based on MHFE-1 findings and preliminary data from these focus groups, the MHFE-2 research interview for the mothers has been enhanced, and we are in the process of designing a complementary interview for their home visitors. Finally, we are pilot-testing standardized measures that assess the quality of the home visitor–client relationships over time.

Continuing Conundrums

However tautly we in the field stretch the evaluation canvas to accommodate the frame of contemporary social programs, there are corners that cannot be covered, for which evaluation as we know it is inadequate. This is true for a host of reasons, some of which are technical limitations (e.g., the absence of good quality measures) and others which have to do with the nature (the depth, embeddedness, and breadth) of the social problems such programs are meant to address. Within MHFE-1, arguably the most difficult of these conundrums was the imperative to undertake "culturally sensitive" research, an approach that is easy to endorse and extremely challenging to operationalize satisfactorily.

We could appropriately call this dilemma a challenge within a challenge. HFM requires individual programs to meet a standard for culturally competent practice; the standard itself is emphatic but somewhat vague and thus open to considerable interpretation (this vagueness may be the wisest course for a funding agency to take, since the concept itself is not yet well-defined). HFM is not alone in this regard; human services agencies across disciplines, domains, and geographical location are exhorted to behave in a culturally competent manner, but there is often little direction as to how this should be done (see Mistry, Jacobs, & Jacobs, in press). Popular practices include matching providers by race and/or ethnicity to clients, having materials translated into the home languages of participants, and having participants and community residents involved in determining the services to be provided. There is little research in this area, so although these and other activities are recommended, their relation to program utilization and effects is not yet established.

In addition, funders and monitors often require culturally competent practice, on the one hand, and adherence to service standards that may well contradict this practice, on the other. For example, HFM programs are required to be both attentive to the goals and operating standards set by MCTF *and* respectful of individual client needs and the parenting customs of the community in which that client lives. In some communities, this might present a contradiction. Consider, for example, the goal of preventing repeat births in communities in which early childbearing is commonplace; in these communities there may be a mismatch between the family's goals on the one hand and the program's goals on the other. To the extent that programs are implemented differently in different cultural communities and pursue somewhat different or additional goals to those articulated by the state agency, their evaluation *as components of a statewide program* is significantly more complicated. An evaluation sensitive to cultural differences would assume these particularities and carefully document them.

Attempting to conduct evaluation in this manner, however, can create a set of its own contradictions; in this case, primarily between the demand to use measures and techniques appropriate to the specific program's participants and community and the professional obligation to meet the more global standards, or adopt the usual practices, of the evaluation field. For example, virtually every outcome evaluation uses a race variable to describe the population and conduct subgroup analyses (as did MHFE-1). However, increasingly over the past two decades, cultural psychologists and service practitioners have questioned the validity of race as a meaningful demographic category (see, for example, Griffin & Miller, 2007; Lee, 2002, 2007). Given the conflation of race and income in this country, it can be argued that race is more correctly a "social address" variable and does not add much to our understanding of program operations or program effects (Burton & Price-Spratlen, 1999; Rogoff & Angellilo, 2002). Furthermore, the available racial categories often do not describe people as they would describe themselves, which creates a reliability problem. Nonetheless, although a stridently culturally sensitive evaluation might choose not to use or report this information, most evaluators, including us, would be hard-pressed to ignore it. Furthermore, it is unlikely that any peer-reviewed journal would accept an article for publication without these data.

Standardized instruments also pose problems for evaluators striving to be mindful of cultural differences among groups of research participants. For MHFE-1, we investigated the populations with which each of our instruments had been used and selected those that focused on the constructs of interest and were considered appropriate for the teenaged population constituting the sample. However, although these instruments met these standards and are well represented and respected in the field, we later questioned the cultural relevance of a number of items within a few of the measures, for example, those assessing "proper" parenting behaviors.

Therein lies the conundrum. *Culturally sensitive evaluation*, as we envision it, requires attention to the particular communities, geographical and otherwise, that create and sustain the cultures of the program participants. These cultures include individual and communal beliefs, attitudes, behaviors, aspirations, and institutions; they differ group to group and generation to generation (Conner, 2004). Much of *conventional evaluation*—research valued within the profession—assumes that the extent and nature of this variation across people and communities is known and can be adequately described in the decontextualized vocabulary of variables and measures that have largely been developed within the "majority" or mainstream culture.

One of the inherent features of a conundrum is that easy solutions are not readily available, and so it is here. The best available approach is to chip away at current practice by viewing traditional assessments of culture with a critical eye and by complicating and deepening our own understanding of participants' cultural locations or affiliations. We did attempt to incorporate both of these perspectives in MHFE-1. As an example of the former, we used data from the outcome study and ethnography to raise questions about the use of standardized instruments to assess and interpret "racial" and "ethnic" differences in parenting (see Mistry, Diez, & Deshmukh, 2005). As an example of the latter, our process study team was able to disentangle, to some extent, the otherwise highly correlated variables of race, income, and geography when analyzing service noncompliance among the HFM teens (see Goldberg, 2006).

Our initial attempts to unpack race and culture in MHFE-1, however, were largely limited to smaller investigations of particular questions in certain communities and population subgroups. In MHFE-2, we have attempted to infuse the consideration of culture into all aspects of our overall design. For example, we have incorporated more localized, sensitive measures of community and environment to capture the contributions of neighborhood contexts, both cultural and spatial. In addition, the protocol now includes measures that may help explain differential HFM program utilization and effects among participants, including a project-developed measure of cultural identity, and a measure that assesses participants' *acculturative stress* (the psychological consequences of belonging to a nonmajority cultural community). Although none of these actions will wholly address the many difficulties inherent in conducting culturally sensitive evaluation, we do expect them to take us a step farther.

CONCLUSIONS: THE VALUE OF THE EVALUATION ENTERPRISE

The science evaluators practice is limited, and the context into which we "let" our evaluation findings limits them even further. Evaluation findings are often trumped by other exigencies of decision making—politics, beliefs, ideology, and interests, to name a few. Furthermore, what evaluation *cannot* do is precisely what is most often asked of it: to settle matters of principles and values. How much is an increase in the self-esteem of a child with special needs worth? What should our town pay for a local school tax override? Should we revamp our services to more closely align with the desires of our clientele? The answers to questions such as these lay outside the purview of evaluation but within the intentions of contemporary social programs.

It should be obvious by now that, in the debate on whether or not evaluations have anything to offer, we come down decisively on the side that promotes the practice. Done well, evaluation can document the needs, concerns, strengths, and preferences of people in and on their own terms. It can help develop new interventions. It can help articulate program theory. It can register satisfaction (or dissatisfaction) among program participants and present their recommendations for change. It can help improve program operations and, in so doing, help programs improve the lives of the participants within them. It can establish program impacts. Evaluation can act as a hedge against the claims of policy makers, program designers, and program directors—well intentioned and otherwise—that a particular intervention "works" (Of course it does; I've seen it happen; Fund me). As a country with a meager civic impulse when it comes to public support of programs for poor and otherwise marginalized people, we cannot afford to spend money on programs that refuse to be reflective, open to change, responsive to information, and able to make good on their promises of results. Good evaluation can, and should, help in all of these ways.

REFERENCES

Barnes, J., Stein, A., & Rosenberg, W. (1999). Evidence-based medicine and evaluation of mental health services: Methodological issues and future directions. *Archives of Disease in Childhood, 80,* 280–285.

Burton, L. M., & Price-Spratlen, T. (1999). Through the eyes of children: An ethnographic perspective on neighborhoods and child development. In A. S. Masten (Ed.), *Cultural processes in child development* (pp. 77–96). Mahwah, NJ: Erlbaum.

Casswell, S. (2000). A decade of community action research. *Substance Use & Misuse, 35*(1&2), 55–74.

Conner, R. F. (2004). Developing and implementing culturally competent evaluation: A discussion of multicultural validity in two HIV prevention programs for Latinos. *New Directions for Evaluation, 102,* 51–64.

Deshmukh-Towery, I., & Oliveri, R. (2005/2006). Engaging stakeholders in professional development and its evaluation. *The Evaluation Exchange, 9(4),* 15.

Duggan, A., Rodriguez, K., Burell, L., Shea, S., & Rohde, C. (2005). *Evaluation of Healthy Families Alaska: Final report: January 21, 2005.* Retrieved June 19, 2006, from http://www.hss.state.ak.us/ocs/Publications/JohnsHopkins_HealthyFamilies.pdf

Easterbrooks, M. A., & Jacobs, F. (2007). *Touchpoints Early Child Care and Education Initiative: Final evaluation report.* Medford, MA: Tufts University.

Fetterman, D., Kaftarian, S., & Wandersman, A. (Eds.). (1996). *Empowerment evaluation: Knowledge and tools for self-assessment and accountability.* Thousand Oaks, CA: Sage.

Fine, M. (2006). Bearing witness: Methods for researching oppression and resistance— A textbook for critical research. *Social Justice Research, 19*(1), 83–108.

Fitzpatrick, J. L., Sanders, J. R., & Worthen, B. R. (2004). *Program evaluation: Alternative approaches and practical guidelines* (3rd ed.). Boston: Pearson.

Fox, J., Bartholomae, S., & Lee, J. (2005). Building the case for financial education. *Journal of Consumer Affairs, 39*(1), 195–214.

Ganey, A., & Bloomberg, L. *Working together for kids.* Report written for the Pew Partnership for Civic Change. Retrieved March 3, 2007, from http://www.pew-partnership.org/pdf/08_working_together.pdf

Goldberg, J. (2006). More than simply "non-compliance": An investigation of missed visits in a home visiting program for young parents (Doctoral dissertation, Tufts University, 2006). *Dissertations Abstracts International, 67,* 1533.

Gomby, D. S., Larson, C. S., Lewit, E. M., & Behrman, R. E. (1993). Home visiting: Analysis and recommendations. *The Future of Children, 3*(3), 6–22.

Griffin, J., & Miller, E. (2007). Reactions to the article "Culturally relevant prevention: Scientific and practical considerations of community-based programs." *The Counseling Psychologist, 35,* 763–778.

Halpern, R. (1984). Lack of effects for home-based early intervention? Some possible explanations. *American Journal of Orthopsychiatry, 54*(1), 33–42.

Jacobs, F. H. (1988). The Five-Tiered Approach to evaluation: Context and implementation. In H. Weiss & F. Jacobs (Eds.), *Evaluating family programs* (pp. 37–68). Hawthorne, NY: Aldine de Bruyter.

Jacobs, F. H. (2003). Child and family program evaluation: Learning to enjoy complexity. *Applied Developmental Science, 7*(2), 62–75.

Jacobs, F. H., Easterbrooks, M. A., Brady, A., & Mistry, J. (2005). *Healthy Families Massachusetts final evaluation report.* Medford: Massachusetts Healthy Families Evaluation.

Jacobs, F. H., & Kapuscik, J. L. (2000). *Making it count: Evaluating family preservation services*. Medford, MA: Family Preservation Evaluation Project/Tufts University.

Johnson, R. B., & Onwuegbuzie, A. J. (2004). Mixed methods research: A research paradigm whose time has come. *Educational Researcher, 33*(7), 14–26.

Kellam, S. G., & Langevin, D. (2003). A framework for understanding "evidence" in prevention research and programs. *Prevention Science, 4*(3), 137–153.

Kristensen, P., & Bjerkedal, T. (2007, June 22). Explaining the relation between birth order and intelligence. *Science, 316*(5832), 1717.

Kutash, K., Duchnowski, A., Johnson, M., & Rugs, D. (1993). Multi-stage evaluation for a community mental health system for children. *Administration and Policy in Mental Health and Mental Health Services Research, 20*(4), 311–322.

Lawrenz, F., & Huffman, D. (2002). The Archipelago approach to mixed method evaluation. *American Journal of Evaluation, 23*(3), 331–338.

Lee, C. D. (2002). Interrogating race and ethnicity in the examination of cultural processes in developmental research. *Human Development, 45*(4), 280–294.

Lee, K. (2007). *The importance of culture in evaluation: A practical guide for evaluators*. Denver, CO: The Colorado Trust.

Lincoln, Y. S., & Guba, E. G. (1985). *Naturalistic inquiry*. Beverly Hills, CA: Sage.

Lincoln, Y. S., & Guba, E. G. (2000). Paradigmatic controversies, contradictions, and emerging confluences. In N. K. Denzin & Y. S. Lincoln (Eds.), *Handbook of qualitative research* (pp. 163–188). Thousand Oaks, CA: Sage.

Mark, M. M., Henry, G. T., & Julnes, G. (2000). *Evaluation: An integrated framework for understanding, guiding and improving policies and programs*. San Francisco: Jossey-Bass.

Mistry, J., Diez, V., & Deshmukh, I. (2005, April). *Understanding community differences in parenting attitudes among young mothers*. Paper presented at the 2005 Biennial meeting for the Society for Research in Child Development, Atlanta, GA.

Mistry, J., Jacobs, F. H., & Jacobs, L. (in press). Cultural relevance as program-to-community alignment. *Journal of Community Psychology*.

Olds, D. L. (1993). Does prenatal and early infancy nurse home visitation have enduring effects on qualities of parental caregiving and child health at 25–50 months of life? *Pediatrics, 93*, 89–98.

Parker, L. (2004). Commentary: Can critical theories of or on race be used in evaluation research on education? *New Directions for Evaluation, 101*, 85–93.

Patton, M. Q. (1978). *Utilization-focused evaluation*. Beverly Hills, CA: Sage Publications.

Patton, M. Q. (2000). Utilization-focused evaluation. In D. L. Stufflebeam & G. F. Madaus (Eds.), *Evaluation models: Viewpoints on educational and human services evaluation* (2nd ed., pp. 425–438). Norwell, MA: Kluwer.

Radhakrishna, R. B. (2001). *Evaluating international agricultural and extension education projects: Problems, challenges, and strategies*. University Park: The Pennsylvania State University.

Rogoff, B., & Angellilo, C. (2002). Investigating the coordinated functioning of multifaceted cultural practices in human development. *Human Development, 45*, 211–225.

Rosecrans, A. M., Gittelsohn, J., Ho, L. S., Harris, S. B., Naqushbandi, M., & Sharma, S. (2008). Process evaluation of a multi-institutional community-based program for diabetes prevention among First Nations. *Health Education Research, 23*(2), 272–286.

Rossi, P. H., & Freeman, H. E. (1993). *Evaluation. A systematic approach* (5th ed.). Newbury Park, CA: Sage.

Rossi, P. H., Lipsey, M. W., & Freeman, H. E. (2004). *Evaluation: A systematic approach* (7th ed.). Newbury Park, CA: Sage.

Ryan, K. (2004). Serving public interests in educational accountability: Alternative approaches to democratic evaluation. *American Journal of Program Evaluation, 25*(4), 443–460.

Scriven, M. (1997). Empowerment evaluation examined. *Evaluation Practice, 18*(2), 165–175.

Senge, P. (1990). *The fifth discipline: The art and practice of the learning organization.* New York: Doubleday.

Small, S. A. (1990). Some issues regarding the evaluation of family life education programs. *Family Relations, 39*(2), 132–135.

Smith, J. K. (1983). Quantitative versus qualitative research: An attempt to clarify the issue. *Educational Researcher, 12*, 6–13.

Upshur, C. C., & Barreto-Cortez, E. (1995). What is participatory evaluation (PE)? What are its roots? *The Evaluation Exchange, 1*(3/4), 7–9.

Weiss, C. (1998). *Evaluation* (2nd ed.). Upper Saddle River, NJ: Prentice Hall.

Wight, D., & Obasi, A. (2002). Unpacking the "black box": The importance of process data to explain outcomes. In J. Stephenson, J. Imrie, & C. Bonell (Eds.), *Effective sexual health interventions: Issues in experimental evaluation* (pp. 151–166). Oxford, England: Oxford University Press.

6

PREVENTION: ETHICS, RESPONSIBILITY, AND COMMITMENT TO PUBLIC WELL-BEING

JONATHAN P. SCHWARTZ AND SALLY M. HAGE

A crisis in mental health services related to the inverse relation between access and supply versus demand has emerged (Satcher, 2000). Research suggests that only 10 to 15% of those with mental illness receive appropriate services (U.S. Surgeon General [USSG], 1999, 2001). Access to mental health services and the cultural appropriateness of those services pose particular problems for minority and low socioeconomic status (SES) populations (USSG, 2001). The disparity of services affects general health care as well as mental health care (Agency for Healthcare Research and Quality, 2004; Institute of Medicine, 2002). The efficacy of prevention to address current national health and mental health needs has been clearly supported in the literature (Durlak & Wells, 1997; Greenberg, Domitrovich, & Bumbarger, 2001). These disparities in the availability of mental health services exert a moral imperative to expand health initiatives to prevent human suffering before it occurs (Albee, 1986) and provide an ethical justification to further augment effective prevention efforts.

Unfortunately, the ethical standards of the professional associations that govern the practice of mental health professionals do not explicitly address many of the unique ethical issues involved in conducting prevention programs (American Counseling Association, 2005; American Psychiatric Association, 2001; American Psychological Association [APA], 2002; National Association of Social Workers, 1999). In particular, interventions that aim to prevent problems before they occur (e.g., primary and secondary prevention practice) and the ecological focus of typical prevention programs, which intervene at multiple systemic levels, raise unique and heretofore unaddressed ethical issues. Insufficient training on ethical issues unique to prevention raises concern about possible harm that could result from prevention efforts that are not informed by an awareness of prevention ethics.

The purpose of this chapter is to explicate and provide guidance in addressing some of the unique ethical issues inherent in prevention work. To accomplish this, the chapter consists of three main sections: (1) reviewing unique ethical issues in prevention, (2) reviewing existing literature on the ethics of prevention, and (3) proposing recommendations to guide prevention ethics.

ETHICAL ISSUES IN PREVENTION

Defining Prevention

One of the challenges in providing ethical guidance for prevention work is defining the expansive field of prevention. Myriad target populations, settings, methodologies, and goals encompass the discipline. The inclusivity of the field of prevention is evident in the definition proposed by Romano and Hage (2000). They define prevention as including one or more of the following five dimensions: (1) stopping problem behavior before it occurs (primary prevention); (2) delaying the onset of problem behavior (secondary prevention); (3) reducing the negative impact of current problem behavior (tertiary prevention); (4) promoting strengths to reduce risks; and (5) promoting structural policies that promote well-being. Hence, the scope of prevention work makes the formulation of a specific set of ethical guidelines for prevention difficult. For example, a primary prevention program focused on reducing drunk driving in a community would encounter different ethical issues than a secondary prevention program focused on preventing violence in high-risk teenagers. The primary prevention program in this example would need to address issues related to informed consent at the level of the whole community, whereas the secondary prevention program would need to address confidentiality issues related to the possible stigma of being identified as high-risk teenagers.

Core Components of Prevention Work

In addressing ethical issues unique to the diverse field of prevention, we begin by reviewing ethical issues that emerge from each of the core components of prevention work. The program development model (Conyne, 2004) will be used to delineate the steps of planning, implementing, evaluating, and providing feedback about both process and outcome in prevention practice and research. Although each step in the program development model raises the possibility of multiple ethical issues, this review will attempt to highlight the most salient ethical issues unique to prevention practice.

Planning

The initial phases of planning a preventive intervention correspond to the typical therapy steps of assessment (i.e., planning for informed consent and choosing a specific intervention), but in prevention these steps are also inherently different. Unlike traditional therapeutic interventions, preventive interventions typically involve a large group of participants who are not actively seeking services (Conyne, 2004). Although some approaches to prevention use a traditional therapeutic modality, such as functional family therapy (Sexton & Alexander, 2000) and multisystemic therapy (Henggeler, Melton, & Smith, 1992), a significant number of prevention programs aim at primary prevention (i.e., stopping problems before they occur in a community or population). Additionally, the success of prevention programs is inextricably linked to the context of the target population (Trickett, 1992, 1998). Unlike traditional therapy, research suggests that successful prevention interventions must address multiple systems (Conyne, 2004; Durlak, 2003; Hage et al., 2007). For example, prevention interventions are often designed to target the individual, family, community, and societal levels. Because behavior and environment are inextricably linked, prevention planning must attend to contextual influences and cultural relevance. Finally, because planning a prevention program typically entails designing an intervention that affects a specific population, the prevention practitioner must consider the additional step of allocating resources in an ethical and equitable manner.

The first step indicated in planning a prevention intervention is assessment. Unique to typical primary prevention programs is the need to conduct a large-scale needs assessment (Romano & Hage, 2000). A needs assessment often involves competence in methodologies designed to understand the individual and the context. Thus, understanding a target population involves assessment beyond individual problem behavior to an understanding of the multiple contexts informing the target behavior. Such procedures sometimes require the use of both qualitative and quantitative research methods (D'Aunno & Price, 1984). Thus, competence for prevention may ethically involve differential training (e.g., research methods) for a broader range of practice.

A lack of competence in assessment at the planning stage can lead to additional ethical concerns. There is an inherent risk of harm in applying interventions without an understanding of the context of behavior (Sue, Arredondo, & McDavis, 1992). That danger can be multiplied in conducting prevention interventions that may affect individuals, their families, and the communities in which they reside (Trickett, 1998). Targeting individual behavior change may result in unplanned systemic or community consequences. Behavior that appears maladaptive may serve an important purpose within a specific context, and the elimination of that behavior may have unforeseen negative consequences. For example, a lack of assertive communication may appear maladaptive related to healthy self-esteem and a successful relationship. However, a prevention program on assertiveness training may have negative consequences in homes that culturally dictate a strict hierarchical family structure. Furthermore, Trickett (1998) argues that prevention interventions are inherently value-laden and typically stem from the cultural viewpoint of the practitioner. Consequently, without comprehensive ecological assessment, there is danger of imposing contradictory and inappropriately applied preventive interventions.

In addition, ethical issues related to the design of prevention programs are numerous. The initial focus, target, and rationale of prevention programs can raise unique ethical issues. For example, a focus on individual change without attention to social forces can unfairly blame individuals, sustaining social inequality (Prilleltensky, 1997; Vera & Reese, 2000). The current APA codes (APA, 2002) do not address the need to promote social change and eliminate social injustice, a focus that is increasingly emerging as the core of ethical prevention work (Hage et al., 2007; Toporek & Williams, 2006). Furthermore, designing prevention programs that lack a theoretical and empirical base of support can pose multiple ethical dilemmas and complicate the provision of fully informed consent. Additionally, prevention efforts that lack a theoretical base and empirical evidence may increase the risk of imposing incongruent values (e.g., if they are largely based on the cultural assumptions, biases, and worldview of the practitioners; Vera & Reese, 2000). Although theoretically based and empirically validated prevention programs are aspirational, this does not preclude necessary exploratory work in prevention. Problematic ethical issues occur when there is a lack of attention to and communication about the specific place of prevention programs in the progression of science (Waldo & Schwartz, 2003).

To avoid imposing one's values, careful attention to the process of informed consent is an additional and necessary ethical issue to consider in the planning stage of prevention. The structure of prevention programs may lead to factors that take away participants' ability to make an autonomous informed choice. Since prevention is linked within multiple ecological levels and the outcomes are often context-specific, true informed consent may be complex. For example, unique to work in prevention is often the lack of a clearly defined client (Bloom, 1996; Pope, 1990). Typically the target population is a group that is not actively seeking help (Conyne, 2004). The imposed nature of the intervention has the potential of exacerbating the typical power imbalance between a practitioner or researcher and participants, as the prevention practitioner is viewed as acting with expertise and authority to address a problem (Danish, 1990; Trickett, 1992, 1998). As the power differential increases, the ability of the participants to make autonomous decisions related to informed consent decreases. Thus the nature of the participant's consent may become more coercive than autonomous. If participants are to make a truly informed decision, they need to be informed about the goals of the research and understand the possible harm and benefits of their participation. Additionally, there could be indirect negative consequences to others in the community (Pope, 1990) and for those who do not want to participate. For example, a prevention program targeted at increasing academic achievement in a school with a high dropout rate could foster community resentment if more young people leave the community.

Finally, psychology professionals who design prevention programs need to be aware of issues related to equal access to those programs. Given the reality of limited resources and the need for well-designed studies using comparison groups, prevention practitioners and researchers often need to make difficult allocation decisions. For example, how does a preventionist determine where to implement a violence prevention program when the data suggests that all the communities he/she is considering (treatment and control) have serious violence problems? Also, new and unique ethical issues related to the allocation of those programs emerge with the emphasis on empirically supported prevention interventions (Greenberg et al., 2001; Nation et al., 2003). For example, considering that few empirically supported treatments have been developed, are preventionists to limit themselves to addressing only those problems for which empirically supported treatments have been developed?

Implementation

Multiple ethical issues are raised in conducting a prevention intervention. Salient issues in prevention are confidentiality, service delivery, overlapping or multiple relationships, and the process of informed consent.

Because risk and protective factors targeted by prevention are found not only in the individual but in the multiple social contexts in which they interact, the goal of prevention programs is to create lasting change at levels beyond the individual (family, school, community; Conyne, 2004; Vera & Reese, 2000). Therefore, because of the multifaceted nature of typical and effective prevention programs, a team of professionals is often necessary for implementation. This team likely involves people with different positions, training, responsibilities, and relationships with the target population, raising issues of who has access to sensitive confidential materials and what standards of confidentiality are being followed.

The use of a group or community as participant can also complicate the process of maintaining confidentiality (Bloom, 1996; Pope, 1990). Therefore, rather than having one confidentiality agreement between the practitioner and client, prevention denotes multiple individuals receiving the intervention and often multiple individuals involved in service delivery. Potentially exacerbating these confidentiality issues is the fact that prevention topics often involve sensitive issues and material (e.g., substance use and abuse, HIV/AIDS, violence). Hence, some interventions, particularly secondary preventions that target high-risk groups, may involve stigma related to participation (Offord, Kraemer, Kazdin, Jensen, & Harrington, 1998). In fact, receiving a prevention intervention denotes a risk to confidentiality. For example, a violence prevention program that targets individuals who have experienced violence in the home poses an immediate confidentiality risk among participants at the time of informed consent. Indeed, the very act of agreeing to participate denotes to others that the individual has experienced violence in the home.

Additionally, although there is increasingly strong epidemiological data on risk and protective factors and growing evidence for the efficacy of preventive interventions to reduce mental disorders and prevent problem behaviors (Durlak & Wells, 1997; Weissberg, Kumpfer, & Seligman, 2003), there is little research on service delivery. For example, it is important to investigate if specific prevention programs are more effective if mental health practitioners deliver the intervention or if individuals in the existing structure (teachers, nurses, parents) are trained to present the intervention. Therefore, a less effective service delivery approach may be offered due to convenience. On the other hand, the program may be more widely available if it can be delivered as effectively by varied professionals and paraprofessionals. In addition to the lack of research on delivery mechanisms, there is a lack of attention to the ethical issues created by the multiple or overlapping relationships necessary to implement prevention interventions. For example, although the dual relationships inherent in a train-the-trainers model (e.g., teachers, nurses, parents) are not necessarily unethical or even problematic, little guidance is available for dealing with potential problems related to the dual relationships (e.g., a teacher being trained to conduct a preventive intervention with his or her students).

Finally, because of the possibility of both direct and indirect harm and the complications inherent in preventive interventions, issues of informed consent are important throughout the process of an intervention. Unforeseen results may become apparent during the course of an intervention (Durlak & Wells, 1997). For example, prevention of one problem (e.g., alcoholism) in a specific context has the potential to create or exacerbate another (e.g., depression). A process approach to informed consent entails ongoing evaluation of the intervention and ensures that participants are informed of unforeseen or negative results of a prevention intervention. Ethical issues of maintaining autonomy and protecting participants from harm are relevant. It is essential that research participants at the individual, community, or systems (e.g., schools, agencies, government) levels be given the information necessary to make knowledgeable choices about involvement in a prevention intervention.

Evaluation

Unique ethical issues are also raised in evaluating prevention programs. Because preventive interventions have an impact on the individual, the individual's immediate system, and larger community (Albee, 1986; Durlak & Wells, 1997), evaluation issues are complicated; the presence of numerous contexts may increase the potential for negative outcomes (Caplan & Caplan, 1994). Outcomes need to be evaluated at multiple levels, along with attention to unforeseen negative outcomes arising across multiple contexts. For example, an effective prevention program often attempts to educate and create awareness and/or behavior change in members of a community and to also effect environmental and cultural change in the community. A dating violence prevention program on a college campus may attempt to create awareness in individuals through presentations in dormitories, to change the environment of the campus through a safe walk program, and to change the culture through programs promoting men intervening with other men. Subsequently, the potential for harm is greater than a typical therapeutic intervention due to the scope of prevention interventions. Thus, there may be unforeseen direct or indirect outcomes across the individual, family, group, or community (Pope, 1990). For example, a prevention program that targeted underage drinking but actually increased the amount of driving under the influence incidences would have negative implications not only for the individuals involved but for the larger community.

Finally, the outcome of prevention programs may be dynamic over time, suggesting the importance of ongoing long-term evaluation (Brown & Liao, 1999) and the danger of misinterpreting immediate results. However, an emphasis on long-term evaluation must also be balanced with the importance of responding to the immediate need for prevention programs in a responsible fashion.

Prevention scholars (e.g., Durlak & Wells, 1997) must also be alert to evidence related to context-specific prevention outcomes. Subtle or unique differences in populations could make an effective prevention program in one population potentially harmful with a different population (Romano & Hage, 2000). Although cultural relevance of therapeutic approaches is an important issue addressed by the APA "Ethical Principles of Psychologists and Code of Conduct" (APA, 2002), it is particularly salient for prevention, which targets individual change and systemic and community change as well (Trickett, 1998). Caplan and Caplan (1994) point out the potential dangers in mass-produced prevention programs that do not address cultural relevance. For example, addressing teen pregnancy by giving out contraceptives within a culture that prohibits contraceptive use would likely be both insensitive and ineffective.

Complicated issues in prevention program evaluation also bring up issues of professional competence (Pope, 1990). In addition to general research competence, prevention practitioners must be competent in specific approaches relevant to evaluation in prevention such as needs assessment, formative and summative evaluation, and long-term follow-up (Romano & Hage, 2000). For example, knowledge of proper assessment regarding how a prevention program is administered throughout is vital to the ultimate conclusions of a program evaluation.

Universal evaluation problems related to poor instrumentation, unclear target variables, infrequent assessment, no long-term outcomes, and researcher bias could contribute to misleading results. Additionally, prevention researchers must be competent in methods to evaluate multiple ecological levels. Program evaluation that focuses on one ecological level (e.g., individual) may only assess gains in knowledge, not behavior change. Finally, prevention focusing on social change often does not fit within a traditional quantitative research design (Prilleltensky & Nelson, 1997). Understanding the subjective experience of participants to understand the context of their behavior necessitates knowledge of qualitative methods.

Feedback About Both Process and Outcome

Because of the large scope of typical preventive interventions, there may be multiple methods of service delivery. If a well-designed prevention program is not evaluated across each of these methods, the causative factors in the outcomes are unclear and cannot be generalized. A lack of formative feedback reduces the replicability of the intervention and ultimately slows down the advancement of prevention science (Durlak & Wells, 1997; Guterman, 2004; Muñez, Mrazek, & Haggerty, 1994; Price, Cowen, Lorion, & Ramos-McKay, 1989; Waldo & Schwartz, 2003). Similarly, the lack of clear summative evaluation poses multiple ethical dilemmas. Problems in research design, outcome measures, targets for evaluation, and/or a lack of long-term outcomes could lead to a misinterpretation of results. Specifically, misinterpretation of outcome data could raise ethical issues regarding the potential negative impact on a community and field (Bloom, 1996) and lead to deleterious effects such as stigmatizing a community or leading to unsuccessful follow-up programs. For instance, lack of positive outcomes in a prevention program to reduce the school achievement gap among Latino/Latina youth may incorrectly assume that Latino parents care little about their children's school success rather than looking at issues that prevent them from being actively involved, such as work demands, family duties, or immigration issues. Ethical practice involves correctly analyzing how prevention research is used to advance the community and inform further prevention programs.

GUIDANCE FOR PREVENTION ETHICS

The need to address the lack of ethical guidelines for the unique issues raised in prevention work has been identified as salient (Bloom, 1996; Hage & Schwartz, 2006; Pope, 1990). Several authors have attempted to provide guidance in the development of a code of ethics for prevention (Bloom, 1993; Pope, 1990) as well as guidance to deal with the unique ethical issues prevalent in prevention (Bond & Albee, 1990; Conner, 1990; Trickett, 1992, 1998). Theoretical advances in the field of prevention and empirical evidence that support best practice guidelines have also been used to inform the ethics of prevention (Durlak & Wells, 1997; Hage et al., 2007; Seligman, 2002). In addition, an integrated feminist, multicultural model has been postulated to guide ethical issues in prevention (Hage & Schwartz, 2006).

Attempts to guide prevention work have often focused on using fundamental ethical principles and rules to address unique aspects of prevention. The main focus of this effort has been to protect consumers from undue risk and maintain their autonomy (Bloom, 1993; Pope, 1990). Trickett (1992, 1997, 1998) explicates an ecological perspective for addressing the ethics of prevention. An ecological perspective views prevention through a lens that recognizes the interdependence of the individual and his or her social, physical, cultural, and political context. Thus, ethical prevention practice involves understanding the context of the target population and creating collaborative and empowering experiences within that context (Trickett, 1998). Ethical practice involves being aware of and guarding against value impositions that are pervasive in prevention programs. Subsequently, ethical practitioners must attend to the power differential between themselves and participants. Clear and autonomous informed consent procedures address this issue. Ethical practice in prevention must endeavor to create empowerment rather then oppressive experiences (Albee, 1986; McWhirter, 1994).

The development of prevention research and practice described in chapter 1 contributes to linkages with theoretical models that can guide prevention activities (Conyne, 2004) and inform ethical practice. For example, the recent interest in "positive prevention," which focuses on building strengths and competencies rather than solely reducing risks (Seligman, 2002), recognizes an ethical imperative to avoid stigmatizing or pathologizing participants in secondary or tertiary prevention programs (Vera, 2000). In addition, social justice (Albee, 1986) and ecological models (Bronfenbrenner, 1979; Conyne & Cook, 2004) conceptualize prevention as addressing multiple levels (individual, family, social, societal) and purposefully addressing societal issues of oppression at all stages of prevention. Therefore, ecological and social justice models suggest an ethical imperative to address the multiple interactions in individuals' lives in the design and evaluation of prevention programs.

Ethical standards for prevention require a new paradigm, a new lexicon, and an agreed-upon standard of care beyond that associated with therapeutic practice (Pope, 1990; Trickett, 1998). Successful prevention programs have been found to have a strong generative base; to address multiple ecological levels (e.g., individual, family, school, community) and multiple mediating factors (e.g., risk and protective); to be culturally relevant, developmentally appropriate, and of sufficient dosage; and to include quality formative and summative evaluation (Durlak, 2003; Nation et al., 2003). Hage et al. (2007) present best practice guidelines for prevention in the area of practice, research, training, and social advocacy. The purpose of the best practice guidelines is to provide a clear standard for the diverse and unique activities psychologists and other mental health workers undertake in conducting all aspects of prevention. In addition to providing a valuable tool for training and practice, the guidelines are an important step for further generating ethical standards for prevention. Having clear guidelines allows for a conceptualization of significant ethical principles.

An integrated feminist, multicultural framework for prevention ethics (Hage & Schwartz, 2006) identifies issues of the cultural context and power dynamics among stakeholders as two core issues of an ethic of prevention. This framework obligates psychologists to be self-aware of their own cultural values, beliefs, and biases. Also, psychologists must be knowledgeable about the community, cultural values, customs, and expertise of the populations they serve. Thus, at each stage of prevention practice, psychologists will seek to understand and attend to the interaction between their own cultural identity and the cultural context(s) that frames their work. Additionally, ethical practice entails knowledge of and attention to the dynamics of power and privilege on multiple levels. This practice includes examining the interaction between the practitioner or researcher and clients, as well as being cognizant of the impact of power and privilege on people's lives.

TOWARD AN ETHICS OF PREVENTION

Further research and multidisciplinary dialogue are needed to establish an ethical code to govern prevention research, practice, and training. The evolution of the field of prevention, the creation of best practice guidelines, and the formulation of a common framework to guide prevention efforts are important building blocks to the eventual establishment of ethical guidelines for prevention. The next section provides five preliminary recommendations to assist the field of prevention in an integrative examination of prevention ethics. These recommendations are meant to provide direction and guidance to prevention practitioners and researchers in the development of an ethics of prevention.

1. *Given the number and complexity of variables with an impact on prevention, preventionists need to incorporate multiple ecological contexts, including families, schools, industry, communities, and government, into their work.*

Programs that focus solely on individual change and ignore multiple ecological influences fail to account for the context of behavior and put undue blame and responsibility on the individual (Prilleltensky, 1997; Vera & Reese, 2000). Addressing both individual and contextual factors is associated with successful prevention programs (Vera & Reese, 2000). Thus, it is imperative that ethical prevention programs create a means for assessing negative outcomes at multiple ecological levels. Systematic methods must be developed for identifying possible harm before it is produced. Attending to multiple causative factors avoids pathologizing participants, leads to a focus on building clients' strengths, and respects the influence of contextual factors. Acknowledging the effect of environmental influences on behavior is empowering in that it does not stigmatize participants and encourages the use of existing resources to succeed.

2. *The cultures of the communities affected by a preventive intervention vary enormously; preventionists must understand their cultural values and biases and avoid imposing them on the targeted population.*

Prevention programs should be collaborative, empowering, and culturally relevant (Hage et al., 2007; Tricket, 1992), so it is imperative that preventionists understand their own culture, values, and biases and that of their prevention work (Sanson-Fisher & Turnbull, 1987; Sparks & Park, 2000) and communicate these clearly with the target population (Watts, 1994). Competent assessment should lead to an understanding and communication of the interaction between the values and assumptions of the prevention program and the targeted population (Rotheram-Boris & Tsemberis, 1989). Behaviors that may seem unhealthy from one contextual perspective may serve an important purpose in another context. Understanding this possibility avoids the unethical behavior of pathologizing individuals based on contextual behavior. Ethical practice involves adjusting programs to fit the cultural and community norms and values of participants (Nation et al., 2003). A collaborative approach should be undertaken so that integral aspects of the prevention program are culturally relevant and focused on facilitating the empowerment of communities rather then imposing program values in multiple ecological contexts.

3. *Prevention programs should be developed from a sound theoretical base, be empirically supported, and address issues of replicability as well as long-term outcomes or effects.*

Current best practices in prevention focus on prevention programs that are developed from a sound theoretical base and are based on empirical evidence (Weissberg et al., 2003). Multiple prevention programs have found short-term success only to have long-term results return to the original level or below (Brown & Liao, 1999). Designing programs that are supported by a strong generative base is a protective factor against value imposition (Heller, 1996) and allows for evidence-based informed consent. A strong generative base also contributes to the progression of prevention science as it leads to replicable programs and empirically supported approaches. This focus does not preclude exploratory prevention work, especially prevention work that meets the contextual needs of diverse groups and addresses issues of oppression. The ethical progression of research on prevention programs includes formative research that identifies core components of change, thus addressing issues of replicability as well as cultural relevance (Kazdin, 2003). In sum, it is important to assess both short- and long-term outcomes or risk missing program effects that develop over time (Bales, 1987).

4. *In all prevention work, dynamics of privilege and power exist between preventionists and community members; prevention research needs to involve the community in determining the research goals and methods to ensure that programs are developed to meet the community's specific needs.*

In typical prevention programs, the participants are not actively seeking help, and the intervention is designed to prevent a problem that may or may not happen. Additionally, the prevention interventions have the potential to create changes not only in the individual but also at multiple ecological levels. With an understanding of these issues, it is imperative to protect the autonomy of participants. This involves actively addressing the dangers of exploitation and undue influence. Ethical practice involves creating collaborative egalitarian relationships, safeguarding against dual relationships, providing alternatives to participation in prevention programs, and providing ongoing informed consent. Furthermore, including community members and other affected parties in planning at each stage of the prevention program is a suggested ethical practice (Nation et al., 2003; Pope, 1990; Weissberg et al., 2003). Participatory action research involves forming a collaborative relationship with members of the target group (Kidd & Kral, 2005). Thus, the participants are encouraged to become involved and empowered, leading to relevant ethical prevention interventions. Furthermore, a focus on building competency rather then addressing risk factors has been conceptualized as being less stigmatizing and more empowering. Dangers of stigmatizing participants can be further addressed by safeguarding confidentiality at each stage of prevention (Bloom, 1993).

5. *Preventionists need to develop and implement transformative preventive interventions with the aim of long-term systemic change that empowers both individuals and communities.*

The allocation of prevention services should be fair, equal, and free of discrimination. An understanding of the central and contributing effects of oppression in mental health as well as the disparity of mental health services for poor and diverse communities underscores the ethical imperative to make prevention in these communities a priority. Additionally, prevention programs should focus on changing societal structures, policies, and systemic barriers that limit equal access to resources (Davidson, Waldo, & Adams, 2006; Toporek & Williams, 2006). Furthermore, prevention should facilitate participants' empowerment to reach their full capacity (Prilleltensky & Nelson, 2002). Ignoring the multiple effects of oppression and the resulting contextual barriers will limit the effectiveness of preventive interventions and ultimately limit the potential of those involved.

CONCLUSION: FUTURE DIRECTIONS IN THE ETHICS OF PREVENTION

Understanding the unique aspects of the field of prevention and reaching a consensus on best practice guidelines are vital steps toward the creation of an ethics code for prevention. The discussion of ethical issues across stages of development explicated earlier in this chapter demonstrates the need for guiding ethical principles. Further research related to prevention is needed.

In addition to well-developed empirical studies, qualitative research is needed to identify common ethical dilemmas encountered by preventionists and the populations with whom they work. Assessing the point of view of participants in prevention programs, along with that of other individuals, groups, and organizations that are part of other ecological levels, is particularly important in helping to develop effective ethical standards for the profession (Pope, 1990). One possible outcome of this research is to increase the dialogue among individuals conducting prevention. Those conducting prevention interventions often come from varied educational backgrounds and may be governed by different ethical codes. Gathering these diverse perspectives can be informative in proactively addressing ethical issues in prevention. Additionally, research that examines the efficacy of ethical prevention practice is needed. For example, research on the efficacy of community-based participatory research, a program designed to collaborate with the members of the target population at each phase of research, has been well supported (Leung, Yen, & Minkler, 2003; Minkler & Wallerstein, 2004). Differential methods for dealing with unique ethical aspects of prevention programs could be examined, including investigating informed consent procedures and training paraprofessionals to deal with dual relationships.

Overall, there is a need to train practitioners and researchers to proactively identify and address the ethical issues involved in prevention. There is also a need for additional training in prevention in graduate programs in counseling and psychology (Hage, 2003; Mathews, 2003). With the myriad of complicated ethical issues, we are in danger of allowing issues of competence to be the primary ethical violation of prevention practitioners. Further integration of a prevention orientation in psychology and psychology-related professions would serve to orient professionals to a *broader application* of their research and practice, with the goal of more effectively and sensitively responding to the tremendous social needs that exist in our communities.

REFERENCES

Agency for Healthcare Research and Quality. (2004). *2004 national healthcare disparities report*. Washington, DC: Author.

Albee, G. (1986). Toward a just society: Lessons from observations on the primary prevention of psychopathology. *American Psychologist, 41,* 891–898.

American Counseling Association. (2005). ACA *code of ethics and standards of practice*. Alexandria, VA: Author.

American Psychiatric Association. (2001). *The principles of medical ethics with annotations especially applicable to psychiatry*. Washington, DC: Author.

American Psychological Association. (2002). Ethical principles of psychologists and code of conduct. *American Psychologist, 57,* 1060–1073. Washington, DC: Author.

Bales, J. (1987). Prevention at its best. *APA Monitor, 18*, 18–19.

Bloom, M. (1993). Toward a code of ethics for primary prevention. *The Journal of Primary Prevention, 13*, 173–182.

Bloom, M. (1996). *Primary prevention practices.* Thousand Oaks, CA: Sage.

Bond, L. A., & Albee, G. W. (1990). Training preventionists in the ethical implications of their actions. *Prevention in Human Services, 8*, 111–126.

Bronfenbrenner, U. (1979). *The ecology of human development: Experiments by nature and design.* Cambridge, MA: Harvard University Press.

Brown, C. H., & Liao, J. (1999). Principles for designing randomized preventive trials in mental health: An emerging developmental epidemiology paradigm. *American Journal of Community Psychology, 27*, 673–711.

Caplan, G., & Caplan, R. B. (1994). The need for quality control in primary prevention. *The Journal of Primary Prevention, 15*, 15–29.

Conner, R. F. (1990). Ethical issues in evaluating the effectiveness of primary prevention programs. *Prevention in Human Services, 8*, 89–110.

Conyne, R. K. (2004). *Preventive counseling* (2nd ed.). New York: Brunner-Routledge.

Conyne, R. K., & Cook, E. P. (Eds.). (2004). *Ecological counseling: An innovative conceptualization for person-environment interaction.* Alexandria, VA: American Counseling Association.

Danish, S. J. (1990). Ethical considerations in the design, implementation, and evaluation of developmental interventions. Ethics in applied developmental psychology: Emerging issues in an emerging field. In C. B. Fisher & W. W. Tryon (Eds.), *Emerging issues in an emerging field* (pp. 93–112). Westport, CT: Ablex.

D'Aunno, T., & Price, R. (1984). Methodologies in community research: Analytic and action approaches. In K. Heller, S. Reinharz, S. Riger, & A. Wandersman (Eds.), *Psychology and community change* (pp. 68–113). New York: Dorsey.

Davidson, M., Waldo, M., & Adams, E. M. (2006). Promoting social justice through preventive interventions. In R. L. Toporek, L. Gerstein, N. Fouad, G. Roysircar, & T. Israel (Eds.), *Handbook for social justice in counseling psychology: Leadership, vision, and action* (pp. 117–129). Thousand Oaks, CA: Sage.

Durlak, J. A. (2003). Effective prevention and health promotion programming. In T. P. Gullotta & M. Bloom (Eds.), *Encyclopedia of primary prevention and health promotion* (pp. 61–69). New York: Kluwer.

Durlak, J. A., & Wells, A. M. (1997). Primary prevention mental health programs for children and adolescents: A meta-analytic review. *American Journal of Community Psychology, 25*, 115–152.

Greenberg, M. T., Domitrovich, C., & Bumbarger, B. (2001). The prevention of mental disorders in school-aged children: Current state of the field. *Prevention & Treatment, 4*, Article 1. Retrieved April 1, 2007, from http://journals.apa.org/prevention/volume4/pre0040002ahtml

Guterman, N. B. (2004). Advancing prevention research on child abuse, youth violence, and domestic violence: Emerging strategies and issues. *Journal of Interpersonal Violence, 19*, 299–321.

Hage, S. M. (2003). Reaffirming the unique identity of counseling psychology: Opting for the "road less traveled by." *The Counseling Psychologist, 31,* 555–563.

Hage, S. M., Romano, J., Kenny, M. E., Matthews, C. R., Schwartz, J. P., & Waldo, M. (2007). Best practice guidelines on prevention practice, research, training, and social advocacy for psychologists. *The Counseling Psychologist, 35,* 493–566.

Hage, S. M., & Schwartz, J. P. (2006). *Ethics in prevention research and practice: Diverse perspectives in counseling psychology.* Unpublished manuscript.

Heller, K. (1996). Coming of age of prevention science: Comments on the 1994 National Institute of Mental Health-Institute of Medicine Prevention Reports. *American Psychologist, 51,* 1123–1127.

Henggeler, S. W., Melton, G. B., & Smith, L. A. (1992). Family preservation using multisystemic therapy: An effective alternative to incarcerating serious juvenile offenders. *Journal of Consulting and Clinical Psychology, 60,* 953–961.

Institute of Medicine. (2002). *Unequal treatment: Confronting racial and ethnic disparities in healthcare.* New York: National Academy Press.

Kazdin, A. E. (2003). *Research design in clinical psychology* (4th ed.). Boston: Allyn and Bacon.

Kidd, S. A., & Kral, M. J. (2005). Practicing participatory action research. *Journal of Counseling Psychology, 52,* 187–195.

Leung, M. W., Yen, I. H., & Minkler, M. (2003). Community based participatory research: A promising approach for increasing epidemiology's relevance in the 21st century. *International Journal of Epidemiology, 33,* 499–506.

Matthews, C. R. (2003, August). Training for prevention competency in counseling psychology. In M. Kenny (Chair), *Competencies for prevention training in counseling psychology.* Symposium presented at the 111th annual convention of the American Psychological Association, Toronto, Ontario, Canada.

McWhirter, E. H. (1994). *Counseling for empowerment.* Alexandria, VA: American Counseling Association.

Minkler, M., & Wallerstein, N. (2004). *Community-based participatory research for health.* San Francisco: Jossey-Bass.

Muñez, R. F., Mrazek, P. J., & Haggerty, R. J. (1994). Institute of Medicine report on prevention of mental disorders: Summary and commentary. *American Psychologist, 51,* 1116–1122.

Nation, M., Crusto, C., Wandersman, A., Kumpfer, K., Seybolt, D., & Morrissey-Kane, E., et al. (2003). What works in prevention: Principles and effective prevention programs. *American Psychologist, 58,* 449–456.

National Association of Social Workers. (1999). *Code of ethics.* Washington, DC: Author.

Offord, D. R., Kraemer, H. C., Kazdin, A. E., Jensen, P. S., & Harrington, R. (1998). Lowering the burden of suffering from child psychiatric disorder: Trade-offs among clinical, targeted, and universal interventions. *Journal of the American Academy of Child and Adolescent Psychiatry, 37,* 686–694.

Pope, K. S. (1990). Identifying and implementing ethical standards for primary prevention. *Prevention in Human Services, 8,* 43–64.

Price, R. H., Cowen, E. L., Lorion, R. P., & Ramos-McKay, J. (1989). The search for effective prevention programs: What we learned along the way. *American Journal of Orthopsychiatry, 59,* 49–58.

Prilleltensky, I. (1997). Values, assumptions, and practices: Assessing the moral implications of psychological discourse and action. *American Psychologist, 52,* 517–535.

Prilleltensky, I., & Nelson, G. (1997). Community psychology: Reclaiming social justice. In D. Fox & I. Prilleltensky (Eds.), *Critical psychology: An introduction* (pp. 166–184). Thousand Oaks, CA: Sage.

Prilleltensky, I., & Nelson, G. (2002). *Doing psychology critically: Making a difference in diverse settings.* Basingstoke, England: Palgrave.

Romano, J., & Hage, S. (2000). Prevention and counseling psychology: Revitalizing commitments for the 21st century. *The Counseling Psychologist, 28,* 733–763.

Rotheram-Boris, M. J., & Tsemberis, S. J. (1989). Social competency training in ethnically diverse communities. In L. A. Bond & B. Compas (Eds.), *Primary prevention and promotion in the schools* (pp. 297–318). Thousand Oaks, CA: Sage.

Sanson-Fisher, R., & Turnbull, D. (1987). 'To do or not to do?': Ethical problems for behavioral medicine. In S. Fairbairn & G. Fairbairn (Eds.), *Psychology, ethics and change* (pp. 191–211), New York: Routledge.

Satcher, D. (2000). Mental health: A report of the Surgeon General – Executive summary. *Professional Psychology: Research and Practice, 31,* 5–13.

Seligman, M. (2002). Positive psychology, positive prevention, and positive therapy. In C. R. Snyder & S. J. Lopez (Eds.), *Handbook of positive psychology* (pp. 3–9). New York: Oxford Press.

Sexton, T. L., & Alexander, J. F. (2000, December). Functional family therapy. *Office of Juvenile Justice & Delinquency Prevention, Juvenile Justice Bulletin,* 3–7.

Sparks, E., & Park, A. H. (2000). The integration of feminism and multiculturalism: Ethical dilemmas at the border. In M. M. Brabeck (Ed.), *Practicing feminist ethics in psychology* (pp. 203–224). Washington, DC: American Psychological Association.

Sue, D. W., Arredondo, P., & McDavis, R. J. (1992). Multicultural counseling competencies/standards: A call to the profession. *Journal of Multicultural Counseling and Development, 20,* 64–88.

Toporek, R. L., & Williams, R. A. (2006). Ethics and professional issues related to the practice of social justice in counseling psychology. In R. L. Toporek, L. Gerstein, N. Fouad, G. Roysircar, & T. Israel (Eds.), *Handbook for social justice in counseling psychology: Leadership, vision, and action* (pp. 17–34). Thousand Oaks, CA: Sage.

Trickett, E. J. (1992). Prevention ethics: Explicating the context of prevention activities. *Ethics & Behavior, 2,* 91–100.

Trickett, E. J. (1997). Ecology and primary prevention: Reflections on a meta-analysis. *American Journal of Community Psychology, 25,* 197–205.

Trickett, E. J. (1998). Toward a framework for defining and resolving ethical issues in the protection of communities involved in primary prevention projects. *Ethics & Behavior, 8,* 321–337.

U.S. Surgeon General. (1999). *Mental health: A report of the surgeon general.* Washington, DC: U.S. Department of Public Health and Human Services.

U.S. Surgeon General. (2001). *Mental health: Culture, race, and ethnicity. A supplement to mental health: A report of the surgeon general.* Washington, DC: U.S. Department of Public Health and Human Services.

Vera, E. M. (2000). A recommitment to prevention work in counseling psychology. *The Counseling Psychologist, 28,* 829–837.

Vera, E. M., & Reese. L. E. (2000). Preventive interventions with school-age youth. In S. D. Brown & R. W. Lent (Eds.), *Handbook of counseling psychology* (pp. 411–434). New York: Wiley.

Waldo, M., & Schwartz, J. P. (2003, August). *Research competencies in prevention.* Symposium conducted at the meeting of Prevention Competencies at the 111th Annual Convention of the American Psychological Association, Toronto, Ontario, Canada.

Watts, R. J. (1994). Paradigms of diversity. In E. J. Trickett, R. J. Watts, & D. Birman (Eds.), *Human diversity: Perspectives on people in context* (pp. 49–80). San Francisco: Jossey-Bass.

Weissberg, R. P., Kumpfer, K. L., & Seligman, M. E. P. (2003). Prevention that works for children and youth: An introduction. *American Psychologist, 58,* 425–432.

7

TRAINING PRIMARY PREVENTIONISTS TO MAKE A DIFFERENCE IN PEOPLE'S LIVES

JAMES M. O'NEIL AND PRESTON A. BRITNER

Few developed models are available for teaching primary prevention in psychology. Prevention skills and training models have been discussed over the last two decades (Conyne, 1997, 2004; Cowen, 1984; Hage et al., 2007; Perry, Albee, Bloom, & Gullotta, 1996; Romano & Hage, 2000; Zolik, 1983), but ambiguity exists about how to teach these skills in the classroom. Surveys of the Council for Accreditation of Counseling and Related Educational Programs (Matthews, 2003) and American Psychological Association [APA]-accredited counseling psychology programs (Matthews, 2003, August) found that the majority of programs offered no prevention-specific courses, although prevention was deemed important and was often infused into other courses. We believe that a defined curriculum and appropriate pedagogical strategies are needed to train students if primary prevention is to become a significant force in mental health service delivery. Furthermore, we take the position that teaching primary prevention can stimulate students to consider social justice commitments as central parts of their career identities.

Primary prevention is entirely compatible with a social justice framework. Many of the causes of societal oppression and discrimination can be prevented by direct involvement and social change activism at the community, institutional, and societal levels. Although many of these social justice issues would appear to be political in nature, they are, in fact, ethically mandated by basic democratic and human rights principles.

This chapter presents conceptual models and provides recommendations on how to teach primary prevention courses. Our models build on previous authors' conceptualizations (Bloom, 1996; Conyne, 1997, 2004; Hage et al., 2007; Romano & Hage, 2000). Our recommendations are based on our own primary prevention experiences and on our experiences teaching primary prevention at the University of Connecticut. Overall, the goal of this chapter is to provide models and methods that advance teaching primary prevention in psychology and related helping professions. We also recommend elements of a complete curriculum to train future preventionists in more systematic ways.

First, this chapter presents a process-oriented prevention problem-solving model that can be taught to students. Second, primary prevention theoretical frameworks and skills are summarized from the previous literature. We present a new skills model that emphasizes theoretical frameworks and essential skills preventionists need to consider in their training. Third, we explain how the prevention process and skills relate to each other. This section elaborates on the skills needed to implement the steps in prevention problem solving. Fourth, we discuss some of the teaching techniques that have been effective for us. The figures and tables in the chapter build on each other sequentially. The two figures provide the conceptual foundation for teaching prevention, and the two tables focus on teaching skills and curricular options. The chapter concludes with recommendations for a prevention curriculum that includes numerous background courses, interventions, and applied experiences. Implementing preventive interventions requires much knowledge and many skills that usually cannot be taught in a single course or setting.

We hope that this chapter will be useful to faculty who are creating or revising their prevention courses and for students learning about prevention and its relationship to social justice. Faculty who are teaching prevention courses or content are encouraged to experiment with our problem-solving model and skill sets, to take our pedagogical examples and try them in their own courses, and to communicate with the authors for clarifications, materials, or ideas about the content of the chapter. This chapter will also be useful to professionals who have not received formal training but want to incorporate a prevention framework into their commitment to social justice and making a difference in people's lives. Our chapter is meant to challenge the field to focus on prevention training in the context of social justice and to promote discussion of effective and important pedagogical elements in courses and curricula.

PREVENTION PROBLEM-SOLVING MODEL: INTEGRATING THE WORK OF BLOOM AND CONYNE

Two major conceptualizations about prevention processes have been presented in the literature. Conyne (1994, 2004) described seven intentional steps in the prevention process, and Bloom (1996) discussed a three-phase process with five problem-solving steps. Both of these models provide important ideas on prevention processes. However, in our opinion, neither of them on their own have sufficient depth or comprehensiveness to teach the primary processes of prevention.

Figure 7.1 depicts a nine-phase prevention problem-solving process model that represents a synthesis of Bloom and Conyne's conceptualizations. The model shows a sequential process of a decision whether to do prevention, specific implementation steps, and a final evaluation and closure process. More specifically, prevention problem-solving phases one to nine represent specific steps to reduce risk and increase protection related to any of a variety of human problems. The steps include a systematic, premeditated approach to assessing prevention problems, conceptualizing and choosing possible interventions, implementing the intervention, evaluating the process and outcomes, exiting the intervention, and finally reporting the results to the scientific community.

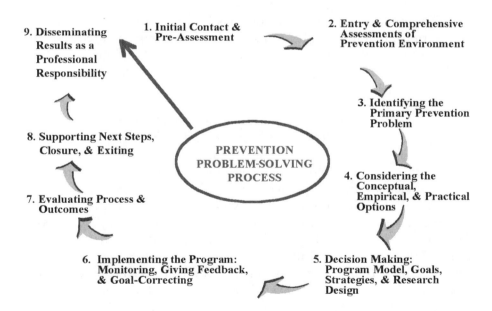

Figure 7.1. Steps in the prevention problem-solving process.

In the initial contact and pre-assessment phase, the preventionist establishes a relationship with a target person or population that seeks prevention services. The preventionist assesses whether change is a realistic option and whether there is a generative base (Conyne, 1994) to make a difference. If the assessment reveals a good possibility for success, then the preventionist completes a comprehensive assessment of the prevention environment (Phase 2) and begins to identify the primary prevention problem (Phase 3). After the prevention problem has been defined using environmental assessments and research literature, the preventionist considers the conceptual, empirical, and practical options (Bloom, 1996) in Phase 4. Decisions are made in Phase 5 regarding what program to implement, which specific goals and strategies to pursue in the prevention program, and how to assess the results and outcomes through research and evaluation. In Phase 6, the preventionist implements the program, makes corrections using feedback, and evaluates the entire process. Phase 7 is the systematic evaluation of the prevention program, using both formative (process) and summative (outcome) research approaches. The preventionist then brings closure to the intervention by exiting (Phase 8), but not before giving maximum support and assistance to ensure an empowering termination to the entire prevention process. The target group is left with the necessary information and tools to determine whether and how to continue the work. In the final phase (Phase 9), the preventionist shares what he/she has learned by summarizing the program's results and disseminating it through published reports and professional publications.

The nine phases provide a step-by-step, schematic overview of how prevention programs can be conceptualized and implemented. For the problem-solving process to be actualized, specific skills are needed. Those skills are reviewed in the next section.

WHAT THEORETICAL FRAMEWORKS AND APPLIED SKILLS ARE NECESSARY?

A question for the prevention educator is: What knowledge and skills should students (and professionals new to the topic) learn, based on the nine phases of prevention problem solving shown in Figure 7.1? This section presents a synthesis of past prevention perspectives and skills (Bloom, 1996; Conyne, 1997, 2004; Romano & Hage, 2000). We have retained some of these authors' training domains, renamed others, and added new ones. Our new training model takes the form of three theoretical frameworks and nine skill areas, as shown in Figure 7.2. In the following sections, these primary prevention frameworks and skills are briefly defined.

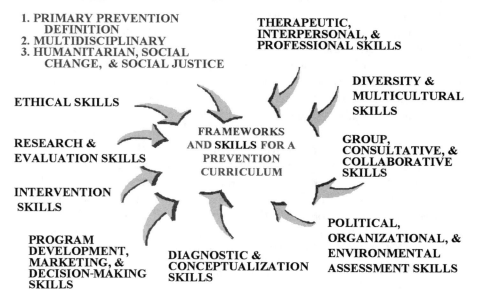

FRAMEWORKS

1. PRIMARY PREVENTION
   DEFINITION
2. MULTIDISCIPLINARY
3. HUMANITARIAN, SOCIAL
   CHANGE, & SOCIAL JUSTICE

THERAPEUTIC,
INTERPERSONAL, &
PROFESSIONAL SKILLS

DIVERSITY &
MULTICULTURAL
SKILLS

ETHICAL SKILLS

FRAMEWORKS
AND SKILLS FOR A
PREVENTION
CURRICULUM

GROUP,
CONSULTATIVE, &
COLLABORATIVE
SKILLS

RESEARCH &
EVALUATION SKILLS

INTERVENTION
SKILLS

PROGRAM
DEVELOPMENT,
MARKETING, &
DECISION-MAKING
SKILLS

DIAGNOSTIC &
CONCEPTUALIZATION
SKILLS

POLITICAL,
ORGANIZATIONAL, &
ENVIRONMENTAL
ASSESSMENT SKILLS

Figure 7.2. Essential frameworks and skills for a prevention curriculum.

Three Primary Prevention Theoretical Frameworks

Albee (2006) reminds us that "no mass disease or disorder has ever been controlled or eliminated through individual treatment" (p. 449); treatment is not as effective as prevention, nor are there enough resources (e.g., numbers of trained psychologists) to come even close to being able to treat the myriad psychological and physical health problems that exist in the United States, much less worldwide.

The first framework implies defining primary prevention and differentiating it from intervention. Most definitions of primary prevention (Bloom, 1996; Bloom & Gullotta, 2003; Conyne, 1997, 2004; Romano & Hage, 2000) imply before-the-fact programs, targeted for healthy or at-risk people, implemented by teams of people, using a variety of risk reduction or health promotion strategies from many different disciplines, to empower others. The definition of primary prevention is critical because without clarity about this complex process, the skills lack an operational context.

The second perspective is a multidisciplinary framework that implies an open intellectual attitude and a willingness to use knowledge outside one's own discipline. For example, a psychologist who wanted to develop a comprehensive HIV prevention program would need to review literatures in epidemiology, demography, public health, medicine, and sociology, prior to engaging the target population and developing the prevention program. Developing a primary prevention program is complex and requires comprehensive knowledge and many competencies. Primary preventionists recognize that knowledge across multiple disciplines is necessary to implement preventive interventions. This perspective implies that preventionists are willing to embrace new theoretical frameworks or approaches when developing their prevention programs.

Humanitarian, social change, and social justice perspectives represent the third framework on prevention. Humanitarian values imply a committed caring about the overall quality of people's lives and activity to alleviate suffering in the world. A social change perspective on prevention includes an activist stance toward unresolved societal problems. The social justice perspective means recognizing that many societal problems disempower people and result from personal and societal oppression and discrimination (Albee, 2006; Joffe & Albee, 1981). Social injustices motivate preventionists to do prevention to combat the causes or the outcomes of societal oppression and discrimination.

Nine Prevention Skill Areas

In some cases, these skills will be developed by students in their graduate training programs. Professionals who are new to prevention may also acquire these skills by collaborating with seasoned colleagues, joining professional networks or interest groups devoted to prevention (e.g., the Society for Prevention Research and APA's Division 17 [Society of Counseling Psychology, Prevention Section], Division 27 [Society for Community Research and Action: Division of Community Psychology, Prevention and Promotion interest group]), and reviewing current syllabi and educational approaches (see the September 2008 special issue of *The Journal of Primary Prevention*, edited by the authors, devoted to teaching prevention). These sources may provide useful information about the prevention skill areas required to effect social change and justice.

Therapeutic, interpersonal, and professional skills affect all other skill areas because, without them, the prevention process can be ineffective, problematic, or prone to failure. Most therapy skills learned by clinicians are relevant to the prevention problem-solving process. For example, the preventionist must develop the interpersonal conditions for trust, risk taking, and hope for positive change to occur. Monitoring resistance and defensiveness and using assessment and conceptualization skills are also important therapy skills relevant to prevention. Yet, the preventionist does not need to be a full-blown clinician to do primary prevention. The real issue is interpersonal and professional competence. Interpersonal competence is demonstrating expert communication skills, showing respect and graciousness to others, and developing working alliances with others. All of these interpersonal qualities can be reduced to Rogerian core conditions like empathy, honesty, genuineness, and positive regard for others. These therapeutic and interpersonal qualities are usually expressed in a professional role. Therefore, effective preventionists aspire to be professional and collegial. Professionalism and collegiality exists when there are mutual commitments to professional collaborations, a sharing of resources, and interpersonal support and solidarity. There is cooperation, challenge, and a commitment to advancing a common goal.

Diversity and multicultural skills include sensitivity to and an ability to work with people of different races, classes, sexes, ages, ethnicities, sexual orientations, and nationalities (Schinke & Matthieu, 2003). Diversity skills also include recognizing the historical, social, economic, and political realities that have caused institutionalized and personal oppression for marginalized groups (Romano & Hage, 2000). Specifically, societal oppression is understood as directly correlating with people's emotional, interpersonal, and health problems. Preventionists must recognize that victims of oppression are often blamed for their problems.

Group skills, including consultation and collaboration skills, reflect the interpersonal and leadership abilities to work collectively with people toward a common goal. These skills include how to form a group, set group norms, facilitate group discussions, develop cohesion, provide feedback, summarize group processes, work through conflict, take action, and bring closure to an activity. Consultation skills are defined as methods of providing preventively oriented psychological and educational services by forming cooperative partnerships and engaging in a reciprocal, systematic, problem-solving process guided by ecobehavioral principles (Zins & Erchul, 2003). Consultation is a set of skills that promotes primary prevention because both processes include similar roles, skills, and intervention strategies. Collaboration implies sharing the work and responsibility of some activity (Conoley & Conoley, 1992). To be collaborative means giving up some control, sharing power, and being able to work for a common goal as a team member. Collaboration skills are critical because prevention activities are rarely solo events and involve professionals pooling resources to promote a common goal.

Political, organizational, and environmental assessment skills imply understanding the political, organizational, and environmental context of any prevention intervention (Conyne, 1997, 2004; Romano & Hage, 2000). The expert preventionist is a competent assessor of overt human dynamics, power structures, norms, alliances, sources of power and abuses, restraining and facilitating forces, and all of the political, organizational, and environmental realities related to an intervention.

Furthermore, like the individual therapist, the preventionist is constantly using *diagnostic and conceptualization skills* to understand what the problem is and how to solve it. Diagnostic appraisals are obtained through quantitative and qualitative measures, interviews, focus groups, observations, and any way to understand the prevention process. The skilled preventionist knows how to obtain these assessments and use them to move through the prevention process. Comprehensive diagnosis facilitates conceptualizing the entire prevention process. Conceptualization skills include the ability to observe a situation or phenomena and to think about it in diverse, critical, and holistic ways. Preventionists use their conceptualization skills to create ways for others to understand knowledge and explain how complex things fit together.

Program development skills, including marketing and decision-making skills, involve the creation of content and processes for any intervention. Program development uses the diagnostic and conceptual information gained during the first three phases of the prevention process and translates them into measurable goals. Marketing skills have been described as an important part of prevention (Conyne, 1994, 2004). The essence of prevention marketing, according to Conyne, is public relations and promotion using persuasion, motivation, sales, advertising, and the use of technological media. Decision making is the systematic process of examining all alternatives for a prevention intervention and choosing the best options. If the preventionist has approached the prevention problem-solving process systemically (see Figure 7.1), many decisions will be based on gathered data, thoughtful conceptualizations, and past empirical results.

Intervention skills are all activities used in actually carrying out the prevention program. All of the skills in Figure 7.2 apply, and which skills are to be used is determined by the prevention problem, the specific processes, and the desired outcomes.

Research and evaluation skills are used from the beginning of primary prevention to the end. These skills imply the use of qualitative, observational, and quantitative data to understand, design, implement, and assess outcomes of any prevention intervention. A proper evaluation can provide program practitioners with useful short-term feedback on how they are recruiting, retaining, and serving their clients; it can put in place the mechanisms to study the long-term effectiveness of the prevention model (Reppucci, Britner, & Woolard, 1997).

Ethical skills are the ability to recognize and take action to remedy any part of the prevention intervention that could cause harm or disrespect or exploit others before, during, or after the intervention. Formal ethical standards do not exist for primary prevention, but the APA Ethical Standards can be used to assess ethical issues or dilemmas during any step of the prevention process (see Figure 7.1 and Schwartz & Hage, chap. 6, this volume).

Integrating the Prevention Problem-Solving Process With the Prevention Skills

This section integrates the prevention problem-solving process (see Figure 7.1) with the prevention frameworks and skills (Figure 7.2). Various authors have described prevention skills (Bloom, 1996; Conyne, 1994, 2004; Romano & Hage, 2000), but how these skills specifically relate to prevention processes has gone unexplained. Therefore, prevention skills have lacked an operational context to be taught. Table 7.1 delineates the specific prevention skills used during the nine problem-solving phases. Our integration underscores how prevention processes are directly related to prevention skills. The connection between the nine prevention problem-solving phases and the primary prevention frameworks and skills moves us closer to articulating a full curriculum for training preventionists. A brief summary of how the prevention skills relate to the problem-solving steps in Table 7.1 follows.

Phase 1, Initial Contact and Pre-Assessment, requires expert interpersonal and assessment skills because the preventionist decides whether there is a generative base for prevention and whether the environment is ready for change and collaboration. Assessment skills are also used to evaluate the organizational, political, and environmental norms and any ethical issues that might affect the prevention. The preventionist needs to know how to make these multiple assessments through interviews and how to make an informed judgment about whether to move forward.

In Phase 2, Entry and Comprehensive Assessment of the Prevention Environment, interpersonal skills are needed to develop a collaborative team of people. A full assessment is required of the positive and negative issues in the environment that may facilitate or restrain the prevention process. Therefore, skills in administering assessment instruments, interviewing, and needs assessment may be necessary to fully understand the prevention environment. In this phase, the prevention relationship is still developing, and a careful analysis of the relationship dynamics is critical. Defensiveness and resistance on the part of the target population must be assessed. Preventionists need to assess their own diversity issues (e.g., how their biases or stereotypes might affect their appraisals of the target population) and the sensitivity to diversity within the target population.

Phase 3, Identifying the Primary Prevention Problem, requires scholarly research on key terms in the literature and data gathering in the community on how the problem is defined (Bloom, 1996). Scholarly literature reviews are critical so that the preventionist may clearly define the problem or issue. Conceptualization skills may be necessary to define fully the problems from a multidisciplinary perspective. Consultation with the local community ensures that there is agreement on what to prevent and how to do it.

TABLE 7.1
Prevention Problem-Solving Phases and Prevention Skills

Prevention problem-solving steps and phases	Skills needed to implement steps and phases
1. Initial Contact and Pre-Assessment	
Identify a generative base	Diagnostic skills
Explore the readiness for change	Interpersonal skills
	Group, consultative, and collaborative skills
	Political and organizational assessment skills
Assess political and organizational setting	Political and organizational assessment skills
	Diagnostic and conceptualization skills
	Ethical skills
Assess local and organizational norms	Group, consultative, and collaborative skills
	Organizational assessment skills
	Diagnostic skills
	Research and evaluation skills
Explore and assess potential to work together	Group, consultative, and collaborative skills
	Organizational and environmental assessment skills
Decide whether to commit to the prevention	Research and evaluation skills program
2. Entry and Comprehensive Assessment of Prevention Environment	
Conduct needs assessment or local assessment	Research and evaluation skills
	Group, consultative, and collaborative skills
Assess environmental positive and negative issues	Organizational and environmental assessment skills
	Diagnostic and conceptualization skills
Assess relevance of diversity and multicultural issues	Diversity and multicultural skills
Form a collaborative team	Intervention skills
	Group, consultative, and collaborative skills
3. Identifying the Primary Prevention Problem	
Activate collaborative team	Intervention skills
	Group, consultative, and collaborative skills
Gather data on the prevention problem in setting	Organizational and environmental assessment skills
	Research and evaluation skills
	Intervention skills
Conduct diagnostic analysis: Forced field analysis of restraining or facilitating factors in environment	Diagnostic skills

TABLE 7.1
(Continued)

Prevention problem-solving steps and phases	Skills needed to implement steps and phases
Generate operational definitions of key terms	Research skills
	Multidisciplinary perspectives
Gather epidemiological and social/psychological research from the literature; create conceptual framework from this knowledge base	Research and evaluation skills Conceptualization skills
Assess potential to stigmatize or stereotype participants	Diversity and multicultural skills

4. Considering the Conceptual, Empirical, and Practical Options	
Review and analyze relevant theoretical models, empirically tested programs, and practical approaches to the problem or issue	Conceptualization skills Research and evaluation skills
Individualize relevant theories, research, and practical programs to the prevention problem or issue	Diagnostic and conceptualization skills
Involve local groups in planning	Group, consultative, and collaborative skills
Consider research and evaluation designs and measures	Research and evaluation skills Diagnostic skills
Consider multiple strategies and programmatic options for implementation	Diagnostic and conceptualization skills Program development skills

5. Decision Making: Program Model, Goals, Strategies, and Research Design	
Decide on the theoretical model for the intervention	Decision-making skills Conceptualization skills
Select multiple strategy sets or program designs	Conceptualization skills Program development skills Decision-making skills
Synchronize individual and collective values and norms of prevention target	Group, consultative, and collaborative skills Diversity and multicultural skills Political and organizational skills
Generate prevention goals and outcomes	Conceptualization skills Program development skills
Decide on research design, measures, and evaluation approaches	Research and evaluation skills
Contract: Who is to do what, with whom, where, when, under what circumstances, and with what measurable outcomes?	Group, consultative, and collaborative skills
Prepare for implementation	Organizational assessment skills
Assess potential ethical dilemmas; brainstorm and implement any strategies to respond	Ethical skills

(continued)

TABLE 7.1
(Continued)

Prevention problem-solving steps and phases	Skills needed to implement steps and phases
6. Implementing the Program: Monitoring, Giving Feedback, and Goal-Correcting	
Implement programmatic goals	Intervention skills
Observe and gather data on participants' reactions	Group, consultative, and collaborative skills
Implement formative and summative evaluation	Research and evaluation skills
Reconceptualize, if necessary, prevention goals or prevention process	Evaluation skills
Locate and use additional resources	Organizational skills
7. Evaluating Process and Outcomes	
Collect systematic process and outcome data	Research and evaluation skills
Analyze and summarize the data	Research and evaluation skills
Disseminate data to target population	Research and evaluation skills
	Group, consultative and collaborative skills
8. Supporting Next Steps, Closure, and Exiting	
Write final report	Conceptualization skills
Disseminate and discuss final report	Group, consultative, and collaborative skills
Leave preventive procedures and processes for target group;	Group, consultative, and collaborative skills
empower group to continue program (if appropriate) and assess next steps	Political, organizational, and environmental assessment skills
Have closure meeting	Political and organizational skills
	Group, consultative, and collaborative skills
9. Disseminating Results as a Professional Responsibility	
Write and report prevention results to community and media	Research and evaluation skills
Publish results in refereed journal	Research and evaluation skills

The preventionist is careful not to stigmatize or stereotype the target population. Group, consultative, collaborative, and research skills dominate this phase of prevention.

Phase 4, Considering the Conceptual, Empirical, and Practical Options, focuses on scholarly reviews of relevant theories, previously tested interventions, and other relevant resources to theoretically ground the prevention intervention (Bloom, 1996). This research is used to generate programmatic options and strategies to implement them. Conceptualization and model development skills are also important. Furthermore, the previous research related to the intervention needs to be individualized to the local community. Polling prevention participants on how to intervene requires group and consultative skills. Research design and evaluation skills are also needed as the method of assessment is considered in the context of the prevention goals, outcomes, and community norms and standards.

In Phase 5, Decision Making, final plans are made regarding the theoretical model, the intervention strategies, and the evaluation methods. Program development and goal-setting skills are needed at this point. Assessment of any individual norm/value conflicts in the targeted environment requires sensitivity to diversity issues. Decisions are made related to who will do what activities and when they will complete them. Marketing skills are needed during this phase to ensure full participation and success. Assessments and discussion of any potential ethical issues are made to ensure no harm is done. Where there are apparent ethical threats, programmatic changes are made or precautions are discussed.

In Phase 6, Implementation, the prevention program is carried out using all the skills necessary to meet the prevention goals and objectives. Research skills are needed when process data are collected and used during the intervention. Ongoing diagnostic and conceptualization skills may be necessary if the formative assessments suggest problems, programmatic changes, or adjustments.

In Phase 7, Evaluating Process and Outcomes, quantitative, qualitative, and observational skills are used to assess whether the program made a difference. The preventionist collects all data, summarizes it, and writes it up into a useful summary for potential dissemination to key collaborators and the community.

In Phase 8, Supporting Next Steps, Closure, and Exiting, group and consultative skills are needed as the intervention is terminated through closure meetings and reviews of the intervention, the procedures used, and measured outcomes. Encouragement and support are given to the targeted population to maintain those parts of the intervention that worked.

Phase 9, Disseminating the Results as a Professional Responsibility, entails sharing results of the prevention effort to the affected community using all forms of media and telecommunications. Furthermore, the results are presented at professional conventions and submitted to journals for scholarly dissemination as part of the preventionist's professional responsibility.

PEDAGOGICAL ACTIVITIES
TO PROMOTE PREVENTION LEARNING

Having established how prevention process and skills relate to each other (see Table 7.1), we turn to a discussion of how to teach this information to students. The specific approaches to teaching prevention have only been addressed by a few authors (Conyne, 2004; Dalton, Elias, & Beck, 1994; Hage et al., 2007). We build on these authors' approaches by discussing various classroom activities, lectures, readings, assignments, papers, practica, and other experiential activities. Table 7.2 shows the prevention skills and frameworks from Figure 7.2 and how learning could occur in and out of the classroom. Teaching options in Table 7.2 include traditional approaches (lecturing, assigned readings, and discussions) and experiential and applied activities. The use of checklists and self-assessment can promote student's self-awareness and greater personalization of the course concepts. Table 7.2 provides many pedagogical possibilities to teach a full prevention curriculum.

We have found certain class activities effective when teaching primary prevention principles and skills. First, before the class begins, we send out a 20-item Prevention Assessment Questionnaire that evaluates students' knowledge and attitudes about prevention. The questionnaire assesses students' knowledge of prevention, interests in becoming a preventionist, motivation to study prevention, feelings about class participation, and attitudes about prevention as a political and social justice issue. One of the most critical questions asked of students is whether they see prevention as part of their professional identity. This assessment establishes critical learning contexts in the course, even before the class has started. We report the assessment data in the first class, and this shapes the collective consciousness of the students and creates positive cohesion and solidarity about studying prevention.

Additionally, in the first class, we ask students to write out their personal definition of primary prevention. We indicate that their definitions are not expected to be full or robust, because no definitions have been provided. The students' definitions are used to derive collectively a clear definition of primary prevention that parallels established definitions in the literature (Albee & Gullotta, 1997; Bloom, 1996; Bloom & Gullotta, 2003; Conyne, 1994).

A third training intervention allows students to assess their knowledge about the prevention frameworks, competencies, and skills shown in Figure 7.2. We administer a 17-item Prevention Skills & Frameworks Checklist that helps students assess (a) the degree to which they understand the five primary prevention frameworks (definitional, multidisciplinary, humanitarian, social change, and social justice) and (b) their perceived degree of competency in the nine skills areas shown in Figure 7.2. This kind of assessment requires students to reflect on the knowledge and skills they currently possess and what skills they need to develop in the

TABLE 7.2
Prevention Frameworks and Skills With Linked Curricular Options
for Teaching and Learning

Frameworks and skills	Pedagogical possibilities
Primary Prevention Framework	—Students write their personal definitions of primary prevention on first day of class with subsequent discussion on the meaning of the concept —Readings that define primary prevention followed with case studies in which students differentiate between primary prevention, secondary prevention, and tertiary intervention —Prevention assessment of students' attitudes about their commitment to primary prevention as a future professional role
Multidisciplinary Framework	—Lecture on the necessity of multidisciplinary cooperation and collaboration —Case examples of how multidisciplinary approaches are essential for success —Readings on the science of prevention and the need to study complex systems (Coie et al., 1993)
Humanitarian, Social Change, Social Justice Framework	—Self-assessment using "Commitment to Humanitarian, Social Change, and Social Justice Checklist" —Debates on the merits of direct treatment versus primary prevention approaches —Read, analyze, and discuss articles by George Albee (e.g., Albee, 2006) and other social activists
Therapeutic, Interpersonal, and Professional Skills	—Coursework in therapeutic listening, interpersonal communication, human relations/family studies, and supervised practicum —Lectures on professionalism, collegiality, and strategies to deal with professional defensiveness and resistance
Diversity and Multicultural Skills	—Coursework on race, class, gender, and diversity —Readings on oppression and emotional and physical health; risk and protective factors in diverse populations (Schinke & Matthieu, 2003; Walsh, DePaul, & Park-Taylor, chap. 3, this volume) —Self assessment using the "Oppression Consciousness Checklist" —Practicum experiences with an emphasis on diversity and multiculturalism

(continued)

TABLE 7.2
(Continued)

Frameworks and skills	Pedagogical possibilities
Group, Consultative, and Collaborative Skills	—Coursework in group theory, group processes, and consultation models and skills —Experiences creating and leading groups —Lecture on the importance of collaboration and case examples demonstrating why it is necessary
Political, Organizational, and Environmental Assessment Skills	—Organizational development or assessment coursework —Readings on organizational and environmental assessment and change, systems theories, uses of power, and empowerment
Diagnostic and Conceptualization Skills	—Experiences in assessment and testing —Organizational development and assessment coursework —Experiences in observational assessment, interviewing, focus groups, and other qualitative data gathering —Experiences in developing theoretical models and paradigms from past theory and research
Program Development, Marketing, and Decision-Making Skills	—Goal-setting and decision-making knowledge and exercises —Experiences in curriculum and program development —Lectures on "How to Market or Publicize an Outreach Program"
Intervention Skills	—Prevention Framework & Skills Questionnaire —Supervised practica and internships in primary prevention programs or other applied experiences
Research and Evaluation Skills	—Coursework in research methods and statistics —Readings on evaluation (Rossi, Lipsey, & Freeman, 2004), prevention evaluation, including single system designs (Bloom, Fisher, & Orme, 2003; Jacobs & Goldberg, chap. 5, this volume; Reppucci, Britner, &Woolard, 1997), and evidence-based practice (APA Presidential Task Force on Evidence-Based Practice, 2006) —Experiences completing critical literature searches —Experiences or coursework in instrument development

TABLE 7.2
(Continued)

Frameworks and skills	Pedagogical possibilities
Ethical Skills	—Readings (Blank, Lorion, & Wolpe, 2003; Bond & Albee, 1990; Schwartz & Hage, chap. 6, this volume; Pope, 1990) —Lecture or review of APA Ethical Standards in the context of primary prevention processes and skills —Lecture on ethical decision making

future. This checklist promotes the personalization of the course content and shapes critical professional identity issues.

A fourth intervention is the use of case studies during the middle and end of the course. Because our course is team taught, various faculty give case studies on actual prevention programs they have developed and implemented. For example, we each present our case studies on reducing institutional racism and sexism in a university setting (O'Neil & Conyne, 1992) and preventing child abuse and neglect through parent education (Reppucci, Britner, & Woolard, 1997). These case studies provide students with vivid examples of primary prevention programs that have been conceptualized, implemented, and evaluated. All faculty are asked to discuss both successes and failures with their programs. These case studies provide a reality base to our course that cannot be fully realized by just reading and discussing published case studies (Albee & Gullotta, 1997). What is most important is that students listen to faculty who are passionate about prevention and making a difference in people's lives.

One assignment used in our prevention class at the University of Connecticut that incorporates many of the teaching options in Table 7.2 is the prevention proposal. The goal of the proposal is to help students apply the course concepts by writing about a prevention program they would like to implement in the future. Students write the proposal using an 18-part outline that addresses many of the issues implied in Figure 7.1 and 7.2. This proposal requires students to define and justify a primary prevention problem, critically review the literature in that area, create a conceptual model that represents the intervention, develop the content of the program, describe how to implement it, and enumerate ways to evaluate outcomes. During the last two classes, students present their proposals in class, bringing closure to the semester's learning. We have found the prevention proposal to be a stimulating and integrative experience for students and one that prepares them for a prevention practicum. An outline of a prevention proposal is available from the authors.

A COMPREHENSIVE CURRICULUM FOR PREVENTIONISTS

Our proposed training models imply that preventionists need comprehensive knowledge and skills to be effective with primary prevention programs. A comprehensive curriculum for a preventionist includes a series of courses and applied experiences supervised by a mentor. Students should first take an introductory course that explains the overall philosophy of primary prevention, including the theoretical perspectives, processes, and essential skills. At the University of Connecticut, we offer a graduate course in the Department of Human Development & Family Studies (HDFS) on "Prevention, Intervention, and Policy" that satisfies this introductory role. This course provides students with a basic understanding of how to conceptualize and implement primary prevention interventions (see Figures 7.1 and 7.2). Our position is that no single course can effectively train preventionists for the many skills necessary to do primary prevention. We recommend that students take a cluster of courses that teach the prevention skills shown in Figure 7.2. At the University of Connecticut, we have relevant courses in the College of Liberal Arts & Sciences Departments of HDFS (e.g., "Grant Writing and Program Evaluation" and "Qualitative Research Methods"), Psychology (e.g., "Organizational Psychology" and "Causal Modeling in Social Psychology"), and Sociology (e.g., "Social Change"); in the Neag School of Education's Department of Educational Psychology (e.g., "Group Dynamics" and "Consultation Theories and Practices"); and through the interdisciplinary PhD program in Public Health (Social and Behavioral Health Sciences) and the University Health Center.

Furthermore, we recommend that students have applied or practical experiences in implementing primary prevention interventions. The prevention practicum would be the final learning experience in a prescribed curriculum for primary preventionists. For example, an applied internship or practicum (not necessarily focused on prevention) is required of HDFS doctoral students and also of students in the graduate program evaluation certificate program, an interdisciplinary effort based in Educational Psychology that also includes faculty from HDFS and Psychology. For those students with an interest in prevention, this practicum opportunity may be tailored to fit the needs of the student and the prevention training experience.

A comprehensive curriculum has some essential components that prevention trainers should consider. First, we recommend coursework that teaches therapeutic, relational, and consultative competencies. Students trained as therapists, consultants, or helping professionals may already have these interpersonal skills. However, these skills need to be adapted to prevention problem-solving processes. Second, these interpersonal competencies need to be learned in the context of diversity, multiculturalism, and the realities of societal oppression. The multiculturally competent preventionist relates to diverse groups of people with sensitivity and effectiveness. Coursework on race, class, gender, and other diversity variables sensitize students to how societal oppression causes personal problems and social injustices. Furthermore, preventionists need to assess their own biases and stereotypes to ensure these attitudes do not negatively affect their prevention efforts.

So much of prevention work is done in groups that our third important curricular area is knowledge about group dynamics and processes. Courses in group dynamics or other group experiences are essential for preventionists. Organizational, environmental, and ecological assessment is another curricular area that affects the entire prevention problem-solving process. Therefore, courses that teach individual, group, and organizational assessment are critical as preventionists engage complex interpersonal and institutional dynamics. Courses in research methodology and program evaluation that emphasize both quantitative and qualitative approaches to data gathering are essential for any preventionist. Additionally, courses that require critical literature searches and authoritative summaries of prior theory and research are needed to develop conceptually based, empirically driven interventions. Finally, courses in professional ethics and ethical decision making are important to ensure that preventionists do no harm during their interventions. We also recommend a one- or two-semester prevention practicum or internship in which the student can actually gain experience in demonstrating the necessary skills. This kind of applied experience gives students the chance to implement a prevention program and receive supervision and feedback during the process.

Interdepartmental collaboration is useful when developing a comprehensive prevention curriculum. Multiple campus departments can create clusters of related courses that help students learn the primary prevention process and skills. One department can provide the introductory course, another can teach prevention research skills or assessment approaches, and another can provide the practica and applied experiences. Interdepartmental and interdisciplinary collaboration may be one of the best ways to create a comprehensive curriculum that trains primary preventionists in the art and science of prevention.

CONCLUSION

There is broad consensus among psychologists, other social scientists, and helping professionals that prevention is important. With proper training in the problem-solving process and the frameworks and skills we have outlined in this chapter, preventionists can be confident that they will be able to help their community partners develop effective—and cost-effective—programs.

This focus on before-the-fact prevention, rather than after-the-fact treatment, is also ethical and consistent with the social justice perspective that permeates this volume. We are aware that our emphasis in this chapter has been on primary prevention, in contrast to treatment or intervention. Many of our pedagogical approaches for primary prevention should apply to other kinds of prevention or intervention. The creative adaptation of our ideas to other forms of prevention is one of the challenges for future prevention educators.

Primary prevention is vital to the ethical and effective practice of social justice psychology. Why, then, are so few graduate programs in psychology and related fields placing the proper emphasis on the training of prevention concepts, methods, and practices? Matthews' (2003; 2003, August) findings and our speculations implicate a lack of training and accreditation requirements. We hope that we have provided some ideas to address the training of preventionists. We would certainly endorse efforts to make prevention coursework and competency a part of accreditation standards for psychologists, counselors, and other preventionists. Without such leverage, programmatic changes on a national scale may not be possible.

Prevention training can play a crucial role in promoting primary prevention practice and the social justice initiatives emphasized throughout this volume. Even with expanded didactic models and required courses, training preventionists will continue to be a challenge. We must help a new generation of professors and students define "what really matters" in their careers by engaging their passions for prevention, social justice, and making a difference in people's lives.

REFERENCES

Albee, G. W. (2006). Historical overview of primary prevention of psychopathology: Address to the 3rd World Conference on the Promotion of Mental Health and Prevention of Mental and Behavioral Disorders, September 15–17, 2004, Auckland, New Zealand. *The Journal of Primary Prevention, 27,* 449–456.

Albee, G. W., & Gullotta, T. P. (Eds.). (1997). *Primary prevention works.* Thousand Oaks, CA: Sage.

APA Presidential Task Force on Evidence-Based Practice. (2006). Evidence-based practice in psychology. *American Psychologist, 61,* 271–285.

Blank, M. B., Lorion, R. P., & Wolpe, P. R. (2003). Ethical consideration in prevention. In T. P. Gullotta & M. Bloom (Eds.), *Encyclopedia of primary prevention and health promotion* (pp. 69–79). New York: Kluwer.

Bloom, M. (1996). Frame of reference for primary prevention practice. In M. Bloom (Ed.), *Primary prevention practices* (pp. 1–23). Thousand Oaks, CA: Sage.

Bloom, M., Fisher, J., & Orme, J. G. (2003). *Evaluating practice: Guidelines for the accountable professional* (4th ed.). Boston: Allyn & Bacon.

Bloom, M., & Gullotta, T. P. (2003). Evolving definitions of primary prevention. In T. P. Gullotta & M. Bloom (Eds.), *Encyclopedia of primary prevention and health promotion* (pp. 9–14). New York: Kluwer.

Bond, L. A., & Albee, G. W. (1990). Training preventionists in ethical implications of their actions. *Prevention in Human Services, 8,* 111–126.

Coie, J. D., Watt, N. F., West, S. G., Hawkins, J. D., Asarnow, J. R., & Markman, H. J. (1993). The science of prevention: A conceptual framework and some directions for a national research program. *American Psychologist, 48,* 1013–1022.

Conoley, J. C., & Conoley, C. W. (1992). *School consultation: A guide to practice and training* (2nd ed.). New York: Allyn & Bacon.

Conyne, R. K. (1994). Preventive counseling. *Counseling and Human Development, 27,* 1–10.

Conyne, R. K. (1997). Educating students in preventive counseling. *Counselor Education and Supervision, 36,* 259–269.

Conyne, R. K. (2004). *Preventive counseling: Helping people to become empowered in systems and settings* (2nd ed.). New York: Brunner-Routledge.

Cowen, E. (1984). Training for primary prevention in mental health. *American Journal of Community Psychology, 12,* 253–259.

Dalton, J. H., Elias, M. J., & Beck, B. L. (1994). Transforming coverage of primary prevention in abnormal psychology courses. *Teaching of Psychology, 21,* 217–222.

Hage, S. M., Romano, J. L., Conyne, R. K., Kenny, M., Matthews, C., Schwartz, J. P., & Waldo, M. (2007). Best practice guidelines on prevention practice, research, training, and social advocacy for psychologists. *The Counseling Psychologist, 35,* 493–566.

Joffe, J. M., & Albee, G. W. (1981). *Prevention through political action and social change.* Hanover, NH: University Press of New England.

Matthews, C. R. (2003). *Training counselors in prevention: How are we doing?* Unpublished manuscript, Penn State University.

Matthews, C. R. (2003, August). Training for prevention competency in counseling psychology. In M. Kenny (Chair), *Competencies for prevention training in counseling psychology.* Symposium presented at the 111th Annual Convention of the American Psychological Association, Toronto, Ontario, Canada.

O'Neil, J. M., & Conyne, R. K. (1992). Reducing institutional racism-sexism in a university setting. In R. K. Conyne & J. M. O'Neil (Eds.), *Organizational consultation: A casebook* (pp. 146–183). Newbury Park, CA: Sage.

Perry, M. J., Albee, G. W., Bloom, M., & Gullotta, T. P. (1996). Training and career paths in primary prevention. *The Journal of Primary Prevention, 16,* 357–371.

Pope, K. S. (1990). Identifying and implementing ethical standards for primary prevention. *Prevention in Human Services, 8,* 43–64.

Reppucci, N. D., Britner, P. A., & Woolard, J. L. (1997). Evaluation for the prevention educator. In N. D. Reppucci, P. A. Britner, & J. L. Woolard (Eds.), *Preventing child abuse and neglect through parent education* (pp. 37–47). Baltimore: Paul H. Brookes.

Romano, J. L., & Hage, S. M. (2000). Prevention and counseling psychology: Revitalizing commitments for the 21st century. *The Counseling Psychologist, 28,* 733–763.

Rossi, P. R., Lipsey, M. W., & Freeman, H. E. (2004). *Evaluation: A systematic approach* (7th ed.). Thousand Oaks, CA: Sage.

Schinke, S. P., & Matthieu, M. (2003). Primary prevention with diverse populations. In T. P. Gullotta & M. Bloom (Eds.), *Encyclopedia of primary prevention and health promotion* (pp. 92–97). New York: Kluwer.

Zins, J. E., & Erchul, W. P. (2003). The use of consultation as a foundation for promoting prevention. In T. P. Gullotta & M. Bloom (Eds.), *Encyclopedia of primary prevention and health promotion* (pp. 80–84). New York: Kluwer.

Zolik, E. (1983). Training for preventive psychology in community and academic settings. In R. Felner, L. Jason, J. Moritsugu, & S. Farber (Eds.), *Preventive psychology: Theory, research, and practice* (pp. 273–289). New York: Pergamon.

II

PREVENTIVE INTERVENTIONS ACROSS CONTEXTS

8

FOSTERING A HEALTHY CLIMATE FOR DIVERSITY

CONNIE R. MATTHEWS, SHANTI PEPPER, AND PEGGY LORAH

Growing evidence suggests a connection between social injustice and a variety of mental health concerns (e.g., Israel, 2006; U.S. Department of Health and Human Services, 2001). Although there are many reasons for confronting social injustice, the link between social conditions and mental health concerns makes this a professionally relevant issue for psychologists and other mental health professionals. The visionary work of George Albee is discussed in the introduction and chapter 1 of this volume and will not be repeated here. Nonetheless, this work provides a framework for what we cover in this chapter. In his call for a "just society" (1986), Albee emphasized the need to simultaneously reduce the impact of environmental stressors by enhancing coping skills, social support, and self-esteem and to accomplish environmental change that eliminates inequities in the social order. It is important that any comprehensive text on prevention address ways to confront injustice that are proactive in creating a climate more appreciative of the diversity that exists in society. The goal of this chapter is to introduce ways to approach such an endeavor.

We examine four contexts in which specific social justice concerns exist and describe prevention programming focused both on ameliorative changes that reduce the impact of environmental stressors and transformative changes designed to create a healthier climate for people from diverse backgrounds. It is impossible to exhaustively include all contexts or all aspects of social injustice that warrant intervention; therefore, we provide a range of contexts and issues that might serve as examples of the kinds of interventions that can be done. We have chosen to address climate issues in secondary schools, colleges and universities, the workplace, and the community because many people interact in these environments and because they reflect a variety of developmental periods.

This chapter is far from exhaustive. It is intended to complement other chapters in this volume, such as chapter 4, which presents a discussion of racism prevention and prevention of homophobia on college campuses, and chapter 13, which addresses bystander behavior in a college context. Our aim is to provide examples to draw upon, expand, and assess.

We recognize that diversity exists in many forms and have tried to reflect this by examining several different aspects of diversity, focusing on one specific group in each context. We first examine sexual orientation and gender identity in secondary schools and the workplace. Although not immediately evident, once revealed, a nonheterosexual orientation or nonconforming gender identity can make one the target of hostile attitudes, discriminatory behavior, or even violence, yet to date there is no broad protection against harassment or discrimination based on sexual orientation or gender identity. Most people spend a substantial portion of their lives in schools and workplaces, so policies and programs that address the immediate environment are critical in the absence of larger social policies. We then consider gender issues in colleges and universities. It was not so long ago that higher education was predominantly the purview of men. Although the enrollment numbers have changed considerably in the past century, the climate on many college and university campuses has continued to provide unique challenges for women. Finally, we explore racial and ethnic concerns in the community, specifically how communities have responded to hate crimes.

FOSTERING A HEALTHY CLIMATE IN SECONDARY SCHOOLS FOR LESBIAN, GAY, BISEXUAL, AND TRANSGENDER (LGBT) YOUTH

A common lament is that "schools aren't safe anymore," as society becomes increasingly aware that schools are not the haven they once were. Harassment, violence, and bullying in schools unfortunately is experienced by a significant number of youth, and research suggests grave consequences for victims of school violence (e.g., Egan & Perry, 1998; Gay, Lesbian and Straight Education Network [GLSEN], 2005; Hodges & Perry, 1999; Kochenderfer & Ladd, 1996; Nansel et al., 2001).

Much research has explored the characteristics of those individuals who participate in bullying and the reasons why some individuals are more likely to bully or be bullied (see, Fekkes, Pijpers, & Verloove-Vanhorick, 2005; GLSEN, 2005; Orpinas & Horne, 2006). GLSEN recently surveyed more than 3,400 students ages 13 to 18 years and more than 1,000 secondary school teachers about their experiences with and attitudes toward harassment. GLSEN's report indicated that the number one reason for harassment was the student's appearance (e.g., body size, the way they look). The second most common reason reported by students was because of perceived or actual sexual orientation.

GLSEN's (2005) report indicated that when compared to their heterosexual counterparts, lesbian, gay, bisexual, and transgender (LGBT) students were three times more likely to feel unsafe at school (22% vs. 7%). Indeed, 92% of LGBT participants (compared to 62% of non-LGBT participants) reported verbal or physical harassment due to perceived or actual sexual orientation, gender expression, race or ethnicity, disability, or religious preference. Clearly, bullying and violence in schools are problems that need continuing attention with respect to all students; however, the school climate for LGBT students is particularly hostile. D'Augelli, Pilkington, and Hershberger's (2002) research on high school victimization experiences of 350 lesbian, gay, and bisexual youth also found striking results. That study suggested that 59% of participants experienced verbal abuse, 24% were threatened with physical violence, 20% reported that their perpetrator threatened disclosure of their sexual orientation, 11% had objects thrown at them, 11% were physically attacked, and 2% were threatened with a weapon.

Strong evidence indicates that individuals who are victims of school violence are likely to use drugs and/or alcohol, perform poorly in school, have lower self-esteem, and experience depression and anxiety (Descamps, Rothblum, Bradford, & Ryan, 2000; GLSEN, 2005; Hodges & Perry, 1999). Interestingly, LGBT individuals who are victims of hate crimes based on sexual orientation experience greater rates of anxiety, anger, depression, and posttraumatic stress when compared to LGBT individuals who experienced crimes unrelated to sexual orientation (Herek, Gillis, & Cogan, 1999). The aforementioned research is indisputable. LGBT youth are experiencing harassment and violence in schools at an alarming rate that is significantly greater than their heterosexual peers, and the consequences of such violence is detrimental to their physical and emotional well-being. Fortunately, programs designed to create safer schools for LGBT students do exist. Due to the limited research available on the effectiveness of specific LGBT antiviolence prevention programs in elementary and secondary schools, we will first discuss how schools have created safer environments. Next, we examine the limited research on evaluating programs to create safer schools for LGBT students.

Although not specifically designed for LGBT students, Fried and Fried (1996) promote a model of intervention that incorporates change on multiple levels, including the individual, family, community, and cultural levels. The individual level may offer individual counseling to victims and bullies as well as education and sensitivity training to individuals to increase awareness of the power of words. The community level may include creating advocacy groups or working toward passing legislation that prohibits institutional prejudice and discrimination. The cultural level might include confronting media violence and its relationship to racism, sexism, and heterosexism (Fried & Fried, 1996).

Following from this framework, a multimodal approach to reduce harassment is optimal for creating a safe and affirmative environment. While one step may focus on intervention at the individual level, the community level may be critical in fostering affirmative and safe schools. Including sexual orientation in harassment policies represents one community level strategy. GLSEN's (2005) study found that more than half of participants (teachers and students) reported their schools included sexual orientation or gender expression in their safety policies. Furthermore, when compared with participants who attended schools without inclusive school safety policies, LGBT students attending schools with inclusive policies described less harassment, felt safer at school, and were less likely to skip class. Although causation cannot be inferred, this study nonetheless suggests a link between inclusive and affirmative policies and LGBT students' increased feelings of safety at school.

Also at the community level, many noteworthy organizations and programs addressing harassment of LGBT students were developed in the mid-1980s to mid-1990s. Such programs seek to foster a sense of community, support friendships, and potentially create a safe place for LGBT individuals and their allies. Such programs include, but are not limited to, GLSEN (Exhibit 8.1), Project 10 (Exhibit 8.2), the California Safe Schools Coalition, Massachusetts Governor's Commission on Gay and Lesbian Youth, and Washington's Safe Schools Project. (For a thorough review of these programs, see Henning-Stout, James, & Macintosh, 2000; and GLSEN, 2000, 2003, & 2005.)

Research examining the effectiveness of strategies for improving the school climate for LGBT students in K–12 education programs remains sparse. However, the available research suggests that programs can be effective in creating safer schools. For instance, Elze's (2003) study of 184 gay, lesbian, and bisexual youths revealed that although the presence of allies did not uniquely contribute to youths' feelings of comfort in schools, comfort was positively related to students' sense of integration with their peers and whether they observed professionals acting on their behalf. Since two of the primary components of the aforementioned school programs were to help

EXHIBIT 8.1
Gay, Lesbian and Straight Education Network (GLSEN)

GLSEN (http://www.glsen.org) was founded in 1990 by local school teachers, and by 1995 it had become a national organization. This nonprofit organization aims to help schools learn to value and respect all students regardless of gender expression and sexual orientation. Its mission includes helping policy makers recognize the need to make schools safe for lesbian, gay, bisexual, and transgender (LGBT) students, empowering educators and principles to learn about LGBT issues, and teaching them how to make schools safe. Two influential components to GLSEN are helping students form Gay-Straight Alliances (GSAs) and Safe Zone Programs in their schools. GSAs are student-led clubs that work to reduce harassment and bullying based on actual or perceived sexual orientation. A unique element of GSAs is that they bring together heterosexual and LGBT students to actively address harassment, bullying, and discrimination through increasing students' knowledge of LGBT issues. This alliance provides support for the LGBT students and addresses the experiences of heterosexual students who wish to serve as allies (i.e., individuals who are affirming of LGBT individuals). Safe Zone Programs, on the other hand, aim to increase the visibility of LGBT individuals and allies by displaying stickers, posters, and/or other signs that indicate that they are a safe person to approach or ask for support (GLSEN, 2003).

LGBT and non-LGBT students come together (in the form of Gay-Straight Alliances, or GSAs) and to increase administrators' and teachers' knowledge and advocacy for LGBT students, Elze's findings found support for these two strategies for creating schools that are safe for LGBT students. A small qualitative study (Lee, 2002) examined the impact of belonging to a high school GSA, and the results confirmed Elze's study. That is, participants reported increased levels of comfort, a feeling of "belonging," confidence, and pride after joining a GSA. Additionally, many of the students reported feeling safer in school because they felt that some teachers, administrators, and their faculty sponsor were there to help protect them. Although students believed that their academic performance had improved

EXHIBIT 8.2
Project 10

Project 10 (http://www.project10.org) was created by Virginia Uribe for the Los Angeles Unified School District in 1984 in response to the prevalence of suicide, school dropout, harassment, and substance use among LGBT students (Uribe, 1994; Uribe & Harbeck, 1991). The primary component of Project 10 is support groups for LGBT youth to process their experiences in a safe place with trained facilitators to improve self-esteem. Other program elements are trainings for administrators, counselors, teachers, and staff on some of the unique obstacles and needs of LGBT youth; increasing LGBT affirming materials in the school library; increasing compliance with nondiscrimination policies, and advocating for LGBT students in high school organizations and in their communities (Henning-Stout, James, & Macintosh, 2000; Uribe & Harbeck, 1991). Thus, Project 10 not only supports LGBT youth individually but also addresses systemic concerns that have made high school difficult for LGBT youth.

as a result of the increased feelings of safety and belonging they experienced, Lee's evaluation of their grades did not confirm students' reports. Their actual grades did not improve noticeably; nonetheless, participants expressed improved attendance, interest, passion, and hope for their futures following their involvement in a GSA. Although limitations exist, Lee's study suggests potentially positive outcomes of GSAs for LGBT youth.

Goodenow, Szalacha, and Westheimer (2006) used data from the 1999 Massachusetts Youth Risk Behavior survey (Massachusetts Department of Education, 2002), where 202 participants who self-identified as Lesbian, Gay, and Bisexual (LGB) or reported same-sex sexual contact were surveyed. Goodenow and colleagues explored how social support, school factors, and administrators' support of LGB youths were related to victimization and mental health consequences. Results indicated that schools with support groups were more likely to also protect LGB students in their harassment policy, and participants in these schools were significantly more likely to report greater safety, less dating violence, less harassment/bullying, and fewer suicide attempts. In summary, research suggests a clear link between increased levels of safety and comfort at school for LGBT students and the presence of prevention programs and inclusive school policies (Elze, 2003; GLSEN, 2005; Goodenow et al., 2006; Lee, 2002).

FOSTERING A HEALTHY CLIMATE FOR WOMEN IN COLLEGES AND UNIVERSITIES

In this section, we examine several areas in which women in college settings may experience oppression. These experiences may affect their ability to function, to be successful students, and sometimes even to remain in school. When colleges and universities provide effective programs that promote a "supportive, equitable, and safe environment for women" (Council for the Advancement of Standards in Higher Education, 1997, p. 1), women students experience improved mental health and are more successful students.

Women students in colleges and universities have many issues with which to struggle, and educators and practitioners in women's centers, counseling centers, and health centers have worked both to ensure safety and to establish prevention programming and advocacy services to help meet their needs. Aside from the usual concerns that all students deal with, women students confront issues of chilly campus and classroom climate, sexual harassment, sexual assault and rape, and dating and relationship violence, which have implications for their mental health and development (Kress et al., 2006).

The first issue we will discuss is sexual harassment. The U.S. Equal Employment Opportunity Commission (n.d.) provides the following definition of sexual harassment:

Unwelcome sexual advances, requests for sexual favors, and other verbal or physical conduct of a sexual nature constitute sexual harassment when this conduct explicitly or implicitly affects an individual's employment [academic status], unreasonably interferes with an individual's work [academic] performance, or creates an intimidating, hostile or offensive work environment. (n.p.)

On campus, this might involve the grades a student receives or academic status a student is granted (e.g., admission into a major or graduate program, awarding of opportunities such as a fellowship or graduate assistantship). Behavior can range from sexual innuendos, jokes, and comments to pressure to engage in sexual activity. A critical issue for colleges and universities is when a student's response to unwelcome behavior becomes the basis for academic decisions about that student and/or when such behavior interferes, or is meant to interfere, with a student's academic performance, thus, creating a hostile learning environment. Best practices in the prevention of sexual harassment include educational programs with the aim to ensure that students, faculty, and staff understand what sexual harassment is and are aware of its causes and consequences. Further, institutions should provide clear and accessible information about policies, including how policies are enforced, how to file formal complaints, and how informal processes work (Sandler & Shoop, 1997).

Sexual assault and rape are another area of concern on campuses. Sexual assault is defined as any unwanted sexual contact, and rape is defined as a sexual assault that involves "the use or threat of force in vaginal, anal, or oral intercourse" (Tjaden & Thoennes, 2006, p. 3). College women are at risk to be victims of sexual assaults, both because of their age group and because of the increased risk factors that come with college attendance, including the sense of independence that comes with living outside of the family environment, assumptions about behaviors in which college women are willing to engage, and the social climate present on many campuses (Shultz, Scherman, & Marshall, 2000). It is estimated that one in five traditionally aged women are raped while in college (Fisher, Cullen, & Turner, 2000), and between 80% and 90% of these victims know their assailants (Karjane, Fisher, & Cullen, 2005).

Dating and relationship violence is a major problem on campuses, with estimates ranging from 20% to 33% of college students being involved in relationships where physical, emotional, psychological, and verbal abuse are present (Schwartz, Griffin, Russell, & Frontaura-Duck, 2006). As is the case with sexual assault, gender-role stereotypes have an impact on dating violence (Schwartz, Magee, Griffin, & Dupuis, 2004). Prevention programs have traditionally addressed prevalence rates for sexual assaults, gender-role stereotypes, rape myths, risk factors, and information about safe dating behavior (Kress et al., 2006). Such programs have usually occurred as part of orientation for new students—both male and female—and have taken the form of speakers who have shared their experiences as victims, lectures and discussions by college staff and peer educators, and interactive theater presentations (Schultz et al., 2000). Research has shown that the attitudes of male and female students who participate in such programming change, and they are less accepting of rape myths (Kress et al., 2006; Schultz et al., 2000), which are "attitudes and beliefs that are generally false but are widely and persistently held, and that serve to deny and justify male aggression against women" (Lonsway & Fitzgerald, 1994, as cited in Kress et al., 2006, p. 150).

There have been some recent changes, however, in prevention efforts to address these issues. For approximately 30 years, college and university women's centers and counseling centers provided educational programming and advocacy services in an attempt to offer information and support for women students and to decrease the number of incidents of sexual assault, sexual harassment, and relationship violence. More recent efforts have begun to use a different language, replacing the term *prevention* with *risk reduction*. Traditional prevention programming often focused on how women can keep these events from happening to them, with women students often reporting that they have felt revictimized by a campus culture that held them responsible for the behaviors of their assailants (Karjane et al., 2005). It remains appropriate to work with women on strategies for maximizing their safety and well-being: encouraging them to attend parties in groups and to leave parties in those same groups, to keep tabs on what friends are doing throughout the evening, and to make sure that one member of the group will not drink alcohol at an event or party and will intervene if she sees a friend in a potentially dangerous situation. At the same time, it is also important to be clear that, while there are things women students can do to reduce their risk, they are not responsible for preventing behavior they neither initiate nor invite.

With the establishment of the Department of Justice Violence Against Women Act (VAWA), and particularly with the development of the Violence Against Women on Campus grant category, the federal government stopped talking about prevention as something women should do. Organizations such as the National Coalition Against Domestic Violence (http://www.ncadv.org) and the National Sexual Violence Resource Center (http://www.nsvrc.org) use the term *risk reduction* to refer to programming directed to women, and they reserve the term *prevention* for programming directed at men. Groups such as these make the point that the only individuals capable of preventing crimes such as sexual assault and rape are the individuals committing them. Recent prevention efforts have also focused more on what men can do (see chap. 13, this volume).

Research indicates that the most effective college and university prevention efforts regarding dating violence, sexual assault, and rape involve peer educators and are interactive (Kress et al., 2006; Schwartz et al.,

2006). Peer education focusing on both individual change and change within campus social systems has shown positive results in limited research studies (Becker, Smith, & Ciao, 2006). In addition, as a way of ensuring that all students understand the dynamics of sexual and relationship violence and the status of women on campus, Pinar (2003) recommends that colleges and universities include women's and gender studies in their general education requirements for all undergraduate students.

In addition to programming geared to individual students and groups of students, larger systemic efforts, which can include legislation, are also important. Until the advent of Title IX of the Education Amendments of 1972, there was no legal mechanism to ensure that women had equal access to education. Title IX prohibits discrimination based on gender in the areas of access and admissions, housing and facilities, courses and other educational activities, career and counseling services, student financial aid, student health and insurance benefits, and athletics (American Association of University Women [AAUW], 2006). Although women are still overrepresented in traditionally female fields and underrepresented in fields such as computer science and engineering, Title IX has ensured that women have access to all fields of study and can prepare for careers in medicine, law, and the sciences. It has also expanded athletic opportunities for women and facilitated the establishment of avenues to address sexual harassment (AAUW, 2006). Although it has taken many years to realize the changes envisioned by proponents of Title IX and many challenges remain, this example of legislative action has shown that over time such efforts can lay the foundation for creating change with respect to gender equity.

Since the 1970s, women's centers on college and university campuses have sponsored programs and advocacy initiatives that seek to empower women to take charge of their education and to maximize their potential. The Council for the Advancement of Standards in Higher Education (1997) addresses the importance of enhancing the educational experiences of women students, focusing on exposure to gender issues and empowerment of women students. The American College Health Association (2005) identifies the importance of supporting student learning by helping students to live healthier lives and by advocating for equal access.

In each of the areas we have discussed in this section, prevention efforts have evolved from single-event presentations to comprehensive educational endeavors. Peer interactions featuring scenarios appear to be effective in providing students with information about these issues. These interactions appear to increase in effectiveness when they are followed by facilitated discussions about ways in which individuals, communities, and systems can be changed (Iverson, 2006). Additionally, educational programming and information should be offered in many forms and venues, including student orientation; curriculum infusion; trainings for students, faculty, and staff on how to help victims of harassment, sexual assault, and relationship violence; varied campus events; and informational materials in paper and electronic forms (Karjane et al., 2005).

Although prevention efforts have evolved, much work remains to foster a healthy climate in colleges and universities. Research efforts that examine outcomes have begun, but much of the available information is anecdotal and focused on breadth of programming rather than on a comprehensive examination of results.

FOSTERING A CLIMATE FOR DIVERSITY IN THE WORKPLACE FOR LESBIAN, GAY, BISEXUAL, AND TRANSGENDER (LGBT) INDIVIDUALS

Although reports of workplace discrimination are believed to be underreported (Badgett, 1997), a review of research suggests that between 25% and 66% of LGBT individuals have reported discrimination in the workplace, and higher rates are reported by individuals who are more open about their sexuality (Croteau, 1996). Moreover, Croteau and Lark (1995) found that of the LGBT individuals surveyed, 44% reported fear of discrimination or anticipated future discrimination at work if their sexual orientation were known. Examples of discrimination are job loss or being passed over for promotions, lower incomes (sometimes up to 27% less), and unequal benefits (e.g., partner health insurance) when compared to their heterosexual counterparts (see Badgett, 1997; Croteau, 1996; Stevenson & Cogan, 2003). Horvath and Ryan (2003) found that lesbian and gay individuals may even experience discrimination before they get an interview if their résumé indicates affiliation or activity in an LGBT organization.

According to Winfeld (2005) and Sobelsohn (2003), LGBT individuals should be fearful. Discrimination based on sexual orientation and gender identity is legal; no federal laws, codes, or statutes that protect against discrimination include sexual orientation or gender identity. Some states, albeit few, have enacted laws to protect LGB individuals, with fewer states protecting transgender individuals (see Sobelsohn, 2003; Winfeld, 2005). Some believe that job discrimination presents one of the gravest threats to civil rights and psychological well-being (Gonsiorek, 1993; Rostosky & Riggle, 2002), and research suggests unmistakable mental and physical consequences for individuals who experience workplace discrimination. For example, Waldo (1999) found that, compared with individuals who perceived less heterosexism in their workplace, LGB individuals who perceived their workplace environment to endorse heterosexism were more likely to report higher rates of personal and job-related consequences. That is, workplace heterosexism was associated with decreased job satisfaction, increased absenteeism, withdrawal from work (e.g., increased tardiness and longer breaks), less productivity at work, higher levels of psychological distress (e.g., depression,anxiety), and health-related problems (e.g., ulcers, headaches, exhaustion). Smith and Ingram (2004) also found a relationship between workplace heterosexism and LGB employees' psychological distress even when the rates of heterosexism were low. Thus, a clear link exists between an individual's mental and physical health and safety and his or her work environment. Creating a healthy, safe, and affirming workplace climate where LGBT individuals can be appreciated and honored is a win-win situation for the employer and the employee; employers benefit from happy, productive, and engaged workers, and employees benefit from greater overall life satisfaction. Fostering such an environment for LGBT individuals is rarely, perhaps never, accomplished with a single intervention or program; however, various approaches are available to enhance the workplace.

First, similar to high schools and universities, organizations should implement antidiscrimination policies that include sexual orientation and gender expression/identity, and they should provide other resources such as domestic partner health benefits to same-sex couples (Winfeld, 2005). Winfeld argues that having such policy protections sends clear messages to management and employees that LGBT individuals are equally valued and protected. Winfeld also argues that without inclusive policies, much of the daily work in the office or in the field cannot be done.

Second, many companies sponsor employee assistance programs (EAPs) that can contribute to the overarching goal of fostering a safe and healthy work climate. Company EAP services to employees and their family members may include individual consultation about life and work stressors, individual counseling, stress management seminars, assessment, referrals, and crisis management. LGBT individuals may also find these resources helpful when navigating antigay jokes in the workplace, discrimination, prejudice, sexism, heterosexism, or family and relationship difficulties. Unfortunately, although these are common struggles faced by the LGBT community in the workplace (e.g., Croteau, 1996; Van Den Bergh,1995), some research suggests that EAP programs/personnel, as well as company policies, do not sufficiently understand or address the needs of LGBT employees (Van Den Bergh, 2000). To that end, Van Den Bergh (1995, 2000) advocates that EAP personnel receive diversity training and education about LGBT concerns. Winfeld (2005) provides an example of how LGBT individuals may be able to use their EAP programs to the fullest. She emphasizes that many EAPs ask employees to describe "family" according to how the employee defines family. This allows LGBT individuals to list their partners so they may also receive the EAP services, which would not be possible if the EAP confined its participants to more traditional definitions of family.

A third step to foster affirmative workplace climate includes diversity training for all employees, which may address a broad spectrum of diversity issues (e.g., race, ethnicity, LGBT, age, religion). Because we believe that discrimination of one group is inextricably connected to oppression of other groups, we believe that addressing each of these issues is vital; however, we recommend a clear and affirmative focus on issues specific to the lesbian, gay, bisexual, and transgender community. To that end, Chrobot-Mason and Quiñones (2002) argue that diversity training should have three fundamental goals: (1) improve the workplace environment for all individuals, (2) enhance coworker relationships with each other by increasing awareness of discrimination, and (3) help employees acknowledge their own biases and prejudices and develop skills to reduce those biases and prejudices. Winfeld (2005) also suggests that trainings should be an ongoing commitment by corporations and organizations. Steps for ongoing commitment include a dedication to open-mindedness (especially from upper management), assessments to evaluate the organizational climate for LGBT individuals, follow-through to use the results of these assessments to develop additional training programs (e.g., a "needs assessment"), and a willingness to reevaluate and update the programs as needed.

A fourth step, recommended by the Human Rights Campaign (2006), is to establish employee network groups, or an Allies program, which typically consists of LGBT affirmative heterosexual individuals working for equal rights. Employee network groups provide a support system for employees, a resource for management to understand their LGBT employees' concerns, and a resource by which companies may better learn how to serve their LGBT consumers/clients.

Large-scale research suggests that changes are being made in the American workforce. For example, a report published by the Human Rights Campaign (2006) stated that 254 (or 51%) of Fortune 500 (F500) companies and 290 colleges and universities currently provide domestic partner health benefits. Sixteen percent of the F500 companies and 562 colleges and universities have a nondiscrimination policy that includes sexual orientation. Although noteworthy improvements have been made for LGB individuals, progress for transgender individuals has been slower. Only 74 colleges and universities have gender expression/identity in their policy, and only 16% of F500 companies have such policies (Human Rights Campaign, 2006). Badgett (1997) and Sobelsohn (2003) contend that there are clear economic benefits to companies that protect their LGBT employees, and research suggests undeniable economic benefits for employees who feel safe at their place of work (see Badgett, 1997; Stevenson & Cogan, 2003; Winfeld, 2005). LGBT individuals who work in organizations with antidiscrimination policies and domestic partner benefits were more likely to be "out" at work and report less workplace discrimination (Day & Schoenrade, 1997; Ragins & Cornwell, 2001; Rostosky & Riggle, 2002). Interestingly, organizational polices and protections have been more effective in decreasing workplace discrimination than city or state legislation (Ragins & Cornwell, 2001). One dilemma for all LGBT individuals is that self-disclosure may lead to greater overall satisfaction (Day & Schoenrade, 1997), but possibly at the expense of a lower salary if antidiscrimination policies and resources are not provided (Ellis & Riggle, 1996). Transsexual individuals going through the process of transition may find this particularly important as the cost of transitioning is very expensive (Walworth, 2003).

Policies, resources, diversity trainings, and support groups are all positive and necessary steps toward fostering an affirmative workplace environment for LGBT individuals, yet they may not be sufficient. Waldo (1999), for example, found that antidiscrimination policies or diversity training alone did not protect LGBT individuals from discrimination. Ragins and Cornwell (2001) found that diversity training that included sexual orientation issues was unrelated to participants' sexual orientation disclosure (i.e., it did not improve feelings of safety to come out). Lesbian and gay support groups at work were marginally related to decreases in workplace discrimination ($p = .056$), but support groups were significantly related to increased disclosure of sexual orientation. Interestingly, Ragins and Cornwell also found a strong association between two subjective experiences: Those individuals who felt their partners were welcomed at company social events also reported less workplace discrimination. In other words, regardless of the "party line" that organizations profess, there is an overall organizational climate that is implicitly or explicitly felt by LGBT individuals, and this climate contributes to the positive and negative experiences in the workplace. It seems, therefore, that efforts to improve workplace climate should concurrently address personal factors, social factors, and political factors.

The aforementioned research suggests workplace discrimination is pervasive for the LGBT community (Croteau, 1996), and many individuals stay closeted because of the fear of future discrimination if their sexual orientation were known (Croteau & Lark, 1995). Due to the negative psychological, medical, and job-related consequences when LGBT individuals work in toxic environments, it is important for organizations to implement multiple and continued interventions to improve the workplace climate. Although some important steps are outlined in this chapter, we found it informative that one of the strongest associations to less perceived workplace discrimination is whether or not a partner is welcomed at a company social event (Ragins & Cornwell, 2001). Regardless of the organization's, or the individual's, unstated beliefs and feeling, LGBT individuals appear to be keen detectors of unsafe situations or people.

FOSTERING A CLIMATE FOR RACIAL
AND ETHNIC DIVERSITY IN THE COMMUNITY

Educational systems and workplaces are important spaces to engage in intentional efforts to combat prejudice and oppression. As somewhat contained places, it is possible to set standards and expectations for participation. Likewise, the population in a school or workplace shares a common purpose. Fostering diversity in the larger community becomes more complex, but many communities are proactively trying to create an environment that affirms and embraces all citizens.

Community level efforts often arise as a result of critical incidents that have occurred within the community. One series of incidents occurred in Billings, Montana, and led to a community response, "Not in Our Town," that has become a model other communities have followed (Public Broadcasting System [PBS], n.d.). These incidents included racist fliers, vandalism in a Jewish cemetery, racist graffiti, bricks through windows where menorahs were placed, and other acts of violence and intimidation. Residents worked together to declare that bigotry and hatred were not acceptable in their town. They did this by supporting their neighbors who had been victims of hate crimes. For instance, newspapers printed full-page menorahs, which thousands displayed in their windows; stores donated paint and painters volunteered their time to paint over racist graffiti; citizens of all denominations attended services in an African-American church that had been targeted. This community mobilization occurred in 1993, and Billings has been free of serious hate crime activity since that time (PBS). The activities in Billings represent an example of the interaction of personal and social involvement. On a personal level, citizens made conscious choices to get to know neighbors who were different in ways that made them targets, thus educating themselves and challenging stereotypes. On a social level, the community came together to change the social climate to one that clearly proclaimed that bigotry was not acceptable.

Because the initial efforts in Billings were in response to acts of violence occurring in the community, they would be classified as secondary prevention (Conyne, 2004). At the same time, the community response and results have led to proactive efforts in other communities and could be considered primary prevention. The Working Group (http://www.theworkinggroup.org) produced a PBS show based on the Billings experience, which continues to be used in communities nationwide as a catalyst for helping them to develop local anti-hate campaigns. Some of these efforts are in response to problems in their own communities (secondary prevention), and others are designed to create a climate that decreases the possibility of such acts (primary prevention).

Other programs are also geared toward helping individuals and communities to respond to bigotry and oppression. For example, the Southern

Poverty Law Center publishes on its Web site (http://www.tolerance.org) *101 Tools for Tolerance*, including activities that can be done on one's own, in the home, in schools, in workplaces, and in the community. Another document on the Web site, *Speak Up: Responding to Everyday Bigotry*, offers suggestions for responding to hate speech and bigoted remarks in everyday settings. This document empowers individuals who want to take action but do not know how by offering practical suggestions on challenging people who perpetuate bigotry and stereotypes in all kinds of settings. Ponterotto, Utsey, and Pedersen (2006) and Sandhu and Aspy (1997) argue that prejudice prevention programs must target both victims of prejudice and those who are or may become perpetrators. The documents offered by the Southern Poverty Law Center also suggest that prevention programs can target bystanders who may not personally be the target of prejudice or oppression but who might nonetheless be affected by the climate it creates for everyone.

On the political level, hate speech and hate crimes legislation can establish community norms that such behavior will not be tolerated and is, indeed, considered criminal. Boeckmann and Turpin-Petrosino (2002) define hate speech as "any form of expression directed at objects of prejudice that perpetrators use to wound and denigrate its recipients" (p. 209). Levin (2002) defines hate crimes as "those offenses committed because of the actual or perceived status characteristic of another, or alternatively, as crimes where the motive is the actual or perceived status characteristic of another—usually, but not necessarily, the crime's victim or target" (p. 227). He reviews a history of legislation dating back to the Thirteenth Amendment abolishing slavery and the Fourteenth Amendment providing equal protection under the law and continuing through to more recent federal, state, and local efforts to enact hate crime legislation.

CONCLUSION

Prevention has long been linked with social justice, especially since it has moved beyond the public health realm of disease prevention to include mental health and behavioral concerns. If prevention practice is to incorporate a social justice focus, it must include proactive efforts to create educational systems, vocational systems, and social systems that foster a climate of health and affirmation for diverse populations. We have provided a sampling of ways in which such activities might be conducted in various settings and at various levels, from individual approaches focused on ameliorative change to environmental approaches seeking more transformative change in a social culture that privileges some and oppresses others. Although we have focused our attention here on specific populations in specific settings, it is important to note that such efforts need not be unidirectional. They merely offer examples of current programming. We have sought to provide information on some of the populations that have been and continue to be targets of oppression and to suggest resources for responding. Ideally, comprehensive programs would incorporate efforts that bring together multiple populations and multiple systems and that direct their efforts to victims of oppression, perpetrators and potential perpetrators, and the larger public who may not directly fall into either category but who nonetheless is affected by the climate created when oppression is tolerated. We have offered examples of programs, approaches, and policies that are being implemented in some settings to begin making the climate more inclusive and affirming for all people. Most of these approaches can boast some anecdotal success; however, there remains a need for programmatic prevention research that helps us to test and refine these models and to more clearly determine their efficacy.

REFERENCES

Albee, G. W. (1986). Toward a just society: Lessons from observations on the primary prevention of psychopathology. *American Psychologist, 41*, 891–898.

American Association of University Women. (2006). *Title IX: Ensuring equity for women and girls*. Retrieved January 19, 2007, from http://www.aauw.org/issue _advocacy/actionpages/positionpapers/titleix.cfm

American College Health Association. (2005). *Standards of practice for health promotion in higher education* (Rev. ed.). Baltimore: American College Health Task Force on Health Promotion in Higher Education.

Badgett, M. V. L. (1997). Vulnerability in the workplace: Evidence of anti-gay discrimination. *Angles: The Policy Journal of the Institute for Gay and Lesbian Strategic Studies, 2*, 1–4.

Becker, C. B., Smith, L. M., & Ciao, A. C. (2006). Peer-facilitated eating disorder prevention: A randomized effectiveness trial of cognitive dissonance and media advocacy. *Journal of Counseling Psychology, 53*(4), 550–555.

Boeckmann, R. J., & Turpin-Petrosino, C. (2002). Understanding the harm of hate crime. *Journal of Social Issues, 58*, 207–225.

Chrobot-Mason, D., & Quiñones, M. A. (2002). Training for a diverse workplace. In K. Kraiger (Ed.), *Creating, implementing and managing effective training and development*. San Francisco: Jossey-Bass.

Conyne, R. K. (2004). *Preventive counseling: Helping people to become empowered in systems and settings* (2nd ed.). New York: Brunner-Routledge.

Council for the Advancement of Standards in Higher Education. (1997). *The book of professional standards for higher education*. Washington, DC: Author.

Croteau, J. M. (1996). Research on the work experiences of lesbian, gay, and bisexual people: An integrative review of methodology and findings. *Journal of Vocational Behavior, 48,* 195–209.

Croteau, J. M., & Lark, J. S. (1995). A qualitative investigation of biased and exemplary student affairs practice concerning lesbian, gay, and bisexual issues. *Journal of College Student Development, 36,* 472–482.

D'Augelli, A. R., Pilkington, N. W., & Hershberger, S. L. (2002). Incidence and mental health impact of sexual orientation victimization of lesbian, gay, and bisexual youths in high school. *School Psychology Quarterly, 17,* 148–167.

Day, N. E., & Schoenrade, P. (1997). Staying in the closet versus coming out: Relationship between communication about sexual orientation and work attitudes. *Personnel Psychology, 50,* 147–163.

Descamps, M. J., Rothblum, E., Bradford, J., & Ryan, C. (2000). Mental health impact of child sexual abuse, rape, intimate partner violence, and hate crimes in the National Lesbian Health Care survey. *Journal of Gay & Lesbian Social Services, 11,* 27–55.

Egan, S. K., & Perry, D. G. (1998). Does low self-regard invite victimization? *Developmental Psychology, 34,* 299–309.

Ellis, A. L., & Riggle, E. D. B. (1996). The relation of job satisfaction and degree of openness about one's sexual orientation for lesbians and gay men. *Journal of Homosexuality, 30,* 75–85.

Elze, D. E. (2003). Gay, lesbian, and bisexual youths' perceptions of their high school environments and comfort in school. *Children and Schools, 25,* 225–239.

Fekkes, M., Pijpers, F. I. M., & Verloove-Vanhorick, S. P. (2005). Bullying: Who does what, when and where? Involvement of children, teachers and parents in bullying behaviors. *Health Education Research, 20,* 81–91.

Fisher, B. S., Cullen, F. T., & Turner, M. G. (2000). *The sexual victimization of college women.* Retrieved from U.S. Department of Justice, Office of Justice Programs, National Institute of Justice: http://www.ncjrs.gov/pdffiles1/nij/182369.pdf

Fried, S., & Fried, P. (1996). *Bullies and victims: Helping your child through the schoolyard battlefield.* New York: M. Evans and Company, Inc.

Gay, Lesbian and Straight Education Network. (2000). *Gay-Straight Alliance handbook.* Retrieved September 16, 2008, from http://www.glsen.org/binary=data/GLSEN_ATTACHMENTS/file/32=1.pdf

Gay, Lesbian and Straight Education Network. (2003). *Safe zone programs.* Retrieved January 2007 from http://www.glsen.org/binary=data/GLSEN_ATTACHMENTS/file/245=1.pdf

Gay, Lesbian and Straight Education Network. (2005). *From teasing to torment: School climate in America. A survey of students and teachers.* New York: Author.

Gonsiorek, J. C. (1993). Threat, stress, and adjustment: Mental health and the workplace for gay and lesbian individuals. In L. Diamant (Ed.), *Homosexual issues in the workplace* (pp. 243–264). Washington, DC: Taylor & Francis.

Goodenow, C., Szalacha, L., & Westheimer, K. (2006). School support groups, other school factors, and the safety of sexual minority adolescents. *Psychology in the Schools, 43,* 573–589.

Henning-Stout, M., James, S., & Macintosh, S. (2000). Reducing harassment of lesbian, gay, bisexual, transgender, and questioning youth in schools. *School Psychology Review, 29,* 180–191.

Herek, G. M., Gillis, J. R., & Cogan, J. C. (1999). Psychological sequelae of hate-crime victimization among lesbian, gay, and bisexual adults. *Journal of Consulting and Clinical Psychology, 67*(6), 945–951.

Hodges, E. V. E., & Perry, D. G. (1999). Personal and interpersonal antecedents and consequences of victimization by peers. *Journal of Personality and Social Psychology, 76,* 677–685.

Horvath, M., & Ryan, A. M. (2003). Antecedents and potential moderators of the relationship between attitudes and hiring discrimination on the basis of sexual orientation. *Sex Roles, 48,* 115–130.

Human Rights Campaign. (2006). *The state of the workforce for gay, lesbian, bisexual and transgender Americans—2005–2006.* Retrieved June 26, 2007, from http://www.hrc.org/workplace

Israel, T. (2006). Marginalized communities in the United States: Oppression, social justice, and the role of counseling psychologists. In R. L. Toporek, L. H. Gerstein, N. A. Fouad, G. Roysircar, & T. Israel (Eds.), *Handbook for social justice in counseling psychology: Leadership, vision, and action* (pp. 149–154). Thousand Oaks, CA: Sage.

Iverson, S. V. (2006). Performing gender: A discourse analysis of theatre-based sexual violence prevention programs. *NASPA Journal, 43,* 547–577.

Karjane, H. M., Fisher, B. S., & Cullen, F. T. (2005). *Sexual assault on campus: What colleges and universities are doing about it.* U.S. Department of Justice, Office of Justice Program, National Institute of Justice: http://www.ncjrs.org/pdffiles1/nij/205521.pdf

Kochenderfer, B. J., & Ladd, G. W. (1996). Peer victimization: Cause or consequence of children's school adjustment difficulties? *Child Development, 67,* 1305–1317.

Kress, V. E., Shepherd, J. B., Anderson, R. I., Petuch, A. J., Nolan, J. M., & Thiemeke, D. (2006). Evaluation of the impact of a coeducational sexual assault prevention program on college students' rape myth attitudes. *Journal of College Counseling, 9,* 148–157.

Lee, C. C. (2002). The impact of belonging to a high school gay/straight alliance. *The High School Journal, 85*(5), 13–26.

Levin, B. (2002). From slavery to hate crime laws: The emergence of race and status-based protection in American criminal law. *Journal of Social Issues, 58,* 227–245.

Lonsway, K. A., & Fitzgerald, L. F. (1994). Rape myths: In review. *Psychology of Women Quarterly, 18*, 133–164.

Massachusetts Department of Education. (2002). *1999 Massachusetts Youth Risk Behavior Survey Results*. Malden, MA: Author.

Nansel, T. R., Overpeck, M., Pilla, R. S., Ruan, W. J., Simons-Morton, B., & Scheidt, P. (2001). Bullying behaviors among US youth: Prevalence and association with psychosocial adjustment. *Journal of the American Medical Association, 285*, 2094–2100.

Orpinas, P., & Horne, A. M. (2006). *Bullying prevention: Creating a positive school climate and developing social competence*. Washington, DC: American Psychological Association.

Pinar, W. F. (2003). The gender of violence on campus. In B. Ropers-Huilman (Ed.), *Gendered futures in higher education: Critical perspectives for change* (pp. 77–93). Albany, NY: State University of New York Press.

Ponterotto, J. G., Utsey, S. O., & Pedersen, P. B. (2006). *Preventing prejudice: A guide for counselors, educators, and parents*. Thousand Oaks, CA: Sage.

Public Broadcasting System. (n.d.). *Not in our town I: The original story*. Retrieved February 12, 2007, from http://www.pbs.org/niot/about/niot1.html

Ragins, B. R., & Cornwell, J. M. (2001). Pink triangles: Antecedents and consequences of perceived workplace discrimination against gay and lesbian employees. *Journal of Applied Psychology, 86*, 1244–1261.

Rostosky, S. S., & Riggle, E. D. B. (2002). "Out" at work: The relation of actor and partner workplace policy and internalized homophobia to disclosure status. *Journal of Counseling Psychology, 49*, 411–419.

Sandhu, D. S., & Aspy, C. B. (1997). *Counseling for prejudice prevention and reduction*. Alexandria, VA: American Counseling Association.

Sandler, B. R., & Shoop, R. J. (1997). What is sexual harassment? In B. R. Sandler & R. J. Shoop (Eds.), *Sexual harassment on campus* (pp. 1–21). Boston: Allyn & Bacon.

Schultz, S. K., Scherman, A., & Marshall, L. J. (2000). Evaluation of a university-based date rape prevention program: Effect on attitudes and behavior related to rape. *Journal of College Student Development, 41*, 193–201.

Schwartz, J. P., Griffin, L. D., Russell, M. M., & Frontaura-Duck, S. (2006). Prevention of dating violence on college campuses: An innovative program. *Journal of College Counseling, 9*(1), 90–96.

Schwartz, J. P., Magee, M. M., Griffin, L. D., & Dupuis, C. W. (2004). Effects of a group preventive intervention on risk and protective factors related to dating violence. *Group Dynamics: Theory, Research, and Practice, 8*, 221–231.

Smith, N. G., & Ingram, K. M. (2004). Workplace heterosexism and adjustment among lesbian, gay, and bisexual individuals: The role of unsupportive social interactions. *Journal of Counseling Psychology, 51*, 57–67.

Sobelsohn, D. C. (2003). Ending employment discrimination. In M. R. Stevenson & J. C. Cogan (Eds.), *Everyday activism: A handbook for lesbian, gay, and bisexual people and their allies* (pp. 105–122). New York: Routledge.

Southern Poverty Law Center. (n.d.). *Speak up: Responding to everyday bigotry.* Retrieved February 12, 2007, from http://www.tolerance.org/speakup/pdf/speak_up_full_document.pdf

Stevenson, M. R., & Cogan, J. C. (2003). *Everyday activism: A handbook for lesbian, gay, and bisexual people and their allies.* New York: Routledge.

Tjaden, P., & Thoennes, N. (2006). *Extent, nature, and consequences of rape victimization: Findings from the national violence against women survey.* Washington, DC: National Institute of Justice.

U.S. Department of Health and Human Services. (2001). *Mental health: Culture, race, and ethnicity. A supplement to Mental Health: A Report of the Surgeon General.* Rockville, MD: Author.

U.S. Equal Employment Opportunity Commission. (n.d.). *Sexual harassment.* Retrieved April 8, 2008, from http://www.eeoc.gov/types/sexual_harassment.html

Uribe, V. (1994). Project 10: A school-based outreach to gay and lesbian youth. *The High School Journal, 77,* 108–112.

Uribe, V., & Harbeck, K. M. (1991). Addressing the needs of lesbian, gay, and bisexual youth: The origins of PROJECT 10 and school-based intervention. *Journal of Homosexuality, 22,* 9–28.

Van Den Bergh, N. (Ed.). (1995). *Feminist practices in the 21st century.* Washington, DC: NASW Press.

Van Den Bergh, N. (Ed.). (2000). *Emerging trends for EAPs in the 21st century.* Binghamton, NY: Haworth Press.

Waldo, C. R. (1999). Working in a majority context: A structural model of heterosexism as minority stress in the workplace. *Journal of Counseling Psychology, 46,* 218–232.

Walworth, J. (2003). *Transsexual workers: An employer's guide.* Bellingham, WA: Center for Gender Sanity.

Winfeld, L. (2005). *Straight talk about gays in the workplace: Creating an inclusive, productive environment for everyone in your organization* (3rd ed.). Binghamton, NY: Harrington Park Press.

9

PROMOTING HEALTHY LIFESTYLES

THERESA L. BYRD AND BELINDA REININGER

Promoting healthy lifestyles is the focus of health education and health promotion programs. Given the amount of health information available, and the number of health education programs that have been developed, one would think there would be few health problems left to resolve. There is some good news about health, with reports of the death rate from cancer being at its lowest since statistics have been collected on the disease. Nevertheless, the prevalence of heart disease, cancer, diabetes, and lung disease, as well as morbidity and mortality related to intentional and unintentional injury, remain high. Underlying many health problems are lifestyle choices. For example, poor diet and lack of physical activity contribute to about 356,000 deaths annually (Mokdad, Marks, Stroup, & Gerberding, 2004, 2005). An additional 440,000 deaths are attributed to tobacco use (U.S. Department of Health and Human Services, 2004). Of course, these lifestyle choices must be interpreted in light of broader social and environmental issues, such as lack of health care coverage, lack of access to care and to other services and resources, poverty, and environmental contamination.

Deaths and associated morbidity occur disproportionately among poor and minority populations (Mokdad et al., 2004). For example, mortality rates for lung, colorectal, and breast cancer are higher among African Americans than Americans of other races or ethnicities ("Recent Trends in

Mortality Rates," 2002). Cervical cancer incidence and mortality rates are higher for Hispanic and African-American women than for non-Hispanic white women. The rate of invasive cervical cancer is twice as high for Hispanic women than non-Hispanic white women (O'Brien, Cokkinides, & Jemal, 2003). The mortality rate for all major causes of death (heart disease, cancer, stroke, accidents, and diabetes) is higher in African Americans than in white Americans (American Cancer Society, 2006). Health promotion practice focuses on those populations who are heavily burdened by death and disease. Often, health educators focus on individual behavior change because more than 40% of mortality in the United States can be attributed to individual behaviors (McGinnis & Foege, 1993). Importantly, however, health promotion practice recognizes that individual behavior is enmeshed in social, environmental, political, and cultural contexts. Moreover, the disparate morbidity and mortality rates seen among marginalized populations require interventions that influence lifestyle choices as well as other ecological factors.

Healthy People 2010 (http://www.healthypeople.gov), a project of the U.S. Department of Health and Human Services (USDHHS), guides the nation's efforts for addressing priority health issues among populations with health disparities. As such, *Healthy People 2010* has two overarching goals: (1) to increase quality and years of healthy life and (2) to eliminate health disparities. The report provides a comprehensive list of objectives for the nation, aimed at setting national priorities to improve health, and includes 28 focus areas, 467 specific objectives, and 10 leading health indicators (Exhibit 9.1). Many of these indicators differ by socioeconomic status and race/ethnicity, and many relate to lifestyle factors. According to the report, 40% of adults do not engage in leisure-time physical activity, but this percentage varies by race/ethnicity, gender, and educational level. This is a leading indicator because it is known that physical activity is associated with lower death rates in adults and decreases the risk of heart disease, diabetes, and some cancers. For example, among adults with less than a ninth-grade education, 73% do not engage in leisure-time physical activity. Women are less likely than men, and African Americans and Hispanics are less likely than non-Hispanic whites, to participate in physical activity. Some objectives in the report focus on changing environmental and health systems, whereas others focus on changing the lifestyle and behavior of individuals. An example of an objective focused on individual lifestyle change is to reduce by 20% the number of adults who engage in no leisure-time physical activity.

An associated health indicator is the rate of overweight and obesity. Attributed to lack of physical activity and poor diet, obesity has become one of the most important health issues of our day, with more than half of adults in the United States being overweight or obese (USDHHS, 2000). Over-

EXHIBIT 9.1
Healthy People 2010: Leading Health Indicators—
10 Major Public Health Issues

1. Physical activity
2. Overweight and obesity
3. Tobacco use
4. Substance abuse
5. Responsible sexual behavior
6. Mental health
7. Injury and violence
8. Environmental quality
9. Immunization
10. Access to health care

Note. From *Healthy People 2010: Understanding and Improving Health,* by the U.S. Department of Health and Human Services, 2000.

weight is also increasing in children and adolescents. According to the Centers for Disease Control and Prevention (CDC, 2007), the rate of overweight among children ages 6 to 11 years has more than doubled over the past 20 years, from 6.5% in 1980 to 18.8% in 2004. The news is even worse for adolescents: Their rates of overweight have tripled in the same time period. As with the other indicators, obesity and overweight are not equally distributed in the U.S. population and occur more often in lower income groups. Among adolescents, twice as many from poor households are overweight compared to those from middle and upper income homes (USDHHS, 2000). Obesity is also more common among Mexican-American and African-American women than non-Hispanic white women (Ogden et al., 2006).

Another health indicator that may not, at first glance, seem to be associated with lifestyle change is mental health. According to *Healthy People 2010*, about 20% of the U.S. population will be affected by mental illness during any given year. The most common of these illnesses is depression. Many people with depression are undiagnosed and not receiving treatment; only 23% of adults diagnosed with depression were receiving treatment in 1997 (USDHHS, 2000). Ethnic minorities may also be less likely to seek treatment for mental illness. African Americans and Hispanics, for example, are less likely to seek treatment for depression than others (Cooper et al., 2003). The *Healthy People 2010* goal is to increase the proportion of adults with recognized depression who receive treatment.

The prevalence of depression among women is between one and a half and three times more than that among men (Kessler, 2000; Kohen, 2000). In addition, higher rates of depression are associated with some medical conditions. For example, rates of depression are twice as high among people with diabetes (Anderson, Lustman, & Clouse, 2000), and especially among diabetics with poor glycemic control (Ciechanowski,

Katon, & Russo, 2000). Population-based studies have documented an association between depression and mortality in heart disease patients and in cancer patients (Unützer, Patrick, Marmon, Simon, & Katon, 2002; Onitilo, Nietert, & Egede, 2006). In addition to this association with physical illness, depression may make it more difficult for people suffering from diabetes and heart disease to follow the prescribed lifestyle changes.

These disparities in morbidity and mortality are troubling. Public health practice must have as its focus social justice, which includes a reduction of health disparities related to race, ethnicity, gender, and socioeconomic status. The role of public health is to ensure conditions in which all people can be healthy. The core functions of public health are *assessment*, or discovering the health issues in populations; *assurance*, making sure that health needs can be met; and *setting in place* policies and laws conducive to health (Institute of Medicine, 2003). In addition, public health should promote healthy lifestyles and prevent disease.

The goal of this chapter is to describe the promotion of health from the viewpoint of public health practice. The chapter comprises four sections. The first section defines health promotion, highlighting the dangers of victim blaming. The second section describes the most widely accepted theories of behavior change and health promotion. The third section describes the process of community assessment that informs an approach to developing or selecting an effective health promotion or disease prevention program. The final section examines a process for identifying effective programs, highlighting the importance of participatory action research and community empowerment.

HEALTH PROMOTION AND THE ECOLOGICAL MODEL

Research in the area of health promotion and disease prevention has shown that appropriate interventions can promote healthy behaviors. As described in other chapters of this volume, prevention-focused interventions have been applied in various settings, including schools, work sites, communities, and other organizations. Before discussing interventions, it is important to define health promotion.

Health promotion has been described as "any combination of educational and environmental supports for actions and conditions of living conducive to health" (Green & Kreuter, 1999, p. 27). Changing knowledge and attitudes through health education is only one component of this definition. Green and Kreuter also encourage consideration of an "ecological model" that extends beyond health education and information for behavior change to include broad goals for community, social, and political change.

Ecological models can be found in many disciplines. In general, these models take into account the individual and the environment when addressing health issues through health promotion efforts (Green, Richard, & Potvin, 1996). McLeroy, Bibeau, Steckler, and Glanz (1988) present an ecological model for health promotion that describes behavior as being determined by factors at the intrapersonal, interpersonal, institutional, community, and public policy levels. (See chaps. 3 and 13, this volume, for further discussion of ecological approaches to prevention and health promotion.)

Understanding health issues from an ecological perspective contributes to more sound, and possibly more effective, programs to promote health (Glanz & Rimer, 1997; Office on Smoking and Health, 1999). An ecological model recognizes health attitudes and values, which is consistent with the theoretical models that are commonly used to change individual behavior. An exclusive focus on changing individuals, however, ignores critical issues beyond the person. The ecological focus on both the individual and the environment prevents victim blaming and promotes attention to all of the factors that may be involved in lifestyle choices. Victim blaming (Ryan, 1976) occurs when the persons who are sick or harmed are blamed for their condition rather than acknowledging the influences from other levels of the ecological model. For example, in the story in Exhibit 9.2, Mary's doctor angrily blamed her for not making the changes in her eating and exercise habits that would lead to a decrease in blood glucose. Mary was at fault, according to her doctor, despite other factors external to her. Victim blaming is a form of social injustice that can become pervasive in public health interventions if care is not taken to examine and implement interventions using an ecological approach.

INDIVIDUAL THEORIES OF HEALTH PROMOTION

An important feature of effective public health interventions is a basis in theory (see chap. 3 for further discussion on the role of theory). Although many interventions have been developed using theories from social psychology and even clinical psychology, theories originating in other disciplines, such as sociology, communications, and political advocacy, have also been valuable.

Several theories commonly used in health promotion, including the Health Belief Model, the Theory of Reasoned Action/Planned Behavior, and the Transtheoretical Model, are aimed at understanding and predicting individual behavior. Another popular theory, Social Cognitive Theory, emphasizes "reciprocal determinism," or the premise that the environment, the person, and the behavior all act upon each other. For this reason, Social Cognitive Theory is often seen as more ecological than the other

EXHIBIT 9.2
Mary's Story

Mary was worried. She knew that this visit with Dr. Black was not going to go well. First of all, she missed the nine o'clock bus, because she had to make breakfast for the kids, get them off to school, and then take the youngest to her neighbor, because he had a fever. She arrived late for her appointment and then had to wait until they could "work her in." Then the nurse just told her that her hemoglobin A1c was way too high. She knew Dr. Black was going to be mad at her. He walked into the room reading her chart and muttering to himself. "Mary," he said in an exasperated tone, "we have talked about getting your sugar under control a million times. Your A1c is 13! Haven't you been following the diet? Have you started the exercise program we talked about? Are you taking your medicine?" "Well I . . ." Mary tried to begin an explanation. "I thought you went to the diabetes class in December. That was six months ago." Dr. Black shook his head, looking quite disappointed in her. "If you were following your program, you would have a much lower A1c by now! I can't understand why you can't get your sugar under control." Mary looked at the floor. "Well," she whispered, "it's harder than you think." Dr. Black continued looking at her chart. "Mary, I'm going to have the health educator come in and talk to you. I want your A1c down next time you come in. Do you understand how serious this is?" Mary didn't answer.

Dr. Black strode into the health educator's office. "Jim, I thought you told me that your new diabetes education program was going to work! Mary's A1c is worse than before. What are you telling these people?" Jim looked startled. "Well, it ought to work; it is based on a proven theoretical framework. As I recall, Mary did well on the posttest. She seemed to understand what she needed to do to get her sugar under control. Her responses to the attitude questions were right on. I have no idea why she is not following her program." Jim agreed to talk to Mary one more time.

"Mary," Jim said as he sat down on the stool across from her, "what is going on? I thought you understood the importance of following the diet and exercise program, and the need to take your medicine every day." Embarrassed, Mary looked at Jim. "Well, I want to do the right thing, but it is hard." Jim looked surprised. "Why?" he asked. "Well," Mary whispered, "the diet is hard to follow. My kids don't like the low-fat stuff, and my husband wants me to cook like I always have. Besides that, fruits and vegetables are so expensive, and the store in my neighborhood doesn't always have them." "Can't you go to another store? And what about the farmer's market we talked about?" Jim asked. "The problem is," Mary explained, "I don't have a car and, even if I did, gas is so expensive. The farmer's market is way on the other side of town, and it takes three buses to get there. Have you ever tried taking three different buses with three little kids in tow?" Jim had to admit that he had not. "And as for the medicine," Mary continued, "I don't have any insurance, and those pills are expensive. I can't afford to take them every day." Jim thought for a minute. "I think we can help you with that. Mary, you should have mentioned all this before." "Well," sighed Mary, "I have tried, but Dr. Black never seems to have the time to listen to me." "Okay, Mary. How about the exercise program? We talked about just walking. That doesn't cost anything!" "I know," Mary nodded, "but there are no sidewalks in my neighborhood, and no lights. Besides that, there are so many loose dogs around. I'm afraid one of them will bite me!"

behavior change theories. In developing interventions, researchers and practitioners also have the power to operationalize constructs in the way they see fit and to mix and match constructs from several theories. Behavior change theories, for example, may have implications for change at both the individual and ecological levels.

The Health Belief Model (HBM; Rosenstock, 1974) was one of the earliest models developed to predict or explain health behavior. It was developed in the 1950s by social psychologists working with the U.S. Public Health Service, who were interested in understanding why people were not accepting low-cost tuberculosis screening (x-ray). Although a new drug effective against the tuberculosis bacillus (TB) was available for the first time, people were reluctant to take advantage of the screening. Reluctance was related to the fact that the public was being asked to be screened for an infection in the absence of symptoms. Furthermore, even if people were infected with TB, they were still unlikely to develop symptoms. Using the HBM, psychologists were able to explain resistance to TB screening behavior to some extent by measuring people's perception of susceptibility to the disease as well as their perception that the screening test would be beneficial. Over the years, the HBM has developed to include six constructs: perceived susceptibility, perceived severity, perceived benefits of the behavior, perceived barriers to the behavior, perceived self-efficacy, and cues to action.

At first glance, this model appears to focus only on people's perceptions, ignoring ecological factors. However, some elements direct attention beyond the individual. Many perceived barriers are quite real and go beyond perceptions of the individual. In addition to personal barriers to screening, such as fear and embarrassment, environmental barriers—such as lack of transportation, poor or no insurance coverage, and lack of adequate screening facilities—might also influence willingness to be screened. These external barriers are clearly important to address; even if people wanted to get screened, they would not be able to do so if the facilities for screening did not exist or were not accessible. HBM has been used to explain, predict, and change a variety of health behaviors, including prenatal care, cancer screening, immunization, dietary intake, and medication adherence (e.g., Adams & Scott, 2000; Byrd, Chavez, & Wilson, 2007; Byrd, Mullen, Selwyn, & Lorimor, 1996; Byrd, Peterson, Chavez, & Heckert, 2004; Cummings, Jette, Brock, & Haefner, 1979; Ma et al., 2007; Sun, Guo, Wang, & Sun, 2006).

The Theory of Reasoned Action (Fishbein & Ajzen, 1975) and the Theory of Planned Behavior (Ajzen, 1991) are similar to the HBM, in that they focus on individual perceptions. Basically, the theories suggest that intention to act is directly linked to actual behavior, and this intention is influenced by attitudes toward the behavior and the "subjective norm." The *subjective norm* refers to what the person believes salient others think she or he should do and how much she or he is motivated to comply with those salient others. The theory of planned behavior adds a construct called *perceived behavioral control,* which focuses on the individual's feelings of control. The ecological model highlights factors in the social system that shape individual beliefs about the expectations of salient others. Ecologically, factors that shape attitudes might also be considered. For instance, if teenagers believe that smoking cigarettes is "cool" and that "everyone does it," attention may be given to how teens are portrayed in the media, how cigarette advertising is targeting teens, and how easily teens can obtain tobacco products in their community. These theories have been used to understand and develop interventions to change many health behaviors, including diet and exercise, safer sex activity, decisions about treatment for depression, and cancer screening (e.g., Barling & Moore, 1996; Basen-Engquist, 1992; Brewer, Blake, Rankin, & Douglass, 1999; Bryan, Fisher, & Fisher, 2002; Sheeran & Orbell, 2000; Smith & Biddle, 1999; Van Voorhees et al., 2005).

Other theories that are commonly used in the practice of health promotion are the Transtheoretical Model (Prochaska & DiClemente, 1983) and Social Cognitive Theory (Bandura, 1986). Similar to the other two theories discussed previously, the Transtheoretical Model focuses on the actions of the individual and takes into account the person's stage of readiness to change and the processes that enhance readiness. The stages of change include precontemplation, in which the person is not even thinking about change; contemplation, in which the person is weighing the pros and cons of changing; preparation, in which the person is planning for change; action, in which the person tries out the change; maintenance, in which the person has continued the changed behavior for some specified period of time; and relapse. According to this theory, different processes of change are useful in different stages for moving the person closer to change and maintenance. People use 10 processes (consciousness raising, dramatic relief, self-reevaluation, environmental reevaluation, self-liberation, helping relationships, counter-conditioning, reinforcement management, stimulus control, and social liberation) in changing their behavior as they move through the stages. Interventions developed using this framework can focus on helping individuals use appropriate processes, depending upon their stage. The model can also be expanded to examine social and political variables, especially as part of the change processes of environmental reevaluation (realizing the impact of behavior on one's social and physical environment) and social liberation (realizing that social norms are changing). This model has been widely used to explain and change a variety of health behaviors, even though it was originally developed for the cessation of addictive behaviors (Prochaska & DiClemente, 1983).

Social Cognitive Theory (Bandura, 1986) offers a number of constructs that can be applied in lifestyle change interventions. It assumes, like other value-expectancy theories, that individuals will consider the outcomes of their behavior (expectations) as well as the value they place upon these outcomes (expectancies). The construct of observational learning assumes that people can learn by watching the actions of others and the outcomes of those actions. Constructs such as environment (those factors external to the person), observational learning (acquiring new behaviors by watching others perform the behavior), and reinforcements (responses to the behavior that act to increase or decrease the behavior) invite us to focus on the organizational, community, and public policy levels.

Armed with theory, health educators and others interested in promoting healthy lifestyles have developed many interventions aimed at changing individual behavior. Mary's story illustrates the kind of frustration that health professionals may face when individual interventions are not effective because other ecological factors are not addressed. Individual knowledge, attitudes, and even good intentions do not always lead to the desired behavior, because factors outside the individual's control are also influential. In Mary's case, in addition to her personal concerns and interpersonal issues with the doctor, there were issues of family, community, the built environment, and policy. In the practice of public health promotion, these multiple levels of influence must be considered.

Because the focus of public health is on population-wide health promotion efforts, identification of relevant factors at various levels of influence can be accomplished through careful community assessment. The purpose of the community assessment is twofold. First, an assessment of the resources and needs of the community will allow the practitioner to develop appropriate interventions, in which the resources of the community are used and needs met. In addition, community assessment is one step in the process of building a sense of community empowerment and capacity. Community empowerment can be defined as a process "by which individuals, communities, and organizations gain mastery over their lives in the context of changing their social and political environment to improve equity and quality of life" (Minkler & Wallerstein, 2005, p. 34). Community capacity implies that community members participate actively in their community and learn to identify problems and resources, mobilize the community, and address problems with or without assistance from outside sources (Minkler & Wallerstein, 2005). To foster community empowerment and capacity, the community should be involved in the assessment and development of health promotion programs.

CONDUCTING A COMMUNITY ASSESSMENT

Before selecting an ecologically based intervention that addresses multiple levels of influence, it is necessary to identify the most important ecological influences placing a population at risk and the most important ecological influences keeping them from harm. Based on the authors' experience and the literature (Minkler, 1997; Reininger, Valentine, & Edwards, 2003; Wallerstein & Bernstein, 1994), we propose the following steps for conducting a community assessment and implementing a proven-effective intervention.

We will begin with a community assessment conducted to specifically select interventions that reduce the identified risks and enhance the identified protective factors. Taking time to assess the needs and assets of a community or population will help the practitioner understand the issues individuals must deal with on a daily basis, along with community-based resources that might be tapped.

Two general data sources should be used in a community assessment: secondary data sources (use of existing data resources) and primary data sources (first-hand collection of data from the population of interest). Community assessment should begin with a review of existing or secondary data sources relevant to the issue of concern. For health issues, this would include epidemiological data. Returning to Mary's story (Exhibit 9.2), it would be important to assess if other women like Mary are also not controlling their diabetes before developing a health promotion program. Therefore, interventionists should review local, state, and national health statistics indicating rates of diabetes and associated health outcomes such as heart disease and obesity. These comparisons provide an estimate of how prevalent the problem is among the populations of interest. Moreover, program planners should review data on behaviors associated with the health issue of interest. For example, physical activity and eating preferences are modifiable behaviors associated with diabetes and should be reviewed to better understand what behavioral patterns are placing the population at risk.

This initial review of secondary data should also include research literature, particularly survey studies regarding the issue and its related determinants. An important reason for the examination of secondary data sources is to identify specific sub-populations (e.g., age, gender, ethnic group) that are particularly burdened by the issue. This provides guidance concerning those specific groups that should be the focus of further assessment and will serve as partners in an intervention.

In the next step of the community assessment, interventionists should collect primary data from the subpopulation with high rates of the health problem and, importantly, with whom the organization has the capacity to work to conduct an intervention. Primary data are needed because secondary data rarely provide enough information for understanding the risks and protective factors associated with the health issue as it is manifested in a geographic and cultural context. Moreover, most secondary data do not provide insight into factors associated with the health outcome across ecological levels. Primary data can be collected by people from one organization or by a coalition of organizations and individuals. Importantly, the community assessment process can enhance empowerment if the assessment is done by working *with* the community rather than doing the assessment *on* the community (Wallerstein, 2002).

Collecting primary data from a sub-population in a particular community can take many forms, including various quantitative and qualitative data collection methods. Selecting the most appropriate assessment methods follows from careful consideration of many factors: the purpose of the assessment, culture and literacy of the population, sensitivity of questions, resources available, need to generalize findings, reporting needs, time, and expertise with each method. No one method is best; in fact, multiple methods can provide a richer understanding of the risk and protective factors (Creswell, 1994). Also, during the primary data collection it is beneficial to use behavioral theory to guide the focus of questions and data analysis. Using theory in this way will help the practitioner focus on relevant ecological factors. For example, the Health Belief Model suggests that barriers and benefits are important influences on behavior. Guided by the Health Belief Model, an assessment related to Mary would include examination of perceived barriers to physical activity and healthful food choices across several ecological levels (e.g., individual's negative attitudes toward exercise, family influence on unhealthful eating, community shopping locales with unhealthful food options, and lack of venues for physical activity) and perceived benefits for increasing physical activity and healthful food choices across ecological levels (e.g., individual positive attitudes and feelings about regular physical activity, family rewards for physical activity and healthful food choices, lower health care costs for better managed diabetes).

Primary data collection provides insight into the ecologically based influences on the health issue. A risk and protective factor assessment should gather data across several levels of the ecological model. Examining risks identifies factors that place people at increased probability for the outcome and examining protective mechanisms identifies those factors that decrease the probability of the adverse health outcome.

In Mary's example, she is not controlling her diabetes through exercise or food choice. Assessment should examine how other diabetic persons living near Mary might also be struggling to control their diabetes. Table 9.1 exemplifies types of risk and protective factors at multiple ecological levels. If Mary's health educator and others conducting the assessment had come into her community, talked to residents, and assessed the lack of social and physical infrastructure to support diabetes management, they might have better understood the difficulties of diabetes management for Mary and others in her community and would have identified the most important and modifiable factors for improving diabetes management. Important influences are those that the literature and the results of the community assessment have shown to contribute to the health issue. Modifiable influences are those that, from a political, economic, and cultural standpoint, can be addressed within a typical intervention period of 3 to 5 years. The final step

TABLE 9.1
Application of Mary's Story to an Ecological Framework

Level of influence	Risk	Protective
Individual (includes factors such as knowledge, attitudes, values, capacities, and maturity)	• Lack of finances to purchase healthier food options	• Knowledge of healthy eating and exercise needs
Interpersonal (includes factors such as relationships with spouses, partners, family, friends, and peers)	• Lack of exercise partners • Family does not want to eat healthy food options	
Organizational (includes factors such as normative support, resources, programs, and policies)	• Physician doesn't have time to spend with patients • Physician not reimbursed for counseling patients	• Health educator at the clinic
Community (includes factors such as media, social networks, social acceptance, and access to goods and services)	• Lack of access to affordable fruits and vegetables • No good public transportation • No child care options	
Policy (includes factors such as local, state, national, and international policy or regulations)	• Lack of enforcement of animal control policies • Lack of health care coverage • Built environment not conducive to exercise	

Note. Risk and protective factors across all levels may not present in all situations and/or may not be assessed in community assessment activities, and some factors may relate to more than one level.

of the assessment is to prioritize the risk and protective factors that are most important and most modifiable. Ultimately, these prioritized factors drive the selection of an evidence-based intervention.

IDENTIFYING PROVEN-EFFECTIVE ECOLOGICAL PROGRAMS TO PROMOTE HEALTHY LIFESTYLES

Interventions are effective when evidence exists that population-wide health outcomes (e.g., improvements in health status, reduction in disease or death rates, increase in protective behaviors, or decrease in risk behaviors) are achieved. Rigorous reviews of potentially effective interventions are underway to promote the implementation of evidence-based interventions in practice and to clearly identify in which areas the development of evidence-based interventions are needed (Zaza, Briss, & Harris, 2005).

Many effective interventions follow from an ecological approach (see chaps. 3 and 13, this volume, for further discussion). Interventions based on an ecological framework, which may also be referred to as *multilevel interventions, systems-approach interventions,* or *social-ecological interventions,* implement strategies to promote health by addressing factors beyond the individual level (Brownson et al., 2005; Elder et al., 2007; McLeroy et al., 1988).

In the case of Mary, a failure to consider ecological factors contributed to the failure of her health plan. An assessment of the community needs and resources might have led to the selection of a more appropriate evidence-based intervention. For example, an appropriate and effective intervention in this case might have included social action strategies to influence city council to provide better transportation services and venues for physical activity. An intervention that involved the community would have had the added benefit of providing opportunities for community empowerment. Moreover, the intervention might have included the establishment of walking groups where women could protect themselves and support one another in reaching their physical activity goals. As it was, the health educator's apparent lack of understanding of the community issues took him down a path that led to failure.

Three important steps when selecting the intervention will help address the most modifiable and important risk and protective factors among a specific sub-population or priority population. Working through these three steps helps to ensure that a participatory process for planning and implementing the intervention is followed, that the intervention will clearly focus on the health issue and determinants present among the priority population, and that the intervention is appropriately adapted to the cultural features of the priority population. (See chap. 3 for further discussion of best practice issues in prevention.) The three steps for selecting an intervention are: (1) forming a planning team, (2) systematically reviewing intervention options, and (3) adapting the intervention to the priority population.

Form a Planning Team

Establishing a planning team—the first step in selecting a proven-effective intervention—is a specific strategy to foster community-based participatory research. This planning team should involve several community members who might be facing the health problem (e.g., persons living with diabetes) or who have constituents who are affected by it (e.g., religious leaders, local business leaders), staff from local organizations who may be addressing the issue (e.g., nonprofit organizations, advocacy groups, health service organizations), and practitioners and researchers who have related expertise. In the end, it will be beneficial to have a diversified group of people who are willing to listen to one another's ideas and to commit to a process of jointly working to select and implement an evidence-based intervention.

Public health is moving toward community-based participatory research, also called *participatory action research* (PAR), as a means of involving community members, organizations, and researchers in an equitable process to address health issues (Israel, 1998). Although a PAR approach does not completely ensure that the community assessment process or the selection of a proven effective intervention will focus on the multiple ecological levels impacting the health issue, it can assist in eliciting various viewpoints about the causes of the problem and insights into solutions. For example, had Mary's health educator been working with multiple people and organizations from the community to select an intervention, he would have had the opportunity to learn about the variety of struggles and roadblocks in managing diabetes and the best strategies for supporting change, rather than blaming or scolding her.

Systematically Review Evidence-Based Intervention Options

The second step in the process is for the planning team to systematically and thoroughly review intervention options. It is important to ensure that the process is both systematic and clearly focused on the issue and determinants found in the priority population. The planning group should create a logic model minimally depicting the health outcome desired, the behaviors related to the health outcome, and the prioritized risk and protective factors that contribute to the presence of the behaviors. Figure 9.1 exemplifies a logic model used for identifying an evidence-based intervention for Mary's community.

Once the intervention is selected, the planning team should create a much more detailed logic model, where the concepts in Figure 9.1 are rewritten as specific objectives with the intervention approach in mind (e.g., time frames and study design). Process objectives focusing on tasks for implementing the intervention should also be added to the logic model. The initial logic model is important for the planning team to develop for two reasons. First, by working together and focusing on those factors—behaviors and outcomes that are crucial for success of the intervention—the planning team sharpens a shared understanding of the issue and identifies a common vision for the intervention. Second, establishing the logic model prior to searching the options for evidence-based intervention keeps the planning team focused on its vision for the intervention rather than being swayed by techniques, marketing, or individual preferences. Several options for logic model development are presented in the literature (Alter & Murty, 1997; Carroll & McKenna, 2001; Millar, Simeone, & Carnevale, 2001; W. K. Kellogg Foundation, 2004).

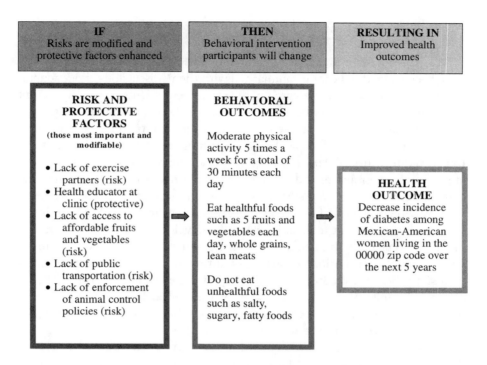

| **IF** Risks are modified and protective factors enhanced | **THEN** Behavioral intervention participants will change | **RESULTING IN** Improved health outcomes |

RISK AND PROTECTIVE FACTORS
(those most important and modifiable)

- Lack of exercise partners (risk)
- Health educator at clinic (protective)
- Lack of access to affordable fruits and vegetables (risk)
- Lack of public transportation (risk)
- Lack of enforcement of animal control policies (risk)

BEHAVIORAL OUTCOMES

Moderate physical activity 5 times a week for a total of 30 minutes each day

Eat healthful foods such as 5 fruits and vegetables each day, whole grains, lean meats

Do not eat unhealthful foods such as salty, sugary, fatty foods

HEALTH OUTCOME
Decrease incidence of diabetes among Mexican-American women living in the 00000 zip code over the next 5 years

Figure 9.1. Example of logic model used for selecting evidence-based intervention. Adapted from "BDI Logic Models," by D. Kirby, 2004, and "Steps to Success in Community-Based HIV/AIDS Prevention," by B. Reininger and C. Collins, 2005. Copyright 2004 by Douglas Kirby. Adapted with permission of the authors.

Once the logic model is in place, it is time to identify relevant evidence-based interventions. The planning team should divide the various sources and ideally use a review sheet to document findings. Reviewing the intervention's priority populations, objectives, health outcomes, strength of evidence of effectiveness for the priority population, and intervention strategies, including ecological levels, theoretical models, implementation requirements (e.g., staff, materials, costs), and evaluation requirements (e.g., evaluation instruments and consultant), will provide the review team with data for selecting the best intervention options. After the team members discuss the results of their intervention review, they can select the intervention option that best fits their logic model, priority population, and budget. Following this decision, the planning team should obtain funding and materials and provide training to move forward into adaptation and implementation.

Adapting the Intervention

Once the team members have obtained the intervention materials and have been trained or become familiarized with them, discussions about adaptation should begin. From a research perspective these discussions are important as the intervention cannot be adapted to change the important elements (e.g., strategies, materials, messages, venues, theoretical underpinnings) of the intervention that make it effective. From a planning perspective, it is important that the intervention elements (e.g., strategies, materials, messages, venues) are culturally appropriate and feasible for the priority population. Finding the balance between program fidelity and local adaptation is the goal of this step.

When considering how to adapt—and for that matter, select—an intervention, it is important to examine what the developers consider the core elements. In some cases this could include the population that receives the intervention, the intervention materials, or intervention strategies, oftentimes related to theoretical constructs. For example, the Social Cognitive Theory construct of self-efficacy can be operationalized through guided practice role plays, where participants receive feedback about their ability to perform a specific skill. By removing the role plays or changing the intervention so that feedback is not given, a core element of the intervention would be missing, thus making it a different, and possibly less effective, intervention. The planning team should consider these unalterable elements as off-limits for modification since changing the elements creates a new intervention, which is no longer scientifically supported. Kelly (2004) describes how poor replication can undermine the effectiveness of an evidence-based intervention. Features of the intervention that are modifiable may include logistics associated with delivery of the intervention, including venues for the intervention, people who deliver the intervention, and times and frequency of intervention sessions.

Once the modifications are completed, it is best to pilot-test the adapted intervention. The pilot initially may include focus groups or interviews with potential participants to review the materials, followed by recruiting, training, and evaluating strategies with the priority population. If the planning team has done a good job of maintaining membership of and listening to its community members, the intervention piloting should provide very few surprises.

Once the pilot testing and final refinement of the intervention strategies are complete, it is time to fully implement and evaluate the intervention. As is clear from this discussion, community assessment results—particularly the risk and protective factor assessment findings—drive the selection of an intervention. Selecting a proven effective intervention is not a quick or necessarily easy process; however, systematically reviewing proven effective interventions and then adapting the intervention for the priority population provides a foundation for improving health outcomes.

CONCLUSION

Assessing needs and assets and implementing interventions requires an understanding of how individuals and groups of people change their behaviors. Using an ecological approach allows interventionists to assess the potential for behavior change in a broad context of influences, including policies, community organizations, interpersonal networks, and individual characteristics. Even though it may be more complicated to plan than interventions focusing on only one level, an ecological approach also allows interventionists to more comprehensively address the factors most likely to influence healthful behaviors. Note that not all interventions using an ecological approach are identical—in fact, far from it. Some ecological interventions focus solely on policy change, whereas others focus solely on community-level, organizational, or interpersonal changes. Other ecologically focused interventions include multiple components to address various features of the ecological model. At this point in intervention research, the elements of an ecological model that are essential to produce positive changes across populations have not been determined. However, many of the options for proven-effective interventions use an ecological framework to help populations make the behavior changes that result in better health outcomes (Kelly et al., 1997; Perry et al., 1997; Stigler, Perry, Komro, Cudeck, & Williams, 2006).

Implementing evidence-based interventions that are developed through community involvement in both the assessment of health problems and the selection of interventions is an important strategy for achieving equity in health outcomes. This community-based research process builds relationships between populations that are bearing the burden of morbidity and mortality and the researchers and practitioners whose careers are devoted to addressing those concerns. Finally, communities and individuals most affected by health issues deserve effective ecological programs, not just band-aid approaches.

REFERENCES

Adams, J., & Scott, J. (2000). Predicting medication adherence in severe mental disorders. *Acta Psychiatrica Scandinavica, 101,* 119–124.

Ajzen, I. (1991). The theory of planned behavior. *Organizational Behavior and Human Decision Processes, 50,* 197–211.

Alter, C., & Murty, S. (1997). Logic modeling: A tool for teaching practice evaluation. *Journal of Social Work Education, 33,* 103–117.

American Cancer Society. (2006). *Cancer facts and figures for African Americans 2005–2006.* Atlanta, GA: Author.

Anderson, R. J., Lustman, P. J., & Clouse, R. E. (2000). Prevalence of depression in adults with diabetes: A systematic review. *Diabetes, 49*, A64.

Bandura, A. (1986). *Social foundations of thought and action*. Englewood Cliffs, NJ: Prentice Hall.

Barling, N. R., & Moore, S. M. (1996). Prediction of cervical cancer screening using the theory of reasoned action. *Psychological Reports, 79*, 77–78.

Basen-Engquist, K. (1992). Psychosocial predictors of "safer sex" behaviors in young adults. *AIDS Education & Prevention, 4*, 120–134.

Brewer, J. L., Blake, A. J., Rankin, S. A., & Douglass, L. W. (1999). Theory of reasoned action predicts milk consumption in women. *Journal of the American Dietetic Association, 99*, 39–44.

Brownson, R. C., Hagood, L., Lovegreen, S. L., Britton, B., Caito, N. M., Elliott, M. B., et al. (2005). A multilevel ecological approach to promoting walking in rural communities. *Preventive Medicine, 41*, 837–842.

Bryan, A., Fisher, J. D., & Fisher, W. A. (2002). Tests of the mediational role of preparatory safer sexual behavior in the context of the theory of planned behavior. *Health Psychology, 21*, 71–80.

Byrd, T. L., Chavez, R., & Wilson, K. M. (2007). Barriers and facilitators of Pap test screening in Hispanic women. *Ethnicity and Disease, 17*, 129–134.

Byrd, T. L., Mullen, P. D., Selwyn, B., & Lorimor, R. (1996). Initiation of prenatal care by low-income Hispanic women in Houston. *Public Health Reports, 111*, 70–74.

Byrd, T. L., Peterson, S. K., Chavez, R., & Heckert, A. (2004). Cervical cancer screening beliefs among young Hispanic women. *Preventive Medicine, 38*, 192–197.

Carroll, J., & McKenna, J. (2001). Theory to practice: Using the logic model to organize and report research results in a collaborative project. *Journal of Family and Consumer Science, 93*(4), 63–65.

Centers for Disease Control and Prevention. (2007). *Childhood overweight*. Retrieved September 5, 2007, from http://www.cdc.gov/nccdphp/dnpa/obesity/childhood/

Ciechanowski, P. S., Katon, W. J., & Russo, J. E. (2000). Depression and diabetes: Impact of depressive symptoms on adherence, function, and costs. *Archives of Internal Medicine, 160*, 3278–3285.

Cooper, L. A., Gonzales, J. J., Gallo, J. J., Rost, K. M., Meredith, L. S., & Rubenstein, L. V. (2003). The acceptability of treatment for depression among African American, Hispanic, and white primary care patients. *Medical Care, 41*, 479–489.

Creswell, J. W. (1994). *Research design: Qualitative and quantitative approaches*. Thousand Oaks, CA: Sage.

Cummings, K. M., Jette, A. M., Brock, B. M., & Haefner, D. P. (1979). Psychosocial determinants of immunization behavior in a swine influenza campaign. *Medical Care, 17*, 639–649.

Elder, J. P., Lytle, L., Sallis, J. F., Young, D. R., Steckler, A., Simons-Morton, D., et al. (2007). A description of the social-ecological framework used in the trial of activity for adolescent girls (TAAG). *Health Education Research, 22,* 155–165.

Fishbein, M., & Ajzen, I. (1975). *Belief, attitude, intention and behavior: An introduction to theory and research.* Reading, MA: Addison-Wesley.

Glanz, K., & Rimer, B. K. (1997). *Theory at a glance: A guide for health promotion practice.* Washington, DC: National Cancer Institute, National Institutes of Health, U.S. Department of Health and Human Services.

Green, L. W., & Kreuter, M. W. (1999). *Health promotion planning: An educational and ecological approach.* Mountain View, CA: Mayfield.

Green, L. W., Richard, L., & Potvin, L. (1996). Ecological foundations of health promotion. *American Journal of Health Promotion, 10,* 270–281.

Institute of Medicine. (2003). *The future of the public's health.* Washington, DC: National Academy Press.

Israel, B. A. (1998). Review of community-based research: Assessing partnership approaches to improve public health. *Annual Review of Public Health, 19,* 173–202.

Kelly, J. A., Murphy, D. A., Sikkema, K. J., McAuliffe, T. L., Roffman, R. A., Solomon, L. J., et al. (1997). Randomised, controlled, community-level HIV-prevention intervention for sexual-risk behaviour among homosexual men in US Cities. Community HIV Prevention Research Collaborative. *Lancet, 350,* 1500–1505.

Kelly, J. A. (2004). Popular opinion leaders and HIV prevention peer education: Resolving discrepant findings and implications for the development of effective community programmes. *AIDS Care, 16,* 139–150.

Kessler, R. C. (2000). Gender differences in major depression. In E. Frank (Ed.), *Gender and its effects on psychopathology* (p. 61). Washington, DC: American Psychiatric Press.

Kirby, D. (2004). *BDI logic models: A useful tool for designing, strengthening and evaluating programs to reduce adolescent sexual risk-taking, pregnancy, HIV, and other STDs.* Retrieved March 15, 2008, from http://www.ihpl.org/pdf/Module_3.pdf.

Kohen, D. (2000). Introduction. In D. Kohen (Ed.), *Women and mental health* (pp. 1–16). Philadelphia: Routledge.

Ma, G. X., Fang, C. Y., Shive S. E., Toubbeh, J., Tan, Y., & Siu, P. (2007). Risk perceptions and barriers to hepatitis B screening and vaccination among Vietnamese immigrants. *Journal of Immigrant & Minority Health, 9*(3), 213–220.

McGinnis, J. M., & Foege, W. H. (1993). Actual causes of death in the United States. *Journal of the American Medical Association, 270,* 2207–2212.

McLeroy, K. R., Bibeau, D., Steckler, A., & Glanz, K. (1988). An ecological perspective on health promotion programs. *Health Education Quarterly, 15*(4), 351–377.

Millar, A., Simeone, R., & Carnevale, J. (2001). Logic models: A systems tool for performance management. *Evaluation and Program Planning, 24,* 73–81.

Minkler, M. (1997). *Community organizing and community building for health.* New Brunswick, N J: Rutgers University Press.

Minkler, M., & Wallerstein, N. (2005). Improving health through community organization and community building: A health education perspective. In M. Minkler (Ed.), *Community organizing and community building for health* (pp. 26–50). New Brunswick, NJ: Rutgers University Press.

Mokdad, A. H., Marks, J. S., Stroup, D. F., & Gerberding, J. L. (2004). Actual causes of death in the United States—2000. *Journal of the American Medical Association, 291,* 1238–1245.

Mokdad, A. H., Marks, J. S., Stroup, D. F., & Gerberding, J. L. (2005). Correction: Actual causes of death in the United States—2000. *Journal of the American Medical Association, 293,* 293–294.

O'Brien, K., Cokkinides, V., & Jemal, A. (2003). Cancer statistics for Hispanics. *CA: A Cancer Journal for Clinicians, 53,* 208–226.

Office on Smoking and Health, National Center for Chronic Disease Prevention and Health Promotion, Centers for Disease Control and Prevention, & U.S. Department of Health and Human Services. (1999). *Best practices for comprehensive tobacco control programs.* Atlanta, GA: Office on Smoking and Health.

Ogden, C. L., Carroll, M. D., Curtin, L. R., McDowell, M. A., Tabak, C. J., & Flegal, K. M. (2006). Prevalence of overweight and obesity in the United States 1999–2004. *Journal of the American Medical Association, 295,* 1549–1555.

Onitilo, A. A., Nietert, P. J., & Egede, L. E. (2006). Effect of depression on all-cause mortality in adults with cancer and differential effects by cancer site. *General Hospital Psychiatry, 28,* 396–402.

Perry, C. L., Sellers, D. E., Johnson, C., Pederson, S., Bachman, K. J., Parcel, G. S., et al. (1997). The child and adolescent trial for cardiovascular health (CATCH) intervention, implementation and feasibility of elementary schools in the United States. *Health Education and Behavior, 24,* 716–735.

Prochaska, J. O., & DiClemente, C. C. (1983). Stages and processes of self-change of smoking: Toward an integrative model of change. *Journal of Consulting and Clinical Psychology, 51,* 390–395.

Recent trends in mortality rates for four different cancers by sex and race/ethnicity— United States 1990-1998. (2002). *Morbidity and Mortality Weekly Report, 51*(3), 49–53.

Reininger, B., & Collins, C. (2005). *Steps to success in community-based HIV/AIDS prevention. How to monitor and measure evidence-based intervention effectiveness: Module 3—Building Evaluation Capacity.* Retrieved March 15, 2008, from http://www.ihpl.org/pdf/module3.pdf

Reininger, B., Valentine, J., & Edwards, K. (2003). *Steps to success in community-based HIV/AIDS prevention: How to determine who is at risk and why.* Atlanta, GA: Centers for Disease Control and Prevention.

Rosenstock, I. M. (1974). Historical origins of the health belief model. *Health Education Monographs, 2*, 328–335.

Ryan, W. (1976). *Blaming the victim*. New York: Random House Press.

Sheeran, P., & Orbell, S. (2000). Using implementation intentions to increase attendance for cervical cancer screening. *Health Psychology, 19*(3), 283–289.

Smith, R. A., & Biddle, S. J. (1999). Attitudes and exercise adherence: Test of the theories of reasoned action and planned behaviour. *Journal of Sports Sciences, 17*(4), 269–281.

Stigler, M. H., Perry, C. L., Komro, K. A., Cudeck, R., & Williams, C. L. (2006). Teasing apart a multiple component approach to adolescent alcohol prevention: What worked in Project Northland? *Prevention Science, 7*, 269–280.

Sun, X., Guo, Y., Wang, S., & Sun, J. (2006). Predicting iron-fortified soy sauce consumption intention: Application of the theory of planned behavior and health belief model. *Journal of Nutrition Education & Behavior, 38*(5), 276–285.

Unützer, J., Patrick, D. L., Marmon, T., Simon, G. E., & Katon, W. J. (2002). Depressive symptoms and mortality in a prospective study of 2,558 older adults. *The American Journal of Geriatric Psychiatry, 10*(5), 521–530.

U.S. Department of Health and Human Services. (2000). *Healthy People 2010: Understanding and improving health* (2nd ed.). Washington, DC: U.S. Government Printing Office.

U.S. Department of Health and Human Services. (2004). *The health consequences of smoking: A report of the Surgeon General*. Retrieved September 16, 2008, from http://surgeongeneral.gov/library/smokingconsequences/

Van Voorhees, B. W., Fogel, J., Houston, T. K., Cooper, L. A., Wang, N. Y., & Ford D. E. (2005). Beliefs and attitudes associated with the intention to not accept the diagnosis of depression among young adults. *Annals of Family Medicine, 3*(1), 38–46.

Wallerstein, N. (2002). Empowerment to reduce health disparities. *Scandinavian Journal of Public Health, 30*, 72–77.

Wallerstein, N., & Bernstein, E. (Eds.). (1994). Community empowerment, participatory education, and health. *Health Education Quarterly, 21*, 141–148.

W. K. Kellogg Foundation. (2004). *W.K. Kellogg Foundation logic model development guide*. Retrieved July 31, 2007, from http://www.wkkf.org/default.aspx?tabid=101&CID=281&CatID=281&ItemID=2813669&NID=20&LanguageID=0

Zaza, S., Briss, P. A., & Harris, K. W. (Eds.). (2005). *The guide to community preventive services: What works to promote health? Task force on community preventive services*. New York: Oxford University Press.

10

DEVELOPING HEALTHY FAMILY RELATIONSHIPS

MICHAEL WALDO, ARTHUR M. HORNE, AND MAUREEN E. KENNY

A fifth-grade Mexican American, Marta, attended her first day of school in New Mexico shortly after moving there from Texas. Marta was just beginning to master English. She had been teased at her previous school for speaking Spanish, and her former teacher was critical of her school performance. Marta's mother had attended meetings with other Spanish-speaking parents to discuss supporting their children's educations. She accompanied her daughter to school and with the help of a translator, explained to Marta's new teacher that her child was very bright and she hoped Marta would get the best education possible at the school. Marta's mother asked to be informed about her daughter's progress and indicated that she would help out at home. On the way home, she told her daughter that she was enrolled in a good school and that she must try very hard. Marta subsequently graduated near the top of her class in high school and pursued a degree in nursing. Marta believes her experiences as an outsider and her being bilingual will enable her to be especially helpful to Mexican-American women.

A 40-year-old husband and father experienced a downturn in his business that caused him to doubt his value as a provider. That night he decided his wife was spoiling their daughter by spending too much time with her as she put her to bed. He told his wife to leave their daughter's room, and when she didn't, he violently grabbed his wife's arms and ushered her out, bruising his wife and terrifying their daughter. Deeply shamed, the man later contemplated suicide but yielded to his pastor's advice and admitted himself to a hospital. After discharge, he joined a men's group focused on preventing domestic violence, and he and his wife participated in a parent education workshop.

These examples from the authors' clinical experience demonstrate the profound impact families have on the development and well-being of their members. Families vary greatly in size, structure, composition, race, culture, religion, and access to societal power and economic resources, but all play critical roles in providing support and nurturance for family members and preparing them for engagement in the world beyond the family. The central role families play in fostering the adjustment and development of their members has been consistently acknowledged in counseling theory since the early work of Freud and Adler. However, despite Adler's advocacy for parent education in child guidance clinics as early as the 1920s (Dreikurs, Corsini, Lowe, & Sonstegard, 1959), psychological interventions with families were not commonly practiced until the 1950s. As is suggested by the examples that began this chapter, engaging in prevention and health promotion efforts with families is particularly compelling.

Families are critically important social systems that have profound effects on their members and the other social systems (e.g., schools, neighborhoods, workplaces) with which they interact (Boyd-Franklin, 2003; Horne, 2000). A family's capacity to provide growth-fostering nurturance and guidance is influenced by internal family processes, which are affected by factors external to the family, such as the experience of societal oppression, stress, discrimination, and access to social, political, and economic resources. Strong and supportive family relationships also promote resilience, enabling family members to cope more effectively with external stressors related to work, school, poverty, and racism (Kumpfer, 1999). Stronger families not only generate stronger individuals but also contribute to stronger schools and communities. As illustrated in the story of Marta, strong families can organize themselves and advocate for improved access to societal resources.

As suggested by general systems theory (VonBertalanffy, 1968) and social ecological perspectives on human development (Brofenbrenner, 1979), the examples at the beginning of the chapter highlight the complex interactions that occur between individuals, families, and society. In both examples, the individuals' characteristics (e.g., ethnicity, development, gender, personality) interacted with the characteristics of the family system (e.g., degree of support, authoritarianism, gender roles), and together these factors interacted with other systems in society (e.g., education, religion, economics). The first example highlights how a family's cultural heritage can be both a target for derision and a source of strength; the second how gender roles can affect the adjustment of family members and how factors external to the family system, such as downturns in the economy resulting in job loss, affect processes internal to the family. The examples illustrate how families can help prepare their members as active and informed citizens and how community services (e.g., school support for parents, group counseling/therapy) can help families fulfill their developmental role.

All interventions with families have the potential for prevention. For example, *primary prevention* interventions, such as premarital couples' communication workshops, have the potential to strengthen couples' problem-solving skills so they will not engage in destructive conflicts that harm them and their future children (Guerney, 1977). Early remedial interventions (referred to as *secondary prevention*, because they strive for early detection and resolution of problems to prevent the problems from getting worse) also have potential primary prevention effects in families because they prevent a problem experienced by one family member from causing problems for other family members. For example, early detection and treatment of a mother's post-partum depression can prevent bonding and developmental problems for her infant (Keitner & Miller, 1990). Similarly, rehabilitation interventions (referred to as *tertiary prevention* because they focus on preventing problems that cannot be eliminated from causing other problems) can serve as primary prevention in families. For example, couples counseling with a family in which the father suffers from chronic alcoholism may limit the negative impact of that disorder on others in the family (O'Farrell, Choquette, & Cutter, 1998).

This chapter focuses on primary, secondary, and tertiary prevention and health promotion with families. The first section describes family systems theories, explains how family systems promote resilience by fostering strengths and preventing dysfunction, and integrates these concepts into a framework for prevention planning. The second section discusses risk/protective factors and social learning in family systems, and principles for effective family-focused prevention. The third section addresses how family prevention programs can be implemented to reduce risks and promote protective factors related to aggression and violence in young people and explains how such programs incorporate social learning and family systems theories. Examples of prevention and early intervention programs that have been developed to have an impact on youth aggression through family systems are also presented.

FAMILY SYSTEMS THEORIES

The many ways families promote positive development and resilience can best be understood through the framework of systems theory (VonBertalanffy, 1968). Researchers and clinicians have employed systems theory to understand family systems from intergenerational (Bowen, 1978), structural (Minuchin, 1980), strategic (Haley, 1976), attachment style (Ainsworth & Bowlby, 1991), conflict resolution (Rahim, 1983), and communication (Satir, 1967) perspectives. These perspectives offer complementary explanations of how family systems function and foster strengths in family members.

Intergenerational Family Systems

Bowen (1978) proposed that healthy families foster the ability of their members to differentiate their thoughts from their emotions and to differentiate themselves from others. Family members need to differentiate themselves, even as they remain connected in adaptive ways (Boyd-Franklin, 2003). Emotional systems in families that are entangled and fused prevent their members from achieving differentiation, resulting in vulnerability to volatile emotions and dependency in relationships. Undifferentiated individuals tend to seek romantic partners who are similarly dependent, in an effort to fulfill their dependency needs. But two undifferentiated partners are rarely able to consistently satisfy each others' needs. Like a two-legged stool, their relationship is inherently unstable. To deal with unmet emotional dependence, the couple will focus emotional needs on a third person or activity, like a third leg for a stool. The process is referred to as *triangulation*. Although activities (gambling, substance abuse, extramarital affairs, work) can perform this role, triangulation often is projected on a child in the family. If the parental family system is emotionally dependent on the child for stability, the triangulated child's ability to differentiate is compromised. That child, as an adult, will seek a partner with a similar lack of differentiation, continuing the cycle and transmitting low levels of differentiation to yet another generation. On the other hand, differentiated individuals tend to partner with similarly mature spouses. Because they are not emotionally dependent, they can promote healthy differentiation in their children. The theory also suggests that major contextual traumatic stressors (e.g., poverty, oppression, war, dislocation) can reduce differentiation in family systems and affect future generations (Lev-Wiesel, 2007). Families that do not suffer traumatic stress are more likely to promote healthy differentiation and pass that to future generations.

Bowen's intergenerational systems theory provides important concepts for understanding how family systems relate to prevention. It explains how promoting healthy family systems can result in greater differentiation and emotional well-being for immediate family members and for subsequent generations (including reducing the likelihood of alcoholism, gambling, etc.). Acknowledging that immediate and future generations of family members' levels of differentiation may be affected by major contextual stressors suggests that protecting families from stress and helping them deal with trauma could result in profound long-term benefits. The theory also provides direction for the development of prevention activities that increase differentiation in family systems. For example, Griffin and Apostal (1993) describe a prevention program for married couples that influences differentiation. Participants learned to identify and express their own emotions and to understand and acknowledge their partners' emotions. After practicing these skills with their spouses, they showed significant gains in levels of differentiation.

Structural Family Systems

Minuchin's (1980) structural approach to family systems focuses on sociological and anthropological perspectives regarding family structure, subsystems within the family system, and boundaries. Minuchin describes the healthy family as one in which parent and child subsystems are separated and delineated by clear boundaries. Unhealthy family structures include subsystems composed of a parent and "parentified" child, or one in which one parent is split away from the family. Minuchin describes a continuum of boundaries in families, ranging from diffuse boundaries in enmeshed family structures to rigid boundaries occurring in disengaged family structures.

Minuchin's structural perspective can explain how differentiation, as described by Bowen, is expressed in family systems (Johnson & Waldo, 1998). Differentiated families develop appropriate boundaries. Lack of differentiation can result in family dysfunction, such as diffuse family boundaries and enmeshed relationships or rigid boundaries erected to overcompensate for unfulfilled dependency. The structural perspective can also inform prevention efforts. Preventive interventions can help families develop healthy boundaries and subsystem structures. Minuchin and his colleagues have successfully employed these principles to promote social justice by building resiliency in families that face the risks associated with poverty (Minuchin, Colopinto, & Minuchin, 1998). Minuchin's structural approach and Bowen's intergenerational approach have been extended by other family systems theorists who recognize the need to understand the role of gender and culture in family processes and to extend work with families to multiple systems, including non-blood kin, churches, community organizations, and medical and social service systems (Boyd-Franklin, 2003; McDaniel, Lusterman, & Philpot, 2001; McGoldrick, 1998; McGoldrick et al., 1999).

Strategic Family Therapy

Jackson, Haley, and Madanes are among a number of authors who have written about the strategic approach to understanding family systems. This approach employs cognitive and behavioral principles to understand families (Haley, 1976; Jackson, 1964; Madanes, 1981). Rather than concentrating on underlying emotional dynamics or the structure of relationships, the strategic approach focuses on repetitive circular sequences of behavior that regulate closeness within family systems. Consider this series of events: A mother becomes extensively invested in work, her husband feels neglected and becomes irritable with their child, the child develops an eating disorder, the mother reduces her time at work and spends more time at home to care for the child, the father becomes less irritable and punitive toward the child, the child's eating disorder subsides, and the mother begins to reinvest in work. The strategic approach exemplifies family systems thinking in its identification of first- and second-order change. First-order change addresses the symptom: reducing the eating disorder. Second-order change addresses the underlying system of circular behaviors that perpetuate the symptom: improving parental closeness and openness.

Circular behavioral exchanges maintain the stability (homeostasis) of the family structure and boundaries described by Minuchin. For example, families with rigid boundaries and disengaged members will behave in ways that maintain these positions. In this type of family system, family members of a husband/father who is remote and abuses alcohol will maintain stasis by making sure he has access to alcohol, making excuses for his absence at family events, and not discussing their feelings about his drinking. The strategic approach also points to preventive interventions for families. For example, direct training in behavior that promotes healthy family structure and boundaries (e.g., prescribing a weekly date for a married couple as a way to prevent their child from forcing parental interaction by exhibiting behavior problems) could promote family strength and prevent problems. Once established, family homeostasis then perpetuates these positive behaviors, increasing the likelihood of sustained and generalized positive change. For example, the Brief Strategic Family Therapy Program (Santisteban et al., 1996) employs structural and strategic techniques to prevent conduct disorder and socialized aggression among Hispanic youth. The program has demonstrated improvements in family functioning and reductions in problem behaviors in comparison to control groups and individual counseling approaches.

Attachment Style and Conflict Resolution

The circular behavioral exchanges described previously have a potential impact on children's development of attachment styles and approaches to conflict. Attachment styles are the internal working models children develop through interaction with their parents regarding their self-worth and the responsiveness of others (Ainsworth & Bowlby, 1991; Bartholomew & Horowitz, 1991). Attachment styles can be expressed in approaches to conflict that reflect levels of concern for self and others (Rahim, 1983). Attachment styles and approaches to conflict correspond to dimensions on the family system boundary continuum described by Minuchin (1980) and levels of differentiation described by Bowen (1978), as follows:

- *Secure attachment* and an *integrative approach* to conflict can emerge from positive views of self and others that develop in healthily engaged families with clear boundaries and high levels of differentiation.
- *Preoccupied attachment* and an *obliging approach* to conflict can emerge from negative views of self and deference to others that develop in enmeshed families with diffuse boundaries and low levels of differentiation.
- *Dismissing attachment* and a *dominating approach* to conflict can emerge from narcissistic views of self and exploitive attitudes toward others that develop in disengaged families with rigid boundaries and low levels of differentiation.
- *Fearful attachment* and an *avoiding approach* to conflict can emerge from negative views of self and others that develop in very enmeshed or disengaged families with very rigid or diffuse boundaries and very low levels of differentiation.

An understanding of maladaptive attachment styles and corresponding conflict resolution behaviors has been incorporated into group interventions that focus on preventing domestic violence. Participants in these groups learn egalitarian orientations toward relationships and positive conflict resolution skills (Rosenbaum & Leisring, 2001). Reductions in domestic violence resulting from improved conflict resolution skills suggest that training in integrative conflict resolution skills could prevent battering and possibly other disorders associated with preoccupied, dismissive, or fearful attachment.

Communication in Family Systems

Communication is perhaps the most immediate and accessible manifestation of family systems (Satir, 1967). It is through communication that conflict resolution and attachment occur, circular behavioral exchanges are expressed, boundaries and family structures are maintained, and differentiation and triangulation are projected. For example, imagine an alcoholic father who is not greeted by his wife or children when he returns from work. Instead of taking initiative to say "Hello," he heads to the refrigerator for a beer. His wife notices this and says to the children "See, the first thing he does is get a beer." Overhearing this, the father shouts, "I drink because of the disgusting way I'm treated in this family!!!!" and storms out of the house. This father is employing a dominating conflict resolution approach that is indicative of a dismissing attachment style and acting in a way that affirms a rigid boundary between himself and his wife and children. He is decreasing the strength of the spousal subsystem and probably increasing the strength of the wife and children subsystem. He is also portraying his lack of differentiation and triangulation (depending on alcohol) in a manner that is likely to reduce the differentiation of his children.

Fortunately, communication may be the most malleable manifestation of family systems (Satir, 1967). Where it may be difficult to directly access and change individuals' levels of differentiation or change a family's structure, it is possible to help families improve their communication. Also, knowledge of what constitutes healthy communication is abundant. The same qualities that typify therapeutic communication (Rogers, 1957) are important in healthy family communication (Guerney, 1977): unconditional positive regard (respect), genuineness (honesty), and empathy (understanding). If the alcoholic father in the previous example exercised healthy communication, he might have said,

> It seems to me that my efforts to support the family are not appreciated, and it bothers me. I noticed no one said 'Welcome home, Dad!' or even 'Hello' when I came in. I'd like to feel like we are all important to each other. I wonder if we could spend some time checking with each other about how our days have gone.

A number of prevention programs promote healthy communication in families. Relationship enhancement, in particular, has consistently demonstrated that improved family communication prevents a wide range of individual and family problems (Giblin, Sprenkle, & Sheehan, 1985).

Integrating Family Systems Concepts

Figure 10.1 depicts the potential relation among family systems concepts. Bowen's concept of differentiation forms the vertical "Y" axis of the figure, and Minuchin's concept of structural boundaries forms the horizontal "X" axis of the figure. Healthy family systems are characterized as high on differentiation (Y axis) and in the healthy middle range (between disengaged and enmeshed) with regard to family boundaries (X axis). Healthy family systems employ assertive and empathic communication, engage in integrative conflict resolution, and promote secure attachment. Family systems with lower levels of differentiation are likely to have either an enmeshed structure with diffuse boundaries or a disengaged structure with rigid boundaries. Enmeshed family structures promote passive communication, obliging conflict resolution behaviors and preoccupied attachment. Disengaged family structures promote aggressive communication, dominating conflict resolution behaviors, and dismissive attachment. Family systems that have very low

X

	Diffuse/ Enmeshed	Clear/ Healthy	Rigid/ Disengaged
High Differentiation			
Communication:		Assertive/Empathic	
Conflict:		Integrative	
Attachment:		Secure	
Boundaries:		Clear	
Structure:		Healthy	
Differentiation:		High	
Low Differentiation			
Communication:	Passive		Aggressive
Conflict:	Obliging		Dominating
Attachment:	Preoccupied		Dismissive
Boundaries:	Diffuse		Rigid
Structure:	Enmeshed		Disengaged
Differentiation:	Low		Low
Very Low Differentiation			
Communication:	Confused	fluctuating radically with	Withdrawn
Conflict:	Avoiding		Avoiding
Attachment:	Fearful	fluctuating radically with	Fearful
Boundaries:	Very Diffuse	fluctuating radically with	Very Rigid
Structure:	Very Enmeshed		Very Disengaged
Differentiation:	Very low		Very low
Boundaries/ Structure:	**Diffuse/ Enmeshed**	**Clear/ Healthy**	**Rigid/ Disengaged**

Y

Figure 10.1. Family systems: Communication, conflict, attachment, structure, boundaries, differentiation.

levels of differentiation may fluctuate between highly disengaged and enmeshed structures. These fluctuations promote withdrawal or confused communication, avoidance of conflict resolution, and fearful attachment.

Understanding family systems concepts can inform preventive interventions. For example, enhancing family communication is an excellent approach to prevent problems before they occur, because teaching communication skills can be efficiently accomplished during relatively brief interventions with multiple families (Guerney, 1977; Reid, Patterson, & Snyder, 2002). Families do not need to have an identified problem to benefit from communication skills training, and typically there is little or no stigma associated with learning communication skills. Nevertheless, improved communication can be a protective factor for families, helping them develop integrative conflict resolution styles, secure attachment, clear boundaries, and increased differentiation (Griffin & Apostal, 1993). And, as was suggested by the case example of the Mexican-American family at the beginning of this chapter, improved ability to communicate within the family, and with external systems such as schools, can help families to deflect the negative influence of environmental barriers to development and promote social justice. The strategic and structural perspectives on family systems can guide secondary prevention—that is, early detection and remediation. These approaches go beyond addressing overt symptoms, focusing instead on correcting problematic behavioral exchanges among family members and establishing healthy family structures. Strategic and structural interventions can prevent future symptoms by alleviating the underlying systemic problems that cause symptoms. For example, when a child's eating disorder symptoms function to bring her disengaged parents together, increasing intimacy between the parents can decrease the need for the child's symptoms. Given family systems' propensity to maintain behaviors and structures that are in place (homeostasis), improvements in families' behaviors and structures are likely to have long-term preventive benefits for family members.

Bowen's concept of differentiation in family systems also offers compelling ideas regarding healthy family development and problem prevention. The notion that levels of differentiation are passed from one generation to the next explains how tertiary prevention—limiting the negative impact of a problem—is essential with families. When persons demonstrate difficulty with differentiation (such as the symptoms associated with severe mental illness, antisocial behavior, or substance abuse), efforts to alleviate those symptoms can promote differentiation not only for the person suffering from the illness, but for that person's family and for future generations. Also, when severe stressors threaten to impact families' levels of differentiation, preventive interventions can support families to promote healthy differentiation among present and future family members. Examples include helping families deal with ongoing environmental stressors like crime, poverty, and racism, and supporting families experiencing acute stressors like caring for a wounded soldier returning from war, grieving the loss of a child to illness, or dealing with natural disasters. Finally, understanding family systems can inform preventive interventions at community, regional, national, and international levels. Recognizing the impact crime, poverty, racism, war, and other stressors have on present and future families provides motivation and guidance for societal efforts to reduce these stressors and for supporting the self-empowerment of families who seek to effect social change (Doherty & Carroll, 2007). Examples include community crime watch initiatives, financial and educational advocacy for impoverished families, affirmative action, and efforts to end violent conflict around the world.

RISK/PROTECTIVE FACTORS AND SOCIAL LEARNING IN FAMILY SYSTEMS

Knowledge of family risk and protective factors supports and complements notions derived from family systems theories in informing the design of family-focused prevention programs intended to promote positive youth development and prevent youth problems. (See chap. 3, this volume, for a discussion of risk and protective factors.) Family risk factors have been linked with a variety of psychological disorders among youth and adults, including substance abuse, anxiety, depression, school failure, eating disorders, violence, and conduct problems. The risk for psychological disorder increases when youth are exposed to more risk factors and decreases when they are exposed to more protective factors (Boyd-Franklin, 2003; Horne, 2000; Orpinas & Horne, 2006; Rutter, 1999). Family factors associated with higher risks for childhood problems include family and marital conflict, use of discipline methods that are either too harsh or too lax, lack of adult supervision, parental depression, family stress and disorganization, a family history of behavior problems, and failure to teach pro social skills and competencies (Kumpfer & Bluth, 2004). Secure attachment, positive parent-child relationships, low levels of parental discord, supportive connections with extended family, effective discipline methods, family involvement and advocacy in the child's education, adult monitoring of child and adolescent activities, and positive family communication are protective factors associated with reduced probability of youth emotional and behavioral problems (Kumpfer, 1999; Kumpfer & Alvarado, 2003).

In addition to the family and ecological system factors discussed previously, the development and maintenance of risk and protective factors in family systems can be understood from a social learning perspective. A social learning family systems model has been developed from the work of

Bandura (1986) and the work of Patterson and his colleagues at the Oregon Social Learning Center (Reid et al., 2002). Social learning emphasizes that behavior is learned in social environments, in part by receiving reinforcement or punishment for engaging in behaviors and in part by observing others engage in behaviors and imitating (modeling) those behaviors. Learning occurs from birth on. Children learn their behavioral patterns by how they are responded to in the family and by observing how their parents behave. Children reared in families with a high rate of coercive interaction or where parents or older siblings use power aggressively learn that those behaviors result in positive outcomes and model their own behavior accordingly. See chapters 11 and 13 in this volume for discussion of the social learning model as applied to prevention in school and community contexts.

FAMILY-FOCUSED PREVENTION PROGRAMS TO PREVENT YOUTH BEHAVIORAL PROBLEMS

Childhood aggression and conduct problems are the primary reasons that families seek child mental health services. These problems are of particular interest as targets for prevention because they are associated with juvenile delinquency and substance abuse in adolescence and beyond (Forehand, Kotchick, Shaffer, & Dorsey, 2002). In an effort to identify characteristics of effective family-focused interventions, Kumpfer and Alvarado (2003) led a national study of 35 programs. Examples of family-focused interventions identified as effective through this study included parent training; family skills training that combined behavioral parent training and social and life skills training for children; and brief family therapy targeted at families with youth who are at high risk for conduct disorder, delinquency, substance abuse, depression, and school problems. A number of these programs incorporated social learning theory principles as well as family systems concepts. The findings complement 3 decades of research documenting the effectiveness of parenting interventions in reducing existing behavioral conflicts and preventing the escalation of behavior problems during adolescence (Forehand et al., 2002; Horne & Sayger, 2006; Reid et al., 2002).

What Kumpfer and Alvarado (2003) learned from their review also highlights a number of the components of best practice guidelines identified by other prevention scholars (see chap. 3, this volume; Hage et al., 2007). For example, effective programs were age and developmentally appropriate and sustained for a sufficient period to achieve impact. Consistent with the emphasis family systems theories place on conflict resolution and healthy family structure, researchers identified the following essential components of effective programs: open communication, family cohesion, efforts to improve family relations, and parental monitoring. Effective programs were also tailored to meet the cultural traditions of participating families. It is important to recognize that what might be considered desirable components of family cohesion and differentiation vary across cultural groups. Family protective factors may also vary by culture. For example, some research suggests that role adaptability, spirituality, racial pride, access to economic resources, and community involvement characterize many resilient African-American families (Kumpfer, 1999). For those families who have experienced oppression related to poverty and racism, effective interventions strive to facilitate the development of skills and opportunities that empower families to gain control over their lives (Boyd-Franklin, 2003).

In addition to parenting programs, effective family-system prevention programs often work concurrently with parents, their children, extended family, and other relevant systems, such as schools. As suggested by the developmental-contextual framework presented in chapter 3, comprehensive programs that address multiple contexts are generally more effective than narrowly focused interventions. Programs that involve both the adult caretakers and their children, for example, are more effective than programs directed only toward adults (Kumpfer & Alvarado, 2003). Moreover, since the family is only one of many systems (e.g., schools, peer groups, neighborhoods) that influence child and adolescent development, addressing multiple systems enhances the protective power of the interventions. Using a systemic framework also alerts preventionists not to place undue blame on families for child and adolescent outcomes. Many biological, societal, and structural factors affect families' capacities to function and parent effectively. Biological, societal, and structural factors include genetic predispositions; health/illness; level of poverty; neighborhood crime; community availability of youth recreation services; housing density; exposure to racial, ethnic, and religious discrimination; school quality; and employment opportunities. Effective prevention must seek to address these systemic issues to create a more just society, even as it recognizes and enhances the strengths of families to thrive in spite of inequity and social oppression (Boyd-Franklin, 2003; Horne, 2000; Kumpfer & Alvarado, 2003).

Exhibits 10.1, 10.2, and 10.3 describe three model prevention and early intervention programs that have demonstrated potential for promoting family strengths and preventing behavior problems among children and adolescents. The programs incorporate the principles of effective family prevention identified previously, including attention to cultural factors, the interrelationship of the family system with other critical systems, and efforts to reduce critical risk factors and foster protective factors. The programs conduct outcome assessments to evaluate their effectiveness.

EXHIBIT 10.1
The Strong African American Families Program

The Strong African American Families Program (SAAF) is an empirically based pre-vention program for rural African-American families that was developed by Brody and Murry, of the University of Georgia. This family-centered preventive intervention was designed to prevent alcohol use and high-risk behaviors among African-American adolescents living in rural areas. SAAF focuses on increasing four parent behaviors: involved-vigilant parenting (characterized by high levels of parental involvement, sup-port, inductive reasoning, and monitoring); clearly articulated expectations regarding alcohol use; communication about sex; and racial socialization.

Youth Targets. In addition to its focus on parenting, SAAF targets five fac-tors that protect youths against the early onset of alcohol use and sexual activity: (1) a planful future orientation, (2) resistance efficacy, (3) negative attitudes toward early alcohol use and sexual activity, (4) negative images of drinking youths, and (5) acceptance of parental influence. The SAAF program is based on the belief that youths who have positive future-oriented perspectives are more likely to plan and monitor their behavior and to avoid substance use.

The SAAF Program. SAAF consists of seven consecutive weekly meetings held at community facilities, with separate parent and child skill-building curricula and a family curriculum. Each meeting includes concurrent training sessions for par-ents and children (1 hour each), followed by a joint parent-child session (1 additional hour), where the families practice the skills they learned in their separate sessions. Parents and youth receive a total of 14 hours of prevention training. Together, family members practice communication skills and engage in activities designed to increase family cohesion and the youth's positive involvement in the family.

Empirical Tests of SAAF's Efficacy. SAAF's efficacy was evaluated in a ran-domized prevention trial, in which participating families' longitudinal outcomes in the targeted behaviors were compared with those of families in a control group. This trial yielded the following results: (a) participating families increased the targeted positive parent and youth behaviors, whereas control families experienced declines in those behaviors (Brody et al., 2004); (b) participating youths were less likely than control youths to have started using alcohol 2 years after the program concluded (Brody, Murry, Gerrard, et al., 2006; Brody, Murry, Kogan, et al., 2006); and (c) SAAF-induced changes in targeted parent and youth behaviors were associated with participating youths' delay of alcohol use initiation (Brody, Murry, Kogan, et al., 2006; Gerrard et al., 2006).

Note. Program description provided by Gene Brody (gbrody@uga.edu) and Velma McBride Murry (vmurry@uga.edu), The University of Georgia.

The Strong African American Families Program (SAAF; Exhibit 10.1) was designed to enhance family protective factors that decrease the likelihood of high-risk behavior among youth (Brody et al., 2004). SAAF seeks to encourage youth to internalize their parents' norms through exposure to clearly articulated expectations about alcohol use, information about sexual-ity, and parent–child relationships that promote discussions about these issues. Because racism is seen as contributing to substance use and compromising African-American youths' psychological functioning, parents participating in SAAF are also taught how to foster racial socialization so that their children will learn effective ways of dealing with racism.

EXHIBIT 10.2
LIFT: A Multimodal Preventive Intervention
for Reducing Childhood Conduct Problems

Linking the Interests of Families and Teachers (LIFT) is a multimodal prevention program comprising parent management training, child social skills training, a recess incentive program, and enhanced school-home communication. Various intervention components occur simultaneously, and the content of the parent and child components is complementary to other components. The parent-focused components of the program are summarized here.

Parent Management Training. Parents are invited to six parenting group sessions, once a week for 6 weeks. The group sessions involve brief lectures, illustrative role plays and video, and discussion. Parenting skills taught include giving encouragement, effective discipline, family problem solving, monitoring, and supervision. Session content is modified for parents of first graders and fifth graders to reflect the developmental challenges typically faced by children and parents during each grade. To maximize participation, researchers offer sessions multiple times each week, provide free babysitting, and if parents do not show up for a group session, offer an individual session at home or the option of receiving written materials and videos through the mail. The varied delivery approaches resulted in 93% of parents receiving all of the parent training materials.

Enhanced Communication Between School and Home. Researchers encourage parents and teachers to communicate with each other frequently. Methods for improving communication are discussed during parent training. Parents receive weekly newsletters describing LIFT activities at school and providing suggestions for activities that parents and children can do at home to reinforce LIFT concepts. Phones and answering machines are placed in each classroom. Teachers update the answering machines weekly with descriptive messages about classroom activities. Parents are encouraged to call and leave messages if they have any questions for teachers, and teachers are encouraged to respond. An average family made 21 calls to their classroom answering machine over the 10-week course of the intervention and identified themselves during 11 of those calls.

Program Outcomes. The efficacy of LIFT for preventing conduct problems has been examined in several studies (Eddy, Reid, & Fetrow, 2000) and is currently being evaluated in a National Institute of Mental Health funded randomized controlled trial involving more than 600 participants. Studies yielded the following results among participants compared to controls: (a) a decrease of observed aggressive behavior during recess among the most physically aggressive children, (b) a decrease in negative behaviors during observed family problem-solving discussions of the most verbally negative parents, (c) an increase in positive teacher perceptions of child social skills, (d) fewer police contacts by the end of middle school, and (e) a lower likelihood of receiving a conduct disorder diagnosis by age 16 years. Because of the numerous positive outcomes related to the program to date, LIFT has been recognized as a promising prevention program by several federally sponsored best practice panels, including the U.S. Department of Education Safe and Drug Free Schools panel and the U.S. Office of Juvenile Justice and Delinquency Prevention Blueprints for Violence Prevention panel (Eddy, Reid, Stoolmiller, & Fetrow, 2005).

Note. Program description prepared by J. Mark Eddy, Research Scientist, Oregon Social Learning Center, 160 E. Fourth Ave., Eugene, OR 97401; marke@oslc.org

Linking the Interests of Families and Teachers (LIFT; Exhibit 10.2) was designed to address social interaction factors that contribute to the development and maintenance of youth behavior problems (Eddy, Reid, & Fetrow, 2000). As noted elsewhere in this chapter, a variety of factors are related to youth conduct problems, including social rejection by peers, parents, and teachers (Reid et al., 2002). LIFT is a multifaceted or "multimodal" intervention that addresses the critical social relationships that occur across the important social settings in children's lives.

The Bully Busters Program was developed to assist schools with bullying problems. It has demonstrated success in a number of elementary and middle schools (Horne, Bartolomucci, & Newman-Carlson, 2003; Howard, Horne, & Jolliff, 2001; Orpinas, Horne, & Staniszewski, 2003). Bully Busters focuses on creating classrooms where all members are treated with respect and dignity, where all engage in democratic problem solving, and where bullying and aggression are not tolerated. A supplemental in-home component (Horne, Stoddard, & Bell, 2008; Exhibit 10.3) was developed to incorporate these same values into families, thus offering a more comprehensive approach to family prevention and early remediation of aggression. The program brings together parents who want their families to become more caring, connected, and supportive and who want to learn to prevent or reduce bullying and victimization, both in family and school contexts.

The initial successes of these programs are cause for optimism regarding the efficacy of preventive interventions with families. Family systems and social learning theories are helpful in understanding the mechanisms that contribute to program efficacy. From a structural family systems perspective, promoting involved and vigilant parenting in the SAAF program, parental monitoring in the LIFT program, and parents' identification of bullying in the Bully Busters for Parents program all encourage appropriate levels of parental engagement, a counter to the rigid boundaries associated with disengagement (Minuchin, 1980). The activities in each program that encourage supportive parenting practices are strategic interventions that increase parents' repertoire of behaviors for providing guidance (Haley, 1976). The focus on communication skills, which is also central to each of the programs, enhances family interaction (Satir, 1967).

Activities specific to each program are also likely to contribute to their success. The focus on racial socialization is a unique and potentially powerful component of the SAAF program. Generations of African-American families have been exposed to racism, potentially impeding differentiation within African-American family systems. Addressing racism directly and providing children with tools for coping with it could be an important step in strengthening racial pride and helping them differentiate (Bowen, 1978) from the negative impact of prolonged oppression. The LIFT program's emphasis on enhanced communication between school and home acknowledges that children's development occurs in multiple interrelated systems

EXHIBIT 10.3
Bully Busters for Parents:
A Family Prevention Model for Bullying Prevention

Bully Busters for Parents (BBP) is a multiple family group prevention approach for reducing aggression, and consists of four 2-hour sessions, facilitated by trained group leaders. The groups are composed of up to eight parents who have expressed interest in participating in the program or who may have been identified by school personnel because their child is currently involved in a bully-victim cycle.

Goals. The goals of BBP are to provide parents with practical means for identifying if their child is either a bully or a victim and to create a supportive forum where parents can discuss their concerns, ask questions, and develop the skills needed to address issues related to bullying and victimization. BBP focuses on the important influence effective and supportive parental communication patterns have on overall family functioning while also recognizing that parenting can be stressful. Self-care is highlighted. Parents are provided with stress management, problem-solving, and coping skills.

Sessions. Each of the four sessions is structured so that parents share a meal together and then engage in activities and discussion focused on the evening's topic. The groups have unstructured elements, as well, including time for parents to share concerns or ask questions that the group may then work to problem-solve. The objectives of the first session are to dispel common myths about bullying, aid parents in understanding the different types of bullies, and introduce the Family Council (a brief, weekly scheduled meeting during which all family members can come together to discuss positive and negative family matters with the aim of engaging in open and honest dialogue while reinforcing the parents' authority). The objectives of the second session are to review successes and difficulties in implementing the Family Council, learn about the different types of victims, and learn a framework for how to efficiently conceptualize and then problem-solve parenting concerns. The objectives of the third session are to review the Family Council, help parents identify and understand the various systemic influences that serve to create and maintain bully-victim dyads, and determine the most effective means of intervening with these systems. The objectives of this last session are to review the activities practiced at home, further to develop the parents' understanding of the importance of parenting with emotional awareness, and to provide parents with information about, and techniques for, self-care and family care.

Results and Feedback From Parents. Efficacy studies are under way for the program. In the completed pilot projects parents have shared that they enjoyed and benefited from the opportunity to engage in the group process with other parents who are similarly struggling with issues related to bullying and victimization. Data collected before and after the intervention indicate an increase in the level of cohesiveness within families, as well as an increase in the parents' and children's perceptions of their ability to handle situations involving aggression, both in and outside of the family. Furthermore, parents experienced a renewed interest in collaborating more closely with the school system to prevent and remediate issues related to aggression and bullying (e.g., parents from one group exchanged contact information to create a parent-based and school-sanctioned bully-victim support network).

Note. Program description prepared by Jennifer Stoddard (velovino@msn.com), Christopher Bell (cbell@uga.edu), and Arthur Horne (ahorne@uga.edu), Bully Research Program, University of Georgia.

(Brofenbrenner, 1979). School and parental systems working together increases the stability of both, decreasing the likelihood of counterproductive triangulation (Bowen, 1978) and increasing appropriate hierarchical boundaries for promoting positive behavior (Minuchin, 1980). The Bully Busters for Parents program promotes differentiation (Bowen, 1978) within the family system by encouraging parents' self-care in the face of stress. This program seems to directly address attachment (Ainsworth & Bowlby, 1991) and conflict resolution (Rahim, 1983), first by assisting families in becoming more caring, connected, and supportive and then by engaging them in Family Council meetings that involve mutual problem solving.

CONCLUSION

Given the pervasive and powerful impact family systems have on the development of individuals and society, the family is a critical setting for prevention work. This chapter has identified prominent family systems theories and their implications for promoting healthy families that will foster the well-being of all family members. Unfortunately, many families in our society confront risks related to both internal family processes and externally imposed stressors, including racism and poverty. Although social change strategies are needed to reduce external stressors, strong families can offer a source of resilience in coping with life stressors. Strong families can work together to improve their access to economic and social resources that are vital to their well-being and social mobility. Fortunately, a growing body of research and practice is emerging concerning prevention and health promotion efforts that serve to reduce family risks and promote family strengths. These efforts to strengthen families are informed by systemic and social learning theories and by research on family risk and protective factors. Efforts to support and strengthen families, to recognize and respect cultural variations in family resources, and to reduce the societal factors that undermine family strengths are critical to promoting positive development and social justice.

REFERENCES

Ainsworth, M. D. S., & Bowlby, J. (1991). An ethological approach to personality development. *American Psychologist, 46*, 333–341.

Bandura, A. (1986). *Social foundations of thought and action: A social cognitive theory.* Englewood Cliffs, NJ: Prentice Hall.

Bartholomew, K., & Horowitz, L. M. (1991). Attachment styles among young adults: A test of a four category model. *Journal of Personality and Social Psychology, 61*, 226–244.

Bowen, M. (1978). *Family therapy in clinical practice*. New York: Jason Aronson.

Boyd-Franklin, N. (2003). *Black families in therapy: Understanding the African American experience* (2nd ed.). New York: Guilford Press.

Brody, G. H., Murry, V. M., Gerrard, M., Gibbons, F. X., McNair, L., Brown, A. C., et al. (2006). The Strong African American Families Program: Prevention of youths' high-risk behavior and a test of a model of change. *Journal of Family Psychology, 20*, 1–11.

Brody, G. H., Murry, V. M., Gerrard, M., Gibbons, F. X., Molgaard, V., McNair, L., et al. (2004). The Strong African American Families Program: Translating research into prevention programming. *Child Development, 75*, 900–917.

Brody, G. H., Murry, V. M., Kogan, S. M., Gerrard, M., Gibbons, F. X., Molgaard, V., et al. (2006). The Strong African American Families Program: A cluster-randomized prevention trial of long-term effects and a mediational model. *Journal of Consulting and Clinical Psychology, 74*, 356–366.

Bronfenbrenner, U. (1979). *The ecology of human development*. Cambridge, MA: Harvard University Press.

Doherty, W. J., & Carroll, J. S. (2007). Families and therapists as citizens: The families and democracy project. In E. Aldarondo (Ed.), *Advancing social justice through clinical practice* (pp. 223–244). Mahwah, NJ: Erlbaum.

Dreikurs, R., Corsini, R. J., Lowe, R., & Sonstegard, M. (1959). *Alderian family counseling*. Eugene, OR: University of Oregon Press.

Eddy, J. M., Reid, J. B., & Fetrow, R. A. (2000). An elementary school-based prevention program targeting modifiable antecedents of youth delinquency and violence: Linking the interests of families and teachers (LIFT). *Journal of Emotional and Behavioral Disorders, 8*, 165–176.

Eddy, J. M., Reid, J. B., Stoolmiller, M., & Fetrow, R. A. (2005). Outcomes during middle school for an elementary school-based preventive intervention for conduct problems: Follow-up results from a randomized trial. *Behavior Therapy, 34*, 535–552.

Forehand, R., Kotchick, B., Shaffer, A., & Dorsey, S. (2002, June). *Behavioral parent training: Accomplishments, challenges, and promises*. Paper presented at the Third International Conference on Child and Adolescent Mental Health, Brisbane, Australia.

Gerrard, M., Gibbons, F. X., Brody, G. H., Murry, V. M., Cleveland, M. J., & Wills, T. A. (2006). A theory-based dual-focus alcohol intervention for preadolescents: The Strong African American Families Program. *Psychology of Addictive Behavior, 20*, 185–195.

Giblin, P., Sprenkle, D. H., & Sheehan, R. (1985). Enrichment outcome research: A meta-analysis of premarital, marital and family interventions. *Journal of Marital and Family Therapy, 11*, 257–271.

Griffin, J. M., & Apostal, R. A. (1993). The influence of relationship enhancement training on differentiation of self. *Journal of Marital and Family Therapy, 19*, 267–272.

Guerney, B. G., Jr. (1977). *Relationship enhancement: Skill-training programs for therapy, problem prevention, and enrichment*. San Francisco: IDEALS.

Hage, S., Romano, J., Conyne, R., Kenny, M., Matthews, C. R., Schwartz, J., & Waldo, M. (2007). Best practice guidelines on prevention in practice, research, training, and social advocacy for psychologists. *The Counseling Psychologist, 35*, 493–566.

Haley, J. (1976). *Problem-solving therapy*. San Francisco: Jossey-Bass.

Horne, A. (2000). *Family counseling and therapy* (3rd ed.). Itasca, IL: Peacock.

Horne, A., Bartolomucci, C., & Newman-Carlson, D. (2003). *Bully busters: Bullies, victims and bystanders—A manual for elementary school teachers*. Champaign, IL: Research Press.

Horne, A., Stoddard, J., & Bell, C. (2008). *A parents' guide to understanding and responding to bullying: A bully busters approach*. Champaign, IL: Research Press.

Horne, A., & Sayger, T. V. (2006). Social learning family intervention. In A. Kilpatrick & T. Holland (Eds.), *Working with families: An integrative model by level of need* (4th ed., pp. 128–144). Boston: Allyn & Bacon.

Howard, N., Horne, A., & Jolliff, D. (2001). Self-efficacy in a new training model for the prevention of bullying in the schools. *Emotional Abuse, 2*, 181–191.

Jackson, D. (1964). *Myths of madness: New facts for old fallacies*. New York: MacMillan Publishing Company.

Johnson, P., & Waldo, M. (1998). Integrating Minuchin's boundary continuum and Bowen's differentiation scale: A curvilinear representation. *Contemporary Family Therapy, 20*, 403–413.

Keitner, G. I., & Miller, I. W. (1990). Family functioning and major depression: An overview. *American Journal of Psychiatry, 147*, 1128–1137.

Kumpfer, K. L. (1999). *Strengthening America's families: Exemplary parenting and family strategies for delinquency prevention*. U. S. Department of Justice, Office of Justice Programs, Office of Juvenile Justice and Delinquency Prevention. Retrieved on July 3, 2007, from http://www.strengtheningfamilies.org/html/lit_review_1999_toc.html

Kumpfer, K. L., & Alvarado, R. (2003). Family-strengthening approaches for the prevention of youth behavior problems. *American Psychologist*, 457–465.

Kumpfer, K. L., & Bluth, B. (2004). Parent/child transactional processes predictive of resilience or vulnerability to "substance abuse disorders." *Substance Use & Misuse, 39*, 671–698.

Lev-Wiesel, R. (2007). Intergenerational transmission of trauma across three generations: A preliminary study. *Qualitative Social Work, 6*, 75–94.

Madanes, C. (1981). *Strategic family therapy*. San Francisco: Jossey-Bass.

McDaniel, S. H., Lusterman, D. D., & Philpot, C. L. (Eds.). (2001). *Casebook for integrating family therapy: An ecosystemic approach*. Washington, DC: American Psychological Association.

McGoldrick, M. (Ed.). (1998). *Re-visioning family therapy: Race, culture and gender in clinical practice*. New York: Guilford.

McGoldrick, M., Almeida, R., Preto, N. G., Bibb, A., Sutton, C., Hudak, J., et al. (1999). Efforts to incorporate social justice perspectives into a family training program. *Journal of Marital and Family Therapy, 25*, 191–209.

Minuchin, S. (1980). *Families and family therapy*. Cambridge, MA: Harvard University Press.

Minuchin, P., Colopinto, J., & Minuchin, S. (1998). *Working with families of the poor*. New York: Guilford.

O'Farrell, T. J., Choquette, K. A., & Cutter, H. S. G. (1998). Couples relapse prevention sessions after behavioral marital therapy for male alcoholics: Outcomes during the three years after starting treatment. *Journal of Studies on Alcohol, 59*, 357–370.

Orpinas, P., & Horne, A. (2006). *Bullying prevention: Creating a positive school climate and developing social competence*. Washington, DC: American Psychological Association.

Orpinas, P., Horne, A., & Staniszewski, D. (2003). School bullying: Changing the problem by changing the school. *School Psychology Review, 32*, 431–444.

Rahim, M. A. (1983). A measure of styles of handling interpersonal conflict. *Academy of Management Journal, 26*(2), 368–376.

Reid, J. B., Patterson, G. R., & Snyder, J. (Eds.). (2002). *Antisocial behavior in children: Developmental theories and models for intervention*. Washington, DC: American Psychological Association.

Rogers, C. R. (1957). The necessary and sufficient conditions for therapeutic personality change. *Journal of Consulting Psychology, 21*, 95–103.

Rosenbaum, A., & Leisring, P. A. (2001). Group intervention programs for batterers. *Journal of Aggression, Maltreatment, & Trauma, 5*(2), 57–71.

Rutter, M. (1999). Resilience concepts and findings: Implications for family therapy. *Journal of Family Therapy, 21*, 119–144.

Santisteban, D. A., Szapocznik, J., Perez-Vidal, A., Kurtines, W. M., Murray, E. J., & LaPerriere, A. (1996). Engaging behavior problem drug abusing youth and their families into treatment: An investigation of the efficacy of specialized engagement interventions and factors that contribute to differential effectiveness. *Journal of Family Psychology, 10*(1), 35–44.

Satir, V. (1967). *Conjoint family therapy*. Palo Alto, CA: Science and Behavior Books.

VonBertalanffy, L. (1968). *General systems theory: Formulations, development, applications*. New York: George Braziller.

11

DEVELOPMENT OF A POSITIVE SCHOOL CLIMATE

KRIS BOSWORTH, PAMELA ORPINAS, AND KATIE HEIN

The educational, social, and physical environment of the school is often referred to as school climate. A positive school climate exists when all members of the school community feel valued and respected, are constructively engaged in their activities, and feel emotionally and physically safe in the school building and its surroundings. These positive perceptions of the environment can exist regardless of the size or location of the school, the socioeconomic class of the students, or the surrounding neighborhood (Rutter, Maughan, Mortimore, Ouston, & Smith, 1979).

Although defining what constitutes a positive school climate may be difficult, most people know how to recognize it: A positive school climate is inviting and nurtures people's best qualities (Orpinas & Horne, 2006). In addition, a positive school climate welcomes students and their families, celebrates diversity of opinions and cultures, and promotes academic excellence. The School Social Competence Development and Bullying Prevention Model developed by Orpinas and Horne integrates eight dimensions of a positive school climate: (1) excellence in teaching, including strong teaching skills, positive classroom management skills, and ability to motivate students; (2) school values that support respect for all members of the community and the belief that all children can learn; (3) awareness of strengths of the school, as well as areas in need of improvement, leading to finding solutions; (4) clear policies that support respectful solutions of problems and a system of accountability for offenders that promotes responsibility rather than blind obedience; (5) caring, respect, and positive rapport among members of the school community, leading to a strong sense of community; (6) teachers' positive expectations of their students and administrators' positive expectations of teachers and staff; (7) mechanisms to support teachers in handling daily stress; and (8) a safe, clean, and aesthetically pleasant physical environment. Although the model was originally developed to prevent bullying, the dimensions of a positive school climate are not exclusive to the violence prevention field. Each of these dimensions enhances students' and teachers' sense of community and connectedness to the school.

Many egregious inequalities exist in schools as a result of unequal distributions of funds for education (Kozol, 1991). However, strong leadership and effective teaching can overcome or mitigate many of these inequalities. As discussed later in this chapter, individuals can create climates that either promote learning and positive behavior or that encourage negative behavior (Hein, 2004). A positive school climate is not only linked to prevention of behavioral and mental health problems, as described later in this chapter, but it is also a social justice imperative. All students benefit from a school that promotes a positive educational and social climate, but this environment is particularly important for students living in impoverished neighborhoods or disorganized family environments or, in general, students who have little or no access to other resources and services outside of school. A free, public education is a powerful tool for social justice. For some students, schools may provide the only alternative to violence, drug use, and other destructive behaviors experienced in the community. Schools can be a safe haven or protective buffer, promoting skills and providing resources to students who cannot access such resources elsewhere. Although many disparities can be documented within the current public school system in the United States (e.g., U.S. Department of Education, 1995), many students of color, girls, and other disenfranchised groups have found public education to be the pathway to opportunity for a more equitable life. Thus, positive school climate promotes social justice precisely because of the leveling of the playing field—and the learning field—in all areas of prevention.

Educators and policy makers struggle to narrow the disparities among groups of students within the education system. The underlying causes of disparities are complex, and some are not limited to the factors that are under control of the school systems. For example, most educational research shows a positive relation between the socioeconomic status (SES) of students and their scores on standardized tests. However, this association is not true for all schools; some schools with a high number of low-income students report high test scores (Fashola & Slavin, 1997; Fullan, 2000; McGee, 2004). Educators in such schools have been successful in creating systems and environments in which disparities can be, and are being, reduced.

Schools that have been successful in reducing disparities focus on three critical aspects of schooling. Each of these three components is necessary, but not sufficient by itself, to ensure academic success for all students and reduce academic disparities.

1. *Curriculum:* Educational research has identified culturally relevant curricula that are more effective at teaching key concepts in reading, math, writing, and science. Educators' daily choices of instructional content can make a difference on reducing disparities (English, 2000).

2. *Instruction:* The quality of teaching is also critical. The methods and instructional strategies teachers use to deliver the curriculum can enhance the effectiveness of the content (Marzano, Pickering, & Pollock, 2001; Slavin et al., 1996). Further, some strategies, such as cooperative learning, can improve race relations, increase academic achievement, and enhance a positive school climate (U.S. Department of Health and Human Services, 2001).

3. *Climate:* A positive school climate, the focus of this chapter, is an essential educational tool, not just a school descriptor (Hein, 2004; Rutter et al., 1979). A positive climate is like rich soil: One can plant good seeds into a pot of fertile soil or a pot of rocks and have very different outcomes, even if the original seeds were identical.

A supportive, organized, and predictable school climate is a powerful tool for social justice within public schools, as a positive school climate benefits every student, regardless of race, sex, level of ability, ethnicity, sexual orientation, or SES. The metaphor "raise the water level in the lake and all boats rise with the water" illustrates this point. To maximize learning, all students must feel safe and accepted, and be aware of being valued members of their school community.

The goal of this chapter is to explain and exemplify the influence of a positive school climate on students' behaviors, which can additionally be a mechanism for increasing student retention and academic achievement, as well as preventing mental health and behavioral problems. This chapter supports the need for interventions that promote a positive school climate, describes several innovative approaches to school climate change, and identifies processes by which school climate change can occur. This chapter is composed of four sections. The first section describes the impact of positive school climate on student behavior and, thus, highlights its importance for prevention. The second section addresses a secondary benefit of promoting a positive school climate: it facilitates the implementation of prevention activities. The third section briefly describes three theories that support the need for a positive school climate and explains the possible mechanisms by which climate has an impact on behavior. The fourth section delineates several strategies to promote a positive school climate. Throughout the chapter, examples of programs designed to promote a positive school climate are described.

IMPACT OF POSITIVE SCHOOL CLIMATE ON STUDENT BEHAVIOR

A positive school climate is critical for healthy student growth and the prevention of behaviors that increase health and social risks, such as early sexual activity; alcohol, tobacco, and other drug use; and violence perpetration or victimization. This section emphasizes three well-researched characteristics (or measures) of a positive school climate: (1) level of connectedness, inclusion, or identification with the school; (2) positive classroom management, which also increases connectedness; and (3) teachers' positive expectations of students.

Schools provide a buffer against risk-taking behavior when students report having an attachment to or bonding with the school and adults there. Research has demonstrated that the sense of connectedness emerges from actions adults within the school take to ensure a safe and accepting environment. For example, Patton and colleagues (2006), in a group-randomized trial of 25 schools in Australia, found that a schoolwide intervention designed to promote social inclusion significantly reduced extreme risk behaviors. Among upper elementary school students, a strong sense of community was significantly associated with low behavioral problems and strong academic performance (Battistich, Solomon, Kim, Watson, & Schaps, 1995). Schools that emphasize social relationships and opportunities within the school and feelings of identification with school, described as *school-as-community*, may buffer some of the detrimental effects that poverty can have on behavior (Battistich et al., 1995). The National Longitudinal Study of Adolescent Health of 2004 brought a similar concept, *school connectedness*, to the forefront. School connectedness was associated with a decrease in many unhealthy behaviors such as the use of illegal substances, emotional distress, suicide, deviant behavior, violence, and pregnancy (Resnick, Ireland, & Borowsky, 2004). Connectedness to the school may be partially a function of school size: In smaller schools (under 600), students on average feel more connected (Blum, McNeely, & Rinehart, 2002).

Classroom management also contributes to connectedness and to the prevention of behavioral problems. Resnick and colleagues (1997) found that well-managed classrooms contributed to a sense of connectedness. In a well-managed classroom, expectations for individual responsibility are clear, teachers consistently acknowledge all students, and students participate in the management of the classroom by performing regular jobs and having input on classroom rules. In a study of middle school students in 12 schools in a poor section of London, two distinct groups of schools emerged. One group of schools had high achievement scores and low delinquency rates, whereas the other group had low achievement scores and high delinquency rates. Classroom behavior was much better in schools where the teacher had prepared lessons in advance and when classrooms were well organized (Rutter et al., 1979). Classroom environment may influence the course of development of aggressive behavior years later, especially in aggressive boys. In a longitudinal study of elementary school-children, aggressive children placed in poorly managed classrooms actually increased aggression, whereas those aggressive students placed in well-managed classrooms maintained or diminished their aggression (Ialongo, Poduska, Werthamer, & Kellam, 2001).

A recent case study of two middle school teachers in a culturally diverse, low SES school identified classroom management strategies to prevent aggressive and disruptive student behavior (Hein, 2004). The two teachers were purposefully selected because administrators and students identified them as being extraordinary at managing their classrooms. The strategies they used are summarized in four areas. First, they maintained high outcome expectations of all students, in relation to academic achievement and classroom behavior. Second, teachers respected and trusted students as demonstrated by listening to them, not interrupting students when adults entered the classroom, allowing students to move about the classrooms much as adults are permitted to move about their workspace, and providing supplies (such as pencil or paper) needed in the classroom rather than wasting instructional time disciplining students for coming to class unprepared. Third, teachers created a climate of self-discipline by including students in rule making, decision making, and problem solving in the classroom. Teachers engaged students rather than controlled them and talked to students about consequences of risk behavior. Fourth, teachers deliberately used culturally responsive teaching strategies to create a safe and inclusive classroom environment. The most commonly used culturally responsive strategies were encouraging peer relationships, promoting collaborative learning, drawing knowledge from students, and using relevant, culturally diverse examples in class. Teachers understood students' home cultures but did not attribute student behavior to the students' home situations.

Numerous psychological and educational research studies have examined the puzzling effect of teachers' expectations on students' behavior (Reyna, 2000; Rosenthal, 1994; Swim & Sanna, 1996). Social stereotypes, such as "women are bad at math" or "Asian Americans are hard working," may influence educators' behavior. Teachers may spend less time, provide less feedback, teach more simplistic materials, or prompt less frequently for answers with students for whom expectations are lower, thus reducing their chances of success. Even in gifted classes where all students are high performing, African-American students are less likely to receive in-class attention from teachers than Caucasian students (Alder, 2000). An evaluation of the Department of Defense schools, which have the narrowest achievement gaps between racial/ethnic groups, highlights a combination of factors leading to this success, including teachers' high expectations for all students (Smrekar, Guthrie, Owens, & Sims, 2001).

SUPPORT FOR PREVENTION CURRICULA

In addition to having a direct impact on student behavior, positive school climate has an indirect effect by enhancing the impact of prevention programs. Prevention curricula are most effective when classroom behaviors are consistent with what is taught in the lessons (Rutter et al., 1979; Williams & Jones, 1993). In the United States, nearly all youth are at school. Thus, schools provide location and easy access for delivering prevention messages. Positive school climate and culture play three important roles in strengthening prevention activities:

1. *Enhance the intervention by providing prosocial models.* Most violence prevention curricula, for example, teach skills to resolve conflicts peacefully. If students observe those same skills practiced in the school environment, the impact of the curriculum is enhanced. Rowling (1996) described the school climate as the "hidden curriculum" that either supports healthy lifestyles or contributes to risk-taking behavior.
2. *Offer opportunities to practice and reinforce positive social skills.* The school culture and climate continually shape student behavior by reinforcing positive prosocial activities. Reinforcement of prosocial skills facilitates the integration of such skills into youths' repertoire of behavior. Hence, a positive environment allows students to practice safely positive prosocial behaviors (Bosworth & Walz, 2005; Lewis, Sugai, & Colvin, 1998).
3. *Facilitate fidelity of implementation.* Fidelity of program implementation depends to a great extent on the quality of the

environment. Based on rigorous evaluations, scientists have identified effective and promising programs and strategies for preventing and reducing violence (Botvin, 2000; Tobler & Stratton, 1997). However, the same results are not guaranteed when these interventions are scaled up to a general population. Schools often do not have the capacity to implement a quality program with fidelity or to sustain the program once funding has ended (Elliott & Mihalic, 2004). Further, positive results may not be obtained when schools are dysfunctional and the school climate is negative. Gottfredson and colleagues (Gottfredson, Jones, & Gore, 2002; Skroban, Gottfredson, & Gottfredson, 1999) found that implementing efficacious programs in disorganized and conflict-prone settings might offer minimal benefits if basic improvements in school environment are not achieved.

Many educators and parents say it is important for schools to promote health, reduce risk behaviors, and help students develop social competence (Markow & Scheer, 2002), yet in practice school leaders rarely embrace prevention programs as an integral part of their educational mission. Prevention curricula are often considered add-on activities not directly related to the school's academic mission and are thus fraught with problems that lead to poor implementation and low sustainability. Consequently, few educators have become involved in prevention research activities, and prevention scientists have expressed frustration at the public school educators' lack of commitment to a prevention philosophy. Educational policies, such as No Child Left Behind, further remove schools from the role of fostering life skills as the role of schools is focused tightly on the conveyance of content. Yet, positive school climate serves as a broad mechanism to foster academic and social development even as it supports school-based, add-on prevention programs. Three significant vulnerabilities for the implementation of prevention programs are the lack of prepared professional staff, inadequate funding, and the impact of unexpected external policies that influence educational priorities.

- *Unprepared professional staff.* Because bringing an external instructor to teach prevention programs does not support the model described in the introduction of this chapter of creating a positive school climate, most successful prevention programs require that educators who implement the program be fully trained in the specific curriculum. Teachers and other school personnel, who are usually overworked, generally view the training as an extra responsibility. Only a few may have a passion for this kind of activity. If the curriculum is implemented in a particular class, such as social studies, all social studies teachers need to be trained. However, it is unlikely that all of them will share equal enthusiasm, skills, and background for delivering the curriculum. Training of teachers is further complicated by staff turnover. Thus, it is difficult to maintain a highly trained staff capable of delivering a curriculum with fidelity over time. To solve these problems and ensure fidelity of implementation, some researchers train non-school staff to deliver their program at schools (e.g., Farrell, Valois, & Meyer, 2002; Meyer, Allison, Reese, Gay, & Multisite Violence Prevention Project, 2004). The drawback is that school personnel are not trained, and the program will most likely end when the grant expires. Other programs, such as the Bully Busters Prevention Program (Newman, Horne, & Bartolomucci, 2000) train school personnel directly, but teachers' "buy-in" is not uniform and the rapid turnover of the teaching staff results in uneven implementation over time.

- *Inadequate funding.* Prevention is rarely a line item on a school or a district budget. The majority of the funding comes from the Safe and Drug Free School Title IV program, state allocations, or grants. The funding from Safe and Drug Free Schools has facilitated the integration of prevention programs into the school curriculum. Although Title IV funding has been consistent since the late 1980s, the threat that the funding will not be renewed or will be renewed at a substantially lower level exists. In fact, in the past two years there have been substantial cuts to Title IV funding. Grants are another source of funding that may provide an opportunity for increased staff involvement and implementation of evidence-based programs. However, because grants are short lived, such an infusion of money may lead to an excellent implementation that spans only a few years. Continuous implementation depends on the commitment of the organization (Swisher, 2000).

- *Impact of external forces.* The No Child Left Behind legislation has provided carrots and sticks for schools to focus primarily on academic programs. Most educators believe that to be academically successful, the education of the "whole" child is paramount. However, all actors in public education—students, teachers, and administrators—are measured by test scores as a single indicator of success. The social skills and emotional competency necessary for healthy development are not assessed. As a result of this legislation, school policy makers, school boards, superintendents, and community members judge their schools primarily on test scores. Often these stakeholders pressure schools to cut back on any activities, including prevention, not perceived as directly increasing academic test scores.

In summary, research overwhelmingly supports that promoting a positive school climate will improve students' well-being and reduce high-risk behaviors, as well as provide a propitious background for prevention programs. However, schools must recognize and overcome obstacles to successful implementation. The next section describes the theoretical support for developing a positive school climate.

THEORIES AND EXAMPLES OF APPLICATION

This section briefly describes three theories that provide a rationale for creating a positive school climate to promote students' well-being and reduce health-risk behavior. The theories depicted are social cognitive theory (Bandura, 1986), attachment theory (Ainsworth & Bowlby, 1991; Bowlby, 1982), and resiliency (Masten, 2001; Werner & Smith, 2001).

Social Cognitive Theory

A primary construct of social cognitive theory is reciprocal determinism, or the continuous interaction among personal cognitions, the environment, and behaviors. The theory posits that a change of any of those three components will affect the others. Thus, modifying the school climate will change students' behaviors and their thoughts about those behaviors. Another construct relevant to positive school climate is observational learning: People learn by observing the behavior of others and the outcomes of those behaviors. A positive school environment, one in which people communicate well and solve problems without resorting to aggression, provides ongoing models of appropriate behavior (Dill & Haberman, 1995; Rutter et al., 1979). Rather than participating in a single lesson on appropriate problem-solving behavior, students observe prosocial behaviors repeatedly throughout the school year. Repeated exposures to positive role models increase the likelihood that students will adopt the modeled behavior into their own behavioral repertoire. Positive Behavioral Support (Exhibit 11.1) is an example of an intervention that uses social cognitive theory for creating a positive school climate, and the Good Behavior Game (Exhibit 11.2) applies these principles at the classroom level.

Attachment Theory

First noted in the relationship between infants and mothers, attachment is critical to children's emotional development (Bowlby, 1982). Two

EXHIBIT 11.1
Positive Behavioral Support

Originally designed to change the disruptive behaviors often found in many children with disabilities, Positive Behavioral Support (PBS; http://www.pbis.org) has become a widespread intervention for violence prevention (Sugai, 2003). This empirically validated approach seeks to reduce challenging behaviors in school by replacing them with pro-social behaviors. Based on social cognitive theory, PBS posits that problem behavior continues because it is rewarded. By changing the environment to provide a single school culture with consistent rules and procedures, misbehavior is less likely to be reinforced and pro-social behavior is more likely to be taught and modeled consistently. Schools that implement the school-wide PBS report increased time engaged in academic activities and improved academic performance. Most schools report 20% to 60% reduction in discipline referrals allowing teachers and administrators to devote more time to academic goals (Lewis, Powers, Kelk, & Newcomer, 2002).

Implementation of PBS requires a number of activities at the local school level. First, faculty members agree on three to five positively stated rules, such as "Be responsible" or "Be respectful." Next, a selected team representing the faculty, administration, parents, and staff puts those rules into operation in various locations in the schools. For example, if a rule is "Be safe," the team defines related behaviors in each school location (e.g., playground, hallways, buses, classrooms, library, cafeteria) and identifies a reward system (e.g., tokens that can be redeemed at the school store, stickers and points toward lunch with the principal, drawings at the end of the week, pizza party). At the beginning of the school year, students learn the rules at each location. To accomplish this objective, teachers take children to each location and demonstrate the expected behaviors. Then, students practice the behaviors at the site. On a regular basis, students and educators identify students who are following the rules and reward them. Signs and posters throughout the school remind students of the rules. To ensure continued implementation, the PBS team at each site meets regularly (usually monthly) to review implementation progress and monitor discipline referrals.

The implementation of PBS is unique to each school. Although each school follows the same process, no two schools' rules, teaching strategies, or reward system are alike. Because each school develops ownership in the structure of their school, the sustainability of PBS is enhanced (Lewis et al., 2002; Sugai, Sprague, Horner, & Walker, 2000).

EXHIBIT 11.2
The Good Behavior Game

The Good Behavior Game (Barrish, Saunders, & Wolf, 1969) is a classroom management strategy designed to reduce aggressive and disruptive behavior of early elementary students, based on a process of group contingencies and clear behavioral goals set by teachers. To begin the process, the teacher targets behaviors that she or he would most like to change in the classroom. To begin the game, the teacher lists a few rules on the board, such as "stay in your seats" or "no talking to classmates," and then divides the class into teams. The teacher then identifies particular times that students are to follow those rules, often as short as 10 minutes. Each individual student is responsible to the rest of the team. The team that has the fewest violations of the rules "wins" the game. All team members immediately receive a small token reward, such as extra time at recess, the opportunity to line up first for lunch, or extra minutes of free time in the classroom. The teacher may announce the game at any time during the day for various periods of time, helping students monitor their behavior during the entire day. Over 20 years of research has shown the efficacy of this strategy to prevent disruptive and aggressive behavior (Embry, 2004). One large-scale longitudinal study also attests to the long-term effect of this strategy, particularly among highly aggressive boys (Kellam, Rebok, Ialongo, & Mayer, 1994).

characteristics central to attachment theory can be nurtured in a school environment. First, all children need a safe haven they can turn to in times of need. Second, children need a secure base of operation that grounds them as they explore the world. Both of these elements are essential not only in preventing risky behaviors, but also for taking academic risks to learn new content and to explore new ideas through various academic pathways. Even for children who have had poor, unattached relationships with their parents, attachment to a caring adult in the school, such as a mentor or a teacher, can help the child overcome emotional difficulties and thrive (Werner & Smith, 1982). The Caring School Community program (Exhibit 11.3) uses peer buddies to promote attachment between older and younger children. Other programs, such as Big Brothers/Big Sisters of America, are based on mentors who act as substitute parents to provide the positive bond the child lacks (Orpinas & Horne, 2006).

Resiliency

Resiliency is the ability to withstand or surmount risk (Masten, 2001). Werner and Smith (1982, 1992, 2001) conducted one of the first longitudinal studies to identify characteristics of resilient children, by following into adulthood children born on Kauai in 1955. Of those babies born with four or more risk factors, more than two-thirds were living successful lives as adults.

In examining the characteristics of these successful adults, the researchers identified three processes that supported the development of resiliency within individual, family, school, and community domains: care and support, meaningful participation, and high expectations (Benard, 1991). Care and support meet students' needs for affiliation and connectedness with family, peers, and schools. In schools, caring relationships that provide guidance and unconditional support can engage a students' intrinsic motivation to learn. Rutter and colleagues (1979) found that in schools with low levels of delinquency, adults gave students responsibilities and opportunities to participate in a range of school activities. High expectations often motivate students to achieve by transmitting the belief that the student, regardless of background, can be successful (Bosworth & Walz, 2005). Henderson and Milstein (2003) described six school characteristics that help develop student resiliency: (1) increase connectedness of students to school, (2) set clear and consistent boundaries, (3) teach life skills, (4) provide a caring and supportive environment, (5) set and communicate high expectations, and (6) provide opportunities for meaningful participation.

These theories have guided the development of a number of interventions that have been effective in changing environmental conditions, as shown in the examples provided in the exhibits. These programs have demonstrated impacts on several outcomes such as reducing discipline referrals, curtailing alcohol and other drug use, and increasing student bonding. These interventions have in common being process oriented— that is, they provide a step-by-step process to enhance a positive school climate. The next section examines some of these guidelines.

GUIDELINES FOR ENHANCING A POSITIVE SCHOOL CLIMATE

Changing school climate is a more complex process than implementing a single curriculum. Creating a positive climate is multidimensional and time consuming, requiring vision, diligence, and patience on the part of school leadership. This section summarizes the process and the roles for successful implementation of school-wide environmental change.

Most models for environmental change lean heavily on principles outlined in the field of community development (Minkler & Wallerstein, 1997). These community development principles and activities are highly process oriented. They do not rely on a prescriptive curriculum or set of intervention tools, although they may be implemented in the context of the development process. Instead, the power is in the process by which the members of the community work together to recognize problems or issues, define goals and solutions, and then identify activities specifically designed

EXHIBIT 11.4
BreakAway

BreakAway is a youth involvement/empowerment model for school change that has been used since the late 1970s (Lofquist, 1983; Lynn & Lofquist, 2002). In the BreakAway process, youth are not the passive recipients of services, but active partners in identifying problems and solutions.

The initial step in a BreakAway process is the training of a team of faculty members and administrators who will work with a group of student leaders and their projects. This training ensures that adults understand the role of youth as participants but do not abdicate their adult roles and responsibilities. Faculty are also trained in principles of prevention, needs assessment, action planning, and organizational change. After the training, educators identify a group of youth leaders to form a core team challenged with the responsibility of improving a situation at their school. The success of this approach lies in identifying leaders from all groups on campus, not just those who rise to the top in the conventional adult view of leadership (e.g., student council). The youth and educators together examine the current environment and develop a vision for an "ideal" school.

From this process, this adult-youth team develops an action plan to help move the school towards the ideal environment. The team also identifies additional student leaders who form the leadership team that will work with the core team to carry out the projects and activities. Some examples of BreakAway activities are students and faculty walking around campus "patrolling" during free time, formation of a human relations club, training of peer mediators and peer counselors, information campaign on how to help a friend with drug abuse, and meetings with local law enforcement to partner on identifying drug dealers. Case studies and anecdotal data have shown that this process reduces discipline infractions, improves overall relationships on campus, and increases engagement and connectedness among students (Lynn & Lofquist, 2002).

---

to change conditions within the community. These community organization principles have guided community activities since the 1950s. Nyswander (1956), among others, posited that the fundamental principle of community development was starting where the people are.

Social involvement alone can be preventive by providing a buffer against risk factors and by teaching social and problem-solving skills in an authentic environment. For example, one school principal who used the BreakAway process (Exhibit 11.4) to reduce racial tension in her school reported that the specific projects developed were secondary to the process by which student leaders from different races and ethnicities joined together to work toward common goals of betterment of the school. She reported that the sense of collaboration among the previously antagonistic groups permeated the school and changed the tone and atmosphere in the entire school. The School Social Competence Development and Bullying Prevention Model (Orpinas & Horne, 2006) and the Protective Schools model (Bosworth, 2000) propose a similar process. Exhibit 11.5 describes the Protective Schools model.

EXHIBIT 11.5
The Protective School Model

A Protective School (http://www.protectiveschools.org) is a vision of a learning community that emphasizes proactive approaches to using resources and knowledge to create a safe and caring environment for the social and academic growth of every child. This model originated as a result of the conclusions of a panel of experts from the fields of prevention, training, health education, and policy (Bosworth, 2000). These experts identified 10 dimensions of a school that would be "protective" for children: vision of success, a positive and protective school culture, commitment from leadership, strong academic program, research-based prevention, continuum of service, ongoing professional development, strong home/school/community relationships, funding and resources, and data-driven decision making.

The process begins by determining the support for the process and identifying a core team. Then, teachers and staff assess the school climate based on the 10 dimensions. The Protective Schools Assessment (PSA) uses an anonymous inventory. The individual responses are collated and, with this assessment tool, school staff can identify strengths as well as opportunities for growth and further achievement. The areas selected by faculty are formalized into a written action plan. The core team works with the administration, other faculty members, parents, and students to implement the changes identified in the action plan. Some of the changes may include the adoption of an evidence-based curriculum. For example, if a concern expressed on the assessment is students not treating each other with respect, the school may adopt a social skills curriculum. The core team would plan, monitor, and evaluate implementation of the curriculum.

More than 70 schools funded by two Safe Schools/Healthy Students grants have implemented the Protective Schools process. A 2-year evaluation has shown the development of a more positive school climate as well as increases in standardized test scores in mathematics, reading, and language arts (Kibble, 2006).

In a variety of school climate and culture change processes, administrators, counselors, and teachers play critical roles to achieve lasting change (Bosworth, 1999).

- *Leadership.* The school principal needs to be 100% supportive of school climate change. Initially, school leaders learn about the specific change process to be implemented, the dynamics of changing an organization, and their role in a successful implementation. Next, leaders must be visibly and actively supportive of the change process. Although it is not practical for leaders to be intimately involved in the day-to-day implementation activities, they are visible in actively supporting the change through a number of activities, such as holding discussions at meetings, allowing staff members to have the time and freedom to pursue innovative change strategies, and setting up a communication process by which the flow of information to the leadership and to the community at large is effectively managed. Leaders need to nurture leadership skills of teachers, counselors, librarians, custodians, and other adults in the school environment so that the change permeates the school culture.

- *Counselors.* School counselors are in a unique position to provide leadership and support for enhancing their school climate. Counselors have strong relationship skills that can provide a foundation for communicating the process and plans for change. Additionally, following the American School Counseling Association (ASCA) model, school counselors are trained in leadership, advocacy, and collaboration skills that are essential to the smooth operations of any implementation plan (ASCA, 2003).
- *Teacher Leaders.* Support and commitment from the administrators is critical, and key facilitation skills of the school counselor are crucial. As important as those factors are, another essential actor in the change process is a teacher leader. Teacher leaders are those who provide excellent instruction in the classroom and have skills and interest in providing leadership for the entire school. These teachers are also opinion leaders in the school. Generally, they have strong positive relationships and influence with their peers. To implement strategies to enhance the positive school climate, teacher leaders sit on committees that review data, develop action plans, actually implement plans, monitor progress, and evaluate success. They also serve as a conduit of communication about the change to other teachers, parents, and students. They can bring concerns from those parties to the attention of the administration and facilitate solutions to issues and problems.

Thus, the implementation of school-wide climate change involves a number of school personnel acting in leadership roles. The principal still plays a key role as gatekeeper of the issues that are the focus in the school and as the arbiter of resources. However, without others taking on responsibilities for the change process, implementation will not occur.

CONCLUSION

Theory and empirical studies support the importance of the school environment in sustaining positive student choices. If prevention of risk behaviors is to be successful, researchers and practitioners must pay attention to the climate of the school. Positive school climate is not merely relevant as a component of a prevention program but is also a critical and necessary tool to promote social justice.

A positive school climate results in students feeling more connected to the school, and such connection reduces risk-taking behavior and increases academic achievement. Additionally, a positive climate can facilitate the adoption and implementation with fidelity of evidence-based curricula. Finally, a positive climate in which prosocial skills are modeled and rewarded and in which students have ample opportunity to practice them can facilitate student mastery of essential prevention skills.

Support at all levels of school administration is essential for implementation of complex culture change. District administration provides for the vision and support, and the leadership from the principal and site administration must be visible and ongoing. School counselors play a fundamental role as leaders and facilitators of the process. Teacher leaders who are respected by their peers provide the time and energy to implement actions plans.

Models to promote a positive school climate are primarily process models, such as BreakAway, Positive Behavior Support, and the Protective Schools model. Each school applies the model to fit within its existing culture, which increases the likelihood of ownership of the process and the outcomes. Time invested at the beginning of the process may be considerable. However, once goals and implementation plans are in place, less time is spent managing student misbehavior.

By creating, enhancing, and maintaining a positive climate in schools, all members of the school community benefit: Teachers spend less time dealing with disruptive behavior that interrupts learning; students and staff are less stressed by being in an inviting, respectful, and safe environment; and students are more willing to pursue academic challenges that can lead to pathways out of situations currently limited by racism, sexism, or other societal discrimination.

REFERENCES

Ainsworth, M. D. S., & Bowlby, J. (1991). An ethological approach to personality development. *American Psychologist, 46,* 333–341.

Alder, N. (2000). Part III: Creating multicultural classrooms. *Multicultural Perspectives, 2,* 28–31.

American School Counseling Association. (2003). *The ASCA National Model: A framework for school counseling programs.* Alexandria, VA: Author.

Bandura, A. (1986). *Social foundations of thought and action: A social cognitive theory.* Englewood Cliffs, NJ: Prentice-Hall.

Barrish, H. H., Saunders, M., & Wolf, M. M. (1969). Good behavior game: Effects of individual contingencies for group consequences on disruptive behavior in a classroom. *Journal of Applied Behavior Analysis, 2,* 119–124.

Battistich, V., Solomon, D., Kim, D. I., Watson, M., & Schaps, E. (1995). Schools as communities, poverty levels of student populations, and students' attitudes, motives, and performance: A multilevel analysis. *American Educational Research Journal, 32,* 627–658.

Battistich, V., Solomon, D., Watson, M., & Schaps, E. (1997). Caring school communities. *Educational Psychologist, 32,* 137–151.

Benard, B. (1991). *Fostering resiliency in kids: Protective factors in the family, school, and community.* Portland, OR: Northwest Regional Educational Laboratory, Western Center for Drug-Free Schools and Communities.

Blum, R. W., McNeely, C. A., & Rinehart, P. M. (2002). *Improving the odds: The untapped power of schools to improve the health of teens.* Minneapolis: Center for Adolescent Health and Development, University of Minnesota.

Bosworth, K. (1999). *Preventing student violence: What schools can do.* Bloomington, IN: Phi Delta Kappa.

Bosworth, K. (2000). *Protective schools: Linking drug abuse prevention with student success.* Tucson: University of Arizona, College of Education.

Bosworth, K., & Walz, G. R. (2005). *Promoting student resiliency.* Alexandria, VA: American Counseling Association Foundation.

Botvin, G. J. (2000). Preventing drug abuse in schools: Social and competence enhancement approaches targeting individual-level etiologic factors. *Addictive Behaviors, 25,* 887–897.

Bowlby, J. (1982). *Attachment and loss, Vol. 1* (2nd ed.). New York: Basic Books.

Dill, V. S., & Haberman, M. (1995). Building a gentler school. *Educational Leadership, 52,* 69–71.

Elliott, D. S., & Mihalic, S. (2004). Issues in disseminating and replicating effective prevention programs. *Prevention Science, 5,* 47–53.

Embry, D. D. (2004). Community-based prevention using simple, low-cost, evidence-based kernels and behavior vaccines. *Journal of Community Psychology, 32,* 575–591.

English, F. W. (2000). *Deciding what to teach and test: Developing, aligning, and auditing the curriculum.* Thousand Oaks, CA: Corwin Press.

Farrell, A. D., Valois, R. F., & Meyer, A. L. (2002). Evaluation of the RIPP-6 violence prevention program at a rural middle school. *American Journal of Health Education, 33,* 167–172.

Fashola, O. S., & Slavin, R. E. (1997). Promising programs for elementary and middle schools: Evidence of effectiveness and replicability. *Journal of Education for Students Placed at Risk (JESPAR), 2,* 251–307.

Fullan, M. (2000). The three stories of education reform. *Phi Delta Kappan, 81,* 581–584.

Gottfredson, G. D., Jones, E. M., & Gore, T. W. (2002). Implementation and evaluation of a cognitive-behavioral intervention to prevent problem behavior in a disorganized school. *Prevention Science, 3,* 45–56.

Hein, K. (2004). *Preventing aggression in the classroom: A case study of extraordinary teachers.* Unpublished doctoral dissertation, University of Georgia.

Henderson, N., & Milstein, M. M. (2003). *Resiliency in schools: Making it happen for students and educators.* Thousand Oaks, CA: Corwin Press.

Ialongo, N., Poduska, J., Werthamer, L., & Kellam, S. G. (2001). The distal impact of two first-grade preventive interventions on conduct problems and disorder in early adolescence. *Journal of Emotional and Behavioral Disorders, 9,* 146–160.

Kellam, S. G., Rebok, G. W., Ialongo, N. S., & Mayer, L. S. (1994). The course and malleability of aggressive behavior from early first grade into middle school: Results of a developmental epidemiologically-based preventive trial. *Journal of Child Psychology and Psychiatry and Allied Disciplines, 35,* 259–281.

Kibble, B. (2006). *Tucson LINKS final report.* Submitted to Substance Abuse Mental Health Service Administration.

Kozol, J. (1991). *Savage inequalities.* New York: Harper Perennial.

Lewis, T. J., Powers, L. J., Kelk, M. J., & Newcomer, L. L. (2002). Reducing problem behaviors on the playground: An investigation of the application of school-wide positive behavior supports. *Psychology in the Schools, 39,* 181–190.

Lewis, T. J., Sugai, G., & Colvin, G. (1998). Reducing problem behavior through a school-wide system of effective behavioral support: Investigation of a school-wide social skills training program and contextual interventions. *School Psychology Review, 27,* 446–459.

Lofquist, W. A. (1983). *Discovering the meaning of prevention: A practical approach to positive change.* Tucson, AZ: Associates for Youth Development.

Lynn, D. D., & Lofquist, W. A. (2002). *BreakAway: A framework for creating positive school communities. A leadership team workbook.* Tucson, AZ: Development Publications.

Markow, D., & Scheer, M. (2002). *The MetLife survey of the American teacher, 2002—Student life: School, home and community* (Rep. No. ERIC # ED471707). New York: MetLife.

Marzano, R. J., Pickering, D. J., & Pollock, J. E. (2001). *Classroom instruction that works: Research-based strategies for increasing student achievement.* Baltimore: Association for Supervision and Curriculum Development.

Masten, A. S. (2001). Ordinary magic: Resilience processes in development. *American Psychologist, 56,* 227–238.

McGee, G. W. (2004). Closing the achievement gap: Lessons from Illinois' golden spike high-poverty high-performing schools. *Journal of Education for Students Placed at Risk, 9,* 97–125.

Meyer, A. L., Allison, K. W., Reese, L. R. E., Gay, F. N., & Multisite Violence Prevention Project. (2004). Choosing to be violence free in middle school: The student component of the GREAT schools and families universal program. *American Journal of Preventive Medicine, 26,* 20–28.

Minkler, M., & Wallerstein, N. (1997). Improving health through community organization and community building. In K. Glanz & F. M. Rimer (Eds.), *Health behavior and health education: Theory, research, and practice* (pp. 241–269). San Francisco: Jossey-Bass.

Newman, D. A., Horne, A. M., & Bartolomucci, C. L. (2000). *Bully Busters: A teacher's manual for helping bullies, victims, and bystanders.* Champaign, IL: Research Press.

Nyswander, D. (1956). Education for health: Some principles and their application. *Health Education Monographs.*

Orpinas, P., & Horne, A. M. (2006). *Bullying prevention: Creating a positive school climate and developing social competence.* Washington, DC: American Psychological Association.

Patton, G. C., Bond, L., Carlin, J. B., Thomas, L., Butler, H., Glover, S., et al. (2006). Promoting social inclusion in schools: A group-randomized trial of effects on student health risk behavior and well-being. *American Journal of Public Health, 96,* 1582–1587.

Resnick, M. D., Bearman, P. S., Blum, R. W., Bauman, K. E., Harris, K. M., Jones, J., et al. (1997). Protecting adolescents from harm: Findings from the National Longitudinal Study on Adolescent Health. *Journal of the American Medical Association, 278,* 823–832.

Resnick, M. D., Ireland, M., & Borowsky, I. (2004). Youth violence perpetration: What protects? What predicts? Findings from the National Longitudinal Study of Adolescent Health. *Journal of Adolescent Health, 35,* 424.e1–424.e10.

Reyna, C. (2000). Lazy, dumb, or industrious: When stereotypes convey attribution information in the classroom. *Educational Psychology Review, 12,* 85–110.

Rosenthal, R. (1994). Interpersonal expectancy effects: A 30-year perspective. *Current Directions in Psychological Science, 3,* 176–179.

Rowling, L. (1996). The adaptability of the health promoting schools concept: A case study from Australia. *Health Education Research: Theory and Practice, 11,* 519–526.

Rutter, M., Maughan, B., Mortimore, P., Ouston, J., & Smith, A. (1979). *Fifteen thousand hours.* Cambridge, MA: Harvard University Press.

Skroban, S. B., Gottfredson, D. C., & Gottfredson, G. D. (1999). A school-based social competency promotion demonstration. *Evaluation Review, 23,* 3–27.

Slavin, R. E., Madden, N. A., Dolan, L. J., Wasik, B. A., Ross, S., Smith, L., et al. (1996). Success for all: A summary of research. *Journal of Education for Students Placed at Risk, 1,* 41–76.

Smrekar, M., Guthrie, J. W., Owens, D. E., & Sims, P. G. (2001). *March toward excellence: School success and minority achievement in department of defense schools* (Rep. No. ERIC # ED459218). Washington, DC: National Education Goals Panel.

Solomon, D., Battistich, V., Watson, M., Schaps, E., & Lewis, C. (2000). A six-district study of educational change: Direct and mediating effects of the Child Development Project. *Social Psychology of Education, 4,* 3–51.

Solomon, D., Watson, M., Battistich, V., Schaps, E., & Delucchi, K. (1996). Creating classrooms that students experience as communities. *American Journal of Community Psychology, 24,* 719–748.

Sugai, G. (2003). Commentary: Establishing efficient and durable systems of school-based support. *School Psychology Review, 32,* 530–535.

Sugai, G., Sprague, J. R., Horner, R. H., & Walker, H. M. (2000). Preventing school violence: The use of office discipline referrals to assess and monitor school-wide discipline interventions. *Journal of Emotional and Behavioral Disorders, 8,* 94–101.

Swim, J. K., & Sanna, L. J. (1996). He's skilled, she's lucky: A meta-analysis of observers' attributions for women's and men's successes and failures. *Personality and Social Psychology Bulletin, 22,* 507–519.

Swisher, J. D. (2000). Sustainability of prevention. *Addictive Behaviors, 25,* 965–973.

Tobler, N. S., & Stratton, H. H. (1997). Effectiveness of school-based drug prevention programs: A meta-analysis of the research. *Journal of Primary Prevention, 18,* 71–128.

U.S. Department of Education, National Center for Educational Statistics. (1995). *Making the cut: Who meets highly selective college entrance criteria?* (NCES 95-732) Retrieved April 8, 2008, from http://nces.ed.gov/pubs/web/95732.asp

U.S. Department of Health and Human Services. (2001). *Youth violence: A report of the Surgeon General.* Rockville, MD: U.S. Department of Health and Human Services; Centers for Disease Control and Prevention, National Center for Injury Prevention; Substance Abuse and Mental Health Services Administration, Center for Mental Health Services; and National Institutes of Health, National Institute of Mental Health.

Werner, E. E., & Smith, R. S. (1982). *Vulnerable but invincible: A longitudinal study of resilient children and youth.* New York: McGraw-Hill.

Werner, E. E., & Smith, R. S. (1992). *Overcoming the odds: High risk children from birth to adulthood.* Ithaca, NY: Cornell University Press.

Werner, E. E., & Smith, R. S. (2001). *Journeys from childhood to midlife: Risk, resiliency, and recovery.* Ithaca, NY: Cornell University Press.

Williams, T., & Jones, H. (1993). School-health education in the European Community. *Journal of School Health, 63,* 133–135.

12

CREATING HEALTHY WORK ORGANIZATIONS

DAVID M. DEJOY AND MARK G. WILSON

Traditionally, worksite health promotion has been primarily concerned with improving the health and well-being of working people through programs and services that seek to improve personal health behaviors and lifestyle decisions. Worksite health promotion programs offer enormous potential for expanding the availability and use of preventive health services and combating health disparities and related equity and social justice issues in the United States (U.S. Department of Health and Human Services, 2000). At the same time, there is growing recognition that efforts to enhance the health of the workforce should be more comprehensive and include efforts to improve the social-organizational context of the workplace and the quality of work life itself (DeJoy & Wilson, 2003; Goetzel & Ozminkowski, 2000; McCunney, Anstadt, Burton, & Gregg, 1997; World Health Organization [WHO], 1999). This chapter argues that job characteristics and work environments can be important facilitating or limiting factors in maximizing the potential of prevention efforts in the workplace.

The term *work organization* is increasingly used to refer to social-organizational attributes—that is, how work processes are structured and managed, including scheduling, job design, human resource practices, management style, and related topics. The National Occupational Research Agenda (NORA) identified work organization as one of the national occupational safety and health research priority areas (National Institute for Occupational Safety and Health, 1996, 2002). The term *healthy work organization* is a logical extension and derives from the idea that it should be possible to distinguish healthy from unhealthy work systems.

The idea of healthy work organization has several attractive features. First, it focuses on environmental and organizational factors as modifiable risk factors for disease and injury in the workplace (Danna & Griffin, 1999; DeJoy & Wilson, 2003; McCunney et al., 1997). Emphasizing how work is structured and organized extends the focus beyond the immediate job–worker interface and provides a more systematic accounting of structural and macro-organizational influences; it fundamentally expands the work–health relationship. Second, work organization is an integrative concept that can bring together researchers and viewpoints from a number of different disciplines, not only traditional workplace health areas such as job stress, but also organizational behavior, human resources management, and economics (Danna & Griffin, 1999; DeJoy & Wilson, 2003). Third, work organization brings a human capital orientation to workplace health and suggests potentially important linkages between enhancing human capital and maximizing business strategy (Becker, Huselid, Pickus, & Spratt, 1997; Goetzel & Ozminkowski, 2000). Healthy organizations should have healthier and more productive employees and therefore be more successful in managing costs and competing in the marketplace.

Healthy work organization also intersects with two mega-trends transforming work life in virtually all advanced industrial economies. The first is the growing prominence of the "knowledge worker." Information-based and service-oriented economies rely much more on "brains" than "brawn" and on interpersonal skills for competitive advantage. The value of human capital has increased markedly and work organization factors are assuming greater prominence as drivers of productivity and employee satisfaction. Second, the basic exchange relationship between employer and employee has been transformed. Most workers no longer expect long-term job security and employment opportunities in exchange for diligence and loyalty. Employees are being asked to assume greater responsibility for managing their own retirement plans, health insurance, and other benefits, and for maximizing their future employability in a rapidly changing labor market. Contract work, self-employment, temporary work assignments, remote- or tele-working, and part-time employment are increasingly common modes of employment. This "flexibilization of worklife" (Aronsson, 1999) goes well beyond the absence of physical and environmental hazards; it involves a different and more complex mix of job design and organizational factors. Attributes such as learning opportunities, autonomy, and flexible scheduling have assumed increased importance in the contemporary workplace.

There is, however, a certain contradiction between these two trends. Although the human element has become more important in the business equation, many organizations now seem to value their employees less. From a social justice perspective, the typical worker seems to have lost ground in terms of return on the exchange for their labor. Presumably, other work characteristics may re-balance the exchange relationship; however, just as the incidence of job-related injuries and illnesses shows clear disparities across racial and ethnic groups (Davis, Rowland, Walker, & Taylor, 1995), it is predictable that these same employee groups are likely to lag in terms of this new exchange relationship.

THEORETICAL AND CONCEPTUAL ANTECEDENTS OF HEALTHY WORK ORGANIZATION

Understanding the *idea* of healthy work organization involves assembling and clarifying the various theoretical perspectives that have converged on the basic concept. What are the central or underlying premises of healthy work organization? Can the jargon and findings from different fields be distilled into a coherent and workable point of view? Writing and research related to healthy work organization can be conveniently grouped into four perspectives: (1) those who approach healthy work organization from a human resources or organizational development perspective; (2) those who advocate an expanded job or occupational stress model; (3) those who emphasize the organizational context in occupational safety and health programming; and (4) those who favor an integrative or multilevel health promotion perspective. Each of these perspectives is discussed in this section.

Human Resources and Organizational Development Perspective

Rosen (Rosen & Berger, 1991) and Jaffe (1995) have addressed the concept of healthy work organization most directly. Rosen coined the term *healthy companies* and, through interviews with corporate leaders, developed a values-based model of the healthy company. These companies share 13 values: open communication, employee involvement, learning and renewal, valued diversity, institutional fairness, equitable rewards and recognition, common economic security, people-centered technology, health-enhancing work environment, meaningful work, family–work life balance, community responsibility, and environmental protection. Rosen's working premise is that healthy people and healthy relationships are at the very core of success in business.

Jaffe argues that healthy work organization implies an expanded notion of organizational effectiveness. Organizational effectiveness traditionally focuses on how well the enterprise meets its profit, production, service, and survival goals. Jaffe's point is that organizational effectiveness should also include the health and well-being of the employees. He concludes that the concept of healthy organization involves a redefinition of the relationships, expectations, obligations, and interactions between employees and organizations (Jaffe, 1995).

Occupational Stress Perspective

A number of job stress researchers have addressed the concept of healthy organization, either directly or indirectly. For example, Cox (1988) has sought to expand the job stress model to incorporate the concept of organizational health. According to Cox, "organizational health represents the integration of what we know about health in relation to work but set in an organizational context" (p. 1). He argues that organizational health is affected by the consistency between the objective organization and the subjective organization. The objective organization is the structure, policies, and procedures, whereas the subjective organization involves the task of the organization, the way the organization solves problems, and the opportunities provided for employee growth and development. The basic implication of this line of thinking is to increase the salience of organizational or contextual factors in the work–health relationship.

Cooper and Cartwright (1994) and Lindstrom (1994) have attempted to identify the job and organizational attributes that characterize healthy or low-stress work environments. These authors focus on psychosocial work organization and emphasize the importance of organizational or contextual factors in diagnosing and remedying the causes of stress within organizations. As an illustration, Cooper and Cartwright, in their front-end approach to addressing organizational stress, suggest a variety of organizational change interventions, in addition to the more traditional individual-oriented strategies typically used to manage job stress.

Occupational Safety and Health Management Perspective

A distinct movement emphasizing the importance of organizational and contextual factors is increasingly evident in occupational safety and health research. The body of research on safety and health climate/culture (e.g., Cox & Howarth, 1990; DeJoy, Murphy, & Gershon, 1995; Ribisl & Reischl, 1993; Zohar, 1980) underscores the importance of the broader organizational context in shaping employee behaviors. Related research on human error (e.g., Reason, 1995) also emphasizes the importance of organizational action or inaction in creating the substrate or backdrop for human error by frontline workers. Several authors have espoused the fundamental importance of management system failures occurring upstream in the chain of causation (e.g., Hale & Hovden, 1998; Hofmann, Jacobs, & Landy, 1995). Research on workplace self-protective behavior and safety performance (e.g., DeJoy, 1996; DeJoy, Gershon, Murphy, & Wilson, 1996; Guastello, 1993; Hofmann et al., 1995) highlights organization-level factors as facilitating or hindering safe behavior in the workplace.

Health Promotion Perspective

Over 20 years ago, Pelletier (1984) argued that worksite health promotion programs should be expanded to include interventions designed to improve organizational and environmental conditions. He offered a spheres of influence model that is depicted by several concentric circles building outward from the individual through the work group and organization and beyond. More recently, ecological models of health promotion (e.g., McLeroy, Bibeau, Steckler, & Glanz, 1988) and the related concept of environments that promote health (Stokols, 1992) elaborate this general systems approach to workplace health. DeJoy and Southern (1993) used an ecological frame of reference as a transition point for addressing environmental and organizational influences in prevention programming. They propose an integrative model of health promotion that features three interactive systems: job demands and worker characteristics, work environment, and extra-organizational influences. The principal goal of integrative programming is to devise complementary behavioral and environmental interventions that will have mutually reinforcing effects on worker health.

Financial and other organizational effectiveness outcomes are gaining visibility in the health promotion literature, in the form of attempts to link investments in prevention programs and services with health care costs, absenteeism, and business performance (e.g., Goetzel, Jacobson, Aldana, Vardell, & Yee, 1998; Ozminkowski et al., 1999). Terms such as *health management, health and productivity management*, and *human capital management* are being used to highlight the business outcomes orientation of this work.

When these four perspectives are viewed together, it becomes evident that they share several features in common (Vandenberg, Park, DeJoy, Wilson, & Griffin-Blake, 2002):

- *The increased salience of the organizational context in the work–health relationship.* The emphasis on organizational factors is hardly surprising in that the organization controls resources, sets priorities, shapes work environments, and sets boundaries for what is possible. Very little can be accomplished in work settings without the overt support of management.
- *The importance of organization-level action in producing positive change.* This second element follows from the first but underscores the fact that improving worker health and productivity

involves making changes in the structure and fabric of the organization itself.

- *The need to modify the traditional employer–employee relationship in terms of increased opportunities for information exchange and employee involvement.* The current business environment often demands increased employee initiative and resourcefulness, and these outcomes are difficult to achieve in the absence of increased employee involvement and autonomy. Increased opportunity for participation is not always a good thing for employees. In some instances, participation is more superficial than substantive and/or may represent an intensification of work demands in the absence of increased decision latitude, resources, or opportunities for skill acquisition (Landsbergis, 2003).
- *The idea that the immediate work situation consists of multiple domains.* This element suggests that the immediate work situation includes more than the physical and psychological demands of the job itself. It also involves the social/organizational environment of the workplace—the workplace context. It acknowledges that the individual's work situation is shaped by a variety of other factors that fall within the broad category of job security and career development.
- *An expanded view of organizational effectiveness that includes employee health and well-being as well as business or mission success.* This element holds that healthy employees are more productive and less costly and that organizations with more productive employees should be more successful in terms of business or mission performance. Linking investments in employee health and well-being to business performance is clearly a growing trend, and, depending on the point of view, this may be good or bad. It may be good in the sense that it brings employee health and human resource considerations into the mainstream of business strategy and to the attention of senior managers. It may be bad because it suggests that absent financial or business ramifications, employee health and well-being may be less legitimate concerns for the organization.

CONCEPTUAL MODEL OF HEALTHY WORK ORGANIZATION

Figure 12.1 presents a conceptual model of healthy work organization. The outcomes of interest are labeled *Effectiveness Outcomes* and include measures addressing employee health and well-being as well as more conventional indices of organizational effectiveness (e.g., productivity, finan-

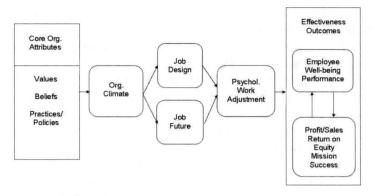

Figure 12.1. Model of healthy work organization. From "Organizational Health Promotion: Broadening the Horizon of Workplace Health Promotion," by D. M. DeJoy and M. G. Wilson; reprinted with permission from *American Journal of Health Promotion* (2003; 17: 339). Copyright 2003 by the *American Journal of Health Promotion.*

cial performance). Healthy work organization is hypothesized as comprising five interrelated components: (1) core organizational attributes, (2) organizational climate, (3) job design, (4) job future, and (5) psychological work adjustment. The first of these components (core organizational attributes) is considered to be exogenous because it is subject to influence by factors outside of the proposed model. Organizations do not exist in isolation; they are subject to a variety of extra-organizational influences, such as economic or market conditions, socialcultural trends, and legislative or legal actions (DeJoy & Southern, 1993).

In the proposed model, core organizational attributes are defined in terms of three variables: organizational values, beliefs, and practices and policies. These three variables delve into the leadership or cultural resources of the organization at three different levels. In many respects, companies are successful because they pay attention to all stakeholders and do not focus exclusively on any single task or constituency (Beer, Eisenstat, & Spector, 1990; Kotter & Heskett, 1992). In terms of organizational values, the healthy organization and the successful organization should both show a good balance between production and employee orientations (Polley, 1987).

At the next level, organizational beliefs involve how the organization views its commitment to and responsibility for employee health and well-being. At least three issues are important here. The first issue concerns general beliefs about the importance of healthy and satisfied employees to the overall success of the enterprise (Ribisl & Reischl, 1993). Of central importance is the idea that employees represent more than units of cost in the business equation. The second involves beliefs about the extent to which employees should be involved in decision making and their attendant needs for relevant information. The third issue refers to a sense of shared responsibility for employee health and well-being, which involves the idea that both individual behavior and organization-level action are important to preventing disease and injury and maximizing worker health and well-being (DeJoy & Southern, 1993).

The third level deals with managerial actions related to employee health and well-being, which essentially reflects how the organization's values and beliefs are translated into policies and programs. Human resources policies affect how employees experience life within an organization, and such policies are among the more readily observable expressions of the organization's basic values and beliefs about its people. Jamieson and O'Mara (1991) argue that the encouragement of personal health within an organization requires policies in four important areas: matching people and jobs, managing and rewarding performance, informing and involving people, and supporting lifestyle and life needs. A fifth area should be added to address the provision of a safe and healthful work environment.

Job design, organizational climate, and job future are central to the model and represent three major domains of work life. In many respects, these domains represent the tangible evidence of healthy work organization. Job design involves the demands and other aspects of the job or task situation itself, or what DeJoy and Southern (1993) refer to as the "immediate job-worker interface." The second domain, organizational climate, focuses on participation, communication, and interpersonal relationships at work, particularly the shared perceptions held by workers about their work group and organization (e.g., Zohar, 1980). The third domain is labeled job future (Sauter, Murphy, & Hurrell, 1990) and includes job security, equity, and related career development considerations.

Psychological work adjustment is included in the model to underscore the importance of subjective evaluation and individual meaning in understanding the effects of various job and organizational factors on employee health and well-being (Lindstrom, 1994). Employees perceive and react to the reality they experience as members of an organization. The subjective or perceived qualities of the organization are at least as important as the objective or actual qualities (Lindstrom, 1994). Furthermore, job satisfaction, organizational commitment, and other widely applied indices of psychological work adjustment represent outcomes that can be used to assess how people are responding to their work environment and are predictive of longer-term consequences on well-being and productivity (Meyer, Stanley, Herscovitch, & Topolnytsky, 2002).

Using data collected from 1,100 employees of a large national retailer, Wilson, DeJoy, and colleagues (Wilson, DeJoy, Vandenberg, Richardson, & McGrath, 2004) used structural equation modeling techniques to provide a cross-sectional test of the model of healthy work organization (Figure 12.1). The service sector is a rapidly expanding segment of the American economy, and the cooperation of this large retail organization provided an excellent opportunity to test the model outside of a corporate headquarters or traditional white collar setting. The model showed good fit across multiple indices as well as significant associations among all of the hypothesized second order latent variables (see Wilson et al., 2004, for details of the model test). In particular, this study supports the important role that employee perceptions and expectations play in organizational outcomes, particularly health and well-being outcomes. The policies, procedures, and actions an organization takes to improve efficiency and effectiveness are filtered through the employees and reflected in their satisfaction with, and commitment to, the job and organization. However, these analyses did not include financial or business performance outcomes, which normally require unit-level data.

MAKING ORGANIZATIONS HEALTHIER

The central importance of organizational level factors in all of the proposed conceptual models of healthy work organization suggests that some type of systematic organizational assessment and change process should be the starting point for making organizations healthier. Undertaking such a process, however, can be a daunting task for an organization. First and foremost, the organization must be willing to openly examine its key organizational policies and structures, important work tasks, and basic modes of operation and decision making. But this is not enough. There also needs to be some type of systematic process or mechanism for identifying problems and for evaluating the actions taken to solve them. Ideally, this process should be participatory, visible, and continuous. In addition, employees throughout the organization need to be involved and empowered to make decisions and to take steps to improve work processes, alter working conditions, and make other changes as needed.

Management Support and Leadership

The adoption of innovative policies and practices within organizations has been studied from a number of different perspectives (Skinner, 2002). As a general rule, adoption is most likely when a match exists between some important organizational problem and the potential solution or innovation at hand. The growing connection between employee health and well-being and organizational effectiveness is clarifying the problem side of this challenge. Today, a fairly strong case can be made for the cost and productivity benefits of having healthy employees (e.g., Goetzel, 2004). The second portion of this challenge is more difficult because any healthy work organization initiative must still compete for a spot on the agenda with other performance-enhancing strategies, many of which have more familiarity and visibility in the business world.

The support of senior management is essential at the beginning of any type of organizational change effort, including healthy work organization. However, the greater challenge is sustaining the attention and support of management in the face of other competing and changing demands and expectations. The establishment of a systematic problem-solving process may help to sustain management support because it can provide a vehicle for linking problems and solutions and provide targeted feedback to management on impact and outcomes. Problem-solving and change orientations are especially important because managers in organizations trying to become healthier should feel free to take steps to create new structures and policies to improve the system or culture (Katz & Kahn, 1978).

Employee Involvement

The research literature on participation and worker involvement shows a wide range of effects in the fields of management, organizational behavior, industrial psychology, and communications (e.g., Cotton, Vollrath, Froggatt, Lengnick-Hall, & Jennings, 1988; Lawler, 1986; Miller & Monge, 1986). Participation serves to enhance the employees' sense of understanding, control (self-efficacy), and communication. Almost by definition, participation increases communication, but it should also increase perceptions of control over events, the upward sharing of information, and knowledge about the organizational context and the individual's role in the organization. Berger and Calabrese (1975) argue that the reduction of uncertainty is an important function of interpersonal communication. Uncertainty exists when one does not know how and why events are occurring and makes it less probable that the individual will believe he or she can act in ways to produce positive outcomes. Participation should lead to all employees having more information about the organization's goals and performance and should help to establish a clearer link between desired performance and distributed rewards. Participation may also increase opportunities for both informational and emotional social support (Marks, Mirvis, Hackett, & Grady, 1986). From an organizational development perspective, broad-based participation is important to continuous improvement and organizational learning (e.g., Senge, 1990). Achieving a sense of empowerment at work typically involves gaining understanding and control, and many empowerment strategies emphasize skill development and the creation of mutual support systems (Zimmerman, 1995). Empowerment activities appear to be critical in facilitating the problem-solving process and helping organizations to improve their work systems and to become healthier and more effective.

Data-Driven Problem-Solving Process

Part of creating a healthy work organization is having norms that value data collection, problem solving, and sharing information to facilitate cooperative or teamwork efforts. Instituting a problem-solving process that is participatory is entirely consistent with the objectives of healthy work organization. A problem-solving process is data-driven to the extent that participants have access to multiple data sources for identifying problems, developing action plans, and evaluating outcomes. Relevant data sources might include financial performance results, injury/illness surveillance data, productivity/quality data, cost analyses, and employee absenteeism/turnover. All of this data exists in most organizations, but it is seldom integrated in any effective manner (DeJoy & Southern, 1993; Goetzel, 2004). Assessing multiple data sources should contribute to objective and convergent verification of problem areas that will be evaluated further as action plans and intervention priorities are created. This data should also be useful in providing insights into the possible causes of identified problems, the types of interventions needed, and the ultimate effectiveness of the selected interventions or actions.

TESTING A HEALTHY WORK ORGANIZATION INTERVENTION

Figure 12.2 outlines an intervention process proposed by DeJoy and Wilson (2003). This process draws from total quality management (TQM) (e.g., Waldman, 1994), organizational learning (e.g., Senge, 1990), and high involvement work processes (e.g., Lawler, 1992). All three approaches emphasize problem-solving and employee involvement as central to organizational change. This intervention process assumes that most of the tangible evidence of healthy work organization shows up in three domains of work life: job design, organizational climate, and job future. Changes in these three domains represent the immediate or proximal outcomes of the change process. As the inputs section of Figure 12.2 indicates, management underwrites the entire process, involving sharing operations-related information with employees, providing opportunities for meaningful participation, and allocating resources sufficient to implement needed structural and operational changes. In the outcomes side of the figure, the problem-solving process shows its effects on organizational effectiveness by influencing the three basic domains of healthy work organization: job design, organizational climate, and job future. Improvements in organizational effectiveness should include employee health and well-being as well as outcomes related to productivity, customer service, and overall financial performance and profitability, which represent the long-term or distal outcomes of the intervention

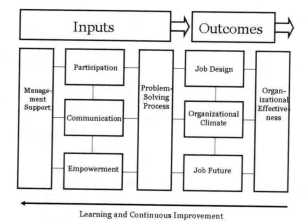

Figure 12.2. Healthy work organization intervention process. From "Organizational Health Promotion: Broadening the Horizon of Workplace Health Promotion," by D. M. DeJoy and M. G. Wilson; reprinted with permission from *American Journal of Health Promotion* (2003; 17: 340). Copyright 2003 by the *American Journal of Health Promotion.*

process. The feedback arrow across the bottom of the figure suggests a learning or continuous improvement process whereby results shape and reinforce the overall organizational change process. In essence, this is designed as an action and results-oriented process.

Study Design and Methodology

Working with the same large retail chain as in the cross-sectional test of our model, 21 stores comprising four operational districts within the southern U.S. region were recruited into the study. Two districts (11 stores) were assigned to the intervention group, and two districts (10 stores) served as control sites. Assignment to intervention and control groups was conducted to make the two sets of stores as comparable as possible in location demographics, employee characteristics, and sales volume. Baseline surveys (organizational audits) were conducted at all 21 sites 6 months prior to the start of the intervention. This same survey with minor modifications was then re-administered approximately 12 months later (post-test 1), and again 24 months later (post-test 2). The intervention process commenced in the intervention stores approximately 6 months following the baseline survey.

An employee problem-solving team, called the "ACTion team," was organized within each intervention store. Each team included approximately 8 to 12 employees who were broadly representative of the employees in each store, and store managers were not eligible to participate on the team. The teams were charged with developing, implementing, and evaluating a tailored plan of action for addressing the issues or problems identified within the store. Summary results from the baseline survey were given to the problem-solving teams, along with monthly reports that tracked business performance for the store.

Assisted by trained facilitators, the ACTion teams developed their action plans using a five-phase problem-solving process: familiarization, skill building, prioritization, action, and reaction. This process provided a simple step-by-step procedure for addressing identified workplace issues. An intervention team manual provided guidance and resource materials for the teams as they worked their way through the successive stages of the intervention process. The level of facilitation was gradually reduced in an effort to help the teams become more independent and self-sustaining. Teams met weekly with their facilitator for 8 weeks, then weekly without the facilitator for 8 weeks. Following this 16-week period, the teams scheduled and conducted their own meetings. Although all intervention stores used this same five-stage intervention process and intervention manual, specific activities and initiatives varied from site to site based on identified needs and specific action strategies adopted by the teams. There were some commonalities in the problems identified in the various stores, specifically, issues related to environmental working conditions, work scheduling, equity, and communication. In control stores, teams were not formed, and organized activities or consultations were not provided.

Assessment of Intervention Effectiveness

Intervention effectiveness was assessed in terms of proximal, intermediate, and long-term outcomes (Table 12.1). All analyses were performed using store-level data (N=21). The proximal outcomes included three sets of scales measuring various dimensions of job design, organizational climate, and job future. These measures were the same as used in our cross-sectional analysis of our model of healthy work organization (Wilson et al., 2004). The intermediate outcomes included a set of measures assessing psychological work adjustment. These are included, in part, based on their demonstrated importance in the cross-section of our conceptual model of healthy work organization (Wilson et al., 2004). The long-term outcomes included sets of measures of employee health and well-being and store business performance.

It is important to note that this longitudinal study took place during a challenging period for the company. In addition to a transition in top corporate leadership soon after the start of the study, the company faced unusually severe competitive pressures, a recessionary national economy, and the occurrence and aftermath of the September 11, 2001, terrorist attack on the World Trade Center and Pentagon. As a result, scores on most of the measures declined across time for both intervention and control stores. This pattern notwithstanding, the intervention still produced

TABLE 12.1
Outcome Measures for the Healthy Work Organization Intervention

Proximal outcomes	Intermediate outcomes	Distal (long-term) outcomes
Job Design • Workload • Control/autonomy • Job content • Role clarity • Physical demands • Environmental conditions • Work schedule **Organizational Climate** • Organizational support • Co-worker support • Involvement/participation • Communication • Workplace safety & health **Job Future** • Job security • Learning opportunities • Flexible work arrangements • Procedural equity • Distributive equity	**Psychological Work Adjustment** • Job satisfaction • Organizational commitment • Work empowerment • Perceived stress	**Employee Health & Well-being** • General health status • Safety at work • Alcohol use • High-risk health behaviors • Preventive health behaviors **Store Business Performance** • Employee turnover • Comparable sales • Sales per labor hour • Average ticket

beneficial effects in several respects. In terms of the proximal outcomes, several of the work dimensions targeted for improvement by the teams did improve significantly in the intervention stores relative to the control stores, specifically, work scheduling, environmental conditions, and equity concerns. Consistent with the participatory focus of the intervention process, significant effects favoring the intervention stores were also found for involvement processes and organizational support. In addition, the intervention stores were better able to retain their strengths during turbulent times. Indeed, the extent of decline in many of the job domain dimensions was less precipitous in the stores receiving the intervention. An essentially similar pattern was evident for psychological work adjustment (intermediate outcomes). Statistically significant intervention effects were obtained for three of the work adjustment measures (job satisfaction, organizational commitment, and job stress); for both job satisfaction and organizational commitment, the rates of decline were steeper for control than for intervention stores. The levels of job stress within the intervention stores remained relatively low and unchanged across time, but stress levels within the control units increased steeply over the same time period.

Shifting to the long-term outcomes, significant intervention effects in the expected direction were obtained for two of the five health and well-being measures: overall perceived health and perceived safety at work. In contrast to the intervention units, which increased slightly on both variables during the duration of this study, the slopes within the control stores indicated steep levels of decline in both health and safety. The effects for alcohol use, engaging in high-risk health behaviors, and undertaking preventive health measures were not statistically significant. For the four financial measures, significant results were obtained for sales per labor hour and employee turnover. In both instances, the outcomes favored those stores receiving the intervention. Examining the trends from Time 2 (which represents the survey administration closest to the intervention process) to Time 3, the intervention stores experienced an actual increase in sales per labor hour and a leveling of employee turnover, whereas control stores experienced a slight decline in sales per labor hour and increased turnover.

Overall, the intervention process seemed to be effective in terms of impact on targeted job domain dimensions and the general climate of the intervention stores. Positive effects were obtained for some traditional measures of psychological work adjustment, including job satisfaction and organizational commitment. The impact on long-term outcomes was less successful, but there were some statistically significant effects for perceived overall health, perceived safety at work, and two business outcomes, which are key indicators for the retail sector.

Lessons Learned

It is difficult to maintain intervention "intensity" across a lengthy intervention period. In essence, the intervention must "compete" and be sustained in the face of other organizational realities and priorities that demand the attention of managers and rank-and-file workers alike. Maintaining sufficient intensity across many months is particularly difficult in the retail sector where business follows wide seasonal variations, employee turnover is high, competition is direct, and work scheduling is variable and often unpredictable. Intervention intensity is critical to producing beneficial effects on health behavior and health risk measures, or in terms of the intervention process converting proximal outcomes into distal outcomes. Health-related outcomes will always be more difficult to achieve because they are influenced by a variety of factors, only some of which are related to an individual's work situation.

Another complicating factor is that each site was free to identify its own priority problems and devise its own solutions. This basic approach makes sense, in that each store presents its own unique environment and socio-organizational context, but this clearly makes it more difficult to demonstrate intervention effectiveness in the conventional manner. Not all stores addressed the exact same problems and, even when the same issues were chosen, the identified solutions were not identical either in terms of potential efficacy or quality of follow-through. This problem is certainly not unique to workplace studies, and similar problems are frequently encountered in participatory action research and community-based public health interventions (Kegler, Twiss, & Look, 2000). Our approach to this problem was to identify certain bellwether outcomes that should be sensitive to general participatory aspects of the intervention and then use broad sets of proximal, intermediate, and distal outcome measures.

Our intervention process acknowledges the central importance of management support but, in American business at least, the attention span of management is often limited by the need to show results on the next quarterly report. The patience for long-term interventions is clearly limited. In our experience with this study, management support, per se, may not be sufficient for this type of intervention to succeed. Our study points to the fine, but important, distinction between management support and management priority. Corporate and district management endorsed this project, and store managers went along with the intervention process and data collection requirements. However, process evaluation data suggest that, for store-level management, the teams were more a novelty than a priority. This may have been different under more favorable business conditions.

This research is unique in at least two respects. First, it represents one of very few work organization studies attempted in the retail sector of the economy. Second, participatory and intensive work organization interventions, by their very nature, are usually applied in settings where the workforce is stable (i.e., low turnover) and where employees have relatively high levels of education and/or job commitment. This is not the case in retail, but we did find that these workers were quite capable of developing and using problem-solving and planning skills in a team-based format. Process evaluation results indicated that participants considered the experience to be beneficial and worthwhile. The problems experienced by the teams were more about lacking the power to implement recommendations rather than not being able to successfully engage in the intervention process itself.

CONCLUSION

This chapter began by arguing that the idea of healthy work organization represents the convergence of trends evident in several different areas of research and practice, including human resources and organizational development, work stress, occupational safety and health management, and worksite health promotion. At this juncture, we have a reasonably good picture of what constitutes healthy work organization. Virtually all of the factors or dimensions identified as being important have been well researched as individual variables. What we are just beginning to do is to examine how these factors interact and operate together in influencing various employee and business outcomes. The development of a conceptual model of healthy work organization is an important step because it: (1) specifies relationships or linkages between components and variables, (2) suggests various leverage points for intervening to improve individual and organizational health, and (3) provides for proximal and intermediate measures of the success or failure of change efforts. Research on healthy work organization is helping to expand the work–health relationship and calling attention to the importance of organizational–environmental factors as modifiable risk factors for disease and injury in the workplace.

Before getting too enthusiastic, we must recognize that there have been only a few preliminary tests of multicomponent models. Testing a model using cross-sectional data is not a particularly complex undertaking. The major requirement is to find an organization that is willing to allow employees to complete a fairly lengthy survey instrument. Testing healthy work organization interventions is another story entirely. First, there is the need to find an organization that is willing to entertain actual organizational and/or operational modifications and to engage in some type of relatively open assessment process in which management will be asked to share some amount of control and relinquish some level of privacy. This is a fairly tall order for many businesses facing today's economic and competitive realities. Secondly, these types of interventions are difficult to evaluate.

The intervention study summarized in this chapter represents one of the first studies to test a healthy work organization intervention and to include both employee health and business performance outcomes. This study also specified sets of proximal and intermediate measures consistent with the intervention logic model. This approach has been recommended for participatory research studies involving multiple study sites where each site has some autonomy in identifying problems and selecting remedies (Kegler, Twiss, & Look, 2000; Parkes & Sparkes, 1998). Although this study occurred during a rather tumultuous period for the host company, the results were quite encouraging. We were able to detect effects on several specific work dimensions that were targeted by many of the store-level intervention teams. Significant effects were also evident for those organizational climate dimensions hypothesized to be most sensitive to the intervention process, particularly involvement processes and organizational support. The intervention process also showed effects on job satisfaction and organizational commitment, two traditionally important indices of psychological work adjustment. Finally, the study yielded effects for some of employee health and business performance measures. Not every long-term outcome was affected, but in comparing intervention and control stores, the pattern of results suggests that the intervention process did extend to these measures.

REFERENCES

Aronsson, G. (1999). Influence of worklife on public health. *Scandinavian Journal of Work and Environmental Health, 25*, 597–604.

Becker, B. E., Huselid, M. A., Pickus, P. S., & Spratt, M. F. (1997). HR as a source of shareholder value: Research and recommendations. *Human Resources Management, 36*, 39–47.

Beer, M., Eisenstat, R. A., & Spector, B. (1990). *The critical path for corporate renewal.* Cambridge, MA: Harvard Business School Press.

Berger, C. R., & Calabrese, R. J. (1975). Some explorations in initial interaction and beyond: Toward a development theory of interpersonal communication. *Human Communication Research, 1*, 99–112.

Cooper, C. L., & Cartwright, S. (1994). Healthy mind, healthy organization—A proactive approach to occupational stress. *Human Relations, 47*, 455–471.

Cotton, J., Vollrath, D., Froggatt, K. L., Lengnick-Hall, M., & Jennings, K. R. (1988). Employee participation: Diverse forms and different outcomes. *Academy of Management Review, 13*, 8–22.

Cox, T. (1988). Editorial: Organizational health. *Work & Stress, 2*(1), 1–2.

Cox, T., & Howarth, I. (1990). Organizational health, culture, and helping. *Work & Stress, 4*(2), 107–110.

Danna, K., & Griffin, R. W. (1999). Health and well-being in the workplace: A review and synthesis of the literature. *Journal of Management 25*(3), 357–384.

Davis, M. E., Rowland, A. S., Walker, B., & Taylor, A. K. (1995). Minority workers. In B. S. Levy & D. H. Wegman (Eds.), *Occupational health: Recognizing and preventing work-related disease* (3rd ed., pp. 639–649). Boston: Little-Brown.

DeJoy, D. M. (1996). Theoretical models of health behavior and workplace protective behavior. *Journal of Safety Research, 27*, 61–72.

DeJoy, D. M., Gershon, R. R. M., Murphy, L. R., & Wilson, M. G. (1996). A work-systems analysis of compliance with universal precautions among health care workers. *Health Education Quarterly, 23*(2), 159–174.

DeJoy, D. M., Murphy, L., & Gershon, R. R. M. (1995). The influence of employee job/task, and organizational factors on adherence to universal precautions among nurses. *International Journal of Industrial Ergonomics, 16*, 43–55.

DeJoy, D. M., & Southern, D. J. (1993). An integrative perspective on worksite health promotion. *Journal of Occupational Medicine, 35*, 1221–1230.

DeJoy, D. M., & Wilson, M. G. (2003). Organizational health promotion: Broadening the horizon of workplace health promotion. *American Journal of Health Promotion, 17*, 337–341.

Goetzel, R. Z. (2004). *Examining the value of integrating occupational health and safety and health promotion programs in the workplace.* Rockville, MD: U.S. Department of Health and Human Services, Public Health Service, Centers for Disease Control, National Institute for Occupational Safety and Health.

Goetzel, R. Z., & Ozminkowski, R. J. (2000). Health and productivity management: Emerging opportunities for health promotion professionals for the 21st century. *American Journal of Health Promotion, 14,* 211–214.

Goetzel, R. Z., Jacobson, B. H., Aldana, S. G., Vardell, K., & Yee, L. (1998). Health care costs of worksite health promotion participants and non-participants. *Journal of Occupational and Environmental Medicine, 40,* 341–346.

Guastello, S. J. (1993). Do we really know how well our occupational accident prevention programs work? *Safety Science, 16,* 445–463.

Hale, A. R., & Hovden, I. (1998). Management and culture: The third age of safety—A review of approaches to organizational aspects of safety, health, and environment. In A. M. Feyer & A. Williamson (Eds.), *Occupational injury: Risk, prevention, and intervention* (pp. 129–165). London: Taylor-Francis.

Hofmann, D. A., Jacobs, R., & Landy, F. (1995). High reliability process industries: Individual, micro, and macro organizational influences on safety performance. *Journal of Safety Research, 26,* 131–149.

Jaffe, D. T. (1995). The healthy company: Research paradigms for personal and organizational health. In S. L. Sauter & L. R. Murphy (Eds.), *Organizational risk factors for job stress* (pp. 13–29). Washington, DC: American Psychological Association.

Jamieson, D., & O'Mara, J. (1991). *Managing workforce 2000: Gaining the diversity advantage.* San Francisco: Jossey-Bass.

Katz, D., & Kahn, R. L. (1978). *The social psychology of organizations* (2nd ed.). New York: Wiley.

Kegler, M. C., Twiss, J. M., & Look, V. (2000). Assessing community change at multiple levels: The genesis of an evaluation framework for the California Healthy Cities Project. *Health Education and Behavior, 27,* 760–779.

Kotter, J., & Heskett, T. (1992). *Corporate culture and performance.* New York: Free Press.

Landsbergis, P. A. (2003). The changing organization of work and the safety and health of working people: A commentary. *Journal of Occupational and Environmental Medicine, 45,* 61–72.

Lawler, E. E., III. (1986). *High involvement management.* San Francisco: Jossey-Bass.

Lawler, E. E., III. (1992). *The ultimate advantage: Creating the high involvement organization.* San Francisco: Jossey-Bass.

Lindstrom, K. (1994). Psychosocial criteria for good work organization. *Scandinavian Journal of Work, Environment, & Health, 20,* 123–133.

Marks, M. L., Mirvis, P. H., Hackett, E. J., & Grady, J. F. (1986). Employee participation in a quality circle program: Impact on quality of work life, productivity, and absenteeism. *Journal of Applied Psychology, 71,* 61–69.

McCunney, R. J., Anstadt, G., Burton, W. N., & Gregg, D. (1997). The competitive advantage of a healthy work force: Opportunities for occupational medicine. *Journal of Occupational and Environmental Medicine, 39*, 611–613.

McLeroy, K. R., Bibeau, D., Steckler, A., & Glanz, K. (1988). An ecological perspective on health promotion programs. *Health Education Quarterly, 15*, 351–377.

Meyer, J. P., Stanley, D. J., Herscovitch, L., & Topolnytsky, L. (2002). Affective, continuance, and normative commitment to the organization: A meta-analysis of antecedents, correlates, and consequences. *Journal of Vocational Behavior, 61*, 20–52.

Miller, K., & Monge, P. R. (1986). Participation, satisfaction, and productivity: A meta-analytic review. *Academy of Management Journal, 29*, 727–753.

National Institute for Occupational Safety and Health. (1996). *National occupational research agenda* (NIOSH Publication No. 96-115). Washington, DC: Author.

National Institute for Occupational Safety and Health. (2002). *The changing organization of work and the safety and health of working people* (DHHS/NIOSH Publication No. 2002-116). Washington, DC: Author.

Ozminkowski, R. J., Dunn, R. L., Goetzel, R. Z., Cantor, R. I., Murnane, J., & Harrison, M. (1999). A return on investment evaluation of the Citibank, N.A., health management program. *American Journal of Health Promotion, 14*, 31–43.

Parkes, K. R., & Sparkes, T. J. (1998). *Organizational interventions to reduce work stress: Are they effective?* Contract Research Report 193/1998. London: Health and Safety Executive Book.

Pelletier, K. R. (1984). *Healthy people in unhealthy places: Stress and fitness at work.* New York: Delacorte Press.

Polley, R. B. (1987). Exploring polarization in organizational groups. *Group and Organization Studies, 12*, 424–444.

Reason, J. (1995). A systems approach to organizational error. *Ergonomics, 38*, 1708–1721.

Ribisl, K. M., & Reischl, T. M. (1993). Measuring the climate for health at organizations: Development of the worksite health climate scales. *Journal of Occupational Medicine, 35*, 812–824.

Rosen, R. H., & Berger, L. (1991). *The healthy company: Eight strategies to develop people, productivity, and profits.* New York: Putnam.

Sauter, S. L., Murphy, L. R., & Hurrell, J. J. (1990). Prevention of work-related psychological disorders. *American Psychologist, 45*(10), 1146–1158.

Senge, P. (1990). *The fifth discipline.* New York: Doubleday Currency.

Skinner, H. A. (2002). *Promoting health through organizational change.* San Francisco: Benjamin Cummings.

Stokols, D. (1992). Establishing and maintaining healthy environments: Toward a social ecology of health promotion. *American Psychologist, 47*, 6–22.

U.S. Department of Health and Human Services. (2000). *Healthy people 2010: Understanding and improving health* (2nd ed.). Washington, DC: U.S. Government Printing Office.

Vandenberg, R. J., Park, K. O., DeJoy, D. M., Wilson, M. G., & Griffin-Blake, C. S. (2002). The healthy work organization model: Expanding the view of individual health and well-being in the workplace. In P. Perrewé & D. Ganster (Eds.), *Research in occupational stress and well-being* (Vol. 2, pp. 57–115). New York: JAI Press/Elsevier Science.

Waldman, D. (1994). The contributions of total quality management to a theory of work performance. *Academy of Management Review, 19*, 510–536.

Wilson, M. G., DeJoy, D. M., Vandenberg, R. J., Richardson, H., & McGrath, A. L. (2004). Work characteristics and employee health and well-being: Test of a model of healthy work organization. *Journal of Organizational and Occupational Psychology, 77*, 565–588.

World Health Organization. (1999). *Regional guidelines for the development of healthy workplaces*. Geneva, Switzerland: Author.

Zimmerman, M. A. (1995). Psychological empowerment: Issues and illustrations. *American Journal of Community Psychology, 23*(5), 581–599.

Zohar, D. (1980). Safety climate in industrial organizations: Theoretical and applied implications. *Journal of Applied Psychology, 65*(1), 96–102.

13

COLLABORATION FOR BUILDING STRONG COMMUNITIES: TWO EXAMPLES

VICTORIA L. BANYARD AND LISA GOODMAN

As previous chapters make clear, scholars and practitioners in the field of prevention have called for a renewed focus on efforts to change broader contexts, not just individuals, and to emphasize positive resource building, not just risk avoidance or reduction (Kenny & Romano, chap. 1). Such a paradigm shift is consistent with more general calls for empowering and emancipatory forms of intervention that counter traditional emphases on individual behavior and intrapersonal variables as causes of difficulty (e.g., Prilleltensky, 1997). This chapter outlines those aspects of prevention that emphasize community as well as individual change and describes two prevention programs (one primary and one tertiary) as examples of more community-based approaches.

Several theorists and practitioners in the broad arena of health promotion and disease prevention have written about the methods they are using within their own fields to accomplish the ambitious goal of community change (e.g., Felner, Felner, & Silverman, 2000; Gullotta, 1994; Nelson, Pancer, Hayward, & Kelly, 2004; Wandersman & Florin, 2003). Those writing in the area of HIV/AIDS prevention have been particularly prolific and persuasive (e.g., Beeker, Guenther-Grey, & Raj, 1998; Trickett, 2002). Three broad principles cut across most of these articulations. First, ongoing collaboration with community members is critical to creating programs that reflect local understandings of both causal factors of health problems and appropriate intervention strategies—two necessary ingredients for true community change (e.g., Beeker et al., 1998; Nelson et al., 2004; Trickett, 2002). Second, the process of identifying determinants of the problem must be grounded in an ecological perspective that considers risk and protective factors at the individual, family, community, and societal levels (e.g., Bogenschneider, 1996; Bronfenbrenner, 1979; Trickett, 2002; see also chaps. 3 and 9, this volume). Third, responses to these problems must be designed to address all levels of the ecological model, with an emphasis on capacity and resource building rather than just problem amelioration, to achieve true community change. This final principle requires that programs move beyond the comfort zone afforded by a traditional approach to prevention that tends to focus on individual behavior change and risk reduction (e.g., Gullotta, 1994; Wandersman & Florin, 2003). In the section that follows, we examine each of these three principles in some detail and then describe their applications in two very different prevention programs.

Community Collaboration

A primary foundation for prevention work that targets community change is collaboration with community members to define the problem at hand and its causes and solutions (see also chaps. 2 and 3, this volume). Collaboration with community members ensures a more accurate assessment of needs, more effective interventions, greater buy-in from participants, and more sustainable programs (Beeker et al., 1998; Trickett, 2002). Coming from the perspective of HIV/AIDS prevention, Trickett argues that any collaboration must be respectful, mutual, and based on assumptions that all have valuable knowledge to contribute to the process. This is no easy proposition, and much has been written about how to define the "community" of interest and how to engage its members. For example, Goodman et al. (2004) discuss the complexities of "giving voice" (p. 31) to community members who hold different perspectives from each other or who set different priorities for goals in a climate of scarce resources. One strategy for giving voice in the arena of educational interventions is to involve peer educators at the levels of curriculum development and dissemination. One HIV prevention program, for example, was designed by members of the community who knew what was missing from their own lives (Kegeles et al., 1996, as cited in Beeker et al., 1998). They helped develop an intervention to decrease risky sexual practices among young gay men that emphasized the creation of spaces for these youth to come together with peers to talk about issues, including HIV prevention. Peer educators have been similarly effective in the violence prevention field (e.g., DeKeseredy, Schwartz, & Alvi, 2000).

Ecological Determinants of Problems

Second, causal models of problems upon which prevention programs are based should consider variables at all levels of the ecological model— that is, factors within the individual and within families, communities, and the broader society as outlined and developed by Bronfenbrenner (1979). In a powerful and well-received critique of conventional models of psychological intervention and prevention, Prilleltensky (1997) described a number of limitations to current individualistic approaches that do not take ecological variables into account, including an overly exclusive valuing of individual independence and autonomy with insufficient attention to sense of community and allocation of resources.

Discussions of empowerment in the community psychology literature imply a similar framework. In this literature, the construct of empowerment builds on the central notion that many forms of oppression and disempowerment exist due to unequal distribution of, and access to, resources. Therefore, setting the conditions for the true empowerment of individuals and communities requires moving beyond the individual level of analysis to a consideration of sociopolitical factors that contribute to this inequality (Zimmerman, 2000). Echoing this idea and critiquing theories of empowerment that emphasize the individual at the expense of the community, Riger (1993) stresses the need to examine the broader context of individual psychological empowerment. She criticizes empowerment theories that focus solely on increasing an individual's perceptions of mastery or efficacy when her or his actual access to power, voice, or resources within the larger system have not changed. Psychological empowerment cannot truly be achieved without actual access to resources and control—that is, political or social empowerment. This type of empowerment requires change at community, institutional, and societal levels. Indeed, McWhirter (1991) specifically discusses empowerment as being beyond solely an individual's experience as it has an impact on the "individual in relation to others, to the community, and to society." (p. 224) Ecological models (e.g., Bronfrenbrenner, 1979) can be helpful in this regard, as they frame individual behavior as occurring within the context of these broader social forces. One of the most widely used of these models is Bronfenbrenner's, who discusses nested levels of influence on individual development from intra-individual factors through aspects of family, school, community, and wider society. For example, empirical research on interpersonal violence pinpoints causes not only within individual perpetrators and their attitudes, but also the role of larger social norms that condone the use of coercion in relationships and support victim-blaming responses to assaults (e.g., Schwartz & DeKeseredy, 1998, 2000). True empowerment for survivors will come only when such community norms are changed and safety nets for survivors are increased. Similarly, facilitating the empowerment of low-income women means not just increasing such things as their own individual feelings of efficacy or their level of job skills. It also means changing their real access to key community resources such as affordable housing and child care.

A variety of empirical work documents the utility of designing prevention efforts with an appreciation of all levels of the ecological model. Trickett (2002), for example, highlights the importance of understanding how specific aspects of a social context differ across communities and therefore differentially impact individual behavior with respect to HIV/AIDS. Specifically, he discusses research showing that in communities where social norms limit women's access to power and resources, women are not empowered to voice their desire for safer sex practices and are therefore at higher risk for HIV/AIDS than are women in other communities. Prevention messages that address specific social norms may work in some communities but be irrelevant in others. Even within a community, ecological factors may critically shape the nature of a problem differentially across particular settings.

In another context, Edwards, Jumper-Thurman, Plested, Oetting, and Swanson (2000) describe the need for an ecological analysis in the implementation of substance abuse prevention programs. They found, for example, that a media campaign that was effective in one community had little impact in another. This contradicting result led them to analyze and describe a community's "readiness to change" in relation to the target problem. A community that, as a whole, refuses to acknowledge the problem of underage drinking, for example, requires a different set of prevention messages and tools than a community that has documented the problem and may even have some preliminary programs in place to address it. Based on interviews with key informants across various communities, Edwards and colleagues developed a model for classifying a broad community or segment of a community in terms of its stage of willingness or ability to deal with a problem such as substance abuse. Understanding a community's level of readiness may be a powerful strategy for prevention and highlights a key aspect of a community's ecology that may often go unassessed.

Actions to Build Community Capacity and Effect Wider Change

A critical part of an ecologically based intervention is capacity building across ecological levels—that is, on individual, family, and community levels (Beeker et al., 1998; Gullotta, 1994). At the individual level, capacity building means increasing individuals' strengths, positive resources, and knowledge and skills relevant to the problem at hand. This may be done through traditional prevention activities such as education workshops or classes, educational brochures, or information groups. Capacity building at the family level of the ecological model involves expanding strengths and improving family relationships through activities such as the well-established home visiting programs that aim to prevent child abuse in at-risk families (Olds, 1988). Capacity building at the community level involves activities that create a stronger sense of community among participants by increasing their sense of connection and value to each other. This may include a variety of activities from strengthening social support networks and people's psychological sense of community to grassroots community organizing for social change and collective action. By strengthening their relationships with each other, programs enable community members to begin to work together toward broader changes in those social conditions that put individuals at risk and enable communities to organize and be more successful at generating needed resources (e.g., Gullotta, 1994).

Foshee and colleagues (1996, 1998) describe a dating violence prevention program that not only targets individuals through an educational curriculum but also includes family education (e.g., parent educational materials) and community supports (e.g., community services for adolescent victims and training of service providers in the community) to deal with the problem. Parents and professionals in the community become more skilled at identifying and supporting survivors and at sending messages to deter perpetrators, thus increasing capacity by creating a broader network of change agents across the community and increasing places where survivors can go for support.

This literature review has drawn out three key considerations for prevention in communities: community collaboration, analysis of problems using an ecological model, and efforts to enhance strengths and build capacity across multiple levels. The remainder of the chapter applies these broad ideas to two specific programs to clearly illustrate their importance. The first example is a tertiary prevention program aimed at improving the emotional and material well-being of low-income women struggling with depression through social support, individual advocacy, and systems change. The program goal is preventing chronic depression. The second example is a primary prevention program aimed at sexual assault prevention through bystander education.

CASE EXAMPLES: DESCRIPTIONS OF THE PROGRAMS

Example 1: ROAD (Reaching Out About Depression)

ROAD (Reaching Out About Depression) is a grassroots mental health and organizing project for low-income women with depressive symptoms in Cambridge, Massachusetts (for a detailed description of ROAD, see Goodman et al., 2007; Smyth, Goodman, & Glenn, 2006). In 1999, the City of Cambridge conducted focus groups with mothers receiving welfare in the wake of welfare reform. A key finding was that participants craved a place to meet regularly to share their struggles coping within the confines of poverty, an ever-shrinking social safety net, and highly stretched informal social support networks. To satisfy this need, the city began sponsoring weekly dinners where low-income women could come together with community activists "around the kitchen table" to talk about their lives and the policies that affect them. In the course of their discussions, each woman described feeling dismissed, misunderstood, labeled, judged, or outright insulted by the social service providers they were told would help and support them, and they spoke of the resultant mistrust these experiences sowed. They expressed longing for a program that would "see" them in comprehensive ways and that would be a community, not just a program, where they could effect some change in the service system.

Eight members of this "Kitchen Table Conversations Project" decided to meet separately with several community activists and local academics interested in community-based prevention. These efforts led to the creation of ROAD as a supportive, action-oriented, and community-building project for low-income women. (Goodman joined the group shortly after it had conceived of ROAD, and she became its lead evaluator). Perhaps not surprisingly given the extent of life crises and obstacles with which they were struggling, all eight of these women coped with various symptoms of depression (which they labeled feeling "blue," "hopeless," "despairing," "depressed," or "down in the dumps") and wanted depression reduction to be a core aspect of the new program.

Consistent with research on depression in low-income communities (e.g., Miranda & Green, 1999; Siefert, Bowman, Heflin, Danziger, & Williams, 2000), the women described the sources of their mental health difficulties at multiple ecological levels, including difficult interpersonal histories, impoverished material circumstances, social isolation, and inherited biological propensities. Given their views concerning the multilayered etiology of their depression, these founding members of ROAD decided to create a program that would address multiple ecological levels simultaneously: The women wanted to be able to talk through their own difficulties with other women in similar circumstances and develop a network of peer supporters; work collaboratively with advocates or volunteers with a range of skills to improve their material circumstances; and gain the skills to be able to work together toward changing the policies that affect their lives.

ROAD's two program components, the Supportive Action Workshop Series and the Advocacy Resource Team, were developed to meet these ambitious goals. The workshop series provides a setting and structure for low-income women to come together to support each other, name and describe their difficulties (especially those related to depression), develop their own strategies for identifying and addressing their needs, and take action to improve service systems for low-income women in their community. The workshop series is composed of 12 sessions, each of which is led by a facilitator team composed of ROAD's founding members and former participants, all of whom receive ongoing training from the program director and other volunteers. The workshops cover a range of topics related to depression in the lives of low-income women. Facilitators are not there to gain the same ends as are participants, of course, but they are also not there to diagnose, label, or treat. Instead, they are active participants in workshop discussions, sharing personal stories, thoughts, and feelings. Each 12-session series also includes a group-determined social action project in which participants take collective action on a problem affecting low-income mothers with depression. For example, participants in one workshop series worked with a local coalition writing letters, talking to neighbors, and visiting politicians to protest the governor's proposed welfare cuts. All participants are invited to repeat the workshop series, which is revised by facilitators after every series. Participants who complete two workshop series are offered the opportunity to train with existing facilitators and the program director to become facilitators themselves.

The Advocacy Resource Team is composed of advocates who are law and psychology volunteer graduate students, supervised by faculty (including the second author) at two local universities. The advocates' role is to provide emotional and instrumental support to members of the ROAD facilitation team, whom the students refer to as their "partners." These advocates work one on one with their ROAD partners once a week for a full year to help them address acute crises (e.g., threatened evictions, loss of benefits, debts, layoffs, health problems, parenting difficulties) and achieve self-determined short- and long-term goals. Advocates approach their work with maximum flexibility, as unencumbered as possible by preconceived notions of what is an "appropriate" goal. Instead, they listen carefully to how their ROAD partners themselves describe their goals and objectives and then brainstorm together about strategies to achieve these "woman-defined" goals (Davies, Lyon, & Monti-Catania, 1998). This process purposefully departs from the more traditional approach of social services that focus on a fixed and predetermined set of outcomes, whether or not these are clients' first priorities (Liang, Glenn, & Goodman, 2005).

The ROAD workshops have so far served 60 ethnically diverse women in Cambridge, recruited through flyers and word of mouth, all of whom self-identify as struggling with symptoms of depression. Evaluation of ROAD is still at an early stage. Quantitative and qualitative methods are being used to explore fully the complex and ever-shifting ways in which the ROAD program and its participants reciprocally influence each other. Preliminary data indicate that the ROAD workshops and Advocacy Resource Team provide a desperately needed opportunity for participants to obtain the skills, confidence, and emotional and instrumental support required to make changes in their lives and communities (e.g., Goodman, Glenn, Bohlig, Banyard, & Borges, 2008). In addition to reporting reduced levels of depression and a greater sense of empowerment over the course of involvement with ROAD, many participants have created substantive changes in their lives by, for example, addressing loan issues, seeking mental health services, focusing on substance abuse problems, reentering the workforce, combating obesity, or applying to go back to school. Others describe feeling less isolated, more empowered to advocate for themselves and for the services they need, and better able to use those services. Facilitators and participants report that having someone on their side who knows them as real and full people and supports their efforts in a truly collaborative way helps them feel that their goals are possible. They feel that the world is not full of people who judge and dismiss them and that they are neither alone in their struggles nor "crazy" for experiencing the difficulties they face.

Collaboration is clearly a theme in how ROAD is structured and run, from its founding partnership among community women, activists, and academics to the consensus process of setting ongoing goals for the program and opportunities for workshop participants to become full ROAD facilitators (and therefore part of the governance structure) upon completion of two workshop series and a 2- to 3-month weekly training meeting. Likewise, the evaluation of ROAD is conducted as a collaborative enterprise. With respect to assessing the impact of the workshops on participants, for example, the ROAD facilitators determine the methods of evaluation to be used and the constructs to be measured. They have also collaborated on choosing specific measures to assess relevant outcomes and, in cases where no measure captured the construct of interest (as in the case of empowerment), they developed their own scale through a lengthy collaboration with the lead evaluator.

As for the application of an ecological perspective, ROAD grew out of the needs of the founding members, all of whom attributed the sources of their depression to causes at individual and community levels. ROAD attends to capacity building in both of these spheres. At the individual level, ROAD provides an opportunity for women to improve their psychological and material well-being, and it helps them to address the structural barriers that inhibit their own efforts to bring about social change. The ongoing facilitator training is a key part of ROAD's capacity-building effort. New facilitators learn communication and leadership skills and content related to each of the workshops. Outside experts are sometimes brought in to discuss specific topics such as domestic violence, substance abuse, or self-care. More experienced facilitators have moved on to learn about other aspects of growing a nonprofit, such as budgeting and grant writing.

At the heart of the ROAD approach, however, is the development of a capacity-enhancing community or peer network for women who have not felt supported—emotionally or materially—in their efforts to overcome depression and poverty (Goodman et al., 2007). Not surprisingly, there is ample evidence to suggest that social support plays a critical role in promoting resiliency and reducing depression in the face of poverty (e.g., Belle, 1982; Galaif, Nyamathi, & Stein, 1999; Green & Rodgers, 2001). ROAD builds on these findings by creating a scaffolding of emotional and instrumental social support (Belle & Doucet, 2003).

Another critical feature of the social support scaffolding is the Advocacy Resource Team. By helping the women with their practical needs, the Advocacy Resource Team enables them to build relationships relatively unburdened by each other's struggles. Some of the time and energy they would otherwise need to spend handling crises in their own lives can now be dedicated to deepening the mutuality and supportiveness of ROAD. For example, with assistance from the Advocacy Resource Team, one ROAD participant was able to help another woman confront a lawyer who had been taking advantage of her financially. The Advocacy Resource Team also enables facilitators to feel more confident about bringing a new group of participants into the ROAD community through the workshops, because they know that the Advocacy Resource Team can help to support this growing network of women (Goodman et al., 2007). Finally, at an even broader level, the social action aspect of ROAD builds on women's enhanced capacity to help them create change in the larger community. As one woman put it, "We get to do something about what we're hollering about."

Example 2: Bringing in the Bystander

Bringing in the Bystander is a primary prevention effort aimed at reducing the rates of sexual violence in communities. The program was developed at the University of New Hampshire by Banyard, Moynihan, and Plante (2007), but it is built on key foundational work by Berkowitz (2002), Foubert (2000), and Katz (1996). Using what Koss and Harvey (1991, p. 114) have termed the "rape avoidance approach," prevention programs most often target men as potential perpetrators and women as potential victims and endeavor to increase individual knowledge about how to avoid both roles and to change attitudes and behavior that put one at risk for sexual assault victimization or perpetration. Many have criticized the relatively narrow focus of these programs (e.g., Berkowitz, 2002; Potter, Krider, & McMahon, 2000; Schewe & O'Donohue, 1993). (See chap. 8, this volume, for further discussion of rape prevention programming on college campuses.)

Bringing in the Bystander, in contrast, takes the approach of educating participants as potential bystanders to incidents of sexual or intimate partner violence before, during, or after the incident. The program model is based on a small but growing area of inquiry making links between social psychological literature on the conditions under which individuals will intervene to help in an emergency and violence prevention (e.g., Banyard et al., 2005, 2007; Banyard, Plante, & Moynihan, 2004; Berkowitz, 2002; DeKeseredy et al., 2000; Foubert, 2000; Foubert & Marriott, 1997; Katz 1996; O'Brien, 2001; Slaby & Stringham, 1994). This program teaches bystanders how to intervene in situations that involve sexual violence. Even as Bringing in the Bystander trains groups of individuals, this model takes a further step toward a broader community approach to prevention through its emphasis on collaboration, grounding in ecological models of causes, and capacity building. The bystander model gives all community members a specific role, including: (1) interrupting situations that could lead to assault before it happens (e.g., walking an intoxicated friend home from a party or advising a housemate not to take an intoxicated partner upstairs at a party) or during an incident (e.g., knocking on the door of a dorm room if you hear someone crying for help); (2) speaking out against social norms that support sexual violence; and (3) having skills to be an effective and supportive ally to survivors (e.g., knowing how to support and not blame a friend who reveals being raped).

This project was developed through explicit collaboration of researchers, local campus crisis center staff, and the statewide coalition against domestic and sexual violence. The context for project and program development was collaborative research focused on community needs assessment related to sexual violence that documented the scope of the problem (Banyard et al., 2005, 2007). These specific community statistics were then used in the educational part of the program. The program also discusses the story of a high-profile case on the campus where the prevention program takes place. Additionally, the program and its evaluation was developed using techniques of formative evaluation, including focus groups with students who provided feedback about changes they thought were needed to the first draft of the program and evaluation tools. Students also gave input about types of specific situations where students were likely to be bystanders and the range of skills they would need to be effective in these contexts.

In addition to using collaborative techniques so that the design of the program was informed by the unique context of community members at whom the program was aimed, the program is grounded in theoretical and empirical work that is clear about the need for understanding sexual violence using an ecological model. For example, feminist theoretical analyses have examined how the role of societal issues, such as gender inequality, form a key part of the foundation of attitudes that support violence in intimate relationships and blame individuals for their own victimization (e.g., Brownmiller, 1975; Koss & Harvey, 1991; Rafter & Stanko, 1982; Sanday, 1996; Stanko, 1995; Yllo, 1993; Yodanis, Godenzi, & Stanko, 2000). Empirical evidence shows that male peer norm support for violence against intimate partners is linked to community rates of sexual violence. Sexual and intimate partner violence is not just a problem of individuals but a problem of communities as well (e.g., Schwartz & DeKeseredy, 1997, 2000; Schwartz & Nogrady, 1996).

The program's grounding in an ecological model of causes and prevention of sexual violence is manifested through direct discussion with participants of the role and responsibility of individuals to their community. Participants discuss sense of community, examples of pro social bystander behavior, and examples of when a bystander had the opportunity to intervene but did not and with what consequences. Group facilitators encourage participants to bring forward examples of when they were helped by others in their own lives. In addition, a great deal of information is presented that locates the causes of sexual violence beyond the individual level of analysis. During the sessions, facilitators present evidence for the role of community norms in support of relationship violence; at the same time, they debunk myths about sexual violence, including the myth that most sexual assaults are falsely reported. In this way participants learn about the problem of sexual violence using an ecological model of its causes, and they directly see evidence for the importance of wider community involvement in efforts to end the problem. At the end of the program, participants create their own "bystander plan," which consists of writing down a set of behaviors they would be willing to engage in—behaviors that would be safe for them and that would be likely to help someone else. For example, students who frequent parties might write that they will make sure they do not leave any friends behind at the party. A business manager might find making a plan for speaking out against sexist remarks or catcalls by their employees more relevant.

The actual program exists in two forms, one 90-minute session or a set of three linked 90-minute sessions. It follows guidelines of best practices from rape prevention literature. For example, it uses peer educators (e.g., DeKeseredy et al., 2000), single-sex groups, and active-learning methods to address knowledge, attitudes, and helping behavior. A woman and a man facilitate as a team to model women and men working together successfully and respectfully. Although this program includes conventional individual education components, the program also has capacity building at its center by seeking to facilitate the empowerment of individuals to play a role in changing those community norms that are key in sexual violence prevalence. For example, participants increase their efficacy and skills as bystanders by role-playing different potential bystander scenarios aimed at challenging community norms along the continuum of sexual violence (e.g., from speaking out against sexist or homophobic jokes, to refusing to be silent when one has information about an assault, to supporting a survivor). Peer leaders also model a range of strategies that participants might use to intervene safely in different contexts and also help group members think through the pros and cons of different decisions they might make. The program includes an exercise to build empathy for victims, a key step in increasing community support for survivors. The program also builds strengths by asking participants to play positive roles in their community (e.g., supporting survivors, challenging social norms that support violence against women) rather than focusing on deficits (e.g., what negative behaviors they need to avoid). In addition, building participants' individual efficacy to intervene involves helping them focus on their own safety as bystanders, something that is stressed throughout the program.

Promoting competency also entails the creation of connections between group members and the larger community. Several parts of the program discussion focus specifically on getting participants to talk about what community means to them and how they see their responsibility to take action within that larger community. An indirect aim is that this discussion promotes a sense of responsibility for creating change around the problem of sexual and intimate partner violence by refusing to be silent and by stepping in to help another. Interestingly, after the program, participants were less likely to agree with the statement, "I don't think there is much I can do about sexual assault on campus," and more likely to agree that "I think I can do something about sexual assault and am planning to find out what I can do about the problem," and "I am actively involved in projects to deal with sexual assault on campus."

In its implementation to date, Bringing in the Bystander has much in common with individually focused and educationally based prevention programs. Though it includes components that extend beyond changing attitudes and knowledge, further work is needed to realize its potential for wider social change, including involving other constituents within the community (e.g., administrators, faculty, staff) and assessing the program's influence on catalyzing broader collective action. What is exciting about this project is that its founding assumptions and guiding framework for the message of sexual and intimate partner violence prevention have the potential to extend into other areas of the theoretical models outlined at the beginning of this chapter. Its broad message about the role of community members in changing community norms and behaviors would seem easily adapted to multiple constituencies within communities. In this example of college campuses, such a program could be adapted for faculty, staff, or administrators. Recently, several researchers have begun adapting and evaluating its use in a media campaign (Potter, Stapleton, & Moynihan, in press) with results showing an impact of the campaign on attitudes. Furthermore, one campus community in which this program was piloted has taken steps to implement the program more widely to train a variety of student groups and leaders and to integrate this perspective into an array of ongoing campus venues. The enthusiasm for more widespread adoption suggests the power that this perspective on prevention may hold for becoming more widely integrated into the community, potentially impacting the way the community as a whole sees the issue and having the effect of improving safety nets and policies that assist survivors and that hold perpetrators accountable.

Despite the need for further efforts to effect wider social change, experimental evaluation suggests that this approach is effective (e.g., Banyard et al., 2007). Nearly 400 students were randomly assigned to either receive the prevention program or not. Compared to the control group, participants reported (a) reduced rape myth attitudes, (b) more knowledge related to sexual violence, (c) more willingness to help others in risky situations, and (d) more actual pro social bystander behaviors (e.g., called 911 when heard someone in the dorm crying for help; walked a friend home from a party; talked to a friend about resources for sexual assault survivors). Participants who attended the program were more likely to believe that they could play a role in ending this problem and expressed greater intention to take on such an active role based on a rigorous experimental evaluation of the program (Banyard et al., 2007). It is believed that as a result of participating in the prevention program, individuals are better positioned to take action and create community change. Several participants also mentioned this in their responses to open-ended questions about the program. For example, one participant wrote, ". . . we all owe it to each other to make the world/community a safer place." Another wrote, ". . . it is filled with good information and it motivated me to get more involved."

CONCLUSIONS AND FUTURE DIRECTIONS

This chapter draws on empirical findings and theoretical discussions to describe three critical ingredients of community-level prevention. It also describes the mechanics and utility of two prevention programs with a wider community focus. Although the two programs differ enormously in structure, focus, target population, and level of prevention (primary vs. tertiary), both have incorporated these three ingredients, at least to some degree, into their program structures. Expanding the reach of prevention beyond individual education to focus on community change and social justice is possible and necessary for ameliorating a variety of community problems. This expansion can be achieved through collaboration with communities in problem definition, intervention design, and implementation, as well as through the use of an ecological lens to develop causal models of problems and the use of interventions to build strengths, resources, and skills at multiple levels.

REFERENCES

Banyard, V. L., Moynihan, M. M., & Plante, E. G. (2007). Sexual violence prevention through bystander education: An experimental evaluation. *Journal of Community Psychology, 35,* 463–481.

Banyard, V. L., Plante, E. G., Cohn, E. S., Moorhead, C., Ward, S., & Walsh, W. (2005). Revisiting unwanted sexual experiences on campus: A twelve-year follow-up. *Violence Against Women: An International and Interdisciplinary Journal, 11,* 426–446.

Banyard, V. L., Plante, E., & Moynihan, M. M. (2004). Bystander education: Bringing a broader community perspective to sexual violence prevention. *Journal of Community Psychology, 32,* 61–79.

Beeker, C., Guenther-Grey, C., & Raj, A. (1998). Community empowerment paradigm drift and the primary prevention of HIV/AIDS. *Social Science Medicine, 46,* 831–842.

Belle, D. (1982). Social ties and social support. In D. Belle (Ed.), *Lives in stress: Women and depression* (pp. 133–144). Beverly Hills, CA: Sage.

Belle, D., & Doucet, J. (2003). Poverty, inequality, and discrimination as sources of depression among U.S. women. *Psychology of Women Quarterly, 27,* 101–113.

Berkowitz, A. D. (2002). Fostering men's responsibility for preventing sexual assault. In P. A. Schewe (Ed.), *Preventing violence in relationships: Interventions across the life span,* (pp. 163–196). Washington, DC: American Psychological Association.

Bogenschneider, K. (1996). Family related prevention programs: An ecological risk/protective theory for building prevention programs, policies, and community capacity to support youth. *Family Relations, 45,* 127–138.

Bronfenbrenner, U. (1979). Contexts of child rearing: Problems and prospects. *American Psychologist, 34,* 844–850.

Brownmiller, S. (1975). *Against our will: Men, women, and rape.* New York: Simon & Schuster.

Davies, J., Lyon, E., & Monti-Catania, D. (1998). *Safety planning with battered women: Complex lives/difficult choices.* Thousand Oaks, CA: Sage.

DeKeseredy, W. S., Schwartz, M. D., & Alvi, S. (2000). The role of profeminist men in dealing with women on the Canadian college campus. *Violence Against Women, 6,* 918–935.

Edwards, R. W., Jumper-Thurman, P., Plested, B. A., Oetting, E. R., & Swanson, L. (2000). Community readiness: Research to practice. *Journal of Community Psychology, 28,* 291–307.

Felner, R. D., Felner, T., & Silverman, M. (2000). Prevention in mental health issues and social intervention: Conceptual and methodological issues in the evolution of the science and practice of prevention. In J. Rapport & E. Seidman (Eds.), *Handbook of community psychology* (pp. 9–42). New York: Plenum.

Foshee, V. A., Bauman, K. E., Arriaga, X. B., Helms, R. W., Koch, G. G., & Linder, G. F. (1998). An evaluation of Safe Dates, an adolescent dating violence prevention program. *American Journal of Public Health, 88,* 45–50.

Foshee, V. A., Linder, G. F., Bauman, K. E., Langwick, S. A., Arriaga, X. B., & Heath, J. L. (1996). The Safe Dates project: Theoretical basis, evaluation design, and selected baseline findings. *American Journal of Preventive Medicine, 12,* 39–47.

Foubert, J. D. (2000). The longitudinal effects of a rape-prevention program on fraternity men's attitudes, behavioral intent, and behavior. *Journal of American College Health, 48,* 158–163.

Foubert, J. D., & Marriott, K. A. (1997). Effects of a sexual assault peer education program on men's beliefs in rape myths. *Sex Roles, 36,* 259–268.

Galaif, E. R., Nyamathi, A. M., & Stein, J. A. (1999). Psychosocial predictors of current drug use, drug problems, and physical drug dependence in homeless women. *Addictive Behaviors, 24*(6), 801–814.

Goodman, L. A., Liang, B., Helms, J. E., Latta, R. E., Sparks, E., & Weintraub, S. R. (2004). Training counseling psychologists as social justice agents: Feminist and multicultural principles in action. *The Counseling Psychologist, 32,* 793–837.

Goodman, L. A., Litwin, A., & Bohlig, A. (2007). Applying feminist theory to community practice: A multi-level empowerment intervention for low-income women with depression. In E. Aldarondo (Ed.), *Advancing social justice through clinical practice* (pp. 265–290). Mahwah, NJ: Erlbaum.

Goodman, L. A., Glenn, C., Bohlig, A., Banyard, V., & Borges, A. (2008). *Feminist relational advocacy: Processes and outcomes from the perspective of low-income women with depression*. Manuscript submitted for publication.

Green, B. L., & Rodgers, A. (2001). Determinants of social support among low-income mothers: A longitudinal analysis. *American Journal of Community Psychology, 29*(3), 419–441.

Gullotta, T. P. (1994). The what, who, why, where, when and how of primary prevention. *The Journal of Primary Prevention, 15*, 5–14.

Katz, J. (1996, Summer). Reconstructing masculinity in the locker room: The Mentors in Violence Prevention Project. *Harvard Educational Review, 65*, 163–175.

Koss, M. P., & Harvey, M. R. (1991). *The rape victim: Clinical and community interventions*. Newbury Park, CA: Sage.

Liang, B., Glenn, C., & Goodman, L. A. (2005). Feminist ethics in advocacy relationships: A relational vs. rule-bound approach. *The Community Psychologist, 38*, 26–28.

McWhirter, E. H. (1991). Empowerment in counseling. *Journal of Counseling and Development, 69*, 222–227.

Miranda, J., & Green, B. L. (1999). The need for mental health services research focusing on poor young women. *Journal of Mental Health Policy & Economics, 2*(2), 73–80.

Nelson, G., Pancer, S. M., Hayward, K., & Kelly, R. (2004). Partnerships and participation of community residents in health promotion and prevention: Experiences of the Highfield Community Enrichment Project (Better Beginnings, Better Futures). *Journal of Health Psychology, 9*, 213–227.

O'Brien, J. (2001). The MVP program: Focus on student-athletes. In A. J. Ottens & K. Hotelling (Eds.), *Sexual violence on campus: Policies, programs, and perspectives* (pp. 98–119). New York: Springer.

Olds, D. (1988). The prenatal/early infancy project. In R. Price, E. Cowen, R. Lorion, & J. Ramos-McKay (Eds.), *Fourteen ounces of prevention* (pp. 9–23). Washington, DC: American Psychological Association.

Potter, R. H., Krider, J. E., & McMahon, P. M. (2000). Examining elements of campus sexual violence policies. *Violence Against Women 6*, 1345–1362.

Potter, S. J., Stapleton, J. G., & Moynihan, M. M. (in press). Designing and implementing a media campaign. Special thematic issue of *Journal of Prevention and Intervention in the Community*.

Prilleltensky, I. (1997). Values, assumptions, and practices: Assessing the moral implications of psychological discourse and action. *American Psychologist, 52*, 517–535.

Rafter, N. H., & Stanko, E. A. (Eds.). (1982). *Judge, lawyer, victim, thief: Women, gender roles, and criminal justice*. Boston: Northeastern.

Riger, S. (1993). What's wrong with empowerment. *American Journal of Community Psychology, 21*, 279–292.

Sanday, P. R. (1996). Rape-prone versus rape-free campus cultures. *Violence Against Women, 2*, 191–208.

Schewe, P. A., & O'Donohue, W. (1993). Rape prevention: Methodological problems and new directions. *Clinical Psychology Review, 13*, 667–682.

Schwartz. M. D., & DeKeseredy, W. S. (1997). *Sexual assault on the college campus: The role of male peer support.* Thousand Oaks, CA: Sage.

Schwartz, M. D., & DeKeseredy, W. S. (1998). *Woman abuse on campus: Results from the Canadian National Survey.* Thousand Oaks, CA: Sage.

Schwartz, M. D., & DeKeseredy, W. S. (2000). Aggregation bias and woman abuse: Variations by male peer support, region, language, and school type. *Journal of Interpersonal Violence, 15*, 555–565.

Schwartz, M. D., & Nogrady, C. A. (1996). Fraternity membership, rape myths, and sexual aggression on a college campus. *Violence Against Women, 2*, 148–162.

Siefert, K., Bowman, P. J., Heflin, C. M., Danziger, S., & Williams, D. R. (2000). Social and environmental predictors of maternal depression in current and recent welfare recipients. *American Journal of Orthopsychiatry, 70*(4), 510–522.

Slaby, R. G., & Stringham, P. (1994). Prevention of peer and community violence: The pediatrician's role. *Pediatrics, 94*, 608–616.

Smyth, K., Goodman, L. A., & Glenn, C. (2006). The full-frame approach: A new response to marginalized women left behind by specialized services. *American Journal of Orthopsychiatry, 76*(4), 489–502.

Stanko, E. A. (1995). [Review of the book *No safe haven: Male violence against women at home, at work, and in the community*]. *Violence Against Women, 1*, 102–105.

Trickett, E. J. (2002). Context, culture, and collaboration in AIDS interventions: Ecological ideas for enhancing community impact. *The Journal of Primary Prevention, 23*, 157–172.

Wandersman, A., & Florin, P. (2003). Community interventions and effective prevention. *American Psychologist, 58*, 441–448.

Yllo, K. (1993). Through a feminist lens: Gender, power, and violence. In R. J. Gelles & D. Loseke (Eds.), *Current controversies on family violence* (pp. 47–62). Thousand Oaks, CA: Sage.

Yodanis, C., Godenzi, A., & Stanko, E. (2000). The benefits of studying costs: A review and agenda for studies on the economic costs of violence against women. *Policy Studies, 21*, 263–276.

Zimmerman, M. A. (2000). Empowerment theory: Psychological, organizational, and community levels of analysis. In J. Rappaport & E. Seidman (Eds.), *Handbook of community psychology* (pp. 43–63). New York: Kluwer/Plenum.

CONCLUSION: PREVENTION AND SOCIAL JUSTICE— NEW LESSONS AND NEXT STEPS

MAUREEN E. KENNY, ARTHUR M. HORNE, PAMELA ORPINAS, AND LE'ROY E. REESE

Based on the articulation set forth in the first half of this work, prevention seeks to promote social justice, which includes the "full and equal participation of all groups in a society," as well as the physical and psychological security of all these groups' members (Bell, 2007, p. 1). Prevention and social justice entail a transformative role for the mental health professional that, based on an understanding of procedural justice, includes multiple stakeholders in decision making and provides the conditions for facilitating empowerment among the clients of an intervention who suffer vulnerabilities in protective assets or a surfeit of risk factors. Preventive interventions that are designed and conducted within an ecological framework of individual and community wellness seek to remedy the toxic social conditions related to poverty and oppression that contribute to emotional and physical disorders. Ideally, such remedies are transformative; they seek to address the "causes of the causes" (Nelson & Prilleltensky, 2005, p. 89). A social justice vision of preventive intervention may not always find the conditions conducive to *primary* prevention, which works to foster wellness and healthy development and build upon cultural strengths. Many, if not most, interventions must tackle prevalent psychopathologies and bad behaviors, but if they must engage in remedial action, at least they can aspire to the ideal of primary prevention's holistic approach toward wellness. Secondary and tertiary prevention is still prevention, which is accomplished (in the best of these cases) contextually and incrementally rather than holistically.

This volume embraces ecological (Bronfenbrenner, 1979) and developmental-contextual (Lerner, 1995) frameworks for preventive interventions, which provide theoretical lenses for examining how the dynamic interactions between the individual and the multiple contexts in which the person is embedded contribute to well-being and social justice. The chapters in Part II, to various degrees, draw on the primary preventive, ecological model for understanding the role of environmental/contextual, rather than individual, factors that affect individual and group well-being. These chapters illustrate how diversity is integral to social justice and describe the dynamic of realizing social justice at the redistributive and therapeutic, individual levels within specific contexts.

The contributions to this volume focusing on healthy families (chap. 10), schools (chap. 11), workplace (chap. 12), and community (chap. 13) contribute to a social justice vision of prevention. These discussions and program examples consider how the salient contexts of human development can be organized to increase access to social, economic, and psychological resources that foster the full participation of all groups in society and thereby promote the augmentation of protective assets and the diminution of risk factors within vital components of the community and within specific community members. Because the school and the family are two critical contexts in the lives of children, they are central in improving children's outcomes. When the educational system provides equal opportunities to children, societal inequities can be alleviated. The chapters on fostering a healthy climate for diversity (chap. 8) and on promoting a healthy lifestyle (chap. 9) cultivate an understanding of factors that cross multiple contexts. Schwartz and Hage (chap. 6) maintain that interventions—along with assessment of outcomes—across multiple environmental/contextual levels are an ethical mandate for social justice prevention.

Ecological and environmental/developmental-contextual frameworks also highlight the reciprocal interactions that occur among contexts. With regard to cross-contextual interactions, schools and families often struggle in developing adaptive interrelationships to support children's learning and development, especially across cultural, linguistic, and social class differences. Nevertheless, families and schools have a tradition of partnership, through mechanisms such as parent-school-community organizations, parent-teacher conferences, and other modes of ongoing communication. Model family prevention programs (chap. 10) often include school components, whereas successful school prevention programs (chap. 11) are likely to include the family. The Boston Connects program (chap. 3) seeks to create systemic change by building capacity across school, family, and community contexts. The partnership of schools and community agencies in this program helps schools to access much-needed community resources for enhancing student learning and family well-being.

Health promotion and prevention programs have traditionally neglected the interface between work organizations and other contexts, although employee assistance programs (see chap. 8), employee benefits, and child care services now focus on these interrelationships. The healthy work organization, as defined by DeJoy and Wilson (chap. 12), presents a complex array of workplace factors that relate to organizational health and, hence, employee well-being. Although not explicitly about social justice or prevention, the experiences of individuals in the workplace are inextricably linked to health promotion and social justice as work influences personal well-being and offers access to social, psychological, political, and economic capital (Blustein, 2006). Adults' experiences in the workplace also have a direct effect on their functioning in home and community settings.

The poverty and oppression that stem from "structural maldistribution" in contemporary American society and other liberal-capitalist systems—and the attendant marginalization associated with race, class, gender and sexual preference, disability, age, and religion—makes any scholarly examination of social justice attentive to diversity concerns. This volume is no exception; its chapters emphasize the importance of cultural relevance in program content and cultural competence among prevention practitioners and researchers. Cultural relevance and understanding of cultural values and cultural biases are imperatives of prevention ethics (chap. 3). Matthews, Pepper, and Lorah (chap. 8) focus attention on developing healthy climates for diversity. Vera, Buhin, and Isacco (chap. 4) describe a program for preventing the development of racism among schoolchildren. Because the impact of this type of program may be limited as long as racism remains prevalent in society, the authors also call for simultaneous efforts in public policy advocacy to effect broader change. Ameliorative and transformative change may complement such attitudinal changes within the context of the school, and indeed it is possible that preventing racism among the young will have long-term transformative effects as they inculcate their friends and family members with new values and beliefs.

As noted, a social justice vision of prevention includes *procedural justice* in addition to distributive justice. Procedural justice, including awareness of privilege and power dynamics and the creation of collaborative egalitarian relationships, is central to ethical prevention practice as conceptualized by Schwartz and Hage (chap. 6). Several chapters in this volume present exemplars of procedural justice. Walsh, DePaul, and Park-Taylor (chap. 3) emphasize the importance of collaboration in prevention best practice and identify the Pathways/Senderos program (Pearlman & Bilodeau, 1999) to illustrate collaborative practice. Both the ROAD and Bringing in the Bystander programs described by Banyard and Goodman (chap. 13) exemplify procedural justice through their ongoing collaboration with community members. As described in chapter 13, the ROAD program supports low-income women in combating depression by providing conditions for fostering collaboration and facilitating empowerment—key therapeutic and dynamic attributes of a wellness-oriented community. Byrd and Reininger (chap. 9) describe an approach to community assessment that actively involves community participants and fosters community empowerment. Reese, Wingfield, and Blumenthal (chap. 2) describe the importance of collaborative efforts in research processes. However, the school and family interventions described by Waldo, Horne, and Kenny (chap. 10) and Bosworth, Orpinas, and Hein (chap. 11) largely rely on the expertise of preventionists or other school personnel or family workers as program developers or leaders. One exception is the BreakAway program (Lynn & Lofquist, 2002) described in chapter 11, which engages youth in program development in schools, thereby building youth investment in the program and fostering their leadership skills. Programs are also emerging that strive to partner family members and professionals in community action and leadership projects (e.g., Doherty & Carroll, 2007). These programs arise from the belief that families will be strengthened only through mutual teaching and learning in community projects.

Efforts to create healthy contexts for development emphasize the promotion of strengths, with less emphasis on remediation of deficits. The chapter authors are clear, however, in their conviction that prevention must continue to address risk reduction. Walsh, DePaul, and Park-Taylor (chap. 3) note that best practices in student support services in school contexts include primary, secondary, and tertiary prevention, as social justice would not be served by ignoring those who are at risk or suffering. The promotion of wellness is inextricably tied to a reduction in toxic social conditions, as Matthews, Pepper, and Lorah make clear in chapter 8. Well-being in the population is increased when oppression and discrimination are decreased. Waldo, Horne, and Kenny (chap. 10) describe how tertiary prevention with adults may be primary prevention for children in the family; to the extent that the problems of adults in the family are lessened, the contexts in which children develop can be improved. In such a way, the ROAD program described by Banyard and Goodman (chap. 13) promotes primary prevention and individual wellness by focusing on group therapeutic approaches to alleviate depression among adult women. Those women also contribute to *systemic* primary prevention in their newfound roles as community activists and advocates.

An examination of prevention practice described in this volume highlights a number of limitations of research and practice related to a social justice vision of prevention. Despite progress in articulating a vision for social justice prevention, prevention practice on the transformative level lags behind ameliorative intervention. Schwartz and Hage (chap. 6) identify "transformative prevention interventions that aim at long-term systemic change" as an ethical standard for prevention. Yet the interventions discussed in this book focus more on individual wellness—how psychotherapeutic techniques can help individual clients of a preventive intervention bolster the protective assets of self-esteem and resilience and minimize environmental risk factors in the service of facilitating empowerment and achieving the crucial state of acceptance of (and perhaps mastery over) their immediate environment. Although such a focus seemingly obscures the macro-level "causes of the causes" in inequitable social relationships, our overriding purpose in this volume is to emphasize the dual nature of social justice in a preventive framework—that is, the interdependence and dynamism of a community's wellness and the physical and psychological wellness of the community's members. In an ideal world of preventive intervention, such dynamism is realized holistically and comprehensively. Most of the time, though, community-wide prevention and wellness are achieved peripherally and incrementally; such efforts can be managed and evaluated only in a couple of contexts—perhaps in just one context alone. Although the school and the family are pivotal in fostering a child's healthy development and preparing youth for full societal participation, their efforts may be undermined by oppressive factors such as racism, poverty, and heterosexism. The healthy work organization focuses on improving processes within the organization and does not address macro-level policies that may have an impact on employee well-being or social justice.

Although the interventions described in this volume are limited in accomplishing transformative change, most of the contributors note the impact of larger social policies and realities for each context. Byrd and Reininger (chap. 9), for example, provide a clear analysis of how health is affected by an array of contextual factors, including public policy. The ROAD program described by Banyard and Goodman (chap. 13) grew out of the awareness among low-income women of the negative impact of the social service system on their emotional well-being. The ROAD Supportive Action Workshops and Advocacy Resource Team were designed to build community capacity and effect wider community change, but Banyard and Goodman acknowledge that these and other community interventions often fall short in achieving transformative societal change. With a social justice vision in mind, Vera, Buhin, and Isacco (chap. 4) encourage mental health professionals to engage in public policy work, outreach, and advocacy that will extend beyond single contexts and potentially effect change at a broader societal level. The programmatic examples provided by Matthews, Pepper, and Lorah in chapter 8 describe interventions at the individual and group levels, but they also document the positive impact of some changes in public policy and media practice at the systemic level.

Although social justice has been a central value of the social work profession for some time (Swenson, 1998), graduate mental health training, especially in counseling and clinical psychology, has emphasized remediation and individual and group intervention, rather than proactive systemic change. Even community psychologists tend to place professional emphasis on remediation rather than preventive wellness. Consider Prilleltensky's take on the principal concerns of community psychologists involved in preventive interventions:

> [M]ost of our efforts in community psychology are ameliorative—as opposed to transformative—in nature. Community interventions strive to alleviate suffering and to minimize the impact of unjust social policies, not to change society in order to prevent problems in the first place. (2001, p. 757)

Yet as some of the contributors to this volume note, there is plenty of optimism regarding some fundamental changes in the way preventionists, particularly mental health professionals, conceptualize, design, and conduct preventive interventions. The training model presented by O'Neil and Britner (chap. 7) teaches students how to make a difference through primary prevention and offers needed guidance to programs in preparing students to effect multiple types of change at multiple levels. Byrd and Reininger (chap. 9) offer a model of community assessment that is important in identifying systemic determinants, rather than individual causes for problems. Students in mental health training would benefit from learning a public health model of assessment of this type. Although this volume describes the multidisciplinary nature of prevention and health promotion, professional training continues to give limited attention to interprofessional collaboration. The advancement of a social justice vision of prevention is limited by the failures of varied professionals and disciplines to share knowledge and organize together to accomplish social change. Reese (2007) recommends that more predoctoral and postdoctoral training be designed to develop competencies in prevention research and practice, including skills in collaboration across disciplines. Professional organizations should collaborate with government agencies and the organizations of other professions to increase training and research partnerships in prevention. Kenny and Romano (chap. 1) note that insurance payments and professional credentialing continue to reward individual and group remediation rather than prevention efforts oriented toward societal change. Mental health professionals need to direct their advocacy efforts toward legislative change on these issues and other health policy issues that impede the attainment of social justice.

Transformative social change is inevitably difficult because it requires a reallocation of social, economic, and political resources. In addition to those political obstacles noted by Kenny and Romano (chap. 1) and Reese,

Wingfield, and Blumenthal (chap. 2), efforts toward societal transformation may also be hampered by insufficient attention to evaluation and research. Top-down approaches to mental health interventions typically draw on health-services research, driven as it is by political and market forces in the provision of adequate and cost-effective delivery systems. Needless to say, such approaches may, more often than not, exclude systemic, trans-contextual causes of pervasive psychopathologies (not to mention "bad behaviors") that plague a community.

Bottom-up approaches that seek out collective community expertise on a particular problem hold the promise of not only a more effective and more encompassing search for the social determinants of health, as reflected in the public health profession, but also of a more invested response by potentially empowered community members. The blending of public health and community-level expertise in evidence-based treatment provides a salutary—and powerful—admixture of individual and community-level wellness, as well as political support, on both sides of the expertise equation. Through public health and psychotherapeutic interventions, community members can become well enough to actively participate in a holistic, ecological approach toward healing their community. This interactive therapeutic process maximizes the potential of Prilleltensky's "partnerships" and emancipatory communitarian responses to social and psychological problems that affect a community's basic functioning. In such a way,

> the community serves the role of leader and activist, aided by research knowledge and political support. Community, practice, and research teams serve complementary roles in understanding local cultural norms and in matching expectations and conflicts in the community with proposed intervention activities. (Wells, Miranda, Bruce, Alegria, & Wallerstein, 2004, p. 959)

Participatory action research, though still in its intellectual and operational adolescence, provides direct, community-level expertise on the broader epidemiology of persistent and pervasive psychopathologies and bad behaviors. It also promotes an important attribute of community identity and, ultimately, of civic participation—of being a stakeholder in positive outcomes for one's own community. As Wells and colleagues (2004) note: "The norms of 'deliberative democracy' proposed by [Norman] Daniels offer one approach for establishing a fair process of integrating community, practice, and research priorities" (p. 960; see also Daniels, 1996).

Research and evaluation evidence could be used to influence those in power and the public at large to recognize the value or common good that could be realized through transformative social change. Reese et al. (chap. 2) maintain that health disparities are sustained in part because advances in prevention knowledge have not been applied to practice. Those authors also identify barriers that have limited progress in research, including difficulty in operationalizing the construct of social justice and determining culturally appropriate approaches to assessment. As noted by Vera, Buhin, and Isacco (chap. 4), documenting the mental health impact of advocacy efforts may be more difficult than assessing the impact of individual or group intervention. The five-tiered approach to program evaluation described by Jacobs and Goldberg (chap. 5) can be used to assess processes and outcomes on multiple levels with multiple indicators at multiple points in time. With some creativity, this type of evaluation can be employed to assess macro policy change as well as more discrete interventions. In addition, Reese, Wingfield, and Blumenthal maintain that evaluation must attend to cost concerns (as programs that are too costly cannot be replicated), to cultural relevance, and to dissemination of research findings to those in the field who can apply the findings to make a difference.

In summary, this volume presents a social justice vision of prevention and related theory, research, and practice. The examples of prevention practice contained in this volume are aligned in many regards with a social justice vision by building environments that promote health and enhance access to social, economic, and psychological resources that allow for full societal participation. Elements of procedural justice, including collaboration and fostering conditions of empowerment, and attention to cultural relevance and competence are evident across many programs. Many of these programs seek to identify and build strengths, promote wellness and reduce oppression related to gender, race, ethnicity, sexual orientation, or other individual or group differences. Despite these aims, most efforts focus on single contexts, are more ameliorative than transformative, and do not create the level of societal change that addresses the "causes of the causes." The chapters in this volume identify some obstacles to the realization of a social justice vision of prevention and also provide some suggestions in how to move forward in that effort. We hope this volume will increase awareness and dialogue concerning the potential for prevention to foster social justice and thereby promote theory, research, and practice that will make this vision a reality.

REFERENCES

Bell, L. A. (2007). Theoretical foundations for social justice education. In M. Adams, L.A. Bell, & P. Griffin (Eds.), *Teaching for diversity and social justice* (2nd ed., pp. 3–16). New York: Routledge.

Blustein, D. L. (2006). *The psychology of working: A new perspective for career development, counseling, and public policy.* Mahwah, NJ: Erlbaum.

Bronfenbrenner, U. (1979). *The ecology of human development*. Cambridge, MA: Harvard University Press.

Daniels, N. (1996). Justice, fair procedures, and the goals of medicine. *Hastings Center Report, 26*(6), 10–12.

Doherty, W. J., & Carroll, J. S. (2007). Families and therapists as citizens: The families and democracy project. In E. Aldarondo (Ed.), *Advancing social justice through clinical practice* (pp. 223–244). Mahwah, NJ: Erlbaum.

Lerner, R. M. (1995). Developing individuals within changing contexts: Implications of developmental contextualism for human development research, policy, and programs. In T. A. Kindermann & J. Valsiner (Eds.), *Development of person-context relations* (pp. 13–38). Hillsdale, NJ: Erlbaum.

Lynn, D. D., & Lofquist, W. A. (2002). *BreakAway: A framework for creating positive school communities. A leadership team workbook*. Tucson, AZ: Development Publications.

Nelson, G., & Prilleltensky, I. (2005). *Community psychology: In pursuit of liberation and well-being*. New York: Palgrave Macmillan.

Pearlman, S. F., & Bilodeau, R. (1999). Academic-community collaboration in teen pregnancy prevention: New roles for professional psychologists. *Professional Psychology, 30*, 92–98.

Prilleltensky, I. (2001). Value-based praxis in community psychology: Moving toward social justice and social action. *American Journal of Community Psychology, 29*(5), 747–778.

Reese, L. E. (2007). Beyond rhetoric: The ABC's of effective prevention practice, science, and policy. *The Counseling Psychologist, 35*, 576–585.

Swenson, C. R. (1998). Clinical social work's contribution to a social justice perspective. *Social Work, 43*, 527–537.

Wells, K., Miranda, J., Bruce, M. L., Alegria, M., & Wallerstein, N. (2004). Bridging community intervention and mental health services research. *American Journal of Psychiatry, 161*(6), 955–963.

AUTHOR INDEX

Numbers in italics refer to listings in the reference sections.

McGoldrick, M., 211, *227*
McGrath, A. L., 256, 257, 261, *269*
McKenna, J., 198, *202*
McKenzie, F. D., 66, *77*
McLeroy, K. R., 189, 197, *203*, 253, *268*
McMahon, P. M., 280, *286*
McNair, L., 220, *225*
McNeely, C. A., 232, *245*
McWhirter, B. T., 18, *33*, 57, *77*
McWhirter, E. H., 10, *13*, 18, 57, *77*, 132,
     138, 273, *286*
McWhirter, J. J., 18, *33*, 57, *77*
McWhirter, R. J., 18, *33*, 57, *77*
Meara, N. M., 65, *77*
Melton, G. B., 125, *138*
Mena, M. P., 71, *78*
Meredith, L. S., 187, *202*
Meyer, A. L., 236, *245*, *246*
Meyer, J. P., 256, *268*
Mihalic, S., 38, 46, *54*, 235, *245*
Millar, A., 198, *204*
Miller, E., 117
Miller, I. W., 209, *226*
Miller, K., 258, *268*
Milstein, M. M., 61, *76*, 240, *245*
Minkler, M., 136, 193, *204*, 240, *246*
Minuchin, P., 211, *227*
Minuchin, S., 210, 211, 213, 222, 224, *227*
Miranda, J., 276, *286*, 295, *297*
Mirvis, P. H., 258, *267*
Mistry, J., 109, 115, 117, *120*, *121*
Mohai, P., 89, *94*
Mokdad, A. H., 185, *204*
Molgaard, V., 220, *225*
Monge, P. R., 258, *268*
Montgomery, G., 88, 89, 91, 92, *96*
Monti-Catania, D., 278, *285*
Moore, S. M., 192, *202*
Moorhead, C., 280, *284*
Morgan, M., 29, *35*
Morrisey-Kane, E., 18, 26, 27, *33*, 48, *54*,
     66, 68, *77*, 127, 132, 134, 135, *138*
Mortimore, P., 229, 231, 233, 234, 237,
     240, *247*
Moynihan, M. M., 280, 283, *284*, *286*
Mrazek, P. J., 18, 20, *33*, 37, *53*, 130, *138*
Mullen, P. D., 191, *202*
Multisite Violence Prevention Project, 236
Muñez, R. F., 131, *138*
Muñoz, R. F., 59, *77*
Murnane, J., 253, *268*

Murphy, D. A., 201
Murphy, F., 43, *53*
Murphy, J. A., 24, *35*, 58, 60, 78
Murphy, L. R., 252, 253, 256, *266*, *268*
Murphy, M. J., 80, *95*
Murray, E. J., 212, *227*
Murry, V. M., 220, *225*
Murty, S., 198, *201*
Myers, L. J., 81, *94*

Najaka, S. S., 84, *96*
Nansel, T. R., 166, *183*
Naqushbandi, M., 101
Nation, M., 18, 26, 27, *33*, 48, *54*, 66, 68,
     77, 127, 132, 134, 135, *138*
National Association of Social
     Workers, 124
National Cancer Institute, 47
National Center for Education Statistics, 83
National Institute for Occupational Safety
     and Health, 250
Nazroo, J., 57, *76*
Nelson, E. S., 87, *94*
Nelson, G., 9, 10, *14*, 18, 23, *34*, 88, 89, *95*,
     130, 135, *139*, 272, *286*, 289, *297*
Nemoto, T., 21, 26, *33*
Neville, H. A., 83, 85, *96*
Newcomer, L. L., 238, *246*
Newman, D. A., 236, *247*
Newman-Carlson, D., 222, *226*
Ngubane, H., 20–21, *33*
Nietert, P. J., 188, *204*
Nieves, L. A., 89, *96*
Nogrady, C. A., 281, *287*
Nolan, J. M., 170, 171, 172, *182*
Northrop, D., 66, *76*
Nussbaum, S., 38, *54*
Nyamathi, A. M., 279, *285*
Nyswander, D., 241, *247*

Obasi, A., 100, 101
O'Brien, J., 280, *286*
O'Brien, K., 186
O'Brien, M. U., 21, 26, 27, 28, *32*, 66, *78*
O'Byrne, K. K., 25, *33*
Ocampo, C., 85, *93*
O'Donohue, W., 280, *287*
Oetting, E. R., 274, *285*
O'Farrell, T. J., 209, *227*
Office on Smoking and Health, 189
Offord, D. R., 128

Ogden, C. L., 187, *204*
Ohara, M., 21, 26
Olds, D., 275, *286*
Olds, D. L., 106, *121*
Oliveri, R., 106, *120*
O'Mara, J., 256, *267*
O'Neil, J. M., 157, *162*
Onitilo, A. A., 188, *204*
Onwuegbuzie, A. J., 100
Orbell, S., 192
Orme, J. G., *162*
Orpinas, P., 69, *77*, 167, *183*, 217, 222, 227, 229, 239, 241, *247*, 292
Ouston, J., 229, 231, 233, 234, 237, 240, *247*
Overpeck, M., 166, *183*
Owens, D. E., 234, *247*
Ozminkowski, R. J., 249, 250, 253, *267, 268*

Pancer, S. M., 272, *286*
Parcel, G. S., 201, *204*
Park, A. H., 133–34
Park, J., 58, 60, *78*
Park, K. O., 253, *269*
Park, N., 91, *94*
Park, Y., 63, *77, 78*
Parker, L., 101–2
Parkes, K. R., 265, *268*
Park-Taylor, J., 24, *35*
Patrick, D. L., 188, *205*
Patterson, G. R., 216, 218, 222, *227*
Patton, G. C., 232, *247*
Patton, M. Q., 101
Pearlman, S. F., 70, 71, 291, *297*
Pederson, P. B., 179, *183*
Pederson, S., 201, *204*
Pelletier, K. R., 253, *268*
Pentz, M. A., 38, *54*
Perez-Stable, E. J., 59
Perez-Vidal, A., 212, *227*
Perry, C. L., 201, *204*
Perry, D. G., 166, 167, *181, 182*
Perry, M. J., 141, *162*
Petersen, S. E., 25, *33*
Peterson, C., 91, *94*
Peterson, S. K., 191, *202*
Pettigrew, T. F., 85, 86, *94*
Petuch, A. J., 170, 171, 172, *182*
Phelps, R., 80, *95*
Philpot, C. L., 211, *226*
Pick, S., 21, 26, *33*
Pickering, D. J., 231, *246*

Pickus, P. S., 250, *266*
Pijpers, F. I. M., 167, *181*
Pilkington, N. W., 167, *181*
Pilla, R. S., 166, *183*
Pinar, W. F., 173, *183*
Pittman, K. J., 25, *33*
Pizarro, M., 86, *95*
Pizzi, L. T., 45, *54*
Plante, E. G., 280, *284*
Plested, B. A., 274, *285*
Plous, S., 87, 88, *95*
Poduska, J., 233, *246*
Polley, R. B., 253, *268*
Pollock, J. E., 231, *246*
Ponterotto, J. G., 79, *95*, 179, *183*
Poortinga, Y. H., 21, 26, *33*, 63–64, *77*
Pope, K. S., 127, 128, 129, 130, 131, 132, 135, 136
Post, J., 60, *76*
Poston, S., 45, *54*
Potter, R. H., 280, *286*
Potter, S. J., 283, *286*
Potvin, L., 189, *203*
Powers, L. J., 238, *246*
Preto, N. G., 211, *227*
Price, R. H., 26, *33*, 41, *55*, 126, 130–31, *137, 139*
Price-Spratlen, T., 117
Prilleltensky, I., 4, 8, 9, 10, *14*, 18, 23, *33, 34*, 41, *55*, 64, 65, 71, 88, 89, 91, *95*, 126, 130, 133, 135, *139*, 271, 273, *286*, 289, 294, *297*
Prilleltensky, O., 41, *55*
Prochaska, J. M., 28, *34*
Prochaska, J. O., 28, *34*, 192
Prochaska, P. J., *204*

Quiñones, M. A., 176, *180*
Quintana, S. M., 85, 86, *95*

Radhakrishna, R. B., 106
Rafter, N. H., 281, *286*
Ragins, B. R., 176, 177, *183*
Rahim, M. A., 210, 213, 224, *227*
Raj, A., 272, 273, 275, *284*
Ramos-McKay, J., 26, *33*, 130–31, *139*
Rankin, S. A., 192, *202*
Rawls, J., *14*, 22, *34*
Reason, J., 253, *268*
Rebok, G. W., 238, *246*
Reed, G. M., 80, *95*

Sutton, C., 211, *227*
Swanson, L., 274, *285*
Swenson, C. R., 4–5, 10, *14*, 65, *78*, 294, *297*
Swim, J. K., 234, *248*
Swisher, J. D., 236, *248*
Szalacha, L., 170, *182*
Szapocznik, J., 212, *227*

Tabak, C. J., 187, *204*
Takaki, R., 85, *96*
Talka, K., 79, 85, 89, *95*
Talleyrand, R. M., 63, *76*
Tan, Y., 191, *203*
Taylor, A. K., 251
Taylor, L., 66, *74*
Taylor, R. J., 82, *96*
Teutsch, S. M., 45–46, *54*
Thakral, C., 29
Thiemeke, D., 170, 171, 172, *182*
Thoennes, N., 171, *184*
Thomas, L., 232
Thompson, C. E., 83, 85, 92, *96*
Tierney, G., 86, *94*
Tjaden, P., 171, *184*
Tobias, M., 57, *76*
Tobler, N. S., 84, *96*, 235
Tolan, P. H., 17, *34*
Tolman, J., 25, *33*
Topolnytsky, L., 256, *268*
Toporek, R. L., 4, *13*, 23, *32*, *34*, 79, 83, 90,
     94, 95, 96, 126, 135
Toubbeh, J., 191, *203*
Trickett, E. J., 70, *76*, 125, 126, 127, 130, 131,
     132, 133, *139*, *140*, 272, 274, *287*
Tsemberis, S. J., 134
Tully, A. W., 79, 85, 89, *95*
Turnbull, D., 133–34
Turner, M. G., 171, *181*
Turner, S. M., 80, *95*
Turpin-Petrosino, C., 179, *180*
Twiss, J. M., 264, 265, *267*

U. S. Department of Education, 230
Unützer, J., 188, *205*
Upshur, C. C., 101
Uribe, V., 169, *184*
U.S. Department of Health and Human
     Services (USDHHS), 4, 20, 38, 40,
     47, 165, 186, 187, 231, 249

U.S. Equal Employment Opportunity
     Commission, 170–71
U.S. Public Health Service, 185
U.S. Surgeon General, 123
Utsey, S. O., 179, *183*

Valentine, J., 193, *204*
Valois, R. F., 236, *245*
Van Den Bergh, N., 175, *184*
Van Hermet, D. A., 63–64, *77*
Van Marter, D., 28, *34*
Van Voorhees, B. W., 192, *205*
Vandenberg, R. J., 253, 256, 257, 261, *269*
Vardell, K., 253, *267*
Vera, E. M., 7, *14*, 24, 26, 27, 28, 29, 30, *34*,
     35, 40, 41, 43, 48–49, 50, *55*, 64,
     78, 80, 81, 83, 85, 86, 88, 89, 91,
     92, 95, 96, 126, 128, 132, 133, *140*
Verloove-Vanhorick, S. P., 167, *181*
Vollrath, D., 258, *266*
VonBertalanffy, L., 208, 209, *227*

Walberg, H. J., 66, *78*
Waldegrave, K., 57, *76*
Waldman, D., 259, *269*
Waldo, C. R., 174, 177, *184*
Waldo, M., 10, *13*, 18, 23, 24, 30, *31*, *32*,
     66, 67, *75*, 125, 126, 132, 133, 135,
     137, *138*, *140*, 141, 142, 154, *161*,
     211, *226*
Walker, B., 251, *266*
Walker, H. M., 238
Wallerstein, N., 136, 193, 194, *204*, *205*,
     240, 246, 295, *297*
Walsh, E., 280
Walsh, M. E., 10, *13*, 24, *33*, 35, 70, *75*, *78*
Walsh, W., 284
Walworth, J., 177, *184*
Walz, G. R., 234, *245*
Wandersman, A., 18, 26, 27, *33*, 42, 48, *54*,
     55, 66, 68, *77*, 90, 92, 96, 101, 127,
     132, 134, 135, *138*, 272, *287*
Wang, N. Y., 192, *205*
Wang, S., 191, *205*
Wang, V. O., 9, *14*, 23, *33*
Ward, S., 280, *284*
Warter, E., 24, *32*
Wasik, B. A., 247
Watanabe, Y., 21, 26

SUBJECT INDEX

Perceived behavioral control, 191
Person-centered prevention, 84, 85–88
Planning, of prevention intervention, 125–27
Planning teams, 197–98
Political skills, 147
Population-based remedies, 5, 6
Positive Behavioral Support, 237, 238
Positive prevention, 132
Positive psychology, 25
Positive youth development, 25
Practice-oriented prevention, 63, 64
Preoccupied attachment, 213
Prevention
    advances in theory and practice, 39–41
    contemporary, 19–21
    core components of, 125–30
    cost-benefit perspective of, 84
    critical controversies, 41–45
    defining, 124
    development tools for community
        building, 272–76
    early definitions of, 21–22
    history of, 7–8, 19–21
Prevention curricula, 234–37
Prevention intervention, cost of, 45–46
Prevention problem-solving model, 143–44
Prevention research, 26–27
Prevention skills, 149–53
Primary data sources, 194–95
Primary prevention, 7–8, 19, 66, 209, 289
Problem-solving class meetings, 239
Problem-solving process, for healthy work
    organizations, 259
Procedural justice, 4, 291
Process evaluation, 99
Professional barriers, as tension area, 29–30
Professional identity, 50
Professional skills, 146–47
Program development skills, 148, 153
Program evaluation
    contemporary orientation, 100–102
    defining, 98–99
    Five-tiered Approach, 102–9
    history of, 99–100
    overview, 97–99
Program evaluation research, 99
Program processes, 100
Protective factors
    developmental contextualism, 61–64
    in family systems, 217–18

Protective Schools model, 241, 242
Psychoeducational intervention, 69
Psycho-educational programs, for
        racism/ethnicism prevention, 86
Psychological empowerment, 273–74
Psychology's social justice agenda
    defining *social justice*, 80–81
    examples of prevention and social
        justice, 85–90
    overview, 79–80
    prevention and promotion of social
        justice, 83–84
    remedial services utilization, 82–83
Psychotropic drugs, 19
Public health methodology, 5

Qualitative skills, 153
Quantitative skills, 153

Racial socialization, 222, 224
Racism
    mental health service utilization
        and, 82–87
    preventing, in children, 85–87
Rape, 171, 172
Readiness to change, of a
        community, 274–75
Redistributive strategies, 66
Relationship violence, 171–72
Remedial intervention, 38
Research and evaluation skills, 148, 153
Resilience, 61, 62–63, 65, 208, 239–40
Result-based evaluation, 99
Richmond, Mary, 19
Risk
    developmental contextualism, 61–64
    prevention and, 64–66
Risk factors, in family systems, 217–18
Risk reduction, for female students, 172
ROAD (Reaching Out About Depression),
        276–79, 293

Safe and Drug Free School, 236
Safe Zone Programs, 169
Satcher, David, 38
School climate
    application theories and
        examples, 237–40
    impact on student behavior, 232–34
    positive, enhancement guidelines
        for, 240–43

Transtheoretical Model, 192
Triangulation, 210

Underserved populations, 79
Universal interventions, 20
U.S. Preventive Services Task Force, 51
Utilization-focused evaluation, 100

Values-based model of healthy
    company, 251
Victim blaming, 189
Violence Against Women Act
    (VAWA), 172

War on Poverty, 19
Washington's Safe Schools project, 168
Wellness, community, 6–7
Women, risks in colleges and universities,
    170–74
Work organizations, 249–50. *See also*
    Healthy work organizations
The Working Group, 178
Workplace heterosexism, 174–75

Youth behavior, family-focused prevention
    programs for, 218–24

ABOUT THE EDITORS

Maureen E. Kenny, PhD, is associate dean at Boston College's Lynch School of Education, and professor of counseling psychology in the Department of Counseling, Developmental, and Educational Psychology at the Lynch School. Dr. Kenny completed her MEd at Teachers College, Columbia University, New York, and her PhD with specializations in counseling and school psychology from the University of Pennsylvania. She is a fellow of the Society for Counseling Psychology (Division 17 of the American Psychological Association) and served as chair of the Section on Prevention of Division 17. Dr. Kenny has published and presented at conferences extensively on topics related to her interests in positive youth development, family relationships, and school-based preventive interventions.

Arthur (Andy) M. Horne, PhD, is distinguished research professor, emeritus, and director of the Educational Policy and Evaluation Center of the University of Georgia in Athens. Dr. Horne completed his PhD at Southern Illinois University in Carbondale. He has been a director of training for counseling psychology at both Indiana State University in Terre Haute and the University of Georgia. He has been active in developing prevention, early intervention, and therapy treatment programs for addressing problems of delinquency, violence, and bullying for 30 years. He has directed research programs in the United States, Europe, and New Zealand, funded by the Centers for Disease Control and Prevention, the U.S. Department of Education, and the National Institute of Mental Health, as well as by foundations and other agencies.

Pamela Orpinas, PhD, MPH, is a professor in the Department of Health Promotion and Behavior in the College of Public Health at the University of Georgia in Athens. She studied psychology at the Catholic University of Chile in Santiago. She received her MPH degree from the University of California, Los Angeles, and her PhD from the School of Public Health at the University of Texas—Houston. Dr. Orpinas has worked in several research projects specifically related to the prevention of violence among children and adolescents, and has been a consultant in the area of violence prevention in several countries. She has published and presented at national and international conferences extensively on this topic.

Le'Roy E. Reese, MD, is an associate professor in the Department of Community Health and Preventative Medicine at the Morehouse School of Medicine in Atlanta, Georgia. He received his PhD in clinical psychology from Ohio State University in Columbus. Dr. Reese conducts community-based health research focused on the development of healthy lifestyles and the reduction of risk behavior among youth and their families residing in underresourced communities. Prior to coming to Morehouse, Dr. Reese was a senior scientist in the Office of the Director at the Centers for Disease Control and Prevention's (CDC) National Center for Injury Prevention and Control, where he helped lead efforts to create research and programmatic priorities for the Center. During his tenure at the CDC, he also served as team leader of the Effectiveness and Evaluation Research Team in the Division of Violence Prevention at the Injury Center. Dr. Reese joined the CDC after spending several years as a faculty member in the Departments of Psychology and Black Studies at Chicago State University, where he co-directed a prevention research team conducting school and community-based prevention research in Chicago.